Cyber Security Standards, Practices and Industrial Applications:

Systems and Methodologies

Junaid Ahmed Zubairi
State University of New York at Fredonia, USA

Athar Mahboob
National University of Sciences & Technology, Pakistan

Senior Editorial Director:	Kristin Klinger
Director of Book Publications:	Julia Mosemann
Editorial Director:	Lindsay Johnston
Acquisitions Editor:	Erika Carter
Development Editor:	Michael Killian
Production Editor:	Sean Woznicki
Typesetters:	Adrienne Freeland
Print Coordinator:	Jamie Snavely
Cover Design:	Nick Newcomer

Published in the United States of America by
Information Science Reference (an imprint of IGI Global)
701 E. Chocolate Avenue
Hershey PA 17033
Tel: 717-533-8845
Fax: 717-533-8661
E-mail: cust@igi-global.com
Web site: http://www.igi-global.com

Library of Congress Cataloging-in-Publication Data

Cyber security standards, practices and industrial applications: systems and methodologies / Junaid Ahmed Zubairi and Athar Mahboob, editors.
      p. cm.
  Includes bibliographical references and index.
  Summary: "This book details the latest and most important advances in security standards, introducing the differences between information security (covers the understanding of security requirements, classification of threats, attacks and information protection systems and methodologies) and network security (includes both security protocols as well as systems which create a security perimeter around networks for intrusion detection and avoidance)"--Provided by publisher.
  ISBN 978-1-60960-851-4 (hbk.) -- ISBN 978-1-60960-852-1 (ebook) -- ISBN 978-1-60960-853-8 (print & perpetual access) 1. Computer networks--Security measures. 2. Computer security. 3. Data protection. 4. Electronic data processing departments--Security measures. I. Zubairi, Junaid Ahmed, 1961- II. Mahboob, Athar, 1971-
  TK5105.59.C92 2012
  005.8--dc22
                              2011009262

British Cataloguing in Publication Data
A Cataloguing in Publication record for this book is available from the British Library.

All work contributed to this book is new, previously-unpublished material. The views expressed in this book are those of the authors, but not necessarily of the publisher.

Table of Contents

Section 1
Mobile and Wireless Security

Section 2
Social Media, Botnets and Intrusion Detection

Section 3
Formal Methods and Quantum Computing

Section 4
Embedded Systems and SCADA Security

Section 5
Industrial and Applications Security

Detailed Table of Contents

Section 1
Mobile and Wireless Security

Victor Pomponiu, University of Torino, Italy

In this chapter, first authors introduce the main wireless technologies along with their characteristics. Then, a description of the attacks that can be mounted on these networks is given. A separate section will review and compare the most recent intrusion detection techniques for wireless ad hoc networks. Finally, based on the current state of the art, the conclusions, and major challenges are discussed.

Wen-Chen Hu, University of North Dakota, USA
Naima Kaabouch, University of North Dakota, USA
S. Hossein Mousavinezhad, Idaho State University, USA
Hung-Jen Yang, National Kaohsiung Normal University, Taiwan

This research proposes a set of novel approaches to protecting handheld data by using mobile usage pattern matching, which compares the current handheld usage pattern to the stored usage patterns. If they are drastic different, a security action such as requiring a password entry is activated. Various algorithms of pattern matching can be used in this research. Two of them are discussed in this chapter.

Rania Mokhtar, University Putra Malaysia (UPM), Malaysia
Rashid Saeed, International Islamic University Malaysia (IIUM), Malaysia

The goal of this chapter is to examine and raise awareness about cyber security threats from social media, to describe the state of technology to mitigate security risks introduced by social networks, to shed light on standards for identity and information sharing or lack thereof, and to present new research and development. The chapter will serve as a reference to students, researchers, practitioners, and consultants in the area of social media, cyber security, and Information and Communication technologies (ICT).

Section 2
Social Media, Botnets and Intrusion Detection

The goal of this chapter is to examine and raise awareness about cyber security threats from social media, to describe the state of technology to mitigate security risks introduced by social networks, to shed light on standards for identity and information sharing or lack thereof, and to present new research and development. The chapter will serve as a reference to students, researchers, practitioners, and consultants in the area of social media, cyber security, and Information and Communication technologies (ICT).

This chapter provides a brief overview of the botnet phenomena and its pernicious aspects. Current governmental and corporate efforts to mitigate the threat are also described, together with the bottlenecks limiting their effectiveness in various countries. The chapter concludes with a description of lines of investigation that could counter the botnet phenomenon.

Due to the rapidly evolving nature of network attacks, a considerable paradigm shift has taken place with focus now on Network-based Anomaly Detection Systems (NADSs) that can detect zero-day attacks. At this time, it is important to evaluate existing anomaly detectors to determine and learn from their strengths and weaknesses. Thus, the authors aim to evaluate the performance of eight prominent network-based anomaly detectors under malicious portscan attacks.

Section 3
Formal Methods and Quantum Computing

Chapter 7

Sellami Ali, International Islamic University Malaysia (IIUM), Malaysia

The central objective of this chapter is to study and implement practical systems for quantum cryptography using decoy state protocol. In particular we seek to improve dramatically both the security and the performance of practical QKD system (in terms of substantially higher key generation rate and longer distance).

Chapter 8

Alfredo Pironti, Politecnico di Torino, Italy
Davide Pozza, Politecnico di Torino, Italy
Riccardo Sisto, Politecnico di Torino, Italy

The objective of this chapter is to give a circumstantial account of the state-of-the-art reached in this field, showing how formal methods can help in improving quality. Since automation is a key factor for the acceptability of these techniques in the engineering practice, the chapter focuses on automated techniques and illustrates in particular how high-level protocol models in the Dolev-Yao style can be automatically analyzed and how it is possible to automatically enforce formal correspondence between an abstract high-level model and an implementation.

Section 4
Embedded Systems and SCADA Security

Chapter 9

Syed Misbahuddin, Sir Syed University of Engineering and Technology, Pakistan
Nizar Al-Holou, University of Detroit Mercy, USA

This chapter proposes a fault tolerant scheme to untangle the RTU's failure issue. According to the scheme, every RTU will have at least two processing elements. In case of either processor's failure, the surviving processor will take over the tasks of the failed processor to perform its tasks. With this approach, an RTU can remain functional despite the failure of the processor inside the RTU.

Chapter 10

Muhammad Farooq-i-Azam, COMSATS Institute of Information Technology, Pakistan
Muhammad Naeem Ayyaz, University of Engineering and Technology, Pakistan

Whereas a lot of research has already been done in the area of security of general purpose computers and software applications, hardware and embedded systems security is a relatively new and emerging area of research. This chapter provides details of various types of existing attacks against hardware devices and embedded systems, analyzes existing design methodologies for their vulnerability to new types of attacks, and along the way describes solutions and countermeasures against them for the design and development of secure systems.

Section 5
Industrial and Applications Security

Chapter 11

The world's critical infrastructure includes entities such as the water, waste water, electrical utilities, and the oil and gas industry. In many cases, these rely on pipelines that are controlled by supervisory control and data acquisition (SCADA) systems. SCADA systems have evolved to highly networked, common platform systems. This evolutionary process creates expanding and changing cyber security risks. The need to address this risk profile is mandated from the highest government level. This chapter discusses the various processes, standards, and industry based best practices that are directed towards minimizing these risks.

Chapter 12

The C4ISR system is a system of systems and it can also be termed as network of networks and works on similar principles as the Internet. Hence it is vulnerable to similar attacks called cyber attacks and warrants appropriate security measures to save it from these attacks or to recover if the attack succeeds. All of the measures put in place to achieve this are called cyber security of C4ISR systems. This chapter gives an overview of C4ISR systems focusing on the perspective of cyber security warranting information assurance.

Chapter 13

Today, nearly 80% of total applications are web-based and externally accessible depending on the organization policies. In many cases, number of security issues discovered not only depends on the system configuration but also the application space. Rationalizing security functions into the application is a common practice but assessing their level of resiliency requires structured and systematic approach to test the application against all possible threats before and after deployment. The application security assessment process and tools presented here are mainly focused and mapped with industry standards and compliance including PCI-DSS, ISO27001, GLBA, FISMA, SOX, and HIPAA, in order to assist the regulatory requirements.

Foreword

The role of cyber infrastructure in the global economy is becoming increasing dominant as this infrastructure has enabled global business and social interaction across cultural and societal boundaries. However, the benefits of this infrastructure can be significantly overshadowed by widespread cyber security incidents as adversarial activities are increasingly international in scope. Online marketplaces for stolen IDs and financial data could be run by criminals maintaining servers across international boundaries and impacting financial enterprises all over the globe. The denial of service (DoS) attack in Estonia is a sobering revelation of how an attack on the cyber infrastructure can severely affect the functioning of an entire nation. With the growing capability of spreading worms over the Internet, the deployment of heterogeneous operating systems, growing number of software patches, sporadic usage of client software (e.g., growing usage of VoIP services with vulnerabilities), and networking technologies (e.g., the on-going aggressive migration towards IPv6) are some of the leading examples diversely impacting the security of the global cyber infrastructure.

The phenomenal adaptation of social networking in the cyberspace is also providing opportunities for attackers. In addition, diverse perspectives and policies adopted by various segments of the cyber infrastructure exacerbate security risks, and further hamper our understanding of security/privacy concerns and the choice of technological and policy measures. To build a secure cyber infrastructure, we need to understand how to design various components of this infrastructure securely. Over the years, we have learned that cyber security needs to be viewed in terms of security of all its components and best practices and standards need to be adopted globally. This understanding has several facets and a holistic approach is required to address security challenges from all the dimensions.

Cyber security has a long way to go, and covering the complete spectrum of this topic is a daunting task. We need not only to learn how to achieve it but also need to realize that it is essential to pursue it. Addressing this need, this book provides a balanced and comprehensive treatment to this vast topic. We expect the readers will greatly benefit from this book and practice the knowledge provided in it.

Arif Ghafoor
Purdue University, USA

Preface

The field of cyber security has assumed utmost importance in today's information age. Cyber security encompasses both information and network security. Information security covers the understanding of security requirements, classification of threats, attacks, and information protection systems and methodologies. Encryption is a key enabling technology for data and information security. Network security, on the other hand, includes both security protocols as well as systems, which create a security perimeter around networks for intrusion detection and avoidance. Network security protocols combine encryption and several related mechanisms, like hashing and digital signatures, along with procedures for key and session management, which allow for parties to establish secure communication links over otherwise insecure communication networks and exchange private information such as personal and financial data.

As part of proactive information security, Security Information Management (SIM) systems are set up by those tasked with managing information security in their respective organizations. These systems consolidate and analyze the information system usage logs in near real-time for alerting and in off-line mode for demonstrating system security and compliance to standards and regulations. At this time real-time audio, video, and instant messaging systems are used ubiquitously over integrated and converged public communication networks. Their security requirements include protection against eavesdropping and end to end authentication. To this end security protocols such as Secure Real Time Protocol (SRTP) for streaming media security have been developed by the Internet Engineering Task Force (IETF).

Cyber security of industrial manufacturing and utility industries, such as power, water, and gas, has assumed national defense status. Most industries, including power generation and manufacturing, use PLC's (programmable logic controllers) that are connected to computers for remote control. SCADA and industrial systems security includes protection of SCADA control units or industrial equipment in production, power generation & distribution, fabrication, refining, public and private infrastructure institutions, and large communication systems. The area of industrial and infrastructure security is very important and various governments have mandated the compliance by all institutions and services to many security regulations.

This book aims to provide a comprehensive reference in cyber security covering all important topics including encryption, authentication, integrity, security infrastructure, and protocols. It covers areas that pertain to digital information encryption techniques, secure networking protocols, security management systems, and industrial and SCADA security standards. We believe that it would not only serve as a reference for existing technologies, it would also become a reference for innovation in this field. It would serve a broad audience including researchers and practitioners in cyber and industrial security, e-commerce and web security experts, academicians, students, and working professionals in utilities, manufacturing, municipal services, government, defense, and networking companies.

Wireless technologies are bringing significant changes to data networking and telecommunication services, making integrated networks a reality. By removing the wires, personal networks, local area networks, mobile radio networks and cellular systems, offer an entirely distributed mobile computing and communications environment. Due to their unique features such as shared medium, limited resources, and dynamic topology, wireless ad hoc networks are vulnerable to a variety of potential attacks. However, the common security measures employed for wired networks are not enough to protect the nodes of the networks against complex attacks. Therefore, a new line of defense, called intrusion detection, has been added. In the first chapter the main wireless technologies are introduced along with their characteristics. Then, a description of the attacks that can be mounted on these networks is given. A separate section reviews and compares the most recent intrusion detection techniques for wireless ad hoc networks. Finally, based on the current state of the art, the conclusions and major challenges are discussed.

Handheld devices like smartphones must include rigorous and convenient handheld data protection in case the devices are lost or stolen. The second chapter proposes a set of novel approaches to protecting handheld data by using mobile usage pattern matching, which compares the current handheld usage pattern to the stored usage patterns. If they are drastically different, a security action such as requiring a password entry is activated. Various algorithms of pattern matching may be used. Two of them discussed in the chapter are (i) approximate usage string matching and (ii) usage finite automata. The first method uses approximate string matching to check device usage and the second method converts the usage tree into a deterministic finite automaton (DFA). Experimental results show this method is effective and convenient for handheld data protection, but the accuracy may need to be improved.

An important part of ISO/IEC 27002 cyber security standard is the conservation of confidentiality that falls under its computer facility protection part which insures that the computer and its stored information can only be accessed by the authorized users. Securing mobile devices and mobile data to ensure the confidentiality, integrity, and availability of both data and security applications requires special consideration to be paid to the typical mobile environment in which a mobile computing device would be utilized. Protecting mobile devices includes multiple security technologies such as the right identification of its particular user, data encryption, physical locking devices, monitoring and tracking software, and alarms. Chapter 3 reviews security-specific hardware and software applied to mobile computing and presents its advantages and drawbacks. Then it considers the concept of usability constraints in context of mobile computing security and introduces the seamless security method for identity proof of a particular user or device.

Social media is transforming the way we find, create, and share information during the course of our personal life and work. The rapid growth of social media and the ubiquitous sharing and access of information through various digital channels has created new vulnerabilities and cyber threats. Chapter 4 provides an overview of the security and privacy implications of social networks and communities. It examines and raises awareness about cyber security threats from social media, to describe the state of technology to mitigate security risks introduced by social networks, to shed light on standards for identity and information sharing or lack thereof, and to present new research and development. The chapter will serve as a reference to students, researchers, practitioners, and consultants in the area of social media, cyber security, and Information and Communication Technologies (ICT).

The Internet, originally designed in a spirit of trust, uses protocols and frameworks that are not inherently secure. This basic weakness is greatly compounded by the interconnected nature of the Internet, which, together with the revolution in the software industry, has provided a medium for large-scale exploitation, for example, in the form of botnets. Despite considerable recent efforts, Internet-based attacks, particularly via botnets, are still ubiquitous and have caused great damage on both national and international levels. Chapter 5 provides a brief overview of the botnet phenomena and its pernicious aspects. Current governmental and corporate efforts to mitigate the threat are also described, together with the bottlenecks limiting their effectiveness in various countries. The chapter concludes with a description of lines of investigation that could counter the botnet phenomenon.

Due to the rapidly evolving nature of network attacks, a considerable paradigm shift has taken place with focus now on Network-based Anomaly Detection Systems (NADSs) that can detect zero-day attacks. At this time, it is important to evaluate existing anomaly detectors to determine and learn from their strengths and weaknesses. Chapter 6 aims to evaluate the performance of eight prominent network-based anomaly detectors under malicious portscan attacks. These NADSs are evaluated on three criteria: accuracy (ROC curves), scalability (with respect to varying normal and attack traffic rates, and deployment points), and detection delay. Based on experiments, promising guidelines are identified to improve the accuracy and scalability of existing and future anomaly detectors. It is shown that the proposed guidelines provide considerable and consistent accuracy improvements for all evaluated NADSs.

Quantum cryptography holds the promise of unbreakable encryption systems and is based in using photons. In chapter 7 the author presents a method to estimate parameters of the decoy state protocol based on one decoy state protocol for both BB84 and SARG04. This method can give different lower bound of the fraction of single-photon counts, the fraction of two-photon counts, the upper bound QBER of single-photon pulses, the upper bound QBER of two-photon pulses, and the lower bound of key generation rate for both BB84 and SARG04. The effects of statistical fluctuations on some parameters of our QKD system have been presented. We have also performed the optimization on the choice of intensities and percentages of signal state and decoy states which give out the maximum distance and the optimization of the key generation rate. The numerical simulation has shown that the fiber based QKD and free space QKD systems using the proposed method for BB84 are able to achieve both a higher secret key rate and greater secure distance than that of SARG04. Also, it is shown that bidirectional ground to satellite and inter-satellite communications are possible with this protocol. The experiment of decoy state QKD has been demonstrated using ID-3000 commercial QKD system based on a standard 'Plug & Play' set-up. One decoy state QKD has been implemented for both BB84 and SARG04 over different transmission distance of standard telecom fiber.

Designing and implementing security protocols are known to be error-prone tasks. Recent research progress in the field of formal methods applied to security protocols has enabled the use of these techniques in practice. The authors' objective in chapter 8 is to give a circumstantial account of the state-of-the-art reached in this field, showing how formal methods can help in improving quality of security protocols. Since automation is a key factor for the acceptability of these techniques in the engineering practice, the chapter focuses on automated techniques and illustrates in particular how high-level protocol models in the Dolev-Yao style can be automatically analyzed and how it is possible to automatically enforce formal correspondence between an abstract high-level model and an implementation.

Not long ago, it was thought that only software applications and general purpose digital systems i.e. computers were prone to various types of attacks against their security. The underlying hardware, hardware implementations of these software applications, embedded systems, and hardware devices were considered to be secure and out of reach of these attacks. However, during previous few years, it has been demonstrated that novel attacks against the hardware and embedded systems can also be mounted. Not only viruses, but worms and Trojan horses have been developed for them, and they have also been demonstrated to be effective. Whereas a lot of research has already been done in the area of security of general purpose computers and software applications, hardware and embedded systems security is a relatively new and emerging area of research. Chapter 9 provides details of various types of existing attacks against hardware devices and embedded systems, analyzes existing design methodologies for their vulnerability to new types of attacks, and along the way describes solutions and countermeasures against them for the design and development of secure systems.

A Supervisory Control and Data Acquisition (SCADA) system is composed of number of remote terminal units (RTUs) for collecting field data. These RTUs send the data back to a master station, via a communication network. The master station displays the acquired data and allows the operator to perform remote control tasks. An RTU is a microprocessor based standalone data acquisition control unit. As the RTUs work in harsh environment, the processor inside the RTU is susceptible to random faults. If the processor fails, the equipment or process being monitored by it will become inaccessible. Chapter 10 proposes a fault tolerant scheme to untangle the RTU's failure issue. According to the scheme, every RTU will have at least two processing elements. In case of either processor's failure, the surviving processor will take over the tasks of the failed processor to perform its tasks. With this approach, an RTU remain functional despite the failure of the processor inside the RTU. Reliability and availability modeling of the proposed fault tolerant scheme have been presented. Moreover, cyber security for SCADA system and recommendations for the mitigation of these issues have been discussed.

The world's critical infrastructure includes entities such as the water, waste water, electrical utilities, and the oil and gas industry. In many cases, these rely on pipelines that are controlled by supervisory control and data acquisition (SCADA) systems. SCADA systems have evolved to highly networked, common platform systems. This evolutionary process creates expanding and changing cyber security risks. The need to address this risk profile is mandated from the highest government level. Chapter 11 discusses the various processes, standards, and industry based best practices that are directed towards minimizing these risks.

C4ISR stands for Command, Control, Communications, Computers, Intelligence, Surveillance & Reconnaissance. C4ISR systems are primarily used by organizations in the defense sector. However, they are also increasingly being used by civil sector organizations such as railways, airports, and oil and gas exploration departments. The C4ISR system is a system of systems and it can also be termed as network of networks and works on similar principles as the Internet. Hence it is vulnerable to similar attacks called cyber attacks and warrants appropriate security measures to save it from these attacks or to recover if the attack succeeds. All of the measures put in place to achieve this are called cyber security of C4ISR systems. Chapter 12 gives an overview of C4ISR systems focusing on the perspective of cyber security warranting information assurance.

A rapidly changing face of Internet threat landscape has posed remarkable challenges for security professionals to thwart their IT infrastructure by applying advanced defensive techniques, policies, and procedures. Today, nearly 80% of total applications are web-based and externally accessible depending on the organization policies. In many cases, number of security issues discovered not only depends on the system configuration but also the application space. Rationalizing security functions into the application is a common practice but assessing their level of resiliency requires structured and systematic approach to test the application against all possible threats before and after deployment. The application security assessment process and tools presented in Chapter 13 are mainly focused and mapped with industry standards and compliance including PCI-DSS, ISO27001, GLBA, FISMA, SOX, and HIPAA, in order to assist the regulatory requirements. Additionally, to retain a defensive architecture, web application firewalls have been discussed and a map between well-established application security standards (WASC, SANS, OWASP) is prepared to represent a broad view of threat classification.

With a wide variety of current topics in Cyber Security treated in this handbook we hope it proves to be a suitable reference to the topics which are covered in various chapters. We hope you have as much pleasure and intellectual fulfillment in reading these chapters as we have had in editing and managing their evolution from original single page chapter proposals to final camera ready drafts that constitute the handbook that you hold.

Junaid Ahmed Zubairi
State University of New York at Fredonia, USA

Athar Mahboob
National University of Sciences & Technology, Pakistan

Acknowledgment

We would like to take this opportunity to thank all the members of the Editorial Advisory Board and the Panel of Reviewers who painstakingly carried out the review and quality assurance processes. Without their contribution and full support we believe this book would not have been able to see the light of the day.

We would also like to acknowledge and thank our respective families for their moral support during the entire period of editing of this book.

Finally, we would like to convey our thanks to the Michael Killian, the managing editor at IGI Global for his timely and constructive reminders and guidelines throughout the whole process of handbook production.

Junaid Ahmed Zubairi
State University of New York at Fredonia, USA

Athar Mahboob
National University of Sciences & Technology, Pakistan

Section 1
Mobile and Wireless Security

Chapter 1
Securing Wireless Ad Hoc Networks:
State of the Art and Challenges

Victor Pomponiu
University of Torino, Italy

ABSTRACT

The wireless technologies are bringing significant changes to data networking and telecommunication services, making integrated networks a reality. By removing the wires, personal networks, local area networks, mobile radio networks, and cellular systems, offer an entirely distributed mobile computing and communications environment. Due to their unique features such as shared medium, limited resources, and dynamic topology, wireless ad hoc networks are vulnerable to a variety of potential attacks. However, the common security measures employed for wired networks are not enough to protect the nodes of the networks against complex attacks. Therefore, a new line of defense, called intrusion detection, has been added. In this chapter, first we introduce the main wireless technologies along with their characteristics. Then, a description of the attacks that can be mounted on these networks is given. A separate section will review and compare the most recent intrusion detection techniques for wireless ad hoc networks. Finally, based on the current state of the art, the conclusions, and major challenges are discussed.

DOI: 10.4018/978-1-60960-851-4.ch001

Figure 1. Different networks types. The intrusion detection techniques for the networks in bold face are the focus of this study.

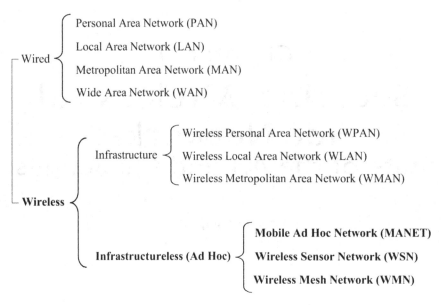

INTRODUCTION

In the last decades, the widespread diffusion of wireless networking has bought crucial changes in modern communication technologies. Wireless networking enables devices with wireless capabilities to communicate without being connected physically to a network. In general, wireless networks aim to increase the user mobility by extending the wired local area networks (LANs).

A *wireless ad hoc network* is a new *decentralized* wireless networking paradigm. It consist of a set of fixed/mobile modes that rely on each other in order to perform the main networking operations (i.e. routing, packet delivery and route discovery) without the aid of any infrastructure (Giordano, 2002). The changing topology and decentralized management, together with pervasive deployment of various services are the main characteristics of the wireless ad hoc networks (Raghavendra, Sivalingam, & Znati, 2004; Stojmenovic, 2002; Xiao, Chen, & Li, 2010). Further, wireless ad hoc networks can be categorized into *mobile ad hoc networks* (MANETs) which are autonomous

systems of mobile nodes, *wireless mesh networks* (WMNs) that are multihop systems in which nodes, organized in a mesh topology and assisted by a wireless card, and *wireless sensor networks* (WSNs). In Figure 1 the main wireless and wired networks types are shown.

Although military and security-strategic operations remain the primary application for ad hoc networks, recently the commercial interest in this type of networks began to grow. For instance, the use of ad hoc networks for emergency missions in case of natural disasters, for law enforcement procedures, for community networking and interaction, for monitoring the weather conditions and for public healthcare (Baronti et al., 2007; Milenkovic, Otto, & Jovanov, 2004; Neves, Stachyra, & Rodrigues, 2008; Perrig et al., 2002).

As the deployment of ad hoc networks spread to numerous application environments, security remains one of the main challenges of these networks. The attacks that can target an ad hoc network can be broadly classified into *passive attacks* and *active attacks*. Passive attacks collect sensitive information from the network without jeopardizing the communications among the nodes. Instead, an active attack interferes and changes the functionality of the network by blocking, forging and modifying the information flow (Wu, Chen, Wu, & Cardei, 2006). Depending on the source of origin, the security attacks could also be split into *outside attacks* and *inside attacks* (i.e. attacks originating from the compromised nodes).

The classical security mechanism employed to protect the wired networks is not suitable for ad hoc networks in many cases. The unique feature that creates these security issues is the lack of centralization, i.e. each node is responsible for routing, packet forwarding and network administration (Molva, & Michiardi, 2003). Contrast to the special-purpose nodes of the wired network (i.e., routers, switches and getaways), the nodes of an ad hoc network are not reliable for accomplishing the critical network operations. Furthermore, authentication and encryption, which both rely on trustworthy cooperation between mobile nodes, are incapable to guard the ad hoc network against inside attacks. Due to these considerations, new techniques which deal with these security issues and, in particular, with intrusion detection have been proposed.

The system that screens the events which occur in a network or node in order to identify potential threats or violations of security rules is called *intrusion detection system* (IDS) (Bace, & Mell, 2001; Denning, 1987). On the other hand, *intrusion prevention systems* (IPSs) are systems that can prevent or stop possible threats. The detection approaches used by IDS can be divided into *signature-based, anomaly-based* and *protocol-based analysis*. The former method, also called *pattern-based detection*, consists of matching the signatures (patterns) of knowing threats with the monitored events to detect security incidents. Instead, the anomaly-based and protocol-based techniques compare the normal activity of the network or its protocols with the occurred events to identify significant anomalies.

The main contribution of this chapter is the investigation of the latest intrusion detection developments proposed in major journals and conferences dedicated to the field (the list of the selected journals and conference is given in section "Additional Reading"). Although the first intrusion detection systems for wireless ad hoc networks were proposed by Zhou and Hass (1999) and by Zang and Lee (2000) more than 10 years ago, we apply this restriction due to the following reasons:

- The growth of the area in the last two years has increased rapidly with many new schemes being proposed, therefore imposing an urgent analysis of their viability and performances.
- There are earlier surveys that cover the former state of the art such those of Zhan and Lee (2000), Molva and Michiardi (2003), Mishra et al. (2004), Parker et al. (2004), Kabiri and Ghorbani (2005), Wu et al. (2006), Anantvalee and Wu (2007), Amini et al. (2007), Krontiris et al. (2007), and Walters et al. (2007). Furthermore, the recent surveys (Barry, & Chan, 2010; Barry, 2009; Farooqi, & Khan, 2009; Giannetous et al., 2009; Madhavi, & Kim, 2008; Mandala et al., 2008; Rafsanjani et al., 2008) are still focusing on the capabilities and performances of the earlier IDS, without taking into considerations the sophisticated algorithms proposed in the last years.
- There are several exhaustive surveys which cover the intrusion detection in the context of wired networks while briefly presenting several IDS for wireless ad hoc networks (Axelsson, 1999; Callegari et al., 2009; Garcia-Teodoro et al., 2009; Lazarevic et al., 2005; Sabahi, & Movaghar, 2008; Wu, & Banzhaf, 2010).

In this chapter, we present the wireless networking along with the challenges and opportunities

Table 1. The major advantages and drawbacks of wireless networks

Advantages	Disadvantages
+ Mobility	- Low security
+ Flexibility	- Interferences
+ Cost	- Low bandwidth

posed by them. A particular section will be devoted to study the threats to which the ad hoc networks are exposed. Then, the major components of wireless intrusion detection systems, together with their characteristics, are presented. Furthermore, a classification of intrusion detection systems based on detection strategy is given and the most important schemes are analyzed, highlighting both advantages and disadvantages. We conclude the chapter by discussing the conclusions and major challenges.

BACKGROUND

This section gives a short background of the wireless networking, along with its fundamental components and architectures. A more detailed attention will be given to wireless ad hoc networks and their variants: MANET, WSN and WMN. It is worth pointing out that this section only provides a high-level overview of wireless networking, as background information for intrusion detection techniques applied in ad hoc networks. For a complete overview of the wireless networking and technologies, we refer to the Gast's definitive guide (Gast, 2002) or the Stojmenovic's handbook (Stojmenovic, 2002).

Wireless Networks

Mobility of the users in wireless networks imposes severe challenges, making classical techniques of networking inadequate. By letting the users to connect to networks only through physical cables, their mobility will dramatically reduce. To tackle this issue, researchers have proposed the wireless connectivity which allows the users to move freely while exploiting useful services.

Wireless networking facilitates devices with wireless capabilities to communicate without being connected physically to a network. The involved devices need only to be within the range of the wireless network infrastructure. A collection of wireless nodes within a limited range, which are capable to transmit data through radio communications, forms a *wireless local area network* (WLAN). Typically, WLANs are devised to extend the existing wired local area networks (LANs), increasing the user mobility.

Independent of the communication protocol used or the transmitted information, wireless networks has several advantages and drawbacks that are pointed out in Table 1. The most important benefit of wireless networks is *mobility,* which permits the users connected to a network to change their location. Another important advantage is *flexibility* that implies the ability to quickly install and deploy network services. Among the major shortcomings that affect these networks we can mention lack of security, reduced bandwidth, and sensibility to noise and interferences caused by weather conditions, obstacles or other wireless devices that operates in the same range using other wireless technologies.

Generally, WLAN architecture comprises two important components: the *stations*, which are mobile nodes that act as endpoints (e.g., personal digital assistants (PDA), portable computers, tablet computers and other electronic devices with wireless capabilities) and the *access points* (i.e., wireless network devices) that connect the wireless *stations* with a wired network infrastructure or an external network like the Internet. The networks that use access points to coordinate the communication among stations are called *infrastructure* (centralized) wireless networks, and offer the advantages of scalability and reliability of transmission. It is important to mention that

Figure 2. An ad hoc network with 10 stations: laptops, cell phones, PDA, smartphones, and table computers

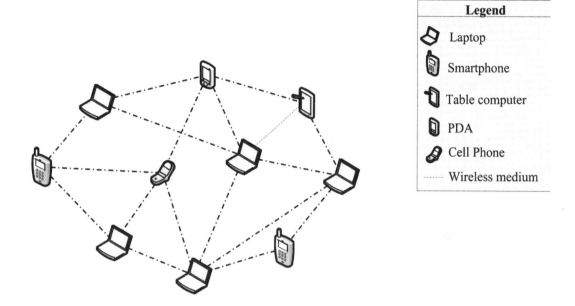

the access points should be well secured since they deal with packet transmission and path discovery.

Wireless Ad Hoc Networks

Unlike to the infrastructure architecture, wireless ad hoc networks consist of a group of mobile nodes (peers) which are able to communicate with each other without the intervention of an access point (see Figure 2). Typically, these types of networks are composed of a small number of stations set up for a particular purpose. The topology of ad hoc networks is dynamic and modeled as a random graph. Other important aspects are the distribution of nodes and their self-organizing ability.

In order to transmit the data packets between stations a wireless medium is used. Several different physical layers are defined: the architecture consents multiple physical layers to be developed to support the medium access. The radio frequency (RF) and infrared physical layers were implemented, although the RF layer has shown to be more reliable.

Depending on their application context, wireless ad hoc networks can be classified into three major categories:

- *Mobile ad hoc networks (MANETs)*. A MANET is system of mobile nodes, where the communication between the nodes is realized via wireless links. Due to the mobility of the nodes, the topology of the MANET is changing frequently.
- *Wireless mesh networks (WMNs)*. In a WMN the mobile/fixed nodes are structured in a mesh topology and communicate through wireless connections. The architecture of WMN comes in three flavors: *backbone WMS*, *client WMS* and *hybrid WMS*. Unlike to MANET, in this network certain nodes can be fixed and, besides the connection among them, they have also an Internet connection.
- *Wireless sensor networks (WSNs)*. A WSN consists of many spatially distributed autonomous devices, called smart sensor nodes, which cooperatively analyze the

Figure 3. Different types of wireless ad hoc networks: a) MANET; b) a hybrid WMN; c) WSN

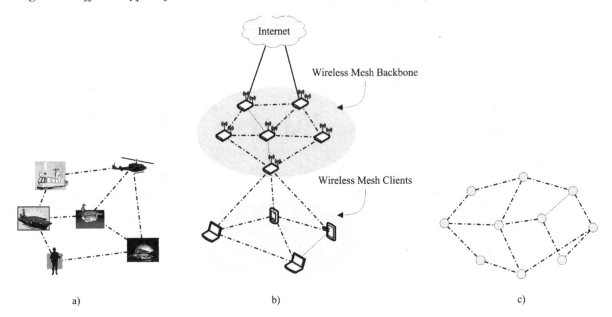

a)   b)   c)

environmental or physical conditions at different locations. Each of these smart nodes comprises the following components: transceiver, a processing unit, a memory unit, the power unit and the sensing unit. Sensor networks may have one or more gateway nodes (or sinks) that collect data from the sensors and forward it to an end-user application. In some rare circumstances, the sensor networks can be without any sink node. The aim of the sink node is to receive information from the network and to allow data aggregation and consumption.

A visualization of the main architectures for wireless ad hoc networks is shown in Figure 3. Note that the hybrid WMN is a joint combination of two layers: mesh client's layer and the mesh backbone layer which comprises the wired/wireless access points of the mesh network.

MANETs, WMSs, and WSNs share many characteristics. Nevertheless, there are some major differences between these networks (Akyildiz, & Wang, 2009), which are summarized in Table 2. The most essential differences between MANETs and other types of ad hoc networks are mobility and the QoS aspects. Instead, for WSNs the fundamental characteristics are the energy requirements and the self-organization.

For more details, the reader can consult several comprehensive surveys that discuss various aspect of MANETs (Stojmenovic, 2002), WMNs (Karrer, Pescapé, & Huehn, 2008; Akyildiz, & Wang, 2009), and WSNs (Bacioccola et al., 2010; Baronti et al., 2007; Stojmenovic, 2005, Xiao, Chen, & Li, 2010).

ATTACKS AND INTRUSIONS IN WIRELESS AD HOC NETWORKS

Due to their inherent vulnerabilities, such as resource constrains, uncontrollable environment, and dynamic network topology, wireless ad hoc networks are subject to a variety of *attacks* and

Table 2. MANET, WMS, and WSN

	Requirements	MANET	WMN	WSN
Goal	Intensive applications (file servers, voice/video transmission)	++++	-	-
	Community and neighborhood networking	-	++++	-
	Healthcare, climate and environmental monitoring, military	-	-	++++
Specification	Energy	++++	+++	+++++
	Multihopping	++++	+++	++++
	Mobility	+++++	+++	+++
	Scalability	+++	++++	++++
	Self-organization, self-healing and self-forming	++++	+++++	+++++
	Quality of Service (QoS)	++++	++	+
Legend: Crucial: +++++ Necessary: ++++ Important: +++ Desirable: ++ Irrelevant: +				

intrusions which could cripple them (Cao, Zhang, & Zhu, 2009; Carvalho, 2008; Cardenas, Roosta, & Sastry, 2009; Karl, & Wagner, 2003; Zhang, & Lee, 2000; Zhou, & Haas, 1999). Many researchers have given various definitions of intrusion and attack terms. According to the definition given in (Lazarevic, Kumar, & Srivastava, 2005, p. 22), "an attack is an intrusion attempt, and an intrusion results from an attack that has been (at least partially) successful."

In the last years, there have been numerous efforts to classify the security attacks in wireless ad hoc networks (Anantvalee, & Wu, 2007; Molva, & Michiardi, 2003; Naveen, & David, 2004; Ng, Sim, & Tan, 2006; Walters, Liang, Shi, & Chaudhary, 2007; Wu, Chen, Wu, & Cardei, 2006; Yang, Ricciato, Lu, & Zhang, 2006; Zhang, & Lee, 2000). From these papers, three taxonomies have been widely adopted: those based on the attack type, based on the localization of the attack, and according to network layers.

The first taxonomy splits the attacks into two classes: *active attacks*, like jamming, spoofing and Denial of Service (DoS), which can modify the information transmitted between the nodes and *passive attacks* such as traffic analysis and eavesdropping, that only gather sensitive information related to the ad hoc network.

Instead, the second taxonomy focuses on the location of the attacker with respect to the network (Amini, Mišic, & Mišic, 2007), and thus, identifies the external attacks that are performed by external agents and internal attacks which are carried out by nodes that belong to the ad hoc network. Unlike to outside attacks, the internal ones are more powerful and severe since the compromised node gained access to the secret information of the network (the cryptographic keys, the node location and identification, etc.).

Finally, the third classification is made according to the International Organization of Standardization (ISO) layer reference model. Table 3 presents the main security attacks in function of the network layers. Some of them, such as eavesdropping, message injection and node impersonation, involve an attacker which has gained the access to the wireless links between mobile stations. Instead, the weaknesses of medium access control (MAC) and of the routing protocols can be exploited by adversaries to devise several attacks such as (Kyasanur, & Vaidya, 2005; Perrig, Szewczyk, Tygar, Wen, & Culler, 2002):

- *Flooding attacks*, in which the attacker deluges the network with data packets in order to consume the node and network resources.

Table 3. Classification of attacks based on ISO layer reference model

Network layer	Attack name	Attack description
Physical	Jamming	Corruption of the wireless medium through strong interferences.
	Eavesdropping	Passive interception of the communication between the nodes.
Link	Disruption of MAC	The MAC specifications are deliberately broken by modifying the frames or the transmission procedure.
	Traffic analysis	Used to identify the communication parties. Generally, the information collected is used to launch further attacks.
	Resource consumption	The resources of target node are exhausted through repeated retransmission attempts.
Network	Flooding	Overwhelms victim's limited resources: memory, processing or bandwidth.
	Location disclosure	Location of the certain nodes and the topology of the network is revealed mainly through traffic analysis techniques.
	Sybil	Multiple attacker personalities are created throughout the network.
	Selective forwarding	The compromised node forward only some packets while dropping the other ones coming from certain nodes.
	Wormhole	Packets at one location in the network are tunneled to another location. It implies the cooperation of two adversaries.
	Blackhole	The compromised node refuses to participate in the routing process by dropping all packets received.
	Sinkhole	The traffic is modified in order to pass through a route that contains the attacker.
	Rushing	A fast side-channel is created between two attackers which acts as an effective DoS.
Transport	SYN flooding	The adversary creates many uncompleted TCP connections with a victim node.
	Session control	The attacker spoofs the IP address of a node and then continues the communication with other nodes.
Application	Repudiation	Denial of participation in communications.
	Virus and Worm	Malicious programs that exploit the vulnerabilities of the applications and operating systems.

- *Routing disturbance attacks*, such as sinkhole, blackhole and wormhole attacks, where the goal of the attacker is to change the route of the data packets.

It is worth pointing out that the attacking mechanism of several attacks can cause damages at multiple layers, being extremely difficult to devise security solutions against them (Anantvalee, & Wu, 2007). Additionally, the proliferation of the attack (i.e., the compromised nodes) and the effects that it generates in a sensor network was extensively studied by De et al. (2009).

Another important aspect is the assumptions related to the threat model. Generally, it is assumed that a single node (or o small set of nodes) is initially compromised through physical capture, and that the attacker is resource-constrained or possess significant computation power and storage space (Karlof, & Wagner, 2003; De, et al., 2009). It is obvious that an attacker equipped with a powerful device can jeopardize and eavesdrop the entire wireless ad hoc network. However, numerous security solutions proposed make idealistic assumption such as considering that *only one* node is compromised at a time and the adversary has limited power resources.

INTRUSION DETECTION SYSTEMS FOR WIRELESS AD HOC NETWORKS

The seminal paper of Zhang and Lee (1999) introduced the first IDS for wireless ad hoc network in 1999; since then numerous prototype systems have been proposed. Although they employ different techniques to analyze the network data, the striking aspect is that majority of them are based on a general framework that consists of the following modules: the data-collecting component, the intrusion detection (ID) engine, the knowledge base, the configurations files of the system and the alert module.

As pointed in (Zhang, & Lee, 1999) and (Anantvalee, & Wu, 2006), to deploy an IDS several considerations should be made. The first assumption asserts that the network activity (i.e., the node activity) is observable. The second important consideration implies the existence of a clear separation between the normal activities and the malicious ones, which permits to the IDS to assess the integrity of the network nodes.

Intrusion detection systems can be classified according to the source of the input information (e.g., audit data, network packets, network traffic, etc.) in either network-based or node(host)-based (Porras, 2009). In the following section, the recent IDSs are classified based on the detection approach used as follows: *misuse (or signature) based detection, anomaly based detection*, and *protocol analysis detection*. To complete their characterization we further divide them in *distributed/cooperative* where the detection process is cooperative and distributed among the nodes, and hierarchical that extend the cooperative detection to the cluster-based networks.

Signature Based Detection

This type of detection uses the information stored in the knowledge base to identify with high accuracy known threats. Due to its low false positive rate, signature based detection is widely employed in commercial IDS for wired networks, but less for wireless ad hoc networks. The main drawbacks of signature-based detection are the inefficiency to detect previously unseen attacks and the lack of understanding the network and applications protocols.

Distributed and Cooperative Techniques

In (Subhadrabandhu, Sarkar, & Anjum, 2006) a decentralized misuse detection algorithm is proposed. In order to work efficiently, the following important assumptions are made:

- The network is composed of two types of nodes: insider nodes which carry out the system tasks (i.e., route discovery, packet analysis, etc.), and outsider nodes (clients) that use the network merely to communicate. Although the task repartition between the nodes is heterogeneous, both types of nodes have the similar characteristics, i.e., limited energy, computation power and storage space.
- The outsider nodes have different security assets, which are independent.
- The adversaries (intruders) can capture *only* the outsider nodes. Hence, all the insider nodes are considered trustworthy. In addition, the network can hold multiple adversaries; their paths and locations are unknown and variable in time.
- The packets transmitted at the network layer are not encrypted (network layer encryption protocols such as IPsec are not supported).

The IDS module is run at the network layer in certain trustworthy (insider) nodes. However, since some insider nodes may not be able to execute the IDS, these nodes are further divided in IDS capable and IDS incapable. All the capable

Figure 4. The working principle of the scheme introduced by Subhadrabandhu et al. (2006). The intruder (i.e., the red node n_3) attacks the target node n_{11}. The nodes n_4, n_7 and n_{10} forward the packets of the intruder to the target node. The IDS capable nodes (i.e., the green nodes n_6, n_8 and n_9) receive the packets since there are in promiscuous mode. Aggregating the reports of the IDS capable nodes, the node n_7 takes the final decision.

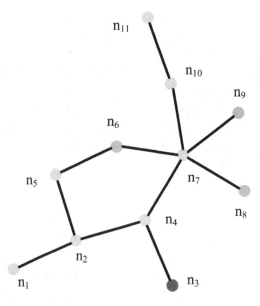

nodes function in promiscuous mode (they sniff any packet that is transmitted by its neighbors).

Adopting this approach, i.e., running the IDS only on some nodes, has the benefit of decreasing the resource consumption but it also rises several issues like: a) the selection of the optimal set of nodes that sniff and analyze the network packets, which have been proven to be an NP-hard problem, and b) the aggregation method used to fuse the decisions given by several capable IDS (see Figure 4). To tackle with the node selection problem Subhadrabandhu et al. (2009) devised two approximation algorithms: the Maximum Unsatisfied Neighbors in Extended Neighborhood (MUNEN) algorithm and the Random Placement (RP) algorithm. The MUNEN algorithm is suitable when the insider nodes move slowly while the RP is useful in the environments where insider nodes are highly dynamic. However, MUNEN performs better than RP regarding the resource consumption. For the second issue, the authors

introduced a distributed data aggregation method based on hypothesis testing and statistical analysis. The main idea is to apply optimal aggregation rules which aims to minimize the system risk. To improve the detection rate each outsider node can be monitored by multiples IDS capable nodes, as illustrated in Figure 4. The experimental results show that the IDS offers a good compromise between complexity and detection accuracy.

Exploiting the game theory, Chen and Leneutre (2009) formulate the intrusion detection problem as a "non-cooperative game." Further, they derive the probable behavior of adversaries together with the minimum necessaries resources and optimal strategy for the defenders (i.e., node that run the IDS module). As in (Subhadrabandhu, Sarkar, & Anjum, 2006) the authors try to determine the optimal strategy for the defenders, i.e., the number of IDS capable nodes necessary to monitor securely the outside nodes, by employing a game theoretical approach. Thus, the problem is seen from two different angles: in (Subhadra-bandhu, Sarkar, & Anjum, 2006) from an optimization angle while in (Chen, & Leneutre, 2009) from a game theoretical angle. In the same study, the authors discus several variants of the main model: Stackleberg ID game which considers the case where the insiders can mount attacks based on the strategy of the defenders or conversely, and ID game with generalized attack model where the adversaries can launch many attacks with different costs and achievements. One of the most important aspects of this general framework is its ability to evaluate and design intrusion detection system, regardless of the detection method used.

ANOMALY BASED DETECTION

Anomaly based detection (Callegari, Giordano, & Pagano, 2009) analyzes the network activity in order to identify possible threats. The activity profiles are constructed by analyzing the characteristics of the network components, e.g., nodes, users or applications. The major advantage of anomaly-based methods is that they are capable to detect efficiently unknown threats. However, these methods produce numerous false positive (i.e., the identification of legitimate activity as being malicious), especially in dynamic systems where allowable activities can easily misclassified.

Distributed and Cooperative Techniques

Shrestha et al. (2009) devised an intusion detection solution with authentication capability in MANET. In their embodiment, which is similar to (Zhang & Lee, 2000), each node is equipped with an IDS module which collects, analyzes and detects local events (e.g., the network packets). Additionally, the nodes communicate with each other in order to detect cooperatively intrusions. To increase the security of the transmitted data an authentication based on hash chains is devised. However, executing IDS in each node consume significant resources like energy, CPU cycles and

memory (Chen, & Leneutre, 2009). Furthermore, the experimental tests are not sufficient to prove the effectiveness of the proposed solution.

Krontiris et al. (2009) devised the first general framework for intrusion detection in WSNs which is focused on the collaboration between sensors. The scheme considers only the case where the IDS attempts to identify a single malicious node since this situation is already very complex. Another important presumption is that each node "sees" its 2-hop neighbors. The intrusion detection evolves in three steps:

- *Alerting.* Each node is installed with an alert module which aim to locally detect attacks. Whenever an alert module of a node (called the alerted node) detects a suspicious activity in its vicinity it outputs the set of suspected nodes (i.e., suspected set). There may by more than one suspected set since many nodes are alerted if a suspicious activity is present.
- *Voting.* The suspected sets, which are cryptographically signed, are interchanged among all the alerted nodes with the aid of a broadcast message-suppression protocol similar to SPIN (Kulik, Heinzelman, & Balakrishnan, 2002). Since the nodes are not synchronized, an attacker can delay and forge its vote during this phase. The algorithm resolves this issue by relaying on the alternatives paths that may exists between the sensor nodes.
- *Revealing.* Each alerted node, which knows the suspected sets of all other alerted nodes, identifies the nodes that appear most frequently and then exposes it. If the alerted nodes cannot reach the agreement regarding the attacker an additional step, called external ring enforcement, is applied which consists in taking into consideration also the results of the neighbors of the alerted nodes. Hence, this procedure

tries to break the uncertain situation by extending the results set.

The memory ROM and RAM requirements of the proposed solution are relatively low, taking as the reference the Tmote Sky sensor architecture which has 10KB of RAM and 48KB of program memory. The communication overhead is between 12 packets to 19 packets, and depends mainly on the topology of the network and the number of the alerted nodes. Several variants of this scheme, which deal with the detection of certain attacks such as the blackhole and sinkhole attacks, can be found in (Krontiris, Dimitriou, & Freiling, 2007; Giannetous, Kromtiris, & Dimitriou, 2009). In addition, in (Kromtiris, Giannetous, & Dimitriou, 2008) is given a lightweight implementation of this intrusion detection method based on mobile agents.

Komninos and Douligeris (2009), proposed a multilayered intrusion detection framework for ad-hoc networks. This type of intrusion detection is denominated low-level IDS by Lauf et al. (2009) since it collects and analyzes the data at the link and network layers. Due to the untrustworthy and distributed environment, the authors state that *each* node needs to have its own intrusion detection module. To perform the *local detection*, firstly the IDS module of the nodes collects the network data by means of a binary tree structure. Secondly, with the aid of the collected data, considered as data points, a unique polynomial is generated through a Lagrange interpolation method. Finally, an attacker is detected if the polynomial generated within the node converges in a predefined interval given by a secret function. In addition, when more information is necessary to improve the detection, the information from the neighborhoods nodes is used. This assumes that a secure connection between the nodes participating in the collaborative detection can be established. The cooperative detection is realized with the help of a linear threshold scheme, i.e., the shares of a secret are distributed to a set of nodes such that the shares form the secret through a linear combination. In the experimental setup the anomaly detection solution, implemented for various proactive routing protocols, shown satisfactory results. However, the detection accuracy depends on the secret function while the distribution of subshares causes a communication overhead for the cooperative intrusion.

In (Creti et al., 2009) a multigrade monitoring (MGM) approach in wireless ad hoc network is introduced. The main idea is to employ sequentially two different intrusion detection approaches: a lightweight method that detects the evidence of attacks and a heavyweight technique that has low false negative rate and no false positive. For the lightweight method, the authors use local monitoring (Zhang & Lee, 2000) which is energy efficient but suffers from high false positive rate. To mitigate this drawback a second technique with high detection performances, called Route Verification (RV), is applied. However, the RV protocol consumes important energy resources due to communication overhead. In essence, the MGM approach provides a modality to equilibrate the security goals and the network resources.

Hierarchical Techniques

Hierarchical IDS techniques were proposed for those ad hoc networks that can be separated into clusters, i.e., a set of nodes that share common characteristics such as links, neighbors, affinities etc.. This type of network is composed of cluster heads, which are similar to switches, routers, or gateway, and monitored nodes. According to the node type, the intrusion detection operates *locally* in each monitored node and *globally* within the cluster heads.

Recently, Chen et al. (2010) proposed an isolation table intrusion detection technique (ITIDS) for hierarchical ad hoc networks. Briefly, this IDS merges to hierarchical intrusion detection methods: the Collaboration-based Intrusion Detection (CBID) (Bhuse, & Gupta, 2006) and the Routing

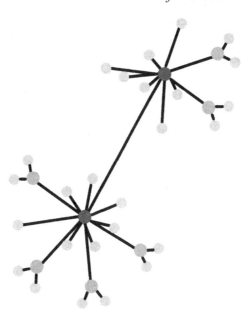

Figure 5. Cluster-base hierarchical ad hoc network: red nodes are the primary cluster heads (PCHs), green nodes are the secondary cluster heads (SCHs) and blue nodes are the member nodes (MNs) for the SCHs. Note that all the green and blue nodes are MNs for the PCHs.

Tables Intrusion Detection (RTID) (Su, Chang, & Kuo, 2006). The CBID uses the cluster heads to monitor and to detect intrusions among the monitored nodes. Instead, the intrusions in RTID are detected with the aid of the routing table. Unlike to CBID, this scheme fragments the network in primary cluster heads, secondary cluster heads and monitored nodes (see Figure 5).

Furthermore, to avoid the energy consumption each malicious node that is detected will be isolated and reordered on the isolation list. However, two aspects are not clear: firstly, the recovery procedure of the isolated nodes and secondly, the memory and communication overhead induced by employing this detection approach.

Mobile agents have been used in IDS due to their capacity to move in large networks. Generally, several mobile agents are attached to each node allowing the execution of the intrusion detection operations. Recently, several intrusion detection techniques that use agents have been devised. For instance, MUSK (Khanum et al., 2010) is an agent-based intrusion detection ar-

chitecture for hierarchical WSNs. Locally, each MUSK agents that detects an intrusion sends an intrusion report to the cluster head (CH) node. Afterwards, CH applies, within the cluster of which is responsible, a voting scheme to assess the intrusion occurrence. If a real intrusion is detected then CH sends a message to the sink node which gives the suitable response. The advantages of the proposed scheme are elimination of duplicate data, reduction of communication overhead and robustness against attacks carried out by nodes belonging to different clusters.

Pugliese et al. (2009), proposed a novel IDS in clustered WSNs based on mobile agents and non-parametric version of Hidden Markov Models (HMMs). A HMM is a stochastic finite state machine (FSM) that is generated by a stochastic process (the real state of the·system). The real state of the system (i.e., the sensor network) is hidden but indirectly observable through another system that generates observable events. HMM and the more general Markov chains have been extensively used in network-based IDS for wired networks (Cheng, 2009; Pugliese et al., 2009). To detect intrusion, the devised system correlates them with the sequences of observable events by applying a set of anomaly rules. The observable events are used to predict the hidden state of the system and assess if an intrusion occurred. To improve the detection accuracy and reduce energy consumption the authors replace the HMMs with the weak process model (WPMs), which are "a non-parametric version of HMMs wherein state transition probabilities are reduced to rules of reachability" (p. 34, Pugliese et al. 2009). The estimation of the threats are reduced to the problem of finding the most probable state sequence of the HMM. In addition, the attacks are classified according to an attack score in low and high potential attacks. However, the scheme assumes that a secure routing protocol (Du, & Peng, 2009) is in place, and the control messages are encrypted and authenticated. Furthermore, the experimental test show that the scheme has a high false positive rate and the detection ability is restricted to flooding, sinkhole, and wormhole attacks.

The nature of ad hoc networks imposes the adoption of IDS that are dynamic and cooperative. Nevertheless, cooperative intrusion detection is a hard problem since the reputation of the nodes cannot be prior assessed. A possible solution is to devise a trust model for the ad hoc network and then to employ it when performing aggregation of multiple detection results. Following this idea Wang et al., (2009) designed an IDS based on a trust model, called IDMTM. The interesting idea is the association of a *trust value* to each node of the network, which is computed in function of his behavior. The IDMTM is running on each node and consist of two modules: the interior and exterior modules. The former monitors several nodes through "evidence chains" and evaluates their trust values, while the latter module carries out the trust recommendations and data aggregation. In order to lower the false positive rate, the trust value is categorized in several levels: compromised, minimum, medium, high, and

highest. The experimental results show good detection performances, performing better than the algorithm proposed by Zhang and Lee (2000).

PROTOCOL ANALYSIS DETECTION

Protocol analysis detection is similar to anomaly-based method the only difference being the admissible profiles which represent the *normal activity of the network protocols*, instead of the network components. Thus, these methods are able to scan and understand the state of network, transport and applications protocols.

Realizing the computational overhead of the low-level IDS (i.e., IDS that analyzes data from the link and network layers), Lauf et al. (2010) proposed an application-level distributed IDS. The abstractions of the application level protocol allow the nodes to model the environment wherein they operate. By focusing on the application layer the IDS is able to identify anomalous patterns through interaction semantic. In order to detect threats, in each node a hybrid IDS, which combines two intrusion detection methods, is installed.

The role of the former method, called Maxima Detection System (MDS), is twofold: (i) to consent the detection of one compromised node and (ii) to train the second detection method. The latter approach, called Cross-Correlative Detection System (CCDS), allows the detection of multiples threats. To generate the behaviors and interactions among the nodes (i.e., the dynamic of the ad hoc network) the hybrid IDS uses an integer labeling system. The proposed solution was tested in several environmental scenarios like aviation sector (Automated Dependent Surveillance) and massively distributed microrobotics, displaying good performances. However, the communication overhead induced is not calculated and there are no comparative tests with other similar schemes. Furthermore, the main problem of this type of detection is that it needs many resources due to the complex analysis involved in checking the integrity of the communication protocols.

CONCLUSION AND FUTURE RESEARCH DIRECTIONS

Due to the increasing demand of wireless ad hoc networks coupled with their inherent vulnerabilities, the security has become a crucial and hard to achieve requirement. The preventive mechanism like encryption, authentication, secure routing and firewalls, are not efficient against many attacks and intrusions. Thus, intrusion detection mechanisms designed especially for wireless ad hoc networks have appeared in the last years.

Throughout this paper, we have reviewed and analyzed the principal IDS that were devised during the last years together with the attacks that can be mount against them. From this investigation emerges several important characteristics:

- Since the attacks that effect ad hoc networks are evolving continuously, e.g., the new jamming attack developed by Law et al. (2009) or the security of route discovery identified by Burmester et al. (2009), the IDSs employ, in principal, the anomaly detection approach. Instead, the schemes that are based on misuse detection (Subhadrabandhu, Sarkar, & Anjum, 2006; Chen, & Leneutre, 2009) suffer from the inability to detect unknown attacks and difficulty to update the detection rules (i.e., the signatures) (Kominos, & Douligeris, 2009).
- The majorities of IDS solutions are cooperative, distributed and hierarchical architectures, trend that is imposed mainly by the nature of wireless ad hoc networks.
- The distributed configuration raises the data fusion problem. When an attack occurs in a certain area of the network, data aggregation is performed *locally*, in a specific node or in a distributed manner. If specified nodes (cluster head nodes) are responsible for data aggregation and computation of the detection result then these nodes can become principal targets for the attackers. Furthermore, since these operations are computation intensive they can quickly exhaust the resource of cluster head nodes (Krontiris, Dimitriou, & Giannetsos, 2008). Instead, the aggregation in a distributed fashion is more suitable for sensor networks but generates complication during the agreement process.
- The IDS process can be performed by all nodes or only by a set of nodes to decrease the resource consumption. The selection of the most suitable nodes can be realized through statistical analysis (Subhadrabandhu, Sarkar, & Anjum, 2006) or by employing the game theoretical approach (Chen, & Leneutre, 2009).
- Several papers started to incorporate concepts derived from the social network analysis such as trust, reputation, and recommendation, into the cooperative IDS (Li, Joshi, & Finin, 2010; Li, Joshi, & Finin, 2010; Wang, Huang, Zhao, & Rong, 2008; Wang, Man, & Liu, 2009; Zhang, Ho, & Naït-Abdesselam, 2010). There are two major drawbacks with this approach: first, the performances of IDS depend on the accuracy of the trust model (Omar, Challal, & Bouabdallah, 2009) and second, the infection caused by a compromised node can propagate via the established trust (De, Liu, & Das, 2009; Khanum, Usman, Hussain, Zafar, & Sher, 2009).
- The experimental tests performed in majority of the IDS are incomplete to draw any conclusion. Among the most important missing information we can mention: the false positive and negative rates, the communication overhead and the resource consumption. Furthermore, the performances of the IDS are not compared with other similar schemes.

Several researchers have used triggers to activate sequentially IDS with increased levels of monitoring. A hybrid intrusion detection architecture tries to combine intelligently advantages of several ID methods while avoiding their limitations (Chen, Hsieh, & Huang, 2010; Creti, Beaman, Bagchi, Li, & Lu, 2009; Lauf, Peters, & Robinson, 2010). There is no much research conducted in this area, thus it could be an interesting research direction.

A variety of attacks affects all the network layers. Depending on the layer, they can have a different behavior, e.g., an attack at the application level cannot raise any suspicion at lower layers (Bellovin et al., 2008). Du to these issues, the development of intrusion detection solutions that operate in all network layers in an interactively manner and provide defense against multiple attacks constitutes another challenge and fruitful area of research.

REFERENCES

Akyildiz, I., & Wang, X. (2009). *Wireless mesh networks*. West Sussex, UK: Wiley and Sons. doi:10.1002/9780470059616

Amini, F., Mišic, V. B., & Mišic, J. (2007). Intrusion detection in wireless sensor networks. In Y. Xiao (Ed.), *Security in distributed, grid, and pervasive computing* (pp. 112-127). Boca Raton, FL: Auerbach Publications, CRC Press.

Anantvalee, T., & Wu, J. (2007). A survey on intrusion detection in mobile ad hoc networks. In Xiao, Y., Shen, X. S., & Du, D.-Z. (Eds.), *Wireless network security* (pp. 19–78). Springer, US. doi:10.1007/978-0-387-33112-6_7

Axelsson, S. (1999). *Research in intrusion-detection systems: A survey. Technical Report*. Goteborg, Sweden: Chalmers University of Technology.

Bace, R., & Mell, P. (2001). *Guide to intrusion detection and prevention systems (IDPS)* (pp. 1–127). National Institue of Standards Special Publication on Intrusion Detection Systems.

Bacioccola, A., Cicconetti, C., Eklund, C., Lenzini, L., Li, Z., & Mingozzi, E. (2010). IEEE 802.16: History, status and future trends. *Computer Communications*, *33*(2), 113–123. doi:10.1016/j.comcom.2009.11.003

Baronti, P., Pillai, P., Chook, V. W. C., Chessa, S., Gotta, A., & Hu, Y. F. (2007). Wireless sensor networks: A survey on the state of the art and the 802.15.4 and ZigBee standards. *Computer Communications*, *30*(7), 1655–1695. doi:10.1016/j.comcom.2006.12.020

Barry, B. I. A. (2009). Intrusion detection with OMNeT++. In *Proceedings of the 2nd International Conference on Simulation Tools and Techniques*.

Barry, B. I. A., & Chan, H. A. (2010). Intrusion detection systems. In Stavroulakis, P., & Stamp, M. (Eds.), *Handbook of information and communication security* (pp. 193–205). Berlin, Germany: Springer-Verlag. doi:10.1007/978-3-642-04117-4_10

Bellovin, S. M., Benzel, T. V., Blakley, B., Denning, D. E., Diffie, W., Epstein, J., & Verissimo, P. (2008). Information assurance technology forecast 2008. *IEEE Security and Privacy*, *6*(1), 16–23. doi:10.1109/MSP.2008.13

Bhuse, V., & Gupta, A. (2006). Anomaly intrusion detection in wireless sensor networks. *Journal of High Speed Networks*, *5*, 33–51.

Burmester, M., & de Medeiros, B. (2009). On the security of route discovery in MANETs. *IEEE Transactions on Mobile Computing*, *8*(9), 1180–1188. doi:10.1109/TMC.2009.13

Callegari, C., Giordano, S., & Pagano, M. (2009). New statistical approaches for anomaly detection. *Security and Communication Networks*, *2*(6), 611–634.

Cao, G., Zhang, W., & Zhu, S. (Eds.). (2009). Special issue on privacy and security in wireless sensor and ad hoc networks. *Ad Hoc Networks*, *7*(8), 1431–1576. doi:10.1016/j.adhoc.2009.05.001

Cardenas, A. A., Roosta, T., & Sastry, S. (2009). Rethinking security properties, threat models, and the design space in sensor networks: A case study in SCADA systems. *Ad Hoc Networks*, *7*(8), 1434–1447. doi:10.1016/j.adhoc.2009.04.012

Carvalho, M. (2008). Security in mobile ad hoc networks. *IEEE Privacy and Security*, *6*(2), 72–75. doi:10.1109/MSP.2008.44

Chen, L., & Leneutre, J. (2009). A game theoretical framework on intrusion detection in heterogeneous networks. *IEEE Transaction on Information Forensics and Security*, *4*(2), 165–178. doi:10.1109/TIFS.2009.2019154

Chen, R.-C., Hsieh, C.-F., & Huang, Y.-F. (2010). An isolation intrusion detection system for hierarchical wireless sensor networks. *Journal of Networks*, *5*(3), 335–342.

Creti, M. T., Beaman, M., Bagchi, S., Li, Z., & Lu, Y.-H. (2009). Multigrade security monitoring for ad-hoc wireless networks. In *Proceedings of the 6th IEEE International Conference on Mobile Ad-hoc and Sensor Systems*.

De, P., Liu, Y., & Das, S. K. (2009). Deployment-aware modeling of node compromise spread in wireless sensor networks using epidemic theory. *ACM Transactions on Sensor Networks*, *5*(3), 1–33. doi:10.1145/1525856.1525861

Denning, D. E. (1987). An intrusion detection model. *IEEE Transactions on Software Engineering*, *13*(2), 222–232. doi:10.1109/TSE.1987.232894

Du, J., & Peng, S. (2009). Choice of Secure routing protocol for applications in wireless sensor networks. In *Proceedings of the International Conference on Multimedia Information Networking and Security*, *2*, 470–473. doi:10.1109/MINES.2009.14

Farooqi, A. S., & Khan, F. A. (2009). Intrusion detection systems for wireless sensor networks: a survey. In Ślęzak, D. (Eds.), *Communication and networking* (pp. 234–241). Berlin, Germany: Springer-Verlag. doi:10.1007/978-3-642-10844-0_29

Garcia-Teodoro, P., Diaz-Verdejo, J., Macia-Fernandez, G., & Vazquez, E. (2009). Anomaly-based network intrusion detection: Techniques, systems and challenges. *Computers & Security*, *28*(1-2), 18–28. doi:10.1016/j.cose.2008.08.003

Gast, M. S. (2005). *802.11 wireless networks: The definitive guide* (2nd ed.). Sebastopol, CA: O'Reilly Media.

Giannetous, T., Kromtiris, I., & Dimitriou, T. (2009). Intrusion detection in wireless sensor networks. In Y. Zhang, & P. Kitsos (Ed.), *Security in RFID and sensor networks* (pp. 321-341). Boca Raton, FL: Auerbach Publications, CRC Press.

Giordano, S. (2002). Mobile ad hoc networks. In Stojmenovic, J. (Ed.), *Handbook of wireless networks and mobile computing* (pp. 325–346). New York, NY: John Wiley & Sons, Inc. doi:10.1002/0471224561.ch15

Jackson, K. (1999). *Intrusion detection system product survey*. (Laboratory Research Report, LA-UR-99-3883). Los Alamos National Laboratory.

Kabiri, P., & Ghorbani, A. A. (2005). Research on intrusion detection and response: A survey. *International Journal of Network Security*, *1*(2), 84–102.

Karlof, C., & Wagner, D. (2003). Secure routing in wireless sensor networks: Attacks and countermeasures. *Ad Hoc Networks*, *1*(2-3), 293–315. doi:10.1016/S1570-8705(03)00008-8

Karrer, R. P., Pescapé, A., & Huehn, T. (2008). Challenges in second-generation wireless mesh networks. *EURASIP Journal on Wireless Communications and Networking*, *2008*, 1–10. doi:10.1155/2008/274790

Khanum, S., Usman, M., Hussain, K., Zafar, R., & Sher, M. (2009). Energy-efficient intrusion detection system for wireless sensor network based on musk architecture. In Zhang, W., Chen, Z., Douglas, C. C., & Tong, W. (Eds.), *High performance computing and applications* (pp. 212–217). Berlin, Germany: Springer-Verlag.

Komninos, N., & Douligeris, C. (2009). LIDF: Layered intrusion detection framework for ad-hoc networks. *Ad Hoc Networks*, *7*(1), 171–182. doi:10.1016/j.adhoc.2008.01.001

Krontiris, I., Benenson, Z., Giannetsos, T., Freiling, F. C., & Dimitriou, T. (2009). Cooperative intrusion detection in wireless sensor networks. In Roedig, U., & Sreenan, C. J. (Eds.), *Wireless sensor networks* (pp. 263–278). Berlin, Germany: Springer-Verlag. doi:10.1007/978-3-642-00224-3_17

Krontiris, I., Dimitriou, T., & Freiling, F. C. (2007). Towards intrusion detection in wireless sensor networks. In *Proceedings of the 13th European Wireless Conference* (pp. 1-10).

Krontiris, I., Dimitriou, T., & Giannetsos, T. (2008). LIDeA: A distributed lightweight intrusion detection architecture for sensor networks. In *Proceeding of the fourth International Conference on Security and Privacy for Communication*.

Kulik, J., Heinzelman, W., & Balakrishnan, H. (2002). Negotiation-based protocols for disseminating information in wireless sensor networks. *Wireless Networks*, *8*(2-3), 169–185. doi:10.1023/A:1013715909417

Kyasanur, P., & Vaidya, N. H. (2005). Selfish MAC layer misbehavior in wireless networks. *IEEE Transactions on Mobile Computing*, *4*(5), 502–516. doi:10.1109/TMC.2005.71

Lauf, A. P., Peters, R. A., & Robinson, W. H. (2010). A distributed intrusion detection system for resource-constrained devices in ad-hoc networks. *Ad Hoc Networks*, *8*(3), 253–266. doi:10.1016/j.adhoc.2009.08.002

Law, Y. W., Palaniswami, M., Hoesel, L. V., Doumen, J., Hartel, P., & Havinga, P. (2009). Energy-efficient link-layer jamming attacks against wireless sensor network MAC protocols. *ACM Transactions on Sensor Networks*, *5*(1), 1–38. doi:10.1145/1464420.1464426

Lazarevic, A., Kumar, V., & Srivastava, J. (2005). Intrusion detection: A survey. In Kumar, V., Lazarevic, A., & Srivastava, J. (Eds.), *Managing cyber threats* (pp. 19–78). New York, NY: Springer-Verlag. doi:10.1007/0-387-24230-9_2

Li, W., Joshi, A., & Finin, T. (2010). (accepted for publication). Security through collaboration and trust in MANETs. *ACM/Springer*. *Mobile Networks and Applications*. doi:10.1007/s11036-010-0243-9

Li, W., Joshi, A., & Finin, T. (2010). Coping with node misbehaviors in ad hoc networks: A multi-dimensional trust management approach. In *Proceedings of the 11th IEEE International Conference on Mobile Data Management* (pp. 85-94).

Lima, M. N., dos Santos, L. A., & Pujolle, G. (2009). A survey of survivability in mobile ad hoc networks. *IEEE Communications Surveys and Tutorials*, *11*(1), 1–28. doi:10.1109/SURV.2009.090106

Madhavi, S., & Kim, T., H. (2008). An intrusion detection system in mobile ad-hoc networks. *International Journal of Security and Its Applications*, *2*(3), 1–17.

Mandala, S., Ngadi, M. A., & Abdullah, A. H. (2008). A survey on MANET intrusion detection. *International Journal of Computer Science and Security*, *2*(1), 1–11.

Milenković, A., Otto, C., & Jovanov, E. (2006). Wireless sensor networks for personal health monitoring: Issues and an implementation. *Computer Communications*, *29*(13-14), 2521–2533. doi:10.1016/j.comcom.2006.02.011

Mishra, A., Nadkarni, K., & Patcha, A. (2004). Intrusion detection in wireless ad hoc networks. *IEEE Wireless Communications*, *11*, 48–60. doi:10.1109/MWC.2004.1269717

Molva, R., & Michiardi, P. (2003). Security in ad hoc networks. In M. Conti et al. (Eds.), *Personal Wireless Communications, 2775*, 756-775. Berlin, Germany: Springer-Verlag.

Naveen, S., & David, W. (2004). Security considerations for IEEE 802.15.4 networks. In *Proceedings of the ACM Workshop on Wireless Security* (pp. 32-42). New York, NY: ACM Press.

Neves, P., Stachyra, M., & Rodrigues, J. (2008). Application of wireless sensor networks to healthcare promotion. *Journal of Communications Software and Systems*, *4*(3), 181–190.

Ng, H. S., Sim, M. L., & Tan, C. M. (2006). Security issues of wireless sensor networks in healthcare applications. *BT Technology Journal*, *24*(2), 138–144. doi:10.1007/s10550-006-0051-8

Omar, M., Challal, Y., & Bouabdallah, A. (2009). Reliable and fully distributed trust model for mobile ad hoc networks. *Computers & Security*, *28*(3-4), 199–214. doi:10.1016/j.cose.2008.11.009

Parker, J., Pinkston, J., Undercoffer, J., & Joshi, A. (2004). On intrusion detection in mobile ad hoc networks. In *23rd IEEE International Performance Computing and Communications Conference - Workshop on Information Assurance*.

Perrig, A., Szewczyk, R., Tygar, J., Wen, V., & Culler, D. E. (2002). SPINS: Security protocols for sensor networks. *Wireless Networks*, *8*, 521–534. doi:10.1023/A:1016598314198

Porras, P. (2009). Directions in network-based security monitoring. *IEEE Privacy and Security*, *7*(1), 82–85. doi:10.1109/MSP.2009.5

Pugliese, M., Giani, A., & Santucci, F. (2009). Weak process models for attack detection in a clustered sensor network using mobile agents. In Hailes, S., Sicari, S., & Roussos, G. (Eds.), *Sensor systems and software* (pp. 33–50). Berlin, Germany: Springer-Verlag.

Rafsanjani, M. K., Movaghar, A., & Koroupi, F. (2008). Investigating intrusion detection systems in MANET and comparing IDSs for detecting misbehaving nodes. *World Academy of Science. Engineering and Technology*, *44*, 351–355.

Raghavendra, C. S., Sivalingam, K. M., & Znati, T. (Eds.). (2004). *Wireless sensor networks*. Berlin/Heidelberg, Germany: Spriger-Verlag. doi:10.1007/b117506

Sabahi, V., & Movaghar, A. (2008). *Intrusion detection: A survey*. In Third International Conference on Systems and Networks Communications (pp.23-26).

Shrestha, R., Sung, J.-Y., Lee, S.-D., Pyung, S.-Y., Choi, D.-Y., & Han, S.-J. (2009). A secure intrusion detection system with authentication in mobile ad hoc network. In *Proceedings of the Pacific-Asia Conference on Circuits, Communications and Systems* (pp.759-762).

Stojmenovic, I. (Ed.). (2002). *Handbook of wireless networks and mobile computing*. New York, NY: John Willy & Sons. doi:10.1002/0471224561

Stojmenovic, I. (Ed.). (2005). *Handbook of Sensor Networks*. England: John Willy & Sons. doi:10.1002/047174414X

Subhadrabandhu, D., Sarkar, S., & Anjum. F. (2006). *A statistical framework for intrusion detection in ad hoc networks*. IEEE INFOCOM.

Vu, T. M., Safavi-Naini, R., & Williamson, C. (2010). Securing wireless sensor networks against large-scale node capture attacks. In *Proceedings of the 5th ACM Symposium on Information, Computer and Communications Security* (pp. 112-123).

Walters, J. P., Liang, Z., Shi, W., & Chaudhary, V. (2007). Wireless sensor network security: A survey. In Y. Xiao (Ed.), *Security in distributed, grid, and pervasive computing* (pp. 367-311). Boca Raton, FL: Auerbach Publications, CRC Press.

Wang, F., Huang, C., Zhao, J., & Rong, C. (2008). IDMTM: A novel intrusion detection mechanism based on trust model for ad hoc networks. In *Proceedings of the 22nd International Conference on Advanced Information Networking and Applications* (pp. 978-984).

Wang, W., Man, H., & Liu, Y. (2009). A framework for intrusion detection systems by social network analysis methods in ad hoc networks. *Security and Communication Networks*, *2*(6), 669–685.

Wu, B., Chen, J., Wu, J., & Cardei, M. (2006). A survey on attacks and countermeasures in mobile ad hoc networks. In Xiao, Y., Shen, X., & Du, D.-Z. (Eds.), *Wireless/mobile network security* (pp. 170–176). Berlin/Heidelberg, Germany: Spriger-Verlag.

Wu, S. X., & Banzhaf, W. (2010). The use of computational intelligence in intrusion detection systems: A review. *Applied Soft Computing*, *10*(1), 1–35. doi:10.1016/j.asoc.2009.06.019

Xiao, Y., Chen, H., & Li, F. H. (Eds.). (2010). *Handbook on sensor networks*. Hackensack, NJ: World Scientific Publishing Co. doi:10.1142/9789812837318

Yang, H., Ricciato, F., Lu, S., & Zhang, L. (2006). Securing a wireless world. *Proceedings of the IEEE*, *94*(2), 442–454. doi:10.1109/JPROC.2005.862321

Zhang, Y., & Lee, W. (2000). Intrusion detection in wireless ad-hoc networks. In *Proceedings of the 6th Annual International Conference on Mobile Computing and Networking* (pp. 275-283).

Zhang, Z., Ho, P.-H., & Naït-Abdesselam, F. (2010). (in press). RADAR: A reputation-driven anomaly detection system for wireless mesh networks. *Wireless Networks*. doi:10.1007/s11276-010-0255-1

Zhou, L., & Haas, Z. (1999). *Securing ad hoc networks. (Technical Report, TR99-1772)*. Ithaca, NY: Cornell University.

ADDITIONAL READING

ACM International Conference on Mobile Computing and Networking (www.acm.org/sigmobile).

ACM Symposium on Mobile Ad Hoc Networking and Computing (http://www.sigmobile.org/mobihoc/). ACM Symposium on Information, Computer and Communications Security.

ACM Transactions on Sensor Networks. (http://tosn.acm.org/).

ACM/Springer Wireless Networks. (http://www.springer.com/engineering/signals/journal/11276).

Choi, H., Enck, W., Shin, J., Mcdaniel, P. D., & Porta, T. F. (2009). ASR: anonymous and secure reporting of traffic forwarding activity in mobile ad hoc networks. *Wireless Networks*, *15*(4), 525–539. doi:10.1007/s11276-007-0067-0

Communications of the ACM. (www.acm.org).

Elsevier Ad Hoc Networks. (http://www.elsevier.com/wps/find/journaldescription. cws_home/672380/description#description).

Elsevier Computer Communications. (http://www.elsevier.com/wps/find/journal description.cws_home/525440/description#description).

Elsevier Computer Networks. (http://www.elsevier.com/wps/find/journaldescription. cws_home/505606/description#description).

Elsevier Computers and Security (http://www.elsevier.com/wps/find/journaldescription. cws_home/405877/description#description).

Elsevier Journal of Network and Computer Applications. (http://www.elsevier.com/wps/find/journaldescription.cws_home/622893/description#description).

Ferreira, A., Goldman, A., & Monteiro, J. (2010). Performance evaluation of routing protocols for MANETs with known connectivity patterns using evolving graphs. *Wireless Networks*, *16*(3), 627–640. doi:10.1007/s11276-008-0158-6

IEEE GLOBECOM. (http://www.ieee-globecom.org/).

IEEE INFOCOM. (www.ieee-infocom.org).

IEEE International Conference on Advanced Information Networking and Applications (http://www.aina-conference.org/). Commercial Intrusion Detection Systems. Retrieved June 01, 2010, from http://www.dmoz.org/Computers/ Security/ Intrusion_Detection_Systems/.

IEEE Transactions on Mobile Computing. (http://www.computer.org/portal/web/tmc).

IEEE/ACM Transactions on Networking. (http://www.ton.seas.upenn.edu/).

International Collaboration for Advancing Security Technology. (iCAST) (2006-2009). Retrieved June 01, 2010, from http://www.icast.org.tw/

International Symposium on Recent Advances in Intrusion Detection (http://www.raid-symposium.org/).

Mobile, A. C. M. Computing and Communications Review (http://www.acm.org/sigmobile/ MC2R).

NIST. Wireless Ad Hoc Networks, Advance Network Technologies Division. Retrieved June, 01, 2010, from http://www.antd.nist.gov/wahn_home. shtml

Simplicio, M. A. Jr, Barreto, P. S. L. M., Margi, C. B., & Carvalho, T. C. M. B. (2010). (in press). A survey on key management mechanisms for distributed Wireless Sensor Networks. *Computer Networks*. doi:10.1016/j.comnet.2010.04.010

Stavrou, E., & Pitsillides, A. (2010). (in press). A survey on secure multipath routing protocols in WSNs. *Computer Networks*. doi:10.1016/j.comnet.2010.02.015

Tarique, M., Tepe, K. E., Adibi, S., & Erfani, S. (2009). Survey of multipath routing protocols for mobile ad hoc networks. *Journal of Network and Computer Applications*, *32*(6), 1125–1143. doi:10.1016/j.jnca.2009.07.002

Wilensky, U. (1999). NetLogo. *Center for Connected Learning and Computer-Based Modeling*. Northwestern University, Evanston, IL Retrievd June 01, 2010, from http://ccl.northwestern.edu/netlogo/

Wiley Security and Communication Networks (http://www3.interscience.wiley. com/journal/114299116/home).

Wireless Sensor Networks Security. (2004-2010). Retrieved June 01, 2010, from http://www.wsn-security.info/index.htm

Zhang, J., & Varadharajan, V. (2010). Wireless sensor network key management survey and taxonomy. *Journal of Network and Computer Applications*, *33*(2), 63–75. doi:10.1016/j.jnca.2009.10.001

Zhang, Z., Zhou, H., & Gao, J. (2009). Scrutinizing Performance of Ad Hoc Routing Protocols on Wireless Sensor Networks. In *Proceedings of the Asian Conference on Intelligent Information and Database Systems (pp. 459-464)*.

Zhu, B., Setia, S., Jajodia, S., Roy, S., & Wang, L. (2010). (in press). Localized Multicast: Efficient and Distributed Replica Detection in Large-Scale Sensor Networks. *IEEE Transactions on Mobile Computing*.

KEY TERMS AND DEFINITIONS

Ad Hoc Network: Consists of a group of mobile nodes (peers) which are able to communicate with each other without the intervention of an access point. Depending on their application, wireless ad hoc networks can be further classified into: mobile ad hoc networks (MANETs), wireless mesh networks (WMNs) and wireless sensor networks (WSNs).

Anomaly Based Detection: Analyzes the network activity in order to identify possible threats. The activity profiles are constructed by analyzing the characteristics of the network components, e.g., nodes, users or applications.

Authentication: Mechanisms that allow an entity to prove its identity to a remote user.

Authorization: Refers to the access control mechanisms and to the ability of an entity to access shared resources.

Cryptography: The since of hiding information. It consists of two main steps: encryption which converts data (i.e., plaintext) into unintelligible gibberish (i.e., ciphertext) through an encryption key, and decryption which performs the reverse operation using the corresponding decryption key. Depending on the cryptographic keys applied, cryptography can be split into: private (symmetric) cryptography which uses the same key to perform encryption/decryption, and public (asymmetric) cryptography that employs different keys to encrypt and decrypt data.

Data Integrity: Refers to methods which assure that data transmitted between two parties has not been changed.

Intrusion Detection System (IDS): A system that screens the events which take place in a network or computer system in order to identify possible threats or violations of security policies.

Protocol Analysis Detection: Constructs admissible profiles of the normal activity of the network protocols, instead of the network components. These methods are able to scan and understand the state of network, transport and applications protocols.

Secure Routing Protocol: A protocol suite which secures the communication in wireless ad hoc networks against routing attacks, i.e., the control plain attack, the blackhole attack, the wormhole attack, etc. The crucial idea is to establish trustworthy communications between the participating nodes by controlling the message integrity and confidentiality, i.e., through message authentication codes (MACs) or digital signatures hash chains.

Signature Based Detection: Uses the information stored in the knowledge base to identify with high accuracy known threats. The main drawbacks of signature-based detection are the inefficiency to detect previously unseen attacks and the lack of understanding the network and applications protocols.

Chapter 2
Smartphone Data Protection Using Mobile Usage Pattern Matching

Wen-Chen Hu
University of North Dakota, USA

Naima Kaabouch
University of North Dakota, USA

S. Hossein Mousavinezhad
Idaho State University, USA

Hung-Jen Yang
National Kaohsiung Normal University, Taiwan

ABSTRACT

Handheld devices like smartphones must include rigorous and convenient handheld data protection in case the devices are lost or stolen. This research proposes a set of novel approaches to protecting handheld data by using mobile usage pattern matching, which compares the current handheld usage pattern to the stored usage patterns. If they are drastic different, a security action such as requiring a password entry is activated. Various algorithms of pattern matching can be used in this research. Two of them are discussed in this chapter: (i) approximate usage string matching and (ii) usage finite automata. The first method uses approximate string matching to check device usage and the second method converts the usage tree into a deterministic finite automaton (DFA). Experimental results show this method is effective and convenient for handheld data protection, but the accuracy may need to be improved.

DOI: 10.4018/978-1-60960-851-4.ch002

INTRODUCTION

Smartphones are extremely popular and convenient these days. People carry them anytime, anywhere and use them to perform daily activities like making phone calls, checking emails, and browsing the mobile Web. However, they are easily lost or stolen because of their small sizes and high mobility. Personal data such as addresses and messages stored in the devices are revealed when the devices are lost (Ghosh & Swaminatha, 2001). Various methods have been used or proposed for smartphone data protection. The methods can be classified into five categories: (i) password/keyword identification, (ii) human intervention, (iii) biometric-based identification, (iv) anomaly/behavior-based identification, and (v) other ad hoc methods. They will be introduced in the next section. This research, an anomaly/behavior-based identification, applies the methods of handheld/mobile usage data matching to smartphone data protection. The idea is to have devices identify the user, analyze usage pattern, and take any necessary actions to protect confidentiality of sensitive data stored. More specifically, we would like to compare statistical anomaly-based or behavior-based user pattern sample activities with typical usage profile known to be normal. To our best knowledge, there is no research work in this area by applying pattern recognition techniques. Experiment results show that this method is effective and easy-to-use.

This research is to design and implement a strategy of smartphone data protection, which includes the following features in order of importance:

- **Rigorous and effective handheld data protection:** It is the major objective of this research.
- **Easy to use and apply:** Many security methods are abandoned because the users are reluctant to learn how to use them.

- **Easy to adapt to each individual owner:** When the device owner is changed, the methods can quickly, easily adapt to the new owner.

A set of novel approaches is proposed in this chapter to protect handheld data by using usage pattern identification. The proposed methods are divided into five steps:

1. **Usage data gathering,** which is to collect the device usage data,
2. **Usage data preparation,** which removes noises from the raw usage data,
3. **Usage pattern discovery,** which finds valuable patterns from the prepared usage data,
4. **Usage pattern analysis and visualization,** which is to analyze and display the discovered patterns for finding hidden knowledge, and
5. **Usage pattern applications,** one of which is smartphone data protection used in this research.

This chapter is organized as follows. A background study consisting of three major subjects is given in the next section. Section III introduces our proposed system using handheld usage pattern matching. Two algorithms of structure similarity are used to check against any possible unauthorized uses: (i) approximate usage string matching and (ii) usage finite automata. The two methods are explained in the following two sections. Section VI shows and discusses some experimental results. Conclusion and some future directions are given in the last section.

BACKGROUND

This research includes three themes:

- **Mobile handheld computing,** which is the computing for (smart) cellular phones.

Figure 1. A system structure of mobile handheld devices

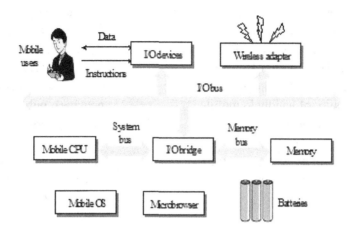

- **Handheld security,** which detects abnormal handheld data accesses and protects the data from unauthorized uses.
- **Approximate string matching,** which is to find the "best" match of a string among many strings.

Related research of these themes will be discussed in this section.

Mobile Handheld Devices

Handheld devices such as smart cellular phones are the must, key component of mobile commerce transactions. People normally have problems understanding the technologies used by devices because they involve various, complicated disciplines such as wireless and mobile networks and mobile operating systems. Figure 1 shows the system structure of a generic mobile handheld device, which includes five major components (Hu, Yeh, Chu, & Lee, 2005):

- **Mobile operating system or environment:** Mobile OSs, unlike desktop OSs, do not have a dominant brand. Popular mobile OSs or environments include: (i) Android, (ii) BREW, (iii) iPhone OS, (iv) Java ME,

(v) Palm OS, (vi) Symbian OS, and (vii) Windows Mobile.
- **Mobile central processing unit:** ARM-based CPUs are the most popular mobile CPUs. ARM Ltd. does not manufacture CPUs itself. Instead, it supplies mobile CPU designs to other chipmakers such as Intel and TI.
- **Input and output components:** There is only one major output component, the screen, but there are several popular input components, in particular keyboards and touch screens/writing areas that require the use of a stylus. Other I/O components include loudspeakers and microphones.
- **Memory and storage:** Three types of memory are usually employed by handheld devices: (i) random access memory (RAM), (ii) read-only memory (ROM), and (iii) flash memory. Hard drives are rarely used.
- **Batteries:** Rechargeable Lithium Ion batteries are the most common batteries used by handheld devices. Fuel cells, a promising technology, are still in the early stage of development and will not be widely adopted in the near future.

Synchronization connects handheld devices to desktop computers, notebooks, or peripherals to transfer or synchronize data. Obviating the need for serial cables, many handheld devices now use either an infrared (IR) port or Bluetooth technology to send information to other devices. The widespread availability of handheld mobile devices and the constantly improving technology that goes into them is opening up new approaches for mobile commerce, which is consequently becoming an increasingly attractive prospect for many businesses.

Handheld Security

The methods of handheld security can be classified into five categories: (i) password/keyword identification, (ii) human intervention, (iii) biometric-based identification, (iv) anomaly/ behavior-based identification, and (v) other ad hoc methods. Details of each category are given as follows:

- **Password/keyword authentication:** It is a fundamental method of data protection and most handheld devices include the option of password protection. However, device users are reluctant to use it because of the inconvenience of password memorization and entry. Data encryption is another data protection method and can be found in many handheld devices. Just the same, it is inconvenient because reading data requires key entry and the decryption takes time and requires extra works. Reviews of encryption algorithms and standards can be found in the article from Kaliski (1993, December). Some of the related research is described as follows:
  - Public keys are used to encrypt confidential information. However, limited computational capabilities and power of handheld devices make them ill-suited for public key signatures.

Ding et al. (2007) explore practical and conceptual implications of using Server-Aided Signatures (SAS) for handheld devices. SAS is a signature method that relies on partially-trusted servers for generating (normally expensive) public key signatures for regular users.
  - Argyroudis et al. (2004) present a performance analysis focused on three of the most commonly used security protocols for networking applications, namely SSL, S/MIME, and IPsec. Their results show that the time taken to perform cryptographic functions is small enough not to significantly impact real-time mobile transactions and that there is no obstacle to the use of quite sophisticated cryptographic protocols on handheld mobile devices.
  - Digital watermarking is particularly valuable in the use and exchange of digital media on handheld devices. However, watermarking is computationally expensive and adds to the drain of the available energy in handheld devices. Kejariwal et al. (2006) present an approach in which they partition the watermarking embedding and extraction algorithms and migrate some tasks to a proxy server. This leads to lower energy consumption on the handheld without compromising the security of the watermarking process. A survey of digital watermarking algorithms are given by Zheng, Liu, Zhao, & Saddik (2007, June).
- **Human intervention:** Several companies such as the device manufacturer HP (2005) and the embedded database vendor Sybase (2006) propose practical handheld security methods, e.g., the owners of lost devices

can call the centers to lock down the devices remotely. Those methods are normally workable, but not innovative. Additionally, they are a passive method. It may be too late when the users find out that their devices are lost.

- **Biometric-based identification:** Advanced devices use biometric measurements such as fingerprint, retina, and voice recognition to identify the owners (Hazen, Weinstein, & Park, 2003; Weinstein, Ho, Heisele, Poggio, Steele, & Agarwal, 2002). This approach is not widely adopted because the methods are not yet practical. For example, an extra sensor may be required for fingerprint recognition. This method also has a reliability problem. For example, if the owner's finger is cut or the owner has a sore throat, it would affect the recognition result.

- **Anomaly/behavior-based identification** (Shyu, Sarinnapakorn, Kuruppu-Appuhamilage, Chen, Chang, & Goldring, 2005; Stolfo, Hershkop, Hu, Li, Nimeskern, & Wang, 2006): This is the approach used by this research. It protects the handheld data by detecting any unauthorized uses by comparing the current usage patterns to the stored patterns. The patterns include application usage, typing rhythm, etc. When the measured activities are outside baseline parameters or clipping levels, a built-in protection mechanism will trigger an action, like inquiring a password, before further operations are allowed to continue.

- **Other Ad Hoc Methods:** Susilo (2002) identifies the risks and threats of having handheld devices connected to the Internet, and proposes a personal firewall to protect against the threats. A method of transient authentication can lift the burden of authentication from users. It uses a wearable token to check the user's presence constantly. When the user and device are sep-

arated, the token and device lose contact and the device secures itself. Nicholson, Corner, & Noble (2006, November) explain how this authentication framework works and show it can be done without inconveniencing the users, while imposing a minimal performance overhead. Shabtai, Kanonov, & Elovici (2010, August) propose a new approach for detecting previously unencountered malware targeting mobile devices. The method continuously monitors time-stamped security data within the target mobile device. The security data is then processed by the knowledge-based temporal abstraction (KBTA) methodology. The automatically-generated temporal abstractions are then monitored to detect suspicious temporal patterns and to issue an alert.

Approximate String Matching

The longest common subsequence searching method is widely used for approximate searches. This method, however, does not always reveal the degree of difference between two strings. This research proposes an approximate method for better characterizing the discrepancies between two strings. Three subjects, (i) longest common subsequences, (ii) string-to-string correction, and (iii) string matching, are related to the proposed string searching method.

Longest Common Subsequences

Finding a longest common subsequence (abbreviated LCS) is mainly used to measure the discrepancies between two strings. The LCS problem (Hirschberg, 1977) is, given two strings X and Y, to find a maximum length common subsequence of X and Y. A subsequence of a given string is just the given string with some symbols (possibly none) left out. String Z is a common subsequence of X and Y if Z is a subsequence of both X and

Y and Hirschberg suggested two algorithms to solve the problem. However, the LCS problem is a special case of the problem of computing *edit distances* (Masek & Paterson, 1980). The edit distance between two character strings can be defined as the minimum cost of a sequence of editing operations, which transforms one string into the other.

String-to-String Correction

The string-to-string correction problem, first suggested by Wagner and Fischer (1974), determines the distance between two strings as measured by the minimum cost sequence of edit operations required to change the first string into the other. The edit operations investigated allow insertion, deletion, and change. Lowrance and Wagner (1975) proposed the extended string-to-string problem to include in the set of allowable edit operations the operation of interchanging the positions of two adjacent symbols. An example of this problem, allowing only deletion and swap operations, was proven to be an NP-complete problem by Wagner in 1975.

String Matching

The string matching problem, given strings *P* and *X*, examines the text *X* for an occurrence of the pattern *P* as a substring, namely, whether the text *X* can be written as $X = YPY'$, where *Y* and *Y'* are strings. Several algorithms for this problem have appeared in the literature (Baeza-Yates & Gonnet, 1992). In some instances, however, the pattern and/or the text are not exact. For example, the name may be misspelled in the text. The approximate string matching problem reveals all substrings in *X* that are close to *P* under some measure of closeness. The most common measure of closeness is known as the edit distance, which determines whether *X* contains a substring *P'* that resembles *P* in at most a certain edit distance from *P* to *P'*. The editing operation, for example,

may change one symbol of a string into another, delete a symbol from a string, or insert a symbol into a string. Some approximate string matching algorithms can be found in the literature (Wu & Manber, 1992).

Smartphone Data Protection Using Handheld Usage Pattern Matching

This research applies user operation patterns to identify and prevent the accesses of unlawful handheld users. This research proposes the following steps to protect sensitive data in a handheld device from unauthorized accesses (Hu, Yang, Lee, & Yeh, 2005):

1. Usage data collection,
2. Usage data preparation,
3. Usage pattern discovery,
4. Usage pattern analysis and visualization, and
5. Usage pattern applications for handheld data protection.

Figure 2 shows the steps and data flows among them. If the system detects a different usage pattern from the stored patterns, it will assume the users are unlawful and block their accesses. The

Figure 2. The structure of the proposed system

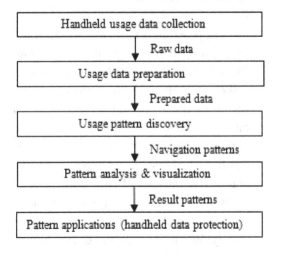

users need to verify their identities such as entering passwords or answering a question in order to continue their operations. This approach has the advantages of convenience and vigorous protection compared to other approaches like password protection and fingerprint recognition.

Usage Data Collection

This stage focuses on collecting data of defined categories in order to construct user usage profile. Based on industry studies and our observations, each handheld user normally follows unique patterns to operate their devices. Possible user pattern measurements include, but not limited to:

- Turn on/off frequency
  - Measured by day and time using the mean and standard deviation
  - Useful for detecting un-authorized users, who are likely to operate a handheld device during off-hours when the legitimate user is not expected to be using the that device
- Location frequency
  - Measures the frequency of operations of a handheld device at different locations
  - Useful for detecting un-authorized users who operates from a location (e.g., a terminal) that a particular user rarely or never visits
- Elapsed time per session
  - Resource measure of elapsed time per session
  - Significant deviations might indicate masquerader
- Quantity of output to location
  - Quantity of output to terminal

Excessive amounts of data transmitted to remote locations could signify leakage of sensitive data (e.g., the method used by an attack via a covert channel).

The usage data should include the user's unique characteristics of using that handheld device. Our research is based on the assumption that every user has a set of distinguishable and identifiable usage behaviors, which can separate this user from others. This assumption has been verified and applied to other information security applications, including intrusion detection. For example, a cell phone user may follow the patterns below to operate his/her phone the first thing in the morning:

- Turn on the cellular phone.
- Check phone messages.
- Check address book and return/make phone calls.
- Check instant messages.
- Reply/write messages.
- Check schedule book.
- Write any notes.
- Turn off the cellular phone.

The above steps are an example of handheld usage patterns. Other patterns exist for the user and each user has his/her own unique usage patterns. To collect usage data, users click on the icon "Pattern" on the interface in Figure 3a to bring up the interface in Figure 3b, which asks users to enter a number of days of usage data collection. The collection duration could be a week or a month depending on the use frequencies. The interface as shown in Figure 3a is re-implemented; so when

Figure 3. (a) The user interface of a device re-implemented to collect usage data and (b) user entry of data collection time

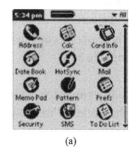 

(a)　　　　　　　　(b)

Figure 4. (a) Users deciding whether or not to modify the threshold values and (b) two input fields for threshold values

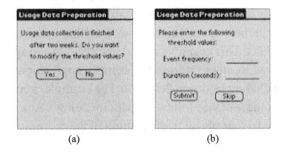

(a)   (b)

an application is clicked, it is recorded and the application is then activated.

Usage Data Preparation

The data collected from the previous step is usually raw and therefore cannot be used effectively. For example, the usage patterns should not include an event of alarm-clock operation if the user rarely uses the alarm clock. Data preparation may include the following tasks (Mobasher, Cooley, & Srivastava, 2000):

- Delete the event whose frequency is less than a threshold value such as 5. For example, if the usage data is collected for a month, data synchronization can be ignored if it is performed twice during that period.
- Remove the event if its duration is less than a threshold value such as 10 seconds. An event lasting less than 10 seconds is usually a mistake.
- Repeatedly performing the same action is considered performing the action one time. For example, making three phone calls in a row is treated as making one call.

The interface in Figure 4. allows users to decide whether or not to modify the default threshold

values. If the user clicks the button "Yes," the interface in Figure .b allows him/her to enter two new threshold values.

After the raw usage data is prepared, a usage tree is created. Figure 5 shows a sample simplified usage tree, where the number inside the parentheses is the number of occurrences. For example, (20) means the event occurs 20 times. This usage tree is only a simplified example. An actual usage tree is much larger and more complicated. Ideally, a directed graph instead of a tree should be used to describe the usage data. However, a directed graph is more complicated and therefore is difficult to process. Using a tree can simplify the processing, but it also creates duplicated nodes, e.g., the event "making phone calls" appears four times in the usage tree of Figure 5.

Usage Pattern Discovery, Analysis and Visualization, and Applications

The stage of usage pattern discovery focuses on identifying the desired usage patterns. Given the complexity and dynamic nature of user behaviors, identified usage patterns could be fuzzy and not that apparent. Advanced AI techniques such as machine learning, decision tree and other pattern matching and data mining techniques can be applied in this stage. Many data mining algorithms are applied to usage pattern discovery. Among them, most algorithms use the method of sequential pattern generations (Agrawal & Srikant, 1995), while the remaining methods tend to be rather ad hoc. The problem of discovering sequential patterns consists of finding inter-transaction patterns such that the presence of a set of items is followed by another item in the time-stamp ordered transaction set.

The major task of the step of pattern analysis and visualization is to pick useful ones from the discovered patterns and display them. If the figure of the usage tree and the usage DFA in the Section

Figure 5. A sample simplified usage tree

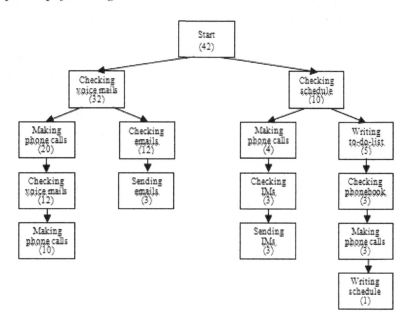

IV can be displayed on the device screen, it will greatly help the mobile users to better manage the proposed methods. However, creating and displaying complicated figures takes much computation time and consumes valuable resources such as memory from the device. Therefore, this research allows users to check the usage data, which may be too complicated to use by users, but not the usage figures.

Usage pattern applications are the last but most important step in user recognition. It applies the final patterns to handheld data protection. A key part of this task is to reduce false positive and false negative while matching actual observed data set with the pre-built user profiles. Usage patterns can be applied to various applications such as recommendation systems (Adda, Valtchev, Missaoui, & Djeraba, 2007) and Web page re-organization (Eirinaki & Vazirgiannis, 2003). This research uses the handheld usage pattern identification to find any illegal uses of the device. Details of pattern applications of handheld data protection will be given in the next two sections.

APPROXIMATE USAGE STRING MATCHING

Using the usage tree to find all illegal usage is not possible because the tree is not able to cover all usage patterns. This research applies two methods of approximate usage matching to mobile data protection without needing all usage patterns stored: (i) approximate string/pattern matching and (ii) finite usage automata. The former method will be covered in this section, while the latter method will be covered in the next section.

Approximate String/Pattern Matching

The string matching problem, given strings P and X, examines the text X for an occurrence of the pattern P as a substring, namely, whether the text X can be written as $X = YPY'$, where Y and Y' are strings. String matching is an important component of many problems, including text editing, bibliographic retrieval, and symbol manipulation. Several algorithms for this problem have appeared in the literature (Baeza-Yates & Gonnet, 1992). In some instances, however, the pattern and/or the text are not exact. For example, the name may be misspelled in the text. The approximate string matching problem reveals all substrings in X that are close to P under some measure of closeness. The most common measure of closeness is known as the edit distance, which determines whether X contains a substring P' that resembles P in at most a certain edit distance from P to P'. The editing operations may include: (i) insertion, (ii) replacement, (iii) deletion, (iv) swap (interchanging any two adjacent characters), and (v) regular expression matching. Some approximate string-matching algorithms can be found in the related literature (Wu & Manber, 1992).

Longest Approximate Common Subsequences

Finding a longest common subsequence (LCS) (Hirschberg, 1977) for two strings occurs in a number of computing applications. A longest common subsequence is mainly used to measure the discrepancies between two strings. An LCS, however, does not always reveal the degree of difference between two strings that some problems require. For example, if $s_0 = \langle a, b \rangle$, $s_1 = \langle b, b \rangle$, and $s_2 = \langle b, a \rangle$, an LCS $\langle b \rangle$ of s_0 and s_1 is the same as an LCS of s_2 and s_0. From the viewpoint of LCS, the resemblance of s_0 and s_1 is the same as the resemblance of s_2 and s_0. However, s_2 has more symbols in common with s_0 than s_1 does, although not in the same order. Approximating an LCS better characterizes the discrepancies between two strings.

A longest approximate common subsequence (LACS) problem produces a maximum-gain approximate common subsequence of two strings (Hu, Ritter, & Schmalz, 1998). An approximate subsequence of a string X is a string edited from a subsequence of X. The only editing operation allowed here is an adjacent symbol interchange. String Z is an approximate common subsequence

of two strings X and Y if Z is an approximate subsequence of both X and Y. The gain function g, which is described later, assigns a nonnegative real number to each subsequence. Formally, the LACS problem is defined as follows: Given two strings X and Y, a weight $W_m > 0$ for a symbol in an approximate common subsequence, and a weight $W_s \leq 0$ for an adjacent symbol interchange operation, a string Z is a longest approximate common subsequence of X and Y if Z satisfies the following two conditions:

1. Z is an approximate common subsequence of X and Y, and
2. The gain $g(X,Y,Z,W_m,W_s) = |Z|W_m + \delta(X,Z) W_s + \delta(Y,Z) W_s$ is a maximum among all approximate common subsequences of X and Y, where $\delta(X,Z)$ is the minimum edit distance from a subsequence of X to Z, and $\delta(Y,Z)$ is the minimum edit distance from Y to Z.

A string Z is said to be at an edit distance k to a string Z' if Z can be transformed to be equal to Z' with a minimum sequence of k adjacent symbol interchanges. The following is an LACS example. Let $X = \langle B, A, C, E, A, B \rangle$, $Y = \langle A, C, D, B, B, A \rangle$, $W_m = 3$, and $W_s = -1$. A longest approximate common subsequence of X and Y is $Z = \langle A, B, C, B, A \rangle$ with the gain $g(X,Y,Z,W_m,W_s) = |Z|W_m + \delta(X,Z) W_s + \delta(Y,Z)W_s = 5 \times 3 + 2 \times (-1) + 1 \times (-1) = 12$.

The LACS problem can be interpreted in another way, known as a *trace* (Wagner, 1975). Diagrammatically aligning the input strings X and Y and drawing lines from symbols in X to their matches in Y provides the trace of X and Y. Figure 6 illustrates the above example through a trace. In an LACS$_i$ trace, each line is allowed to have a maximum of i line-crossings, i.e. the symbol touched by the line may make no more than i adjacent symbol interchanges. The total number of line-crossings in a trace is $\delta(X, Z) + \delta(Y, Z)$.

Figure 6. An LACS2 illustrated through a trace

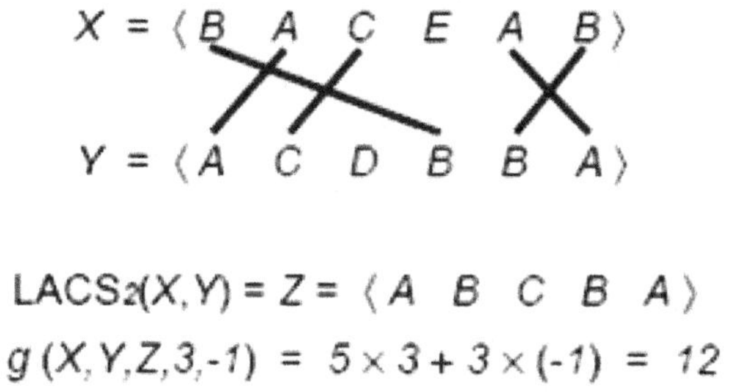

$$X = \langle\ B \quad A \quad C \quad E \quad A \quad B\ \rangle$$
$$Y = \langle A \quad C \quad D \quad B \quad B \quad A \rangle$$

$$LACS_2(X, Y) = Z = \langle\ A \quad B \quad C \quad B \quad A \rangle$$
$$g(X, Y, Z, 3, -1) = 5 \times 3 + 3 \times (-1) = 12$$

Usage Finite Automata

Finding a sequence from the usage tree is costly because the running time of the matching is at least $O(|V_1\|V_2|)$, where V_1 and V_2 are the node sets of the sequence and tree, respectively. To speed up the searches, this research applies the finite-automaton technologies (Aho, Lam, Sethi, & Ullman, 2006) to usage-pattern matching. A usage finite automaton M is a 5-tuple $(Q, q_0, A, \Sigma, \delta)$ where

- Q, which is a finite set of states,
- $q_0 \in Q$, which is the start state,
- $A \subseteq Q$, which is a distinguished set of accepting states,
- Σ, which is a set of events, and
- δ, which is a function from $Q \times \Sigma$ into Q, called the transition function of M.

For a prepared usage tree from the Part B of the previous section, a usage DFA (deterministic finite automaton) M can be constructed by following the steps below:

1. Each path starting at the root and ending at a leaf is a regular expression. For example, the regular expression of the path Checking schedule (H) → Making phone calls (P) → Checking IMs (I) → Sending IMs (M) is "HPIM" where the letters are the shorthands of the events in Figure 5.

2. Combine all regular expressions into a regular expression by using the "or" operator '|'. For example, the result regular expression of the usage tree in Figure 5 is "VPVP|VEL|HPIM|HTBPW."

3. Convert the regular expression into an NFA (nondeterministic finite automata).

4. Convert the NFA to a DFA where
   o An edge label is an event such as making phone calls.
   o An accepting state represents a match of a pattern.

For example, the DFA of the usage tree in the Figure 5 is given in Figure 7, where the nodes of double circles are the accepting states.

Using a DFA to store usage patterns and search for patterns is an effective, convenient way, but this approach also suffers the following shortcomings:

- The DFA may accept more patterns than the usage tree does. For example, the pattern Checking schedule → Making phone calls → Checking voice mails → Checking emails → Sending emails is accepted by the DFA according to its DFA path: $0 \rightarrow 1 \rightarrow 4 \rightarrow 2 \rightarrow 5 \rightarrow 8$ where the final state 8 is an accepting state, but the pattern does not exist in the tree. However, this feature may not be considered harmful because it may accept more "reasonable" patterns. For example, the above pattern is very legitimate, i.e. the users may as well operate their devices by using the pattern "checking schedule, making phone calls, checking voice mails, checking emails, and sending emails."

- This approach misses an important piece of information, the event frequency. The Step B, Usage Data Preparation, of this method removes events with frequencies lower than a threshold value. Otherwise,

Figure 7. A deterministic finite automaton of the prepared usage tree in Figure 5

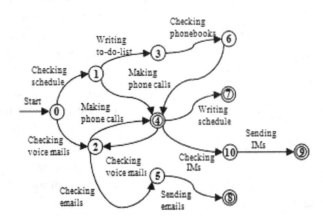

this DFA does not use the frequency information, which could be very useful.

- The pattern discovery is virtually not used in this research because the DFA uses all paths from the usage tree. Without using much pattern discovery, the usage tree and DFA may grow too large to be stored in the device.

EXPERIMENTAL RESULTS

Two algorithms of structure similarity, approximate string matching and usage finite automata, are used in this research to find unlawful handheld uses. Their experimental results are given in this section.

Approximate Usage String Matching

The approximate string matching can be used to find unlawful uses, whose gains are below a threshold value. On the other hand, the user actions are accepted if their gains are equal to or above the threshold value. For example, a sequence of handheld actions is as follows:

S_0 = Checking voice mails → Checking emails → Checking schedule → Check-

ing IMs → Making phone calls → Sending IMs

S_1 = Checking schedule → Making phone calls → Checking IMs → Sending IMs

The gain is $g(s_0, s_1, z, 3, -1) = 4 \times 3 - 1 = 11$ because there are 4 matches and 1 line-crossing and z, such as s_1, is one of the $LACS_2(s_0, s_1)$. No security action is taken if the threshold value is 10. Another sequence of actions is as follows:

S_2 = Checking voice mails → Making phone calls → Sending IMs → Making phone calls → Checking IMs

The gain is $g(s_0, s_2, z', 3, -1) = 3 \times 3 - 1 = 8$ because there are 3 matches and 1 line-cross and z', such as $s_1 - \langle Checking\ schedule \rangle$, is one of the $LACS_2(s_0, s_2)$. A security action is taken if the threshold value is 10. A typical action is to ask the user to enter a password as shown in Figure 8a before he/she is allowed to continue the operations. If the password submitted is incorrect, the interface in Figure 8.a stays. Otherwise, the system displays the interface in Figure 8b, which allows user to decide whether to continue applying the methods, in case the user does not want the proposed methods to keep interrupting his/her works. The

Figure 8. (a) A security alert after detecting suspicious handheld uses and (b) user entry of whether to continue using this method

 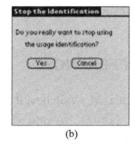

(a) (b)

interface in Figure 3a is then displayed and the user resumes his/her operations.

This method is convenient and effective. The time used for the usage string matching is $O(|X||Y||Z|)$ or $O(|m||n|)$ where X is the total usage patterns, Y is a usage pattern, and Z is the sequence of current user actions, or m is the nodes in the usage tree and n is the current user actions. The actual time could be lower because many patterns can be skipped without matching, e.g., none of the user actions appears in the patterns.

Usage Finite Automata

This sub-section discusses the applications of the usage finite automata. For example, a sequence of handheld actions is as follows:

```
Checking voice mails → Making phone
calls → Checking voice mails → Making
phone calls → Checking IMs → Sending
IMs
```

```
Checking voice mails → Checking
emails → Checking schedule → Making
phone calls → Checking IMs
```

These searching automata are very efficient: they examine each user action exactly once. The time used—after the automaton is built—is therefore $O(m)$ where m is the number of user actions

in the sequence. However, the time used to build the automaton can be large. One major disadvantage of this method is the accuracy problem. For example, many times the owner's operations were interrupted because he/she was trying new functions/patterns. Sometimes, presumed unlawful uses were undetected because the usage DFA includes too many patterns.

CONCLUSION

Handheld devices are easily lost because of their small sizes and high mobility. Personal data like addresses and telephone numbers stored in the devices are revealed when the devices are lost or used by unauthorized persons. This research proposes two novel approaches of handheld usage data matching for handheld data protection. The proposed methods are divided into five steps:

1. **Usage data collection:** This step is to collect the device usage data such as making phone calls and sending emails.
2. **Usage data preparation:** The data collected from the previous step is usually raw and can not be used effectively. The noises have to be removed before it can be further processed.
3. **Usage pattern discovery:** This step finds valuable patterns from the prepared usage data,
4. **Usage pattern analysis and visualization,** which is to analyze and display the discovered patterns for finding hidden knowledge, and
5. **Usage pattern applications,** one of which is handheld data protection used in this research.

Handheld usage data is collected and stored before applying the methods. Usage data is then checked against the stored usage data by using the proposed methods. When unusual usage data such as an unlawful user trying to access the handheld data is detected, the device will automatically lock itself down until an action, like entering a password, is taken. The proposed method includes the following advantages:

- **Convenience:** It is convenient compared to the password-based method because no user intervention is required after the usage patterns are saved unless suspicious actions are detected.
- **Accuracy:** The accuracy of owner identification should be higher than fingerprint or retina recognition, which is still in an early stage of development. Further experiments may be required to support this claim.
- **Flexibility:** The users are able to adjust the level of security by trying various durations of data collection or entering different threshold values.

Experimental results show the methods are effective and convenient for handheld data protection. However, accuracy problem must be solved before they can be put to actual uses. This problem is related to the following questions:

- **Usage data collection:** How much time should be spent to data collection or how much usage data should be collected?
- **Data preparation:** What is the frequency threshold value for removing trivial events?
- **Pattern discovery:** This research uses strings and a deterministic finite automaton to store usage patterns. They are effective, but patterns stored may be too many or may not be optimal. Will the sequential pattern discovery (Agrawal & Srikant, 1995), the most popular pattern-discovery method, or other pattern-discovery methods such as association rules (Agrawal & Srikant, 1994) help?

This chapter only gives general users' experiences about the system. Formal evaluations of this system and finding answers for the above questions will be our future research directions.

REFERENCES

Adda, M., Valtchev, P., Missaoui, R., & Djeraba, C. (2007). Toward recommendation based on ontology-powered Web-usage mining. *IEEE Internet Computing, 11*(4), 45–52. doi:10.1109/MIC.2007.93

Agrawal, R., & Srikant, R. (1994). Fast algorithms for mining association rules in large databases. *Proceedings of 1994 Int. Conf. Very Large Data Bases (VLDB'94)*, (pp. 487-499), Santiago, Chile, Sept.

Agrawal, R., & Srikant, R. (1995). Mining sequential patterns. *Proc. 1995 Int. Conf. Data Engineering (ICDE'95)*, (pp. 3-14). Taipei, Taiwan.

Aho, A. V., Lam, M. S., Sethi, R., & Ullman, J. D. (2006). *Compilers—Principles, techniques, and tools* (2nd ed.). Addison-Wesley.

Argyroudis, P. G., Verma, R., Tewari, H., & D'Mahony, O. (2004). Performance analysis of cryptographic protocols on handheld devices. *Proc. 3rd IEEE Int. Symposium on Network Computing and Applications*, (pp. 169-174). Cambridge, Massachusetts.

Baeza-Yates, R. A., & Gonnet, G. H. (1992, October). A new approach to text search. *Communications of the ACM, 35*(10), 74–82. doi:10.1145/135239.135243

Ding, X., Mazzocchi, D., & Tsudik, G. (2007). Equipping smart devices with public key signatures. *ACM Transactions on Internet Technology, 7*(1). doi:10.1145/1189740.1189743

Eirinaki, M., & Vazirgiannis, M. (2003, February). Web mining for Web personalization. *ACM Transactions on Internet Technology, 3*(1), 1–27. doi:10.1145/643477.643478

Ghosh, A. K., & Swaminatha, T. M. (2001). Software security and privacy risks in mobile e-commerce. *Communications of the ACM, 44*(2), 51–57. doi:10.1145/359205.359227

Hazen, T. J., Weinstein, E., & Park, A. (2003). Towards robust person recognition on handheld devices using face and speaker identification technologies. *Proc. 5ᵗʰ Int. Conf. Multimodal Interfaces*, (pp. 289-292). Vancouver, British Columbia, Canada.

Hewlett-Packard Development Company. L.P. (2005). *Wireless security*. Retrieved January 12, 2010, from http://h20331.www2.hp.com/Hpsub/downloads/Wireless_Security_rev2.pdf

Hirschberg, D. S. (1977). Algorithms for the longest common subsequence problem. *Journal of the ACM, 24*(4), 664–675. doi:10.1145/322033.322044

Hu, W.-C., Ritter, G., & Schmalz, M. (1998, April 1-3). Approximating the longest approximate common subsequence problem. *Proceedings of the 36ᵗʰ Annual Southeast Conference*, (pp. 166-172). Marietta, Georgia.

Hu, W.-C., Yang, H.-J., Lee, C.-w., & Yeh, J.-h. (2005). World Wide Web usage mining. In Wang, J. (Ed.), *Encyclopedia of data warehousing and mining* (pp. 1242–1248). Hershey, PA: Information Science Reference. doi:10.4018/978-1-59140-557-3.ch234

Hu, W.-C., Yeh, J.-h., Chu, H.-J., & Lee, C.-w. (2005). Internet-enabled mobile handheld devices for mobile commerce. *Contemporary Management Research, 1*(1), 13–34.

Kaliski, B. (1993, December). A survey of encryption standards. *IEEE Micro, 13*(6), 74–81. doi:10.1109/40.248057

Kejariwal, A., Gupta, S., Nicolau, A., Dutt, N. D., & Gupta, R. (2006). Energy efficient watermarking on mobile devices using proxy-based partitioning. *IEEE Transactions on Very Large Scale Integration (VLSI) Systems, 14*(6), 625–636.

Lowrance, R., & Wagner, R. A. (1975). An extension of the string-to-string correction problem. *Journal of the ACM, 22*(2), 177–183. doi:10.1145/321879.321880

Masek, W. J., & Paterson, M. S. (1980). A faster algorithm for computing string edit distances. *Journal of Computer and System Sciences, 20*, 18–31. doi:10.1016/0022-0000(80)90002-1

Mobasher, B., Cooley, R., & Srivastava, J. (2000). Automatic personalization based on Web usage mining. *Communications of the ACM, 43*(8), 142–151. doi:10.1145/345124.345169

Nicholson, A. J., Corner, M. D., & Noble, B. D. (2006, November). Mobile device security using transient authentication. *IEEE Transactions on Mobile Computing, 5*(11), 1489–1502. doi:10.1109/TMC.2006.169

Shabtai, A., Kanonov, U., & Elovici, Y. (2010, August). Intrusion detection for mobile devices using the knowledge-based, temporal abstraction method. *Journal of Systems and Software, 83*(8), 1524–1537. doi:10.1016/j.jss.2010.03.046

Shyu, M.-L., Sarinnapakorn, K., Kuruppu-Appuhamilage, I., Chen, S.-C., Chang, L., & Goldring, T. (2005). Handling nominal features in anomaly intrusion detection problems. *Proc. 15ᵗʰ Int. Workshop on Research Issues in Data Engineering (RIDE 2005)*, (pp. 55-62). Tokyo, Japan.

Stolfo, S. J., Hershkop, S., Hu, C.-W., Li, W.-J., Nimeskern, O., & Wang, K. (2006). Behavior-based modeling and its application to email analysis. *ACM Transactions on Internet Technology, 6*(2), 187–221. doi:10.1145/1149121.1149125

Susilo, W. (2002). Securing handheld devices. *Proc. 10ᵗʰ IEEE Int. Conf. Networks,* (pp. 349-354).

Sybase Inc. (2006). *Afaria—The power to manage and secure data, devices and applications on the front lines of business.* Retrieved June 10, 2010, from http://www.sybase.com/files/Data_Sheets/Afaria_overview_datasheet.pdf

Wagner, R. A. (1975). On the complexity of the extended string-to-string correction problem. *Proc. 7ᵗʰ Annual ACM Symp. on Theory of Computing,* (pp. 218-223).

Wagner, R. A., & Fischer, M. J. (1974). The string-to-string correction problem. *Journal of the ACM, 21*(1), 168–173. doi:10.1145/321796.321811

Weinstein, E., Ho, P., Heisele, B., Poggio, T., Steele, K., & Agarwal, A. (2002). Handheld face identification technology in a pervasive computing environment. *Short Paper Proceedings, Pervasive 2002,* Zurich, Switzerland.

Wu, S., & Manber, U. (1992). Text searching allowing errors. *Communications of the ACM, 35*(10), 83–91. doi:10.1145/135239.135244

Zheng, D., Liu, Y., Zhao, J., & Saddik, A. E. (2007, June). A survey of RST invariant image watermarking algorithms. *ACM Computing Surveys, 39*(2), article 5.

ADDITIONAL READING

Aho, A. V., Lam, M. S., Sethi, R., & Ullman, J. D. (2006). *Compilers: Principles, Techniques, and Tools* (2nd ed.). Addison Wesley.

Cormen, T. H., Leiserson, C. E., Rivest, R. L., & Stein, C. (2001). *Introduction to Algorithms* (2nd ed.). Cambridge, Massachusetts: The MIT Press.

Hall, P. A. V., & Dowling, G. R. (1980). Approximate string matching. *ACM Computing Surveys, 12*(4), 381–402. doi:10.1145/356827.356830

Kahate, A. (2009). *Cryptography and network security* (2nd ed.). McGraw-Hill Education.

Michailidis, P. D., & Margaritis, K. G. (2001). On-line string matching algorithms: survey and experimental results. *International Journal of Computer Mathematics, 76*(4), 411–434. doi:10.1080/00207160108805036

Navarro, G. (2001). A guided tour to approximate string matching. *ACM Computing Surveys, 33*(1), 31–88. doi:10.1145/375360.375365

KEY TERMS AND DEFINITIONS

Approximate String Matching: The approximate string matching problem, given strings P and X, reveals all substrings in X that are close to P under some measure of closeness. The most common measure of closeness is known as the edit distance, the number of operations required to transform one into the other. It is to determine whether X contains a substring P' that resembles P in at most a certain edit distance from P to P'.

Finite Automaton: It is an abstract machine that consists of a finite number of states, transitions between those states, and actions. The operation of a finite automaton begins from a start state, goes through transitions based on various input, and may end in an accept state.

Handheld/Mobile/Smartphone Data: It is the data stored in mobile handheld devices. The data is usually stored in non-volatile memory like flash memory and is changed from time to time. Typical mobile data includes contacts, schedules, audio/image/video files, etc.

Handheld/Mobile/Smartphone Security: It is a branch of computer technology applied to mobile handheld devices for protection of devices and its data from theft, corruption, or natural disaster.

Mobile Handheld Devices: They are small, general-purpose, programmable, battery-powered computers that are capable of handling the front end of mobile applications such as location-based services and can be operated comfortably while being held in one hand and enables mobile users to interact directly with mobile applications.

Smartphones: They are a kind of mobile handheld devices with phone capability or mobile phones with advanced features. A typical smartphone includes five components: (i) mobile operating system, (ii) mobile central processing unit (CPU), (iii) input and output components such as keyboard and screen, (iv) memory and storage, and (v) batteries.

String Matching: The string matching problem, given strings P and X, examines the text X for an occurrence of the pattern P as a substring, namely, whether the text X can be written as $X = YPY'$, where Y and Y' are strings.

Chapter 3
Conservation of Mobile Data and Usability Constraints

Rania Mokhtar
University Putra Malaysia (UPM), Malaysia

Rashid Saeed
International Islamic University Malaysia (IIUM), Malaysia

ABSTRACT

An important part of ISO/IEC 27002 cyber security standard is the conservation of confidentiality that falls under its computer facility protection part which insures that the computer and its stored information can only be accessed by the authorized users. Securing mobile devices and mobile data to ensure the confidentiality, integrity, and availability of both data and security applications requires special consideration to be paid to the typical mobile environment in which a mobile computing device would be utilized. Protecting mobile devices includes multiple security technologies such as the right identification of its particular user, data encryption, physical locking devices, monitoring and tracking software, and alarms. This chapter reviews security-specific hardware and software applied to mobile computing and presents its advantages and drawbacks. Then it considers the concept of usability constraints in context of mobile computing security and introduces the seamless security method for identity proof of a particular user or device.

DOI: 10.4018/978-1-60960-851-4.ch003

INTRODUCTION

Within the much broader arena of cyber security, organizations may be able to provide the physical and environmental security but this does not cover the mobile data that is stored in mobile devices including mobile computing devices such as laptops and palmtops and mobile storage devices such as USB drives. Several laptop manufacturers, such as Acer, Compaq, MPC and IBM, have added security focus features to certain models. Other vendors have focused on augmenting laptop vendor's systems with hardware-based encryption engines, such as CryptCard, and security-specific authentication and encryption software, such as SafeBoot (Sharp 2004).

Scantily administered mobile computing devices significantly raise the possibility for security failures and data compromise. Stolen or lost mobile computing/storage device carrying restricted data, such as secret e-mails, customer data and financial reports, pose the risk of falling into the wrong hands. The loss of highly restricted data and the potential connected media scandal is a massive problem in itself, but the impact might be greater if failure to protect certain sensitive data can be interpreted as a defiance of regulations. Security requirements for the protection of sensitive mobile data in mobile computing context are still lacking in the current literature of cyber security. The purpose of this chapter is twofold; address the mobile computing security policies within the map of cyber security requirements and investigate the seamless security tools and mechanisms that take into account user's usability constraints.

BACKGROUND

Most initial mobile computing devices were considered useful, but not something to be protected. This continued for a number of years until the importance of mobile data was truly realized. When mobile computing applications were developed to handle secure organizational and personal data, the real need for mobile data security was felt like never before. It's been realized that mobile data on mobile computing devices is an extremely important aspect of modern life.

Mobile computing is realized strongly and has become very trendy because of the expediency and portability of mobile computing devices. Mobile computing devices are responsible for employees to store, process, transmit, or access organizations restricted data. The use of mobile computing devices provides flexibility and enhanced communications that allow organizations to be more productive.

In some organizations, the notebook has eclipsed the desktop as the standard computing platform in order to enable employees to take their work home with them and maximize productivity. In others, personal data assistants are the computing platform de jour. But organizations need to put the proper tools in place to ensure that their mobile devices and networks are not compromised as a result of this increase in mobility. However, mobile computing creates threats to the stored mobile data and fixed devices/data based on their ability for internet connectivity to static resources and/or upon their intranet connectivity e.g. virus spreading which lacks the internal protections afforded by organization such as firewalls. Protecting the mobile computing devices and the sensitive data they may store or have access to be critical security issue that must be addressed (security policies 4-007, 2007).

Various threads and risks intimidate the mobile computing devices in different degrees, such as:

- Threatened by loss or thievery defined as physical hazard.
- Illegal access risk. Accessing the device by an illegitimate user.
- Foreign network risk. Mobile computing devices may use different networks connection in the move. Although all networks

are susceptible to possibility of attack, mobile wireless networks are the most insecure because of their potencies, agility, flexibility, node independence and self organization. Wireless networks as well prove to be practically defenceless against radio frequency distortion and malicious packet-level disruption and intrusion. Therefore the mobile devices are susceptible to be attacked via/by foreign networks devoid of recognition.

- The above risks are inherited by the mobile data storage device such as removable hard disk and USB drives.
- Mobile computing devices are also subject to the risks that attack the fixed devices like virus, worms and application threat.

DEVICE PROTECTION IN ISO/IEC 27002 CYBER SECURITY STANDARD

ISO/IEC 27002 cyber security standard addresses physical and environmental security for the protection of the computer facilities in its twelve main sections and provides general outlines as well as specific techniques for implementing physical security. Thus it enables organizations to practice physical security to minimize the number of successful attacks which are increasing against the control systems used in current critical infrastructures (Ward, 2008).

Physical and environmental security describes both measures that prevent or deter attackers from accessing a facility, resource, or information stored on physical media and guidance on how to design structures to resist various hostile acts. It can be as simple as a locked door or as elaborate as multiple layers of armed security guards and guardhouse placements. Physical security is not a modern phenomenon. Physical security exists in order to deter persons from entering a physical facility. Historical examples of physical security include city walls, moats, etc. The key factor is the

technology used for physical security has changed over time. While in past eras, there was no Passive Infrared (PIR) based technology, electronic access control systems, or Video Surveillance System (VSS) cameras, the essential methodology of physical security has not altered over time. Physical and environmental security does not support mobile computing and teleworking considerations

Mobile Computing and Data Protection Principles

Desktop systems that are located inside the organization network border have the benefit of network security setup such as antimalware and firewall protection employed at the network level, as well as the physical security in attendance at the office site. Organizations have to make sure that the mobile computing devices have a device security to protect it. Administrators require implementing security solutions at the device level to preserve against infection and unauthorized access, and protect the data stored on the device. In addition, administrators need to make certain that the organization's network is confined from compromising by a wandering device and/or wandering data. There are many ways that confidential or private data can leave an organization's network. Data can be intentionally or inadvertently sent out via e-mail, which makes it tough to protect against information leakage.

Mobile computing devices engaged outside secure area are subject to particular security threats such as lost, stolen, depiction to unauthorised access or tampering. Mobile computing devices carried abroad may also be at danger, for example confiscated by police or customs officials. The loss of a Mobile computing device will mean not only the loss of availability of the device and its data, but may also lead to the disclosure of patent or other sensitive information. This loss of confidentiality, and potentially integrity, will often be considered more serious than the loss of the physical asset. Where large quantities of data are held on a single laptop (or any other storage medium) risk assessments must consider the impacts of loss of all the data. Note that deleted files should be assumed to persist on the laptop's hard disk (NIST, 2009).

Cyber security standard such as ISO/IEC 27002, Code of practice for information security management, the NHS Information Security Management Code of Practice, and the NHS Information Governance Toolkit set out values applicable to mobile computing devices, such as:

ISO/IEC 27002, 9.2.5. (Security of Equipment Off-Premises)

- Security should be applied to off-site equipment taking into account the different risks of working outside the organisation's premises;
- Regardless of ownership, the use of any information processing equipment outside the organisation's premises should be authorised by management;
- Security risks, e.g. of damage, theft or eavesdropping, may vary considerably between locations and should be taken into account in determining the most appropriate controls.

ISO/IEC 27002, 11.7.1. (Mobile Computing and Communications)

- A formal policy should be in place, and appropriate security measures should be adopted to protect against the risks of using mobile computing and communication facilities;
- Special care should be taken to ensure that business information is not compromised. The mobile computing policy should take into account the risks of working with mobile computing equipment in unprotected environments;

- The mobile computing policy should include the requirements for physical protection, access controls, cryptographic techniques, back-ups, and virus protection. This policy should also include rules and advice on connecting mobile facilities to networks and guidance on the use of these facilities in public places.

CYBER SECURITY POLICIES FOR MOBILE COMPUTING

Mobile computing devices can be categorized into two categories from the cyber security prospective: the organization-managed mobile devices which comprise the devices under authority of organization and the organization specifies and enforces the exact security requirements. And personal owned mobile devices. Cyber security policies and procedures for mobile devices are to be determined in accordance with device category. The policies are to be applied to protect organization static data as well as mobile data.

The policies for organization-managed mobile computing address the following requirements to protect organization system or static data (ISSP-22-0410 Policy Draft, 2004).

- Implement Registry and management system for all mobile devices.
- Minimize amount of sensitive data stored on mobile computing/storage devices
- Usage control policies and restrictions. Mobile computing devices are to be configured to use access controls policies.
- Connection control, approve only connection that meet restriction. Furthermore, wireless connection is to be authenticated and encrypted according to wireless security policy
- Immobilizes functions that allow involuntary execution of code on mobile devices without user track

- Travel consideration: apply special and strong security configuration to travelled mobile device and rechecked upon return.
- Issues process for random reviews/inspections for mobile devices and the information stored on those devices by defined security officials.

The policies and procedures used for Personal mobile devices consider the following requirement to protect organization system:

- Confine the use of personally owned mobile computing devices, writable, removable media in organizational information systems.
- Wireless access control, scan and monitor for unauthorized wireless.
- Disallowing the use of removable media in organizational information systems when the media has no identifiable owner.

The protection of sensitive mobile data requires definition and implementation of other set of policies and procedures for mobile devices used by individuals.

Loss and Theft

To deal with loss and theft, the security control must have physical security procedure like alarms or locking cable to be used with mobile devices, auto backup and recovery system that auto-run when the device is connected to organization's network to insure the organization have a recent copy of mobile data. Fast inform to organization and police is desirable in the case of lost or theft of mobile computing device. Record system with all mobile devices information must be available with organization for fast dealing with case.

Illegal Access

The use of strong authentication method for user authorization is critical security control for mobile devices. Mobile computing devices maybe left in unattended/unsecured place, this strongly pos the risk of unauthorized access to device and data. Well-built and frequently changed password, biometric authentication, administrative account, and encryption techniques are key strategies must be implemented in mobile computing devices to avoid illegal access.

Connection Control

The organization must provide virtual private network VPN for mobile computing device to enhance connection security through foreign networks. Furthermore the connection time to or via foreign network must be minimized; and the mobile computing device must have its own firewall installed.

Encryption

The mobile data must be stored in encrypted format that need authentication, or the mobile device may use a full disk encryption have need of pre-boot authentication. Furthermore, the mobile device has to use encryption method when the data is transferred across a foreign network. Confining the use of wireless networks for devices that not capable of using encryption.

OS and Application

The organization must form a procedure to guarantee mobile computing devices are using the latest operating system (OS), application scrapes, anti-virus software & descriptions and firewall settings.

Table 1. Laptop security technologies

Technology	Principle
Encryption	Protect data
User authentication	Confirm the authorized user; prevent unauthorized access
Physical locking devices	Prevent theft
Monitoring and tracing software	Locate and assist in recovery of stolen computers
Alarms	Prevent theft

MOBILE DATA ENCRYPTION AND ACCESS CONTROL TOOLS

There are two main classes of technology that are most relevant to mobile devices and other three classes. These are summarized in the Table 1.

Encryption

Robust OS-level authentication systems prevent unauthorized access to the laptop's operating system. However, if the hard drive is removed to another machine, or if boot-up from a floppy disk is enabled in the stolen machine, the files can be accessed. Unless a hard drive lock option is available and implemented, the only way to protect files from this type of attack is to encrypt them. Encryption requires the use of a digital key to encrypt and decrypt the data. In "symmetric" systems, the same key is used for both encryption and decryption. In Public Key Infrastructure (PKI)-based applications, asymmetric encryption is used, with two keys: a public key for encryption and a private key for decryption.

In many current encryption products, the keys are stored on the hard drive, making them vulnerable to attack. Encryption experts such as RSA Security recommend protecting keys by storing them in tamper-resistant hardware devices that can handle cryptographic functions internally and do not permit the keys to be exported outside the hardware. This is the basis of cryptographic cards and tokens, as well as IBM's Embedded Security Subsystem (ESS), available in ThinkPad laptops.

ESS consists of a built-in cryptographic security chip, which supports key storage, encryption and digital signatures, and a downloadable software component that provides the user and administrative interface and the interface to other applications. Because critical security functions take place within the protected environment of the chip, not in main memory, and not relying on the hard drive to store cryptographic keys, the system is more secure than software only solutions.

Identity, Authentication and Authorization

Authentication is the first step in any cryptography solution. Because unless the device knows who is using it there is no point in encrypting what is being stored on it. The whole purpose of encryption file system is to secure the stored information, without the authentication an unauthorized user can access the information. The whole idea of authentication is based on secrets.

On any computer system, the user presenting identity is the starting point to establishing what rights and privileges, or authorization, if any, is granted the user. Obviously, if an unauthorized person can falsely authenticate him or herself as someone who is trusted, all security measures are irrelevant. The goal of strong authentication systems is to ensure the person authenticating is exactly, and in all cases, the person who should be authenticating.

User authentication is needed in order to identify users. All the authentication mechanism uses one of three possible things (Chen, 2000) to base identification on:

1. Secret based methods such as Passwords, PIN codes, pass phrase, secret handshakes, etc
2. Token based methods based on physical token owned by the user such as id badge, (physical) key, driving license, uniform, etc
3. Biometrics methods based on user's physical characteristics (Evans 1994) such as fingerprints, voiceprints, facial features, iris pattern, retina pattern, etc.

Secret-Based Methods

The simplest and the cheapest form of authentication mechanism that is used by many computer operating systems, a user authenticates himself/herself by entering a secret password known solely to him/her and the system (Kahate 2003). The system compares this password with one recorded in a Password Table, which is available to only the authentication program. The integrity of the system depends on keeping the table secret. This technique is called the clear text password. There are several disadvantages to this scheme. First, it depends for its success on the correct operation of a very large part of the operating system--the entire access control mechanism. Second, the System Administrator can know all of the passwords. There is no reason why he should know them, or even be able to know them. Third, an unauthorized person, even if obtained for a valid purpose, may inadvertently see any listing of the Password Table. Fourth, anyone who can obtain physical access to the computer, such as an operator, may well be able to print the file. A final disadvantage is that it cannot be implemented at all in an environment whose file system security does not protect against unauthorized reading of files.

The clear text password has been enhanced by a password scheme, which does not require secrecy in the computer. All aspects of the sys-

tem, including all relevant code and databases, may be known by anyone attempting to intrude. The scheme is based on using a function H that the would-be intruder is unable to invert. This function is applied to the user's password and the result compared to a table entry, a match being interpreted as authentication of the user. The intruder may know all about, and have access to the table, but he can penetrate the system only if he can invert H to determine an input that produces a given output. Most of operating system in the market uses this type of authentication; some of them with some enhancement, Palm OS can automatically lock the device on power off, at a specific time, or after a certain period of inactivity (Clark 1990). The major drawback of password systems is indeed the threat of capture of user id and associated password – in a widely used system, for example a bank's ATM network, the user's password (PIN code) is static for, in many cases, the lifetime of the cardholder's account. These problems with the password make it unsuitable for the laptop devices which has low physical security and always vulnerable to thefts. The one who steals the laptop for the data has enough time to use any attack strategy to compromise the password such as:

- Try all possible passwords (combinatorial)
- Try many probable passwords (dictionary attack)
- Try passwords likely for the user
- Exploit access to the system list of passwords
- Ask the user

Token-Based Methods

In computer environment the user can use a something owned for access control. The most common method to achieve two-factor authentication is by augmenting the standard user name and password, as 'something you know', through the use of or 'something you have'. Usually some form of electronic 'token'. These tokens tend to fall into four main areas:

1. Magnetic or Optically read cards
2. Smart cards
3. Password Generators
4. Personal Authenticators

Magnetic or Optically Read Cards

This is a prime example of the enhancement of the password by the addition of something owned. Commercially available physical access control systems where the card is used to log on to computer keyboard and allow it to communicate with its processor unit ('soft' lock). Attacks on such token are relatively straightforward. Generally the magnetic strip variety conforms to well publish standard, and reader/writer units are commercially available. To duplicate a token is thus easy and quickly. Optical card are a little more difficult to forge – particularly since the writer mechanisms are not as freely available as their magnetic counterparts.

Smart Cards

Unlike magnetic or optical cards, smart cards retain their data within a protected environment inside the card. Smart cards have simple microprocessor architecture, a controlling program, which resident on the card, only permits data to be divulged from the card's protected area once a valid PIN has been given to card itself. The smart card is more secure than magnetic or optical card since it is data cannot be freely inspected and duplicated but costing more.

Password Generators

Cryptographically based same size of credit card, but slightly thicker. Incorporate an LCD display, which displays a unique password for fixed time duration. Not protected by PIN code.

Personal Authenticators

Hand held same size as mall pocket calculator, protected by unique user PIN. Two type are available – challenge/response and synchronized sequence. The former relies on the host system issuing a challenge to the user which the user types in to his/her authenticator, which then computes and displays a response. This response can be returned to the host computer for verification by an attached crypto-controller. The synchronized sequence device dose not requires a challenge but generates a sequence of cryptographically related session PIN's (SPINS) which traced and verified at the computer in the same way. Main problem with 'something the user has' scheme is that it fetched for the authority at amount time that mean long-term authority; these remain in force until the user consciously revokes it. Even if fetched periodically, a user would be tempted to leave the smart card in the machine most of the time.

Biometric Based Methods

It is a permanent type of verification technique known as biometric authentication that is based on verification of personal physical characteristics. Many researches have been carried out in this field, fingerprint (Intel. 2002), and voice verification, retinal scans, which are commercially available techniques. And some unexpected study of lip prints, head bumps and footprint. Biometrics can be used to augment 'something you know', such as a user ID and password, with 'something you are', namely something unique to your person, such as fingerprints, retinal or facial recognition. Adding biometrics creates a second tier of identity and authentication, which is easy for users to utilize. For example, identity and authentication can be improved through the use of the built-in biometric fingerprint scanner in some models of Acer, Compaq and MPC laptops as shown in Figure 1. When the biometric identification devices are built into the laptop proper, without requir-

Figure 1. Built-in biometric fingerprint scanner

ing additional external hardware, the biometric scanner hardware and authorization software can be used earlier in the boot up process, denying access more quickly to invalid attempts to boot the system. Pre-boot identification and authentication ensures no access will be gained through operating system or application vulnerabilities, or potentially other backdoors such as remote control software, keyboard loggers or viruses/worms that could be exploited after the system is booted. As an example, biometric identification and authentication could be implemented at the BIOS level as simply another form of BIOS password.

Choices in the BIOS such as '[text password] off', '[text password] on', or 'fingerprint'. The MPC laptop BIOS has additional features to protect against brute force attempts to disable the biometric authentication. After three invalid attempts to identify and authenticate, the BIOS will prevent you from attempting again without a reboot. If attempts are made to remove the boot password (text or fingerprint identification), the system will eventually hard lock and will require shipping the laptop to the vendor to unlock it. Once the operating system is booted, options typically exist to use the stored biometric information or match it with a user ID/password for login purposes, as well as providing authorization to applications, which may not have native biometric or other application security. After market

hardware is available for those laptops, which do not have biometrics built-in, providing the fingerprint reader within a mouse or PCCard, for instance. Biometrics at this level will not secure the laptop hardware itself, but may provide additional software-only authentication services, such as the operating system login and/or individual program execution. The disadvantage with biometric authentication technique, it suffers from several usability problems. They have a large false negative rate, and are not easy to revocable – if someone has a copy of your thumbprint, you cannot easily change it. Also biometric authentication often requires some conscious action on the part of the user. The one exception is iris recognition (Negin, 2000).

SECURITY METHODS AND USABILITY CONSTRAINTS

Authentication systems for desktop and mobile computing device are always done once and hold until these are explicitly revoked by the user, or frequently asking the user to reestablish his identity which encourages him to disable the authentication (Noble, 2002). As described by this chapter, many security technologies exist in both hardware and software to provide a laptop security solution for multiple-factor (up to three) authentication and encrypting confidential data in a portable and convenient manner. Security only needs to be one step stronger than the thief is willing to pursue.

There is no point in storing data in a cryptography file system; such a system asks the user to imbue them a long-term authority for decryption. If an illegitimate user gets access to laptop, he or she will get access to the user's data. Furthermore the encryption and decryption functions affect system performance. In real life most (if not all) users need to make sure that no other person can access their machines but few of them goes to the use of an encryption technique as a solution, instead they try to find and apply strong authentication strategy. No single authentication technique will keep a determined thief from the goal of accessing user laptop given enough time by absence of user. Instead having a simple and effective re-authentication mechanism will provide defense-in-depth strategy and will ensure that your defenses are strong enough to protect your data. Applying strong and frequent re-authentication mechanism for system security will slow the progress made by a thief, and hopefully, force the thief to abandon the pursuit, at the least, resale of the stolen property, and at worst, of confidential corporate data.

Interaction of Bluetooth Technology in Mobile Computing Security

The architecture of the Bluetooth system has considered the security issue from the very beginning. The Bluetooth security architecture considers a group of cryptographic protocols to accomplish authentication, integrity and confidentiality. Bluetooth Generic Access Profile characterizes three special modes of security. Each Bluetooth device can activate only one security mode at a particular time. Mode one defines the no-security mode which is planned for applications where the security is not necessary. Security Mode two, also known as service-level security, manages access to services and to devices based on different security polices and trust levels, the Bluetooth start the security procedure after channel initiation request has been received or a channel establishment procedure has been started by itself. Security Mode three, known as link-level security, is a built-in security mode where the Bluetooth device commences security procedures before the physical channel is established. This mode supports authentication (unidirectional or mutual) and encryption and not aware of any application layer security that may exist, as:

- *Authentication* ensures the identity of Bluetooth devices. It authenticates the device at the other end of the link. Authentication is accomplished by using a stored link key or by pairing (entering a PIN).
- *Pairing* is a procedure that authenticates two devices based on a common passkey, thereby creating a trusted relationship between those devices. An arbitrary but identical passkey must be entered on both devices. As long as both devices are paired, the pairing procedure is not required when connecting those devices again (the existing link key is used for authentication). Devices without any input method, like headsets, have fixed passkeys.
- *Authorization* is a process of deciding if a device is allowed to have access to a specific service. User interaction may be required unless the remote device has been marked as "trusted." Usually the user can set authorization on/off to every remote device separately. Authorization always requires authentication.
- *Encryption* protects communication against eavesdropping. For example, it ensures that nobody can listen to what a laptop transmits to a phone. The length of the encryption key can be between 8 and 128 bits.

The security mode three enables Bluetooth to propose a new model of authentication for mobile devices using a Bluetooth-enabled device (e.g. mobile phone).

Seamless Security Mechanisms

In this model the user uses his Bluetooth-enabled device (Bluetooth security token), which works as an authentication token that provides the authentication for mobile computing device over a Bluetooth short-range wireless link. The user

Figure 2. Laptop- cell phone- authentication system

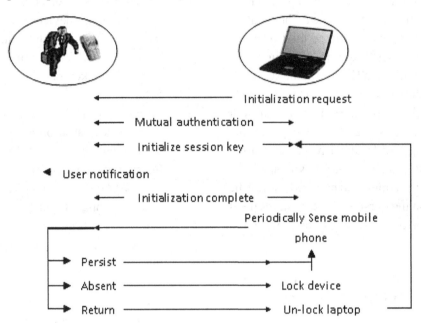

authenticate with the Bluetooth-enabled device infrequently. And, the Bluetooth-enabled device continuously authenticate with the mobile computing by means of the short-range wireless link. This model insures that an illegal user's Bluetooth-device cannot provide authentication services to other user's mobile computing devices, and it uses security mode three which is authenticated and encrypted Bluetooth wireless link to insure that there is no observation, modification, and insertion of messages traveled over the link. The security application of this authentication model performs four functions between mobile computing devices and Bluetooth security token:

- Mutual authentication
- User notification
- Create session key
- Polling, disconnection and reconnection

The overall processes of authentication system are illustrated in Figure 2.

COMMUNICATION MODEL AND SECURITY LEVEL OF SERVICES

The authentication system consists of two parts: the security applications in mobile computing device and Bluetooth- security token and communication module over the short-range wireless link.

Mutual Authentication

The mutual authentication is the first step in the authentication system. In this step the system performs a challenge–response function between the laptop and Bluetooth security token in order to authenticate each other based on public key system. The Bluetooth security token and laptop have predefined key pair, (em, dm) and (el, dl) respectively. The e's are the public keys and the d's are the private keys. rm and rl are random numbers (challenge) generated by Bluetooth security token and laptop, respectively. Each of the Bluetooth security token and laptop exchange their random numbers. The other end receive the challenge decrypt it with its private key, since these

Figure 3. Laptop- cell phone- mutual authentication

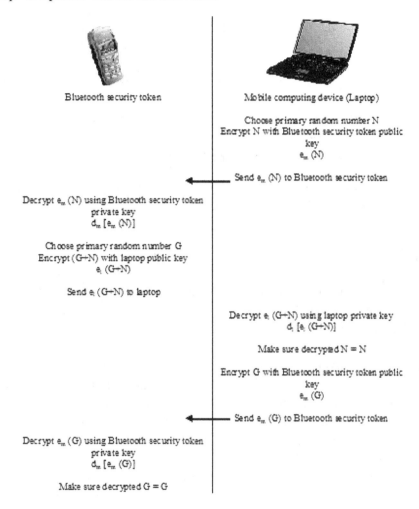

numbers are encrypted with public key, only the holder of the corresponding private key can open and view the number. So the return of the correct information identified each of them as legitimate or not. Figure 3 shows three–way exchange. The Bluetooth security token responds with laptop's challenge and indicates its own challenge. The mutual authentication function combines public key authentication and Diffie–Hellman Key Exchange Agreement/Algorithm [14], were the exchanged challenge consider as base random numbers for Diffie–Hellman Key Exchange.

User Notification

User notification is the next step in authentication system. After mutual authentication between the laptop and Bluetooth security token in order to authenticate user agreement for the connection, the Bluetooth security token informs the user about the connection that has been established, and asks for user permission. Once the user agrees for the connection, the system does not ask him/her again and the Bluetooth security token (cell phone) takes all responsibility for authentication system.

Figure 4. Session key creation

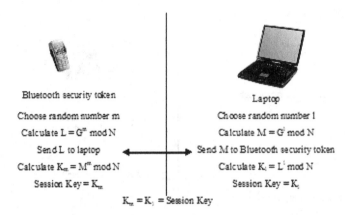

Bluetooth security token

Choose random number m

Calculate $L = G^m \bmod N$

Send L to laptop

Calculate $K_m = M^m \bmod N$

Session Key = K_m

Laptop

Choose random number l

Calculate $M = G^l \bmod N$

Send M to Bluetooth security token

Calculate $K_l = L^l \bmod N$

Session Key = K_l

$K_m = K_l$ = Session Key

Session Key Creation

The session key is used to encrypt laptop–Bluetooth security token communication. Once session key is established, all information that transfers over the wireless link will not be in clear text format; instead it will be encrypted and authenticated using a session key. The creation of a session key is done based on Diffie–Hellman Key Exchange Agreement/Algorithm. The beauty of this schema is that the two parties can agree on a symmetric key using this technique. This key can then be used for encryption/decryption. Also the Diffie–Hellman Key Exchange/Agreement based on mathematical principle, can be implemented on Mobile Information Device Profile (MIDP) application (MIDlet) programs. Diffie–Hellman Key Exchange provides perfect forward security; session keys cannot be reconstructed, even if private keys of both endpoints are known. Creating session key works as shown in Figure 4.

Polling, Disconnection and Reconnection

In this function the system periodically sense Bluetooth security token to ensure that the user is still present, when the Bluetooth security token is out of the range the laptop take step to secure itself. For this function we define 'present check'

message to be periodically sent to Bluetooth security token, the Bluetooth security token must acknowledge this message to show the presence of user. There are two possibilities:

The laptop sends the 'present check' message and receive the acknowledgement, as shown in Figure 5; here it will do nothing and continue the rechecking of the presence of the user periodically.

The other possibility is that the laptop sends the 'present check' message but not receive the acknowledgement for it. In the situation the laptop will resend the 'present check' message in the hope to receive the acknowledgment. If the laptop sends the 'present check' message three times without receiving the acknowledgment as shown in Figure 6, it will declare user absent and disconnect him from the system and stop his/her access to the machine by running a simple security application similar to the screensaver. At the same time the system will continue rechecking the presence of the user periodically.

There are two reasons why the laptop does not receive a response from the Bluetooth security token, the Bluetooth security token and the user are truly away, or the link may have dropped the packet. For the latter, the system uses expected Round Trip Time (RTT) between the laptop and Bluetooth security token, because this is a single, uncontested network hop, this time is relatively stable. The laptop retries request if responses are

Figure 5. Polling, laptop-mobile phone

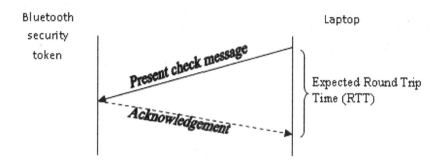

not received within twice the expected round trip time. The continuous rechecking process will periodically sends the 'present check' message and waits for the acknowledgement. Whenever the laptop receives an acknowledgment it declares the presence of the user and reconnect him/ her back to the system, stop security application, and gives the user access to his/her machine.

ZERO INTERACTION AUTHENTICATION (ZIA)

Zero Interaction Authentication, or ZIA, is a cryptography file system that can deal with this type of transient authentication (Corner, 2002). ZIA is a system that allows an owner of a laptop to authenticate to the laptop with no actual effort on the user's part (hence the name Zero-Interaction Authentication). The threat model addressed by ZIA is essentially physical theft of the laptop while

the legitimate user is still authenticated: since the laptop wouldn't know the difference between the attacker and the real user, the attacker could obtain the user's data. One solution to this is to require the user to re-authenticate frequently. Unfortunately, many users find this annoying, and as a result, may disable security features, leaving them vulnerable to attack. ZIA attempts to find a "happy medium" between security and convenience by letting the user authenticate without having to do anything.

The basic idea of ZIA is as follows. All on-disk files are encrypted, but for performance reasons, cached files are not. The user has a token in the form of a wearable device. The laptop has a set of keys for encrypting the contents of its file system, and for each of these keys, the token contains a key-encrypting key that is used to store the corresponding key on the laptop in encrypted form. The laptop polls the token periodically to determine if the user is present. When the token is near the laptop, the keys and file cache on the

Figure 6. Declaring the absence of user after three 'present check' message(s) without acknowledgements

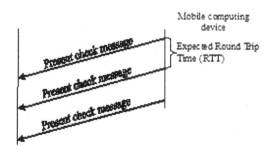

laptop can stay decrypted and the laptop is usable. If the laptop detects that the token is not near, it assumes that the user has left, flushes its cached keys, and re-encrypts everything. This prevents an attacker who gains physical possession of the laptop from obtaining any data. When the user returns, the laptop fetches keys and decrypts the file cache, returning to the state it was in when the user left.

Wireless Link Security

The authentication system preserves against exploitation of Bluetooth wireless link between the mobile computing device and the Bluetooth security token. It protects against observation, modification, and insertion of messages. The system provides confidentiality for messages that exchanged between the mobile computing device and the Bluetooth security token by encrypting it using the symmetric session key that has been created in both side and the AES algorithm.

Because the system uses the encrypted challenge as the primary numbers in the process of creation the session key, it supports against man-in-the-middle attack (also called bucket brigade attack), which works against Diffie-Hellman key exchange algorithm, causing it to fail.

This system implemented through the Java APIs for Bluetooth, which support secure client and server connections. The Bluetooth security token (server) connection specified as secure before the connection is established using a connection URL that specifies the security parameters.

CONCLUSION

The use of mobile computing devices provides flexibility and enhanced communications that allow more productivity. However, the use of these devices poses risks to mobile and fixed resources. Therefore, additional security measures must be implemented to mitigate increased security risks

presented by mobile computing This chapter discuss threat and risks of mobile computing and explore the cyber security standardization extracts considering mobile computing security; furthermore, the chapter discuss the transient authentication mechanism to consider usability constraint.

REFERENCES

Chen, L., Pearson, S., & Vamvakas, A. (2000). *On enhancing biometric authentication with data protection.* Fourth International Conference on Knowledge –Based Intelligent Engineering System and Allied Technologies, Brighton, UK.

Clark, A. (1990). *Do you really know who is using your system?* Technology of Software Protection Specialist Group.

Corner, M. D., & Noble, B. D. (2002). Zero interaction authentication. In *Proceeding of the ACM International Conference on Mobile Computing and Communications* (MOBICOM'02), Atlanta, Georgia, USA.

Corner, M. D., & Noble, B. D. (2002). *Protecting applications with transient authentication.* MOBICOM'02, Atlanta, Georgia, USA.

Evans, A., & Kantrowitz, W. (1994). *A user authentication schema not requiring secrecy in the computer.* ACM Annual Conf. M.I.T. Lincoln Laboratory and Edwin Weiss Boston University.

Hardjono, T., & Seberry, J. (2002). *Information security issues in mobile computing.* Australia.

Intel. (2002). *Biometric user authentication fingerprint sensor product evaluation summary.* ISSP-22-0410. (2004). *Policy draft: Mobile computing.* Overseas Private Investment Corporation.

Kahate, A. (2003). *Cryptography and network security* (1st ed.). Tata, India: McGraw-Hill Company.

National Institute of Standards and Technology. (2009). *Special publications 800-114, 800-124.*

National Institute of Standards and Technology (NIST). (2009). *Special publication 800-53, revision 3: Recommended security controls for federal information systems and organizations.*

Negin, M., Chemielewski, T. A. Jr, Salgancoff, M., Camus, T., Chan, U. M., Venetaner, P. L., & Zhang, G. (2000, February). An iris biometric system for pubic and personal use. *IEEE Computer, 33*(2), 70–75.

Noble, B. D., & Corner, M. D. (September 2002). The case for transient authentication. In *Proceeding of 10th ACM SIGOPS European Workshop*, Saint-Emillion, France.

Sharp, R. I. (2004). *User authentication.* Technical University of Denmark.

University of Central Florida. (2007). *Security of mobile computing, data storage, and communication devices.* University of Central Florida.

Ward, R. (2008). *Laptop and mobile computing security policy.* Devon PCT NHS.

KEY TERMS AND DEFINITIONS

Access Control: is a mechanism that limits availability of information or information-processing resources only to authorized persons or applications.

Authentication: is a process of verifying identity of an individual, device, or process.

Mobile Communication Device: Cellular telephones, smart phones, and mobile computing devices equipped with wireless or wired communication capability.

Mobile Computing Device: a mobile computing device is any Portable device that is capable of storing and processing information with information storage capability (e.g., notebook/laptop computers, personal digital assistants, cellular telephones), and is intended to be used outside of an organization office.

Mobile Data: Data that are stored in a mobile computing/storage device and are considered sensitive, as defined in data classification and protection policy.

Mobile Storage Device: is any device that is capable of storing but not processing information and is intended to be used outside of an organization office.

Section 2
Social Media, Botnets and Intrusion Detection

Chapter 4
Cyber Security and Privacy in the Age of Social Networks

Babar Bhatti
MutualMind, Inc., USA

ABSTRACT

Social media is transforming the way we find, create, and share information during the course of our personal life and work. The rapid growth of social media and the ubiquitous sharing and access of information through various digital channels has created new vulnerabilities and cyber threats. This chapter will provide an overview of the security and privacy implications of social networks and communities. The goal of this chapter is to examine and raise awareness about cyber security threats from social media, to describe the state of technology to mitigate security risks introduced by social networks, to shed light on standards for identity and information sharing or lack thereof, and to present new research and development. The chapter will serve as a reference to students, researchers, practitioners, and consultants in the area of social media, cyber security, and Information and Communication technologies (ICT).

INTRODUCTION

The goal of this chapter is to provide information about online social networks and the security and privacy issues which are associated with them. The chapter talks about online social networks, their scale and reach in the society, what actions are taken on these networks and what are the consequences for security and privacy. This chapter also includes recent examples of security and privacy issues associated with online social networks.

The chapter also looks at what efforts have been made to control and solve the problems and provides references for related research. It provides references to research papers, blogs and other media articles related to social media security and privacy.

DOI: 10.4018/978-1-60960-851-4.ch004

BACKGROUND

The proliferation of social networks is a relatively new phenomenon. Social media and digital content is getting embedded in our private lives and work culture. The novelty, scale and velocity of this change introduce a multitude of issues including security and privacy. It is against this background that we review the current state of cyber security and privacy.

The rapidly shifting nature of social networks and web 2.0 has made it difficult to define standards, boundaries and mechanisms to secure identities and information for individuals and groups. There is active research going on to identify and address various facets of security and privacy issues related to social networks. Industry practices and literature review shows novel approaches and experimentation to address public, business and government concerns. The references section at the end of the chapter is a good starting point. We expect new tools and industry standards for security and privacy to emerge in the next few years.

Further sections in the chapter provide information about the specific social networks and their vulnerabilities, how and where social networks are accessed and used and what all of this means for lay persons and security practitioners.

IMPACT OF SOCIAL MEDIA ON CYBER SECURITY AND PRIVACY

As described in introduction section above, the new modes of communication and sharing introduced by social media necessitates that we re-examine security and privacy. This section looks at the impact of social media. We start with some numbers which give an idea of the scale of social media, discuss the core security and privacy issues related to social media and provide examples of recent security and privacy breaches in the realm of social media.

Social Media Growth

The rapid growth of social media over the last few years has changed the way people create, share and distribute digital content, whether it is messages, photos or other items.

Here are a few statistics for 3 popular social networks – the numbers will surely have changed by the time you read this:

- Facebook has more than 500 million active users
- LinkedIn has over 75 million members
- Twitter has over 150 million registered users and 180 million unique visitors every month

The growth of user generated content is staggering: an average user of Facebook creates 70 pieces of content each month. Estimates by (Rao, 2010) suggest that Twitter users create about 70 million messages – known as Tweets in social media speak – a day.

Most of the growth has taken place in the last 5 years or less, causing disruptions in the way communication and information flows. For instance, breaking news can spread fast due to the viral sharing characteristic of Twitter. In same way, malware can be transmitted rapidly through Twitter. This proliferation of social media and the accompanied user generated content and sharing changes the landscape of privacy and security. In many cases, the standards and recommendations have not kept up with the changes brought up by social media. This environment provides new opportunities for those with malicious intent to exploit user information or to use the viral nature of social media to disperse viruses and malware.

Security concerns of social media applications include Phishing, Scams, Social engineering attacks and Identity Spoofing. There are a number of well-documented incidents related to social media security or privacy. These incidents include phishing, scams, direct hacks, bugs which reveal

Figure 1. Sophos study shows that spam, phishing and malware reports are going up (Adapted from Sophos (2009))

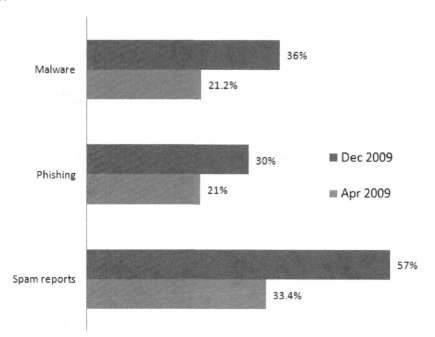

personal info, access to wrong data, inadvertent data leaks by employees, third party applications which abuse data and more.

According to a (Sophos, 2009) survey conducted in December 2009, 60% of respondents believe that Facebook presents the biggest security risk of the social networking sites, significantly ahead of MySpace, Twitter and LinkedIn. Figure 1 shows that security breaches on social networks have increased during the period between April 2009 and December 2009.

The report found that:

- More than half of all companies surveyed said they had received spam via social networking sites, and over a third said they had received malware.
- The survey results show that the perception that social media can be harmful is on the rise as well.

- Over 72% of firms believe that employees' behavior on social networking sites could endanger their business's security.

FACEBOOK, TWITTER AND THE STATE OF CYBER SECURITY

In this section we take a look at Facebook and Twitter, two of the most popular social networks, and provide a high level review of how users and application developers interact with these platforms. We discuss security issues related to these platforms and how these platforms have tackled those security concerns.

Here's a list of a few security breaches and issues associated with social media and social networks.

Let's take a look at the application ecosystem and security apparatus for Facebook and Twitter platforms.

Figure 2. Facebook application access

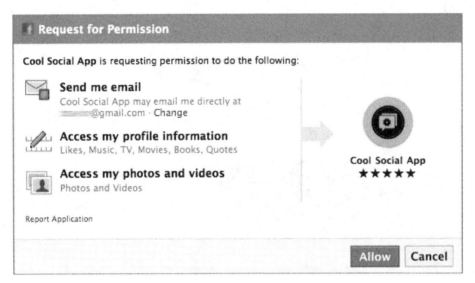

Facebook

As of September 2010, Facebook – world's largest social networking site - had reached 500 million users. With over one million developers and 550,000 active applications using Facebook platform, the situation poses unique security challenges. The previous section listed a few of the public security and privacy incidents.

Let's take a look at how Facebook platform applications work and their security implications. Facebook allows independent developers to build custom applications which can run within Facebook.com platform. Besides applications, there are other ways in which websites and content can be integrated with Facebook: Facebook Connect, Social Plugins. Mobile phone applications are also available.

All platform applications need to follow Facebook guidelines and policies. Once an application is successfully deployed to Facebook, users can access it by following an authentication process which verifies that the user allows certain level of information and publishing access to the application. As an example, the top applications on

Facebook are reported to have over 60 million active users per month (Allfacebook, 2010).

Over time, Facebook has beefed up the way it allows the independent developers to access and use user data (see Figure 2). Recently Facebook took some solid steps for improving application security. As of June 30, 2010, applications were allowed to access only a user's public data unless the user grants your application the extended permissions it needs.

These changes are documented at Facebook Developer website (2010).

Twitter

Twitter is a social network which allows users to share short messages with others. Unlike Facebook, Twitter only allows text messages which are limited to 140 characters. Most of the information posted on Twitter is meant to be shared with others in an asymmetric manner. The asymmetric networking results in faster sharing of content – which includes both information and security threats.

Table 1. Examples of social media exploits

Security Issue	Details
Facebook has been the subject of a number of attacks and phishing scams which resulted in privacy breaches, data exposure and stolen information. Koobface was a mass-mailing virus which targeted Facebook users and directed victims to a site asking to download a Trojan masked as an Adobe Flash update.	Vamosi (2008) covers the details of Koobface incident. McCarthy (2010) describes how phishing scam on Facebook could ensnare company board member. Siciliano (2010) writes how company employees could be tricked on Facebook to share their login info, which can then be used to steal company data. Vascellaro (2010) wrote about a Facebook glitch which exposed Private chats.
Twitter web site was successfully attacked a few times by hackers.	Multiple DDOS attacks caused Twitter.com to go down in August 2009. In 2010 a hacker managed to exploit Twitter API to change user information.
Twitter Security Issues (Short link malware and spam).	Cluley (2010) reports on the Twitter "on mouse over" security flaw, one in a series of security issues with Twitter. The official Twitter Blog (2010) provided an update on Trust and Safety enhancements. Another Twitter Blog (2010) post presented Twitter's efforts to fight spam.

Figure 3. Example of a Twitter short link

Twitter also has a large number of application developers. However Twitter has simpler public/private settings than that of Facebook. Even so, Twitter has been a popular target for hackers and malware distributors. A search for "Twitter Malware" yields over 8 million results in a search engine. We mentioned a few of those in Table 1. Prince (2009), and Naraine & Danchev (2009) have written about Twitter malware.

Since Twitter messages are text based, links are the main mechanisms of spreading malware. To make matters difficult, links on Twitter are not the full URLs but a short form such as http://bit.ly/c0CwHX (see Figure 3). These short URLs serve the purpose of conserving characters on a limited length message but on the other hand, they obfuscate the descriptive information which is usually part of a web link. This introduces a vulnerability which has been exploited many times.

Figure 4. Example of a Bit.ly link warning

STOP - there might be a problem with the requested link

The link you requested has been identified by bit.ly as being potentially problematic. We have detected a link that has been shortened more than once, and that may be a problem because:

- Some URL-shorteners re-use their links, so bit.ly can't guarantee the validity of this link.
- Some URL-shorteners allow their links to be edited, so bit.ly can't tell where this link will lead you.
- Spam and malware is very often propagated by exploiting these loopholes, neither of which bit.ly allows for.

The link you requested may contain inappropriate content, or even spam or malicious code that could be downloaded to your computer without your consent, or may be a forgery or imitation of another website, designed to trick users into sharing personal or financial information.

Bit.ly suggests that you

- Change the original link, and re-shorten with bit.ly
- Close your browser window
- Notify the sender of the URL

Or, continue at your own risk to

Usage of short links was made popular at Twitter but it quickly became an essential part of online content sharing and is not limited to Twitter: it has been adopted by Google and Facebook, among others and these links are often found in email messages.

There are two main ways in which links are shared on Twitter: through updates which are shared with all the followers and direct messages, which are private message between users. Both types of messages can be automated using Twitter's API. Twitter security team has made many changes to effectively detect and combat spam and malware. Any Twitter user can report a Twitter account for abuse and Twitter support reviews such incidents.

As further response to security issues, Twitter started managing the link obfuscation and shortening. The first set of improvements applied to direct messaging as it had created security problems. Twitter announced on June 8, 2010 that all links will be wrapped by a special short URL.

The details of this are available at (Twitter blog, 2010. Links and Twitter).

Link shortening service providers such as Bit.ly have partnered with security companies such as Verisign, which can screen IP addresses, domains and URLs based on its reputation database. When a user clicks on a short URL which points to a suspicious site, Bit.ly shows a warning that the destination site may not be safe (Figure 4).

PRIVACY ON SOCIAL MEDIA

In this section we review the issue of privacy on social media and mention two major social media case studies which caused public uproar due to privacy concerns.

Let's start with a basic question: Who owns your data on social networks?

The question of who owns your data on social networks has been debated intensely. Users are bound to the terms and services of the social

Figure 5. Facebook privacy policy timeline

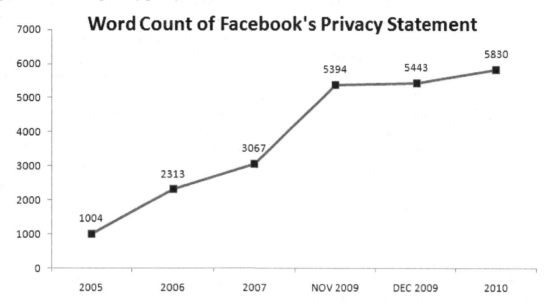

network that they use and that agreement defines how the data can be used. We have discussed this in reference to third party applications where these apps can access most of a user's information. In theory, users can fine tune the privacy settings to decide what to share. In reality, users are found to be either negligent, careless or confused about all the details of privacy and data use policies. Some recent studies have suggested that certain segments of well-informed online users have started getting more serious about their privacy settings. It is clear that majority of users are not yet in control of how their online information is accessed and used.

The second big question is about the use of your data and information and it touches upon the concepts of consent and disclosure. One of the major controversies regarding social media is around the use of personal data for commercial purpose. Due to its size and global popularity, Facebook is in the middle of this debate. The next section talks about how Facebook platform has evolved with respect to privacy.

It is interesting to note that certain regions have stricter privacy laws for data use by companies,

regardless of where the company and its infrastructure resides. In other words, Facebook has to comply with EU laws for users in European region. The European Union Data Protection Directive regulates processing of personal data in Europe.

The Ever Changing Privacy Policies of Facebook

Facebook's privacy policies have been the center of discussions in online and other media. The main reason for this attention is that Facebook made significant changes to their policy recently and then revised the policies over the next few months in response to public backlash. According to an article (New York Times, 2010) the Facebook privacy policy in 2010 was 5830 words long. In 2005 Facebook privacy policy was only 1004 words. Figure 5 shows how the word count of Facebook privacy policy increased over the years.

Here are a few of the major complaints about Facebook privacy policy:

- Default privacy settings compromise user privacy by sharing too much of information which was previously set to private. The burden of information control is on the user.

- Privacy settings are too complicated and can lead to unexpected ways in which a user data could be processed, stored and used. The settings span directory information, status updates, what appears in public search, block lists, personalization etc.
- Information about a user (interests, profile details, pictures, status updates etc) can be shared by their friend or applications, even without the knowledge of their friends. It is difficult for users to understand and control what information from their profile can be shared by third party applications.
- New features such as Social Plugins allow external websites to display Facebook information. Facebook. Depending on the privacy settings and a user's interactions with the external websites, data is exchanged between Facebook and the external websites. This is a difficult concept for many users to grasp.

It is easy to see how the "default settings" can impact the way privacy is compromised. Most people tend to start using applications without fully reviewing and changing the default settings. These default settings tend to be in favor of companies. As Bruce Schneier points out, if given the choice corporations will choose the defaults which will make them the most money, not necessarily the ones which are best for an individual. Critics such as Rowan (2010) are not convinced that it is safe to use Facebook.

Application privacy settings for Facebook are explained at (Facebook privacy policy, 2010). The excerpt below, taken from the above link, sheds more light on how applications access user information.

When you connect with an application or website it will have access to General Information about you. The term General Information includes your and your friends' names, profile pictures, gender, user IDs, connections, and any content shared using the Everyone privacy setting. We may also make information about the location of your computer or access device and your age available to applications and websites in order to help them implement appropriate security measures and control the distribution of age-appropriate content. If the application or website wants to access any other data, it will have to ask for your permission.

We give you tools to control how your information is shared with applications and websites that use Platform. For example, you can block all platform applications and websites completely or block specific applications from accessing your information by visiting your Applications and Websites privacy setting or the specific application's "About" page. You can also use your privacy settings to limit which of your information is available to "everyone".

You should always review the policies of third party applications and websites to make sure you are comfortable with the ways in which they use information you share with them. We do not guarantee that they will follow our rules. If you find an application or website that violates our rules, you should report the violation to us on this help page and we will take action as necessary (Facebook privacy policy, 2010).

Launch of Buzz Turns into a Privacy Fiasco for Google

In February 2010, Google launched a new social networking tool called Buzz which was built around Gmail, a free email service provided by Google with over 170 million users.

As soon as Buzz was introduced, Gmail users started expressing concerns about privacy of their email accounts. Blogs and Twitter messages were abuzz with the potential privacy intrusion introduced by Google Buzz. Users felt that their email connections were made public. Google faced a barrage of complaints, criticism and anger over this. Eventually, Google apologized, changed the default settings on Google Buzz to address the privacy concerns and introduced other changes.

The story of Google Buzz offers some useful insights into the changing perceptions of online privacy. People think of email as a very private mode of communication and they were upset by the notion of a social network invading their privacy. Obviously Google underestimated the level of sensitivity to a product which apparently combined email with social networking.

Lessons Learned

The above examples provide a glimpse into the ongoing controversies associated with online and social network privacy. In near future, it is to be expected that public and government officials will scrutinize the social networking products more closely. As more data becomes available about the use of personal information and mainstream awareness increases, social network platforms will take further steps. We also expect that legislation changes will be a major driver for privacy enhancements. Various privacy watchdog groups have been working on these issues and have issued statements and recommendations.

Sometimes it may be better to take a different approach to manage online privacy, as suggested here.

In a computational world, privacy is often implemented through access control. Yet privacy is not simply about controlling access. It's about understanding a social context, having a sense of how our information is passed around by others, and sharing accordingly. As social media mature,

we must rethink how we encode privacy into our systems. (Boyd, 2010, online article)

SOCIAL NETWORKING ON PORTABLE INTERNET DEVICES

People access social media using a wide variety of devices, ranging from home or work PCs, laptops and other devices. One of the most important digital trends of the last few years is that social networking use is growing rapidly on portable connected Internet devices such as mobile phones, tablets, netbooks and other gadgets. It so happened that the rise in popularity of social networks coincided with the introduction and availability of a new generation of smart phone applications.

That resulted in rapid adoption of social apps on mobile devices. Apple's iPhone app store offered a centralized platform through which users could download applications directly. These "apps" were developed by third party developers and approved by Apple after it reviews the application for compliance with its business policies and technical requirements such as compatibility with iPhone's proprietary operating system. Android platform – an open source operating system for phones and other devices - was introduced by Google. Android also offers a mobile application store. BlackBerry, another popular OS has also launched a mobile application service.

Most popular social sites offer a mobile version for the popular platforms. For instance Facebook application is available on iPhone (Figure 6), Android and BlackBerry mobile operating systems. Usage data shows that people who have social network applications on their phone are likely to spend more time per day using these social applications compared with the users who only access them on a computer.

Since these devices are portable, social networking applications on these devices are likely to be used more frequently. With the rise in popularity of third party applications, users are

Figure 6. Facebook on iPhone

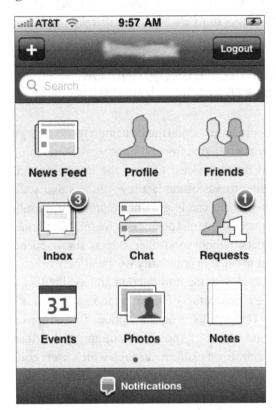

likely to have more sensitive information. This means that if these devices get lost then there is more information at risk. Mobile malware is a problem as well.

Mobile apps are exposed to not only mobile malware and security threats but they are particularly vulnerable to privacy breaches and the risk of data theft. Financial transactions are one of the primary targets of hackers.

The biggest issue with mobile phones is the breadth of security problems with third party applications. Ante, S. (2010) talks about the issues with mobile applications and notes that unlike Apple, "Google doesn't examine all apps before they are available for users to download." According to the article, some security experts believe Google's Android Market is more vulnerable than other app stores.

There are a number of software- and hardware-based approaches to secure mobile devices and

to mitigate the impact of a device falling in the wrong hands. In case of BlackBerry, for example, a centralized architecture model is used to handle secure provisioning, messaging and data stores.

LOCATION-BASED SOCIAL APPLICATIONS

Location based applications allow users to identify a location of a person or object, such as discovering the nearest hospital or restaurant. Used mostly with GPS-based devices or mobile phones, these services fit well with the social networking sites. Location applications come in various favors: mobile applications such as Foursquare (Figure 7), Loopt and Latitude by Google; general social networking sites such as Twitter which allows the option to add location info to all or individual tweets. Facebook is said to introduce location features for updates soon.

As usual, the benefits of these services come with disadvantages and security threats. There are many ways in which location information can be collected, shared and used by applications and hackers. Puttaswamy and Zhao (2010) list references which document a few real-world examples of the cases involving harmful use of location bases social applications. The website "Please Rob Me" (http://pleaserobme.com) is an example of the threats associated with careless or inadvertent "over-sharing" of location information.

Blumberg and Eckersley (2009) define Location privacy as "*the ability of an individual to move in public space with the expectation that under normal circumstances their location will not be systematically and secretly recorded for later use.*"

Most applications realize the implications for security and privacy and have clear policies about how they collect, use and share location information. For instance, Twitter provides an option for users to delete the location info from their messages.

Figure 7. Foursquare locations

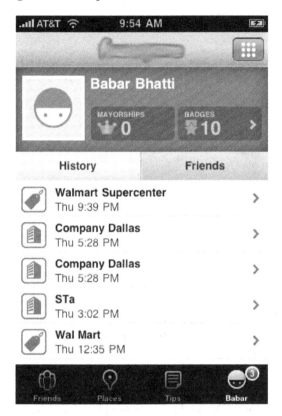

Location applications are likely to see a huge uptake in the coming years and it will stand to benefit from user data. We expect to see active development around location-based services. That will result in a battle between privacy advocates, security experts and those who are creating the new location services and applications. Figure 8 shows how Twitter location feature works.

SOCIAL MEDIA USE INSIDE ORGANIZATIONS

As we have noted before, public social media sites are accessed from work locations and used for various forms of networking and communication among colleagues. The organizations could be a private companies, schools, government offices or non-profits.

There are both opportunities and threats posed by social media in the enterprise. A common prob-lem faced by organizations is that their internal systems do not allow easy sharing of information among authorized users. Taking a page from social media playbook can help companies and organizations. This is one of the primary reasons for creating customized business social networks or communities. Other uses involve customer service and support.

In the early days, many companies decided to block social sites, due to productivity and secu-rity reasons. The trend is changing slowly but a number of companies are still grappling with the policy issues. Should open access to public social sites be allowed using company networks? What filtering should be in place?

Social networking sites are now a vital part of many marketing and sales strategies so there is a need for better protection against security issues. While some organizations have started developing acceptable use policies for social media, for many businesses and companies it remains a challenge to manage the use of social media at work.

Use of social media by government agencies brings up well-justified concern about sensitive information and data leaks. On one hand the gov-ernments in developing countries pride themselves on transparency but on the other hand there is the risk of providing too much access.

Various US government agencies have re-viewed the case of social media and web 2.0 and have issued policy guidelines on what is allowed and what is inappropriate (Godwin, B., et al., 2008). Here are some sources which provide more information about Government and social web.

- Social Media and Web 2.0 in Government
- http://www.usa.gov/webcontent/technol-ogy/other_tech.shtml
- Barriers and Solutions to Implementing Social Media and Web 2.0 in Government
- http://www.usa.gov/webcontent/docu-ments/SocialMediaFed%20Govt_BarriersPotentialSolutions.pdf

Figure 8. Twitter location feature

- http://www.futuregov.net/articles/2010/
  feb/05/govts-warned-about-social-media-
  security-risks/

Drapeau, M. and Wells, L. (2009) at the National Defense University have articulated four specific use cases of social media within the Federal Government. These four use cases include Inward Sharing, Outward Sharing, Inbound Sharing, and Outbound Sharing. The report offers the following recommendation.

The safe use of social media is fundamentally a behavioral issue, not a technology issue. Policy addressing behavior associated with protecting data would likely cover current social media technologies as well as future technologies (Drapeau and Wells, 2009).

To effectively deal with challenges related to security, privacy and compliance, organizations should involve legal, security, and human resource professionals. These groups should build out policy and governance models.

To conclude, an approach which provides granular access control, secure encryption and data monitoring, and comprehensive malware protection is mandatory for businesses to operate flexibly.

IDENTITY AND AUTHENTICATION

One major problem for users of social web is that of multiple identities (user names) to login to various social networks. Each of the major social networks requires users to use its own registration and credentials. This creates silos of user profiles and information.

Currently there is no central authority on the social web which can provide secure and reliable way of managing identity. This remains an issue and major social networks and companies are promoting their solutions. As an example, Microsoft services require LiveID while Google services require Google account / profile, Facebook uses its own login., One approach to solve this problem (to the extent possible) is offered by *OpenID*.

OpenID is an open, decentralized standard for authenticating users that can be used for access control, allowing users to log on to different services with the same digital identity where these services trust the authentication body (Figure 9). Both Facebook and Google support OpenID. This means that a user can register for Facebook using Gmail account provided by Google. This is a faster, streamlined way for users to get started.

Facebook Connect enables third party websites to implement the Facebook login on their own site. Users can use Facebook credentials on third party sites instead of starting from scratch. As is usual with social media, this convenience comes with some risk.

With the popularity of Twitter and the ready availability of its API, many third party application developers have created applications which use Twitter API. These Twitter-based applications only work with Twitter credentials. One cannot use any other login – not even OpenID - for Twitter or the applications built on Twitter, thus defeating the concept of a single universal login.

Social Data Exchange and Portability: OAuth

OAuth or Open Authorization allows a user to grant a third party site access to their information stored with another service provider, without sharing their access permissions or the full extent of their data.

With OAuth, the process of sharing information across an ecosystem of applications becomes more trustworthy and secure. The user is in control of how and when applications are allowed access to their account. For example, social media analytics applications aggregate various metrics for business use. These applications can use OAuth to request credentials for Twitter (Figure 10), Facebook, or Google accounts.

FUTURE RESEARCH DIRECTIONS

Social media is changing the way information flows and transactions happen. The initial excitement over social networks, websites and applica-

tions will give way to social commerce, social customer relationships and other transactional events. Given the rapid change, social media software and security is focus of many studies and research. The major topics include the following: identity management, identity theft protection, application and content security, ways to process information for security threats.

Here are a few research opportunities:

- Developing social customer relationship software with privacy in mind
- Providing a privacy score based on a user profile
- Creating privacy nudges (Lohr, 2010) – software which automatically sends reminders to users about the privacy consequences of their online sharing and other actions
- Making the location based social networks more secure
- Improving software which connects offline and online actions to detect security issues
- Managing corporate and government use of social media and to avoid data leaks

It is expected that innovative new ways will be applied to solve these challenging problems. As an example, here is abstract from the paper by Dwyer et. al (2010), which explains their approach to privacy scoring.

Users may unintentionally reveal private information to the world on their blogs on social network sites (SNSs). Information hunters can exploit such disclosed sensitive information for the purpose of advertising, marketing, spamming, etc. We present a new metric to quantify privacy, based on probability and entropy theory. Simply by relying on the total leaked privacy value calculated with our metric, users can adjust the amount of information they reveal on SNSs. Previous studies focused on quantifying privacy for purposes of data mining and location finding. The privacy metric in this

Figure 9. OpenID

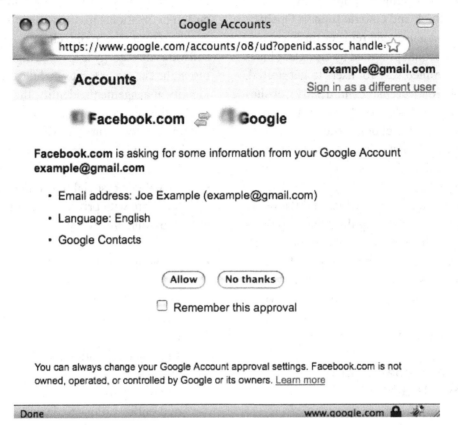

paper deals with unintentional leaks of information from SNSs. Our metric helps users of SNSs find how much privacy can be preserved after they have published sentences on their SNSs. It is simple, yet precise, which is proved through an experimental evaluation (Dwyer et. al.).

CONCLUSION

Social networks are in their early stages of development and adoption. This chapter has provided an overview of the security and privacy aspects of social media and provided information on how various efforts are being made to deal with these security and privacy issues.

Examples of social media exploits are provided. We discuss the challenges and how the major platforms have reacted to these security at-

tacks and privacy breaches. We provide examples of the difficulties faced by lay person to manage and control their privacy settings, especially when privacy policies are in flux.

As this is an area of active research, we talk about new approaches and provide references for further reading. We also discuss how mobile technology and location data adds to the challenges of social media privacy and security.

One should remember that cyber security and privacy is not only a technical issue but a social and policy issue as well. Therefore the appropriate solutions have to address technical, behavioral and policy matters. Attention is also drawn to balance out the benefits of social media with cautious approach towards security and privacy.

The changes and features introduced by social network platforms cause new threats to emerge on a regular basis. Security experts need to con-

Figure 10. Example of OAuth with Twitter

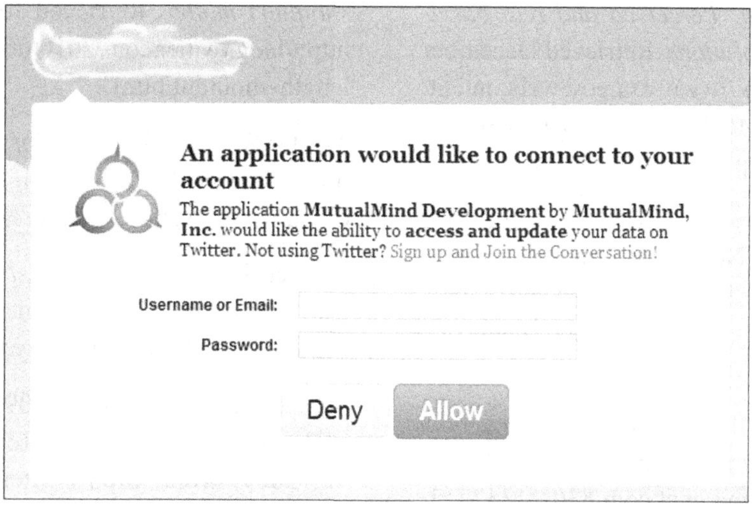

tinuously monitor the situation and educate and inform the public about the threats and how to remove them.

As the topic is so broad and dynamic, it is not possible to provide a comprehensive review of all the topics. Please browse the references and additional reading resources for further resources.

REFERENCES

All Facebook. (2010). *Facebook application leaderboard*. Retrieved September 2010, from http://statistics.allfacebook.com/applications/leaderboard/

Ante, S. (2010). *Dark side arises for phone apps*. Retrieved June 3, 2010, from http://online.wsj.com/article/SB10001424052748703340904575284532175834088.html

Boyd, D. (2010). *Why privacy is not dead*. Retrieved September 2010, from http://www.technologyreview.com/web/26000/

Cluley, G. (2010). *How to protect yourself from Facebook Places*. Retrieved September 17, 2010, from http://www.sophos.com/blogs/gc/g/2010/09/17/protect-facebook-places/

Cluley, G. (2010). *Twitter "onmouseover" security flaw widely exploited*. Retrieved September 21, 2010, from http://www.sophos.com/blogs/gc/g/2010/09/21/twitter-onmouseover-security-flaw-widely-exploited/

Drapeau, M., & Wells, L. (2009). *Social software and security: An initial net assessment*. Washington, DC: Center for Technology and National Security Policy, National Defense University.

Dwyer, C., Hiltz, S. R., Poole, M. S., Gussner, J., Hennig, F., & Osswald, S. ... Warth, B. (2010). *Developing reliable measures of privacy management within social networking sites*. 43rd Hawaii International Conference on System Sciences, (pp. 1-10).

Facbook. (2010). *Privacy policy*. Retrieved September 2010, from http://www.facebook.com/privacy/explanation.php#!/policy.php

Facebook. (2010). *Developers*. Retrieved September 2010, from http://developers.facebook.com/

Gates, G. (2010). *Facebook privacy: A bewildering tangle of options*. Retrieved May 12, 2010, from http://www.nytimes.com/interactive/2010/05/12/business/facebook-privacy.html

Godwin, B., et al. (2008). *Social media and the federal government: Perceived and real barriers and potential solutions*. Retrieved December 23, 2008, from http://www.usa.gov/webcontent/documents/SocialMediaFed%20Govt_Barriers-PotentialSolutions.pdf

Lohr, S. (2010, February 28). *Redrawing the route to online privacy*. New York Times. Retrieved March 27, 2010, from http://www.nytimes.com/2010/02/28/technology/internet/28unbox.html

McCarthy, C. (2010). *Facebook phishing scam snares company board member*. Retrieved May 10, 2010, from http://news.cnet.com/8301-13577_3-20004549-36.html?

Puttaswamy, K. P. N., & Zhao, B. Y. (2010). *Preserving privacy in location-based mobile social applications*. Paper presented at HotMobile'10, Annapolis, Maryland.

Rao, L. (2010). *Twitter seeing 6 billion API calls per day, 70k per second*. TechCrunch. Retrieved from http://techcrunch.com/2010/09/17/twitter-seeing-6-billion-api-calls-per-day-70k-per-second/

Rowan, D. (2010). *Six reasons why I'm not on Facebook*. Retrieved September 18, 2010, from http://www.wired.com/epicenter/2010/09/six-reasons-why-wired-uks-editor-isnt-on-facebook/

Siciliano, R. (2010). *Social media security: Using Facebook to steal company data*. Retrieved May 11, 2010, from http://www.huffingtonpost.com/robert-siciliano/social-media-security-usi_b_570246.html

Sophos. (2010). *Security threat report*. Retrieved January 2010, from http://www.sophos.com/sophos/docs/eng/papers/sophos-security-threat-report-jan-2010-wpna.pdf

Twitter Blog. (2010). *Links and Twitter: Length shouldn't matter*. Retrieved June 8, 2010, from http://blog.twitter.com/2010/06/links-and-twitter-length-shouldnt.html

Twitter Blog. (2010). *State of Twitter spam*. Retrieved March 23, 2010, from http://blog.twitter.com/2010/03/state-of-twitter-spam.html

Twitter Blog. (2010). *Trust and safety*. Retrieved March 9, 2010, from http://blog.twitter.com/2010/03/trust-and-safety.html

Twitter Help Resources. (2009). *About the Tweet with your location feature*. Retrieved November 12, 2009, from http://twitter.zendesk.com/forums/26810/entries/78525

Vamosi, R. (2008). Koobface virus hits Facebook. *CNET*. Retrieved December 4, 2008, from http://news.cnet.com/koobface-virus-hits-facebook/

Vascellaro, J. (2010). *Facebook glitch exposed private chats*. Retrieved May 5, 2010, from http://online.wsj.com/article/SB10001424052748703961104575226314165586910.html

ADDITIONAL READING

Blumberg, A., & Eckersley, P. (2009). *On Locational Privacy, and How to Avoid Losing it Forever*. Retrieved August 2009, from http://www.eff.org/wp/locational-privacy

Carey, R., et al. (2009). *Guidelines for Secure Use of Social Media by Federal Departments and Agencies*. Retrieved September 2009, from http://www.cio.gov/Documents/Guidelines_for_Secure_Use_Social_Media_v01-0.pdf

Chen, X., & Shi, S. (2009). A Literature Review of Privacy Research on Social Network Sites. Mines, vol. 1, pp.93-97, 2009 *International Conference on Multimedia Information Networking and Security, 2009*.

Cramer, M., & Hayes, G. (2010). Acceptable Use in the Age of Connected Youth: How Risks, Policies, and Promises of the Future Impact Student Access to Mobile Phones and Social Media in Schools. *IEEE Pervasive Computing, 01 Apr. 2010.* IEEE computer Society Digital Library.

Eston, T. Privacy and Security of Open Graph, Social Plugins and Instant Personalization on Facebook. Retrieved April 23, 2010, from http://www.spylogic.net/2010/04/privacy-of-open-graph-social-plugins-and-instant-personalization-on-facebook/

Facebook (2010). *Press Room*. Retrieved September 2010, from http://www.facebook.com/press.php

Hawkey, K. (2009). Examining the Shifting Nature of Privacy, Identities, and Impression Management with Web 2.0. Cse, vol. 4, pp.990-995, 2009 *International Conference on Computational Science and Engineering, 2009.*

Ho, A., Maiga, A., & Aimeur, E. (2009). Privacy protection issues in social networking sites. Aiccsa, pp.271-278, 2009 *IEEE/ACS International Conference on Computer Systems and Applications.*

LinkedIn. (2010). *About Us*. Retrieved September 2010, from http://press.linkedin.com/

Marwick, A. E., Murgia-Diaz, D. & Palfrey, J. G (2010).Youth, Privacy and Reputation. *Berkman Center Research Publication No. 2010-5.*

Meister, E., & Biermann, E. (2008). Implementation of a Socially Engineered Worm to Increase Information Security Awareness. Broadcom, pp.343-350, *Third International Conference on Broadband Communications, Information Technology & Biomedical Applications.*

Mitra, A. (2009). *Multiple Identities on Social Networks: Issues of Privacy and Authenticity. Workshop on Security and Privacy in Online Social Networking.* Retrieved 2009, from http://www.sis.uncc.edu/LIISP/WSPOSN09/index.html

Nagy, J., & Pecho, P. (2009). Social Networks Security. Securware, pp.321-325, *Third International Conference on Emerging Security Information, Systems and Technologies.*

Ngoc, T. H., Echizen, I., Komei, K., & Yoshiura, H. (2010). New Approach to Quantification of Privacy on Social Network Sites. Aina, pp.556-564, 2010 *24th IEEE International Conference on Advanced Information Networking and Applications.*

Nielsen (2009). *Global Faces and Networked Places*. Retrieved March 2009, from http://blog.nielsen.com/nielsenwire/wp-content/uploads/2009/03/nielsen_globalfaces_mar09.pdf

Rosenblum, D. (2007). What Anyone Can Know: The Privacy Risks of Social Networking Sites. *IEEE Security and Privacy*, 5(3), 40–49. doi:10.1109/MSP.2007.75

Schneier, B. (2010). *Keynote speech by Bruce Schneier at Higher Education Security Summit, Indiana University*. Retrieved April 2010, from http://bit.ly/d0le8N and from http://www.indiana.edu/~uits/cacrsummit10/program.html

Wikipedia (2010). *Data Protection Directive*. Retrieved from http://en.wikipedia.org/wiki/Data_Protection_Directive

Wikipedia (2010). *Facebook Privacy Criticism*. Retrieved from http://en.wikipedia.org/wiki/Criticism_of_Facebook

Worthen, B. (2010). *Web Watchdogs Dig for Privacy Flaws, Bark Loud*. Retrieved June 2010, from http://online.wsj.com/article/SB10001424052748704312104575298561398856680.html

KEY TERMS AND DEFINITIONS

API: application programming interface. A way for software programs to share data with other programs.

Connections: users on social sites which are connected to each other so that they can share and see each other's information to the extent governed by user and site.

"Everyone": a term used by Facebook to define all users on Internet. This is used in the context of other Facebook terms such as "friends" and "friends of friends".

Follower: someone who subscribes to a user's updates and content stream.

OAuth: is an open industry standard that allows users to share their private resources across web sites by using tokens instead of asking users for their username and password.

Short Links: Converting a long URL (web address) into a short one. For example, http://bit.

ly provides a link shortening service. Short links were made popular for use on Twitter, where message length is limited to 140 characters and each character matters.

Social Networking Sites: Websites which allow individual users to create profile, connect with other users and to create and share digital content and resources.

Tweets: 140-character messages on Twitter

Twitter: a social network which allows posting and sharing 140-character messages with others via web or through sms.

Unfriend: To remove someone as a "friend" on a social networking site such as Facebook.

Chapter 5
Botnets and Cyber Security:
Battling Online Threats

Ahmed Mansour Manasrah
National Advanced IPv6 Center, Malaysia

Omar Amer Abouabdalla
National Advanced IPv6 Center, Malaysia

Moein Mayeh
National Advanced IPv6 Center, Malaysia

Nur Nadiyah Suppiah
National Advanced IPv6 Center, Malaysia

ABSTRACT

The Internet, originally designed in a spirit of trust, uses protocols and frameworks that are not inherently secure. This basic weakness is greatly compounded by the interconnected nature of the Internet, which, together with the revolution in the software industry, has provided a medium for large-scale exploitation, for example, in the form of botnets. Despite considerable recent efforts, Internet-based attacks, particularly via botnets, are still ubiquitous and have caused great damage on both national and international levels. This chapter provides a brief overview of the botnet phenomena and its pernicious aspects. Current governmental and corporate efforts to mitigate the threat are also described, together with the bottlenecks limiting their effectiveness in various countries. The chapter concludes with a description of lines of investigation that could counter the botnet phenomenon.

DOI: 10.4018/978-1-60960-851-4.ch005

INTRODUCTION

A botnet is a collection of computers connected to the Internet that can interact to accomplish distributed activities, usually of an illegal nature. Such systems comprise a set of compromised machines, called *drones* or *zombies*, that run a malicious software application called a *bot*. The bot allows each individual system to be controlled discretely, without the owner's knowledge. And given the nature of the Internet and the prevalence of insecure systems, vast botnets can be created that have very large combined computing power. They can be used as a powerful cyber weapon to take down online services or as an effective tool for making illicit profits. Of course, the owner of a botnet could be located anywhere—another city, country, or continent—but importantly, the Internet is structured in such a way that the botnet can be controlled anonymously. Bots can be controlled either directly using built-in commands, or indirectly via a control centre or other compromised machines on the network.

The growth of botnets, and the increasingly inventive ways in which they are being used to steal personal data, harm government and business operations, or deny users access to information and services represents a serious threat to the Internet economy, to individuals' online privacy, and to national security. Unfortunately, whenever an attack occurs or an exploit is found, the underlying technology, being the easiest to blame, is held at fault. However, legal and political frameworks can be as powerful as technology in addressing cyber-security threats, and any technical solution must be aligned with community standards and values. Therefore, attempts to mitigate the botnet threat should not be limited to purely technical solutions. Although it is clear that technology is an important starting point, we still need to view the challenge with a clear and broad perspective as, perhaps, a mission integration challenge. In fact, it may be that the botnet threat can only be met through an integration of technology, strategy,

policy, and legislation. This is supported by the fact that the substantial national and international efforts of various organizations to raise awareness, track malware, develop or amend legal frameworks, strengthen law enforcement, and improve the response to new threats in general have had little effect.

Thus, we argue that technology alone cannot make everything possible. Moreover, it is not enough for one country or one community to independently self-organize to try and address the problem, if others do not do so as well. Therefore, an international cross-border cyber security platform is needed. The platform should define a global research and development agenda by developing a global cyber security technology framework that can be used to establish an effective mechanism for knowledge dissemination at the national and global level. Moreover, the framework should also provide a better and dynamic global coordinated response to new attacks by possibly increasing monitoring activities at the global scale. Only a holistic approach involving an integrated mix of policy, operational procedure, and technical ingenuity can ensure effective and integrated information sharing, co-ordination, and cross-border co-operation. The success of such efforts would require the active engagement of all stakeholders. Such an effort, moreover, would demonstrate significant advances in the international community's ability to overcome obstacles to executing global co-ordinated actions. This chapter attempts to provide a comprehensive background on extant efforts and challenges faced by different organizations in the battle with botnets.

BACKGROUND

The term bot, short for *robot*, is derived from the Czech word *robota*, which means "work" (Saha & Gairola 2005). Usually, a network of tens to hundreds of thousands and, in some cases, several millions of bots constitute what is known as

Table 1. MessageLabs survey results: Ranking of active botnets

Cutwail	Without doubt the largest botnet around. Since March 2009, it has doubled in size and output per bot.
Rustock	Still sending in bursts, but when active, this botnet shows the scale of its spamming ability. Frequently goes through periods of zero activity.
Grum	Still patchy in output, it has become more active in recent months.
Donbot	Though still one of the top botnets, it has been less active recently.
Xarvester	Earlier in 2009, it was one of the major botnets, but in recent months, it has drastically reduced in size and output.
Mega-D	The top botnet at the start of 2009, it has been steadily declining in size since then. Still one of the hardest working botnets in terms of spam per bot per minute.
Gheg	A smaller botnet, but with consistent output.
Asprox	Patchy output, has recently started working its bots harder to increase output.
Darkmailer	A very small botnet, but has managed to get attention by the sheer volume of spam it sends per bot per minute.

botnet. These bots are handled and commanded by a single, or sometimes a group, of commanders (attacker/botmaster) who have the ability to remotely instruct bots to perform certain tasks. Since the backbone of any botnet is the individual compromised host, botnets are seen in a variety of computer systems—on computers at homes, schools, business places, and governmental offices—all of which may contain valuable data that can provide financial benefits to the attacker (Cooke, Jahanian, Mcpherson, & Danny 2005; Dagon et al., 2005; Gu 2008).

MessageLabs, owned by Symantec, performed a survey in 2009 to identify the most active botnets (Symantec 2009). As shown in Table 1, Cutwail was the largest active botnet, which sent out 74,115,721,081 spam E-mail messages a day with a size of 1400–2100 KB each. Brazil, with 14% of infected hosts, was the country most affected by Cutwil. In addition, note that even Darkmailer, the lowest ranked botnet, sent out 93,954,453 spam E-mail messages a day with an estimated size 1 KB each (Symantec 2009).

Although viruses and worms still pose a significant threat, they do not represent a global threat to critical national infrastructure as do botnets. Botnets perform large-scale coordinated attacks using multiple infected hosts to target either a single or multiple victims (Green, Marchette, Northcutt, & Ralph 1999). These coordinated attacks can take down vital Internet-based resources. An example of such an attack is one performed by Mydoom.M (F-Secure 2009b), a mass-mailing worm that targets port 1034/TCP and sends out E-mails that mimic mail system errors. W32.Randex.E (Symantec 2007) is an IRC Trojan controlled via the IRC protocol. POLY-BOOT-B* (Trendmicro 2003) is an encrypted, memory-resident boot virus that damages the boot sector of hard drives and floppy drives. Note that each attack must be prepared well before the attack itself can take place. Therefore, attackers need to continuously create new means and methods to compromise a wider range of machines for effective and untraceable attacks. To this end, attackers will always try to recruit new hosts while working to maintain existing ones. New members are enlisted by exploiting different vulnerabilities through vulnerability scans, worm exploits, Web-based malware exploits, and botnet takeovers (Cole, Mellor, & Noyes 2007).

The difference between today's bots and traditional viruses or worms is that bots contain a payload that searches for more vulnerable hosts over the Internet by scanning IP addresses. In addition, bots can communicate with the botmaster through a command and control (C&C) centre/ server to receive updates. The process of hiring malicious application on victim propagation has been improved from a single to a multiple automated propagation (Bailey, Cooke, Jahanian, Xu, & Karir 2009). Once an attacker succeeds in infecting enough machines (i.e. turning them into zombies), the attacker will run a "shellcode" that downloads the bot binary from a remote server. The bot will install itself into a configurable directory on the zombie and start each time the system starts (Rajab, Zarfoss, Monrose, & Terzis 2006). Communication with the C&C server can occur via different kinds of network topologies using protocols such as those commonly used for P2P and the IRC and HTTP protocols (Rajab, et al. 2006). This communication pattern allows fast, reliable, and yet anonymous and untraceable, communication with the bots. As result, the attacker can continue launching various types of attacks to maximize financial gains (Rajab, et al. 2006; Saha & Gairola 2005).

For instance, Google discovered a highly sophisticated and targeted attack on its corporate infrastructure originating from China that led to theft of its intellectual property (CNet News, 2010). The attack on Google involved attempts to access the Gmail accounts of Chinese human rights activists, but only two accounts were accessed and the contents of e-mails were not exposed. Separately, Google discovered that accounts of dozens of Gmail users in the U.S., China, and Europe who are human rights advocates appear to have been routinely accessed by third parties, not through a security breach at Google, but most likely as a result of phishing scams or malware placed on the users' computers.

In May 2007, a series of cyber attacks were launched against Estonian government and commercial websites. Some attacks involved vandalizing websites, and replacing the pages with Russian propaganda or bogus information. Up to six sites were rendered inaccessible at various times, including those of the foreign and justice ministries. Most of the attacks were launched using botnets comprised of many thousands of ordinary

computers. The attack was primarily defended through filtering – blocking connections from outside Estonia. For example, Estonia's second largest bank, SEB Eesti Uhispank, blocked access from abroad to its online banking service while remaining open to local users (Sydney morning herald, 2007). Three weeks after the attacks ended, one researcher identified at least 128 separate attacks on nine different websites in Estonia. Of these 128 attacks, 35 were reportedly against the website of the Estonian Police, another 35 were reportedly against the website of the Ministry of Finance, and 36 attacks were against the Estonian parliament's, prime minister's, and general government websites (Lemos and Robert, 2007).

CURRENT EFFORTS

Many efforts have been initiated by academic, corporate, and governmental organizations to address the problem of botnets as a step towards mitigating risk, tracing back attackers, and countering threats. For instance, the Cyber Force Center (CFC) of the National Police Agency of Japan developed a methodology to capture malware and track botnets (Ono, Kawaishi, & Kamon 2007). They use honeypots (EU 2008; Honeynet Project 2005, 2006) to capture malware and then analyse their Internet traffic to identify potential bots. The CFC performs real-time classification of these data on the basis of destination port, source country, and time-line. Unfortunately, there is no proper linkage or coordination between the CFC and other global law enforcement agencies to value the findings and act accordingly. Yet, the inter-countries problem is still an obvious constraint.

Microsoft also contributed to the battle against botnet through a project known as "Operation b49" which took down a major spambot called Waledac (Cranton 2010). Waledac is a worm that spreads as an E-mail attachment sent from every infected machine. Once installed, it will search local files for E-mail addresses to further propagate. It can be sent commands via a remote server (F-Secure 2009a). Statistics show that Waledac is one of the 10 largest botnets in the USA, with hundreds of thousands of infected computers that can send up to 1.5 billion spam E-mail messages per day. This effort has cut off traffic to Waledac at the source, the ".com" or domain registry level. This action is the most crucial, for it severs the connection between the command and control centers of the botnet, and its thousands of zombie computers around the world. Additional technical counter-measures have been implemented to downgrade much of the remaining communication at the peer-to-peer command and control level within the botnet has also taken place. From the other hand, this was a needed effort and solution, we don't have enough information whether such effort still exists; and if exists, is it at a global level or a country designated efforts.

Cisco researchers developed a detection technique that allowed them to discover the techniques that botmasters use to compromise machines. This method is focusing on IRC as the C&C channel, because the IRC protocol uses a nonstandard port for malicious activity and is open to customization (Cisco 2009b). The Cisco ASA 8.2 software and Cisco ASA 5500 series of devices allow filtering of botnet traffic (Cisco 2009a) by monitoring all protocols and ports to identify and stop C&C traffic. However, the software has a limited database that requires frequent updates and can only identify known botnets activity patterns. These updates can only be made available through a matured and wide global collaboration; through a proper information sharing channels. This is because of the fact that one attack in one country may not be repeated –at the time being- in another country. Thus, preparing and learning the attack and its patterns could be the very first step to avoid such attack in the future.

The International Telecommunication Union (ITU), based in Geneva, Switzerland, with 191 member states and more than 700 sector members (ITU 2010), is another large organization that has

also tried its hand at mitigating the botnet threats. The ITU's Botnet Mitigation Toolkit employs a kind of multipronged and multistakeholder strategy to identify and take down every domain that is found to be related to malware or botnet activity (Sector, 2008). However, the toolkit still in the proposing phase and it is not being implemented yet. Moreover, the toolkit does not thoroughly address the social aspects of infection that explain why machines are compromised and the user's role.

National governments have also made efforts to improve Information security by establishing and issuing rules and regulations. For instance, the People's Republic of China's "Computer Information System Security Protection Rules and Regulation" was issued as early as 1994 (APEC, 2008). And in April 2002, the Japanese Ministry of Internal Affairs and Communication promulgated an anti-spam law (The Law on Regulation of Transmission of Specified Electronic Mail) to address the danger of spam (APEC, 2008). The Republic of Korea, quite experienced with spam, ratified the "Act on Promotion of Information and Communication Network Utilization and Information Protection, etc." in 2001 (APEC, 2008). In July 2002, the European Union authorized the "EU Privacy and Electronic Communications Directive" (APEC, 2008). The countries such as Italy, Britain, Denmark, Spain and others that are members of EU should not send business email in EU without the previous agreement of the recipient based on this treaty (EU, 2008). Many other countries have also invested effort and money to address Internet security. However, the above measure and regulations are only effective with the spam cases. Knowing that spam could be an action of a botnet, but it is well known that worms and other threads are also involved in such activity. Thus, botnets threats are not being collaboratively addressed within any internet security acts, roles or regulations at a global level.

ISPs, responsible for providing Internet, E-mail, and other services, represent a strong target for the attackers. Organization such as MAAWG (MAAWG, 2010), IETF (IETF, 2010), and IAB (IAB, 2008) have conducted considerable research in this area (Sector, 2008). Technical solutions include filtering of inbound E-mail such as HELO filtering (Inc, 2004); outbound filtering to prevent infection of other ISPs, router-level filtering, including filtering of spoofed source address traffic (NISCC, 2004) using the Border Gateway Protocol (BGP); management of port 25 (MAAWG, 2010); and authentication mechanisms such as DKIM (DKIM, 2009), sender ID (Microsoft, 2006), and SPF (SPF, 2008). ISPs play a vital role in such a war. There should be a proper information sharing channel between ISP and various players worldwide. An attack may occur targeting one ISP network will be technically kept hidden from the public as a matter of reputation. This indeed a very important step toward the big picture of battling the internet thread such as botnet by collaboratively disseminate attack information to the security communities, agencies and bodies for learning and early prevention.

EXISTING CONSTRAINTS TO BOTNET MITIGATION

Why have none of these techniques or policies been effective? Some blame a lack of awareness among stakeholders due to the lack of pertinent statistics (Bergstrand, Borryd, Lindmark, & Slama 2009). Indeed, we know that most ISPs do not follow up on complaints regarding botnets because most work with only estimates of the scale of the problem. For instance, the Swedish Post and Telecom Agency (PTS) estimates that less than 1% of computers in Sweden with broadband connections are infected (Bergstrand, et al. 2009). Another aspect is user behaviour, which can negate all the safeguards provided by the ISP. The problem stems from a lack of skill and awareness regarding information security (Bergstrand, et al. 2009). Thus, the solution lies in training people, both information

security professionals and normal users. The first government to begin training users was the USA, where in 1987, rules were enforced that made it mandatory for new staff to undergo periodic information security training (APEC, 2008). This is indeed a very good practice, but we do not have enough information on whether such courses are still conducted. However, because botnets are a global threat, efforts made in only one country will not solve the problem.

Currently, governments, industry, and civil society are all trying to put in place rules and policies for their end-users. However, several issues prevent success, particularly the lack of the resources to deal with the impact of botnets. Furthermore, because all the different efforts generally share the same features, considerable repetition of work has occurred. Hence, it is better to group stakeholders in a systemic manner, such as on the basis of geography or roles and policy. To depute these communications, there should be coordination between them (Sector, 2008).

SOLUTIONS AND RECOMMENDATIONS

Many would agree that the damage caused by malware is significant and needs to be reduced although its economic and social impacts may be hard to quantify. That said, who should consider in assessing what action to take, and several factors, against botnets. These include: the roles and responsibilities of the various participants, the incentives under which they operate as market players as well as the activities already undertaken by those communities more specifically involved in fighting botnets. Among the various participants, those concerned by malware are:

- Users (home users, small and medium-sized enterprises (SMEs), public and private sector organizations) whose data and information systems are potential targets and who have different levels of competence to protect them.

- Software vendors who have a role in developing trustworthy, reliable, safe and secure software.
- Anti-virus vendors who have a role in providing security solutions to users (such as updating anti-virus software with the latest information on malware).
- Internet Service Providers (ISPs) who have a role in managing the networks to which the aforementioned groups connect for access to the Internet.
- Law enforcement entities, which have a mandate to investigate and prosecute cybercrime.
- Government agencies, which have a role to manage risks to the security of government information systems and the critical information infrastructure.
- Governments and inter-governmental organizations, which have a role in developing national and international policies and legal instruments to enhance prevention, detection and response to malware proliferation and its related crimes.

Better understanding of the nature, successes and limitations of ongoing action by communities more specifically involved in fighting malware is also important to assessing how to enhance prevention of and response to malware. Substantial efforts by various participants have been made within countries and economies and at the international level to, inter alia, raise awareness, measure malware, develop or amend legal frameworks, strengthen law enforcement, and improve response. For example:

- Many websites and resources exist to help end users and organizations secure their information systems.
- Many entities track, measure and sometimes even publish data on their experience with malware and related threats (CME 2007). Furthermore, schemas (CERT 2006) exist to provide single, common identifiers to new virus threats and to the most prevalent virus threats in the wild to reduce public confusion during malware incidents.
- Numerous countries across the world have legal provisions against hacking, spam, data interference, and system interference. Furthermore, the Convention of the Council of Europe on cybercrime is the first and only legally binding multilateral treaty addressing the problems posed by the spread of criminal activity online and 43 countries across the globe are now party to the Convention.

Fighting malware is complex and would benefit from more comprehensive measurement, co–ordination and policy solutions. While many ongoing initiatives (OECD 2008) are contributing important resources to combating malware, there remain a number of areas for improvement such as:

A Global Partnership Against Botnets

The need for a consistent approach to a global problem is not new but malware presents particular complexities due to the wide variety of actors with responsibility for combating malware. The communities involved in fighting malware, whether governments, businesses, users, or the technical community, need to improve their understanding of the challenges each of them faces and co-operate – within their communities and across communities – to address the problem. Furthermore, their co-operation must occur at the global level. It is not enough for one country or one community to effectively self organize if others do not do so as well.

Proactive Prevention Strategies Framework

This framework is to examine and promote further efforts that can be made to improve online users awareness of the risks related to malware and of the measures they should take to enhance the security of their information systems. Improve standards and guidelines by updating the security manuals such as the IETF Security Handbook RFCs should be encouraged to include new challenges such as those presented by malware. And encourage R&D activities such as malware detection and analysis, security usability - how people interact with machines, software and online resources.

Policy Frameworks/Law Enforcement

This framework is to examine the government efforts to provide mutual assistance and share information for the successful attribution and prosecution of cybercriminals. As well as examining and initiating Co-operation between CSIRT teams and law enforcement entities. Finally, examining resources necessary for specialized cybercrime law enforcement agencies to be able to investigate and prosecute cybercrime in co-operation with other concerned public and private stakeholders.

Technical Measures Framework

This framework could examine the technical measures such as filtering, and many others could be examined to understand how they would help fight malware. And how users might be provided with better tools to monitor and detect the activities of malicious code, both at the time when a compromise is being attempted and afterwards.

In summary, only a holistic approach involving an integrated mix of policy, operational procedure and technical defenses can ensure that information sharing, co–ordination and cross–border co-operation are effectively integrated and addressed. The success of such a global "Anti-botnet Partnership" would require active engagement from all participants. Such an effort, however, would demonstrate significant advances in the international community's ability to overcome obstacles to addressing a global threat like botnet through global coordinated action. Governments on the other hand, should create specific budgets devoted to information security, which should cover the creation of international treaties, the development of stronger security software, educating and training of users to raise general awareness, and fortify organization security. Furthermore, several countries have enacted laws with strict penalties for Internet crime such as implementing DDOS attacks and sending out spam (APEC, 2008). However, there exist no special laws and regulations specifically targeting botnets. Therefore, governments should unite at international conferences and meetings to create special rules that can be applied anywhere in the world.

FUTURE RESEARCH DIRECTIONS

Most current research is focused on the political issues and very little work has been done on the social, educational, and technological aspects of the problem. However, on the basis of the previous and ongoing efforts, we briefly list here several facets of cyber security related to botnets that require attention but are not addressed anywhere else:

1. **Domestic and international law enforcement.** A hostile party on an Internet-connected computer can conduct an attack on another that may be thousands of miles away as easily as if it were next door. It is often difficult to identify the perpetrator of such an attack, and even when a perpetrator is identified, criminal prosecution across national boundaries is often problematic.

2. **Education.** Individual Internet users need to continually maintain and update their

system security. Corporations and large organizations must also be informed of the best practices for effective security management. For example, some large organizations now have policies that set strict security guidelines for all systems on the premises. Automated updates are sent to all computers and servers on the internal network, and no new system is allowed online until it conforms to the security policy.

3. **Information security.** Information security refers to measures taken to protect or preserve information on a network as well as the network itself. Thus, it also involves physical security, personnel security, criminal law and investigation, economics, and other issues. These factors need to be included in the curriculum for cyber security practitioners, and supporting law and technologies need to be made available.

4. **Sociological issues.** There are several areas relating to cyber security in which there may be conflicting interests and needs, and such tensions will need to be addressed as part on any comprehensive approach to cyber security. For example, as part of the effort to prevent attacks or to track down cyber criminals, it may be necessary to determine the origin of data packets on the Internet. But such knowledge may be perceived by some to conflict with an individual's right to privacy or anonymity. To cite another example, what some nations or individuals may perceive as a necessary filtering of data may be perceived by others as unwanted censorship. Such issues involve ethics, law, and societal concerns as much as they do technology. All these non-technological issues make the cyber security problem even more challenging.

As a result, a cyber security platform that mainly focuses on botnets activities and brings together academics, researchers, organizations and governments is a favored solution. The Cyber security platform should aims to produce a cyber-security research platform to define a national and international R&D agenda to produce the technologies that will protect our information systems and networks into the future. The cyber security platform may consists (mainly) of

1. Strategies Platform to increase the user awareness by hosting and arranging for international cyber security conference worldwide. In addition, the strategy platform should also try to standardize and coordinate cyber security awareness and education programmes across the countries hand in hand with existing bodies and law regulators. This will also lead to establish progressive capacity building programmes for national law enforcement agencies. This itself will be an effective mechanism for the cyber security knowledge dissemination at the national and global level. The strategy platform should not be on its own, it should also contribute to the technical aspects of the problem by providing important inputs towards examining how people interact with the IT infrastructure, with a focus on ethics, culture, behaviour, and other factors that can lead to non-technology security lapses. Moreover, the platform should also facilitate various studies to address the sociological and the behavioural phenomena that may lead people to commit acts of cyber crime. This should also be considered within any policy framework to address various sociological/behavioural factors to be taken into consideration.

2. Where the Engineering Platform is to innovate and produce detection, monitoring and traceback mechanism that will directly help and assist building a standard cyber security risk assessment framework. This framework should also provide various cyber security requirement controls and baselines. These

controls and baselines can be the kick off to develop an effective cyber security incident reporting mechanisms. As well as providing better dynamic protection that can react when attacks are detected, possibly by increasing monitoring activities at various scale. The engineering platform should also facilitate the development of various tools based on improved models that characterize "normal" traffic behavior. That should also identify the origin of the cyber attacks, including traceback of network traffic, identify attackers based on their behaviour and collecting evidence in uncooperative network environments for further research.

3. Finally, Policies Platform that should review, analyze and to further enhance countries existing cyber laws to address the dynamic nature of cyber security threats (botnets) by closing the gaps that may exists in the existing countries Cyber Laws in the area of botnet threats. As well as analyzing the conflicts that arises from these Cyber Laws between botnet cybercrimes and privacy legislations. And to guide and monitor of systems to ensure that they meet declared security policies before any action can take place. And then provide consideration of international laws and standards and the impact of both on cyber security technologies, policies, and implementation. These considerations should consider the various technical, sociological and behavioural factors from the engineering and the strategy platforms.

CONCLUSION

Attacks are becoming more sophisticated and the attackers are becoming smarter. Therefore, defences should be improved and updated. In this chapter, we discussed extent botnet mitigation efforts in terms of three main domains: govern-

ments or communities, ISPs, and individuals users. For governments, we suggested long-term plans to train managers and experts on emerging security threats and the implementation of relevant policies and regulations. ISPs, given their crucial role in providing Internet services, should strengthen their infrastructure with more powerful defence systems, use filtering policies for certain sources, and also sharing botnet information with other ISPs. Individual users, currently the most vulnerable, should be prepared for and warned of vulnerabilities, and depute the technological aspects of the problem and the detection as well as educating them how to use or utilize it.

In sum, it is not useful or effective for countries or communities to independently self-organize and establish policies for their networks. Rules and policies in each country are limited by international borders, whereas attackers are not. Hence, governments and communities must establish robust communication channels at the functional level for rapid sharing of information and co-ordinated resolution, and to also institute specific policies to respond to threats that originate from anywhere at any time.

REFERENCES

APEC. (2008). *Guide on policy and technical approaches against botnet*. Lima, Peru.

AusCERT. (2002). Increased intruder attacks against servers to expand illegal file sharing networks. (Advisory AA-2002.03). Retrieved March 27, 2010, from http://www.auscert.org.au/render. html?it=2229&cid=1

Bailey, M., Cooke, E., Jahanian, F., Xu, Y., & Karir, M. (2009). A survey of botnet technology and defenses. Paper presented at the 2009 Cybersecurity Applications \& Technology Conference for Homeland Security.

Bergstrand, P., Borryd, K., Lindmark, S., & Slama, A. (2009). Botnets: Hijacked computers in Sweden (No. *PTS-ER*, *2009*, 11.

Bort, J. (2007). How big is the botnet problem? Network World. Retrieved March 27, 2010, from http://www.networkworld.com/research/2007/070607-botnets-side.html

Canavan, J. (2005). The evolution of malicious IRC bots.

CERT Coordination Center. (2006). List of CSIRTs with national responsibility. Retrieved from http://www.cert.org/csirts/national/contact.html

Cisco. (2009). Cisco ASA botnet traffic filter. Retrieved March 27, 2010, from http://www.cisco.com/en/US/prod/vpndevc/ps6032/ps6094/ps6120/botnet_index.html

Cisco. (2009). Infiltrating a botnet. Retrieved March 27, 2010, from http://www.cisco.com/web/about/security/intelligence/bots.html

CNet News. (Jan 2010). InSecurity complex, Behind the China attacks on Google (FAQ). Retrieved from http://news.cnet.com/8301-27080_3-10434721-245.html?tag=mncol;txt

Cole, A., Mellor, M., & Noyes, D. (2007). Botnets: The rise of the machines. Paper presented at the 6th Annual Security Research Associates Spring Growth Conference.

Common Malware Enumeration (CME). (2007). Data list. Retrieved from http://cme.mitre.org/data/list.html

Cooke, E., Jahanian, F., & Mcpherson, D. (2005). The zombie roundup: Understanding, detecting, and disrupting botnets. In Workshop on Steps to Reducing Unwanted Traffic on the Internet (SRUTI), (pp. 39–44).

Cranton, T. (2010). Cracking down on botnets. Retrieved March 27, 2010, from http://microsoftontheissues.com/cs/blogs/mscorp/archive/2010/02/24/cracking-down-on-botnets.aspx

Dagon, D., Gu, G., Zou, C., Grizzard, J., Dwivedi, S., Lee, W., et al. (2005). A taxonomy of botnets. Paper presented at the CAIDA DNS-OARC Workshop.

DKIM. (2009). DomainKeys identified mail (DKIM). Retrieved March 27, 2010, from http://www.dkim.org/

EU. (2008). About European Union. Retrieved March 27, 2010, from http://europa.eu/index_en.htm

F-Secure. (2009). Email-Worm: W32/Waledac.A. Retrieved March 27, 2010, from http://www.f-secure.com/v-descs/email-worm_w32_waledac_a.shtml

F-Secure. (2009). Mydoom.M. Retrieved April 07, 2010, from http://www.f-secure.com/v-descs/mydoom_m.shtml

freed0. (2007). ASN/GeoLoc reports and what to do about them. Retrieved March 27, 2010, from http://www.shadowserver.org/wiki/pmwiki.php/Calendar/20070111

Gandhi, M., Jakobsson, M., & Ratkiewicz, J. (2006). Badvertisements: Stealthy click-fraud with unwitting accessories. *Journal of Digital Forensic Practice*, *1*(2). doi:10.1080/15567280601015598

Green, J., Marchette, D., Northcutt, S., & Ralph, B. (1999). Analysis techniques for detecting coordinated attacks and probes. Paper presented at the Intrusion Detection and Network Monitoring, Santa Clara, California, USA.

Gu, G. (2008). Correlation-based botnet detection in enterprise networks. Unpublished Dissertation, Georgia Institute of Technology, Georgia.

Honeynet Project. (2005). Know your enemy: GenII honeynets. Retrieved from http://old.honeynet.org/papers/gen2/

Honeynet Project. (2006). Know your enemy: Honeynets. Retrieved March 27, 2010, from http://old.honeynet.org/papers/honeynet/

IAB. (2008). IAB documents and current activities. Retrieved March 27, 2010, from http://www.iab.org/documents/index.html

IETF. (2010). Operational security capabilities for IP network infrastructure (OPSEC). Retrieved March 27, 2010, from http://datatracker.ietf.org/wg/opsec/charter/

ITU. (2008). ITU botnet mitigation toolkit: Background information.

ITU. (2010). About ITU. Retrieved March 27, 2010, from http://www.itu.int/net/about/#

Lemos, R. (2007). Estonia gets respite from web attacks. Security Focus. Retrieved from http://www.securityfocus.com/brief/504

Li, C., Jiang, W., & Zou, X. (2009). Botnet: Survey and case study. Paper presented at the Fourth International Conference on Innovative Computing, Information and Control (ICICIC).

MAAWG. (2010). MAAWG published documents. Retrieved March 27, 2010, from http://www.maawg.org/published-documents

Messmer, E. (2009). America's 10 most wanted botnets. Retrieved March 27, 2010, from http://www.networkworld.com/news/2009/072209-botnets.html

Micro, A. T. (2006). Taxonomy of botnet threats.

Microsoft. (2006). Sender ID. Retrieved March 27, 2010, from http://www.microsoft.com/mscorp/safety/technologies/senderid/default.mspx

Microsoft. (n.d.). Windows products. Retrieved March 27, 2010, from http://www.microsoft.com/windows/products/

OECD Ministerial Background Report. (2008). DSTI/ICCP/REG(2007)5/FINAL, malicious software (malware): A security threat to the Internet economy.

Myers, L. (2006, October). Aim for bot coordination. Paper presented at 2006 Virus Bulletin Conference (VB2006).

National Infrastructure Security Co-Ordination Centre. (2004). Border gateway protocol.

Ono, K., Kawaishi, I., & Kamon, T. (2007). Trend of botnet activities. Paper presented at 41st Annual IEEE International Carnahan Conference on Security Technology.

Puri, R. (2003). Bots & botnet: An overview.

Rajab, M. A., Zarfoss, J., Monrose, F., & Terzis, A. (2006). A multifaceted approach to understanding the botnet phenomenon. Paper presented at 6th ACM SIGCOMM conference on Internet measurement.

Saha, B., & Gairola, A. (2005). Botnet: An overview.

Sink, C. (July 2004). Agobot and the kit.

SPF. (2008). Sender policy framework.

Symantec. (2007). W32.Randex.E. Retrieved March 27, 2010, from http://www.symantec.com/security_response/writeup.jsp?docid=2003-081213-3232-99

Symantec MessageLabs. (2009). MessageLabs intelligence: Q2/June 2009.

Symantec. (n.d.). Learn more about viruses and worms.

Szor, F. P. a. P. (2003). An analysis of the slapper worm exploit.

The Shadowserver Foundation. (2007). Botnets. Retrieved March 27, 2010, from http://www.shadowserver.org/wiki/pmwiki.php/Information/Botnets#toc

The Sydney Morning Herald. (2007). Cyber attacks force Estonian bank to close website. Retrieved from http://www.smh.com.au/news/breaking-news/cyber-attacks-force-estonian-bank-to-close-website/2007/05/16/1178995171916.html

Trendmicro. (2003). POLYBOOT-B*. Retrieved from http://threatinfo.trendmicro.com/vinfo/virusencyclo/default5.asp?VName=POLYBOOT-B*

ADDITIONAL READING

Akiyama, M., et al. (2007) A proposal of metrics for botnet detection based on its cooperative behavior. Proceedings of the Internet Measurement Technology and its Applications to Building Next Generation Internet Workshop (SAINT 2007). pp. 82-82.

Bacher, P., Holz, T., Kotter, M., & Wicherski, G. (2005) Know your Enemy. Available from URL: http://www.honeynet.org/papers/bots/

Castillo-Perez, S., & Garcia-Alfaro, J. (2008) Anonymous Resolution of DNS Queries. Lecture Notes in Computer Science, International Workshop on Information Security (IS'08), International OTM Conference. pp. 987–1000.

Choi, H., Lee, H., Lee, H., & Kim, H. (2007) Botnet Detection by Monitoring Group Activities in DNS Traffic. Seventh IEEE International Conference on Computer and Information Technology (CIT 2007). pp. 715-720.

Cooke, E., Jahanian, F., & Mcpherson, D. (2005) The Zombie Roundup: Understanding, Detecting, and Disrupting Botnets. In The 1st Workshop on Steps to Reducing Unwanted Traffic on the Internet (SRUTI 2005). pp. 39-44.

Dagon, D. (2005) Botnet Detection and Response. The Network is the Infection, OARC Workshop, 2005. Available from URL: http://www.caida.org/workshops/dns-oarc/200507/slides/oarc0507-Dagon.pdf

Global Secure Systems, M. A. P. S. (2008). Introduction to the Realtime Blackhole List (RBL). Retrieved March 27, 2010, from http://www.mail-abuse.com/wp_introrbl.html.

Gomes, L. H., Cazita, C., Almeida, J. M., Almeida, V., & Meira, J. W. (2004). Characterizing a spam traffic. Paper presented at 4th ACM SIGCOMM Conference on Internet Measurement, Taormina, Sicily, Italy, (pp. 356–369).

Gower, J. C. (1971). A general coefficient of similarity and some of its properties. *Biometrics*, *27*(4), 857–871. doi:10.2307/2528823

Gu, G. (2008) Correlation-Based Botnet Detection In Enterprise Networks. Ph.D thesis, College of Computing. Georgia Institute of Technology, Georgia. pp. 1-6.

Harris, E. (2003). The Next Step in the Spam Control War: Greylisting. PureMagic Software – Projects. Retrieved March 27, 2010, from http://projects.puremagic.com/greylisting/index.html.

Husna, H., Phithakkitnukoon, S., Palla, S., & Dantu, R. (2008). Behavior analysis of spam botnets. 3rd International Conference on Communication Systems Software and Middleware and Workshops (pp. 246–253).

Ianelli, N., & Hackworth, A. (2005). *Botnets as a Vehicle for Online Crime* (pp. 1–28). CERT Coordination Center.

Jian, Z., Zhen-Hua, D., & Wei, L. (2007). A Behavior-Based Detection Approach to Mass-Mailing Host. Paper presented at International Conference on Machine Learning and Cybernetics (pp. 2140–2144).

Kim, M. C., & Choi, K. S. (1998). A comparison of collocation-based similarity measures in query expansion. *Information Processing & Management*, 19–30.

Kristoff, J. (2004) Botnets. North American Network Operators Group (NANOG 32). Available from URL: http://www.nanog.org/mtg-0410/kristoff.html

Kugisaki, Y., Kasahara, Y., Hori, Y., & Sakurai, K. (2007) Bot Detection based on Traffic Analysis. International Conference on Intelligent Pervasive Computing (IPC). pp. 303-306.

Lim, T. M., & Khoo, H. W. (1985). Sampling Properties of Gower's General Coefficient of Similarity. *Ecology*, 66(5), 1682–1685. doi:10.2307/1938031

Miao, Y., Qiu-Xiang, J., & Fan-Jin, M. (2008). The Spam Filtering Technology Based on SVM and D-S Theory. First International Workshop on Knowledge Discovery and Data Mining (WKDD) (pp. 562–565).

Mockapetris, P. (1987) Domain Names - Concepts And Facilities. RFC 1034. Available from URL: http://www.faqs.org/rfcs/rfc1034.html

Mockapetris, P. (1987) Domain Names - Implementation And Specification. RFC 1035. Available from URL: http://www.faqs.org/rfcs/rfc1035.html

Oikarinen, J., & Reed, D. (1993) Internet relay chat protocol. RFC 1459. Available from URL: http://www.faqs.org/rfcs/rfc1459.html

Qiong, R., Yi, M., & Susilo, W. SEFAP: An Email System for Anti-Phishing. In Proceedings of the ICIS 6th IEEE/ACIS International Conference on Computer and Information Science (pp. 782–787).

Ramachandran, A., & Feamster, N. (2006). Understanding the network-level behavior of spammers. *SIGCOMM Comput. Commun. Rev.*, 36(4), 291–302. doi:10.1145/1151659.1159947

Ramachandran, A., Feamster, N., & Dagon, D. (2006) Revealing botnet membership using dnsbl counter-intelligence. 2nd Workshop on Steps to Reducing Unwanted Traffic on the Internet (SRUTI 2006).

Rieck, K., Laskov, P. & Klaus-Robertmuller. (2006) Efficient Algorithms for Similarity Measures over Sequential Data: A Look Beyond Kernels. Proc of 28th DAGM Symposium (LNCS). pp. 374–383.

Sandford, P. J., Sandford, J. M., & Parish, D. J. (2006). Analysis of SMTP Connection Characteristics for Detecting Spam Relays. Paper presented at International Multi-Conference on Computing in the Global Information Technology (pp. 68–68).

Sauver, J. S. (2005). Spam Zombies and Inbound Flows to Compromised Customer Systems. Paper presented at MAAWG General Meeting, San Diego, 2005.

Schiller, C. A., Binkley, J., Harley, D., Evron, G., Bradley, T., Willems, C., & Cross, M. (2007). *Botnets: The Killer Web App* (pp. 77–93). Syngress Publishing. doi:10.1016/B978-159749135-8/50005-6

Schonewille, A., & Helmond, D.-J. V. (2006). *The Domain Name Service as an IDS. Master's Project* (pp. 5–14). Netherlands: University of Amsterdam.

Symantec (2007) Internet Security Threat Report White Paper. Available from URL: http://www.symantec.com/

Tu, H., Li, Z.-T., & Liu, B. (2007). *Detecting Botnets by Analyzing DNS Traffic* (pp. 323–324). Intelligence and Security Informatics.

Weimer, F. (2005) Passive DNS Replication. In 17th Annual FIRST Conference on Computer Security Incident Handling (FIRST 2005).

Whyte, D., Oorschot, P. C. v., & Kranakis, E. (2006). Addressing SMTP-Based Mass-Mailing Activity within Enterprise Networks. In Proceedings of the 22nd Annual Computer Security Applications Conference (pp. 393–402). IEEE Computer Society.

Wills, C. E., Mikhailov, M., & Shang, H. (2003) Inferring Relative Popularity of Internet Applications by Actively Querying DNS Caches. Proceedings of the 3rd ACM SIGCOMM conference on Internet measurement. PP. 78-90.

Xie, Y., Yu, F., Achan, K., Gillum, E., Goldszmidt, M., & Wobber, T. (2007) How Dynamic are IP Addresses. In Proceedings of the 2007 conference on Applications, technologies, architectures,and protocols for computer communications (SIGCOMM 2007).

Yoshida, K., Adachi, F., Washio, T., Motoda, H., Homma, T., Nakashima, A., et al. (2004). Density-based spam detector. Paper presented at Tenth ACM SIGKDD International Conference on Knowledge Discovery and Data Mining, Seattle, WA, USA (pp. 486–493).

Zhaosheng, Z., Guohan, L., Yan, C., Fu, Z. J., Roberts, P., & Keesook, H. (2008). Botnet Research Survey. Paper presented at 32nd Annual IEEE International Conference on Computer Software and Applications (COMPSAC '08) (pp. 967-972).

Zou, C. C., & Cunningham, R. (2006) Honeypot-Aware Advanced Botnet Construction and Maintenance. Proceedings of the 2006 International Conference on Dependable Systems and Networks (DSN 2006). PP. 100-208.

Chapter 6
Evaluation of Contemporary Anomaly Detection Systems (ADSs)

Ayesha Binte Ashfaq
National University of Sciences & Technology (NUST), Pakistan

Syed Ali Khayam
National University of Sciences & Technology (NUST), Pakistan

ABSTRACT

Due to the rapidly evolving nature of network attacks, a considerable paradigm shift has taken place with focus now on Network-based Anomaly Detection Systems (NADSs) that can detect zero-day attacks. At this time, it is important to evaluate existing anomaly detectors to determine and learn from their strengths and weaknesses. Thus we aim to evaluate the performance of eight prominent network-based anomaly detectors under malicious portscan attacks. These NADSs are evaluated on three criteria: accuracy (ROC curves), scalability (with respect to varying normal and attack traffic rates, and deployment points) and detection delay. Based on our experiments, we identify promising guidelines to improve the accuracy and scalability of existing and future anomaly detectors. We show that the proposed guidelines provide considerable and consistent accuracy improvements for all evaluated NADSs.

DOI: 10.4018/978-1-60960-851-4.ch006

INTRODUCTION

With an increasing penetration of broadband Internet connectivity and an exponential growth in the worldwide IT infrastructure, individuals and organizations now rely heavily on the Internet for their communication and business needs. While such readily-available network connectivity facilitates operational efficiency and networking, systems connected to the Internet are inherently vulnerable to network attacks. These attacks have been growing in their number and sophistication over the last few years (Symantec, 2002-2008). Malware, botnets, spam, phishing, and denial of service attacks have become continuous and imminent threats for today's networks and hosts (Symantec, 2002-2008; McAfee, 2005). Financial losses due to these attacks are in the orders of billions of dollars. In addition to the short-term revenue losses for businesses and enterprises, network attacks also compromise information confidentiality/integrity and cause disruption of service, thus resulting in a long-term loss of credibility.

Since the CodeRed worm of 2001, malware attacks have emerged as one of the most prevalent and potent threats to network and host security. Many network-based anomaly detection systems (NADSs) have been proposed in the past few years to detect novel network attacks (Williamson, 2002 – Cisco NetFlow). Since malicious portscans are the vehicle used by malware and other automated tools to locate and compromise vulnerable hosts, some of these anomaly detectors are designed specifically for portscan detection (Williamson, 2002 - Ganger, 2002), (Zou, 2003), while other detectors are more general-purpose and detect any anomalous traffic trend (Mahoney, 2001 - Soule, 2005), (Gu, 2005). Most of the network-based anomaly detectors, model and leverage deep-rooted statistical properties of benign traffic to detect anomalous behavior. A variety of theoretical frameworks–including stochastic, machine learning, information-theoretic and signal processing

frameworks–have been used to develop robust models of normal behavior and/or to detect/flag deviations from that model.

The main challenge of NADSs is to define a robust model of normal traffic behavior. In particular, an accurate model needs to cater for changes in normal traffic behavior over time. Such changes in normal traffic behavior lead to potentially low detection rates and high false alarm rates of NADSs. In view of the vast existing literature on network anomaly detection, it is important to evaluate existing NADSs. While a comprehensive performance evaluation facilitates study of various aspects of contemporary anomaly detectors, more importantly they should reveal the strengths and shortcomings of existing NADSs and consequently lead to promising design guidelines that can be used to improve the accuracy of NADSs.

In this chapter, we evaluate prominent Network-based Anomaly Detection systems to learn from their strengths and to propose promising guidelines to improve the accuracy of current and future anomaly detectors. In order to quantify and compare the accuracies and delay characteristics of prominent NADSs proposed in the last few years, we also perform a comparative performance evaluation of a diverse set of anomaly detection systems. The anomaly detectors compared in this chapter were proposed in (Williamson, 2002), (Jung, 2004), (Schechter, 2004), (Mahoney, 2001), (Lakhina, 2004), (Soule, 2005), (Gu, 2005) and (NIDES). These NADSs are chosen because they employ very different traffic features and theoretical frameworks for anomaly detection. Moreover, most of these detectors are frequently used for performance benchmarking in the intrusion detection research literature (Sellke, 2005), (Weaver, 2004– Ganger, 2002), (Mahoney, 2002), (Mahoney, 2003), (Lakhina, 2004), (Lakhina, 2005), and (Zou, 2003). Some of these NADSs have been designed for and evaluated at endpoints while others have been tailored towards organization/ISP gateways. Similarly, some detectors are designed for portscan detection, while others are general-purpose NADSs. This diversity allows us to determine how much, if any, performance improvement is provided by portscan NADSs over general-purpose ADSs.

We evaluate these NADSS on three criteria: accuracy, scalability, and detection delay. Accuracy is evaluated by comparing ROC (false alarms per day versus detection rate) characteristics of the NADSs. Scalability is evaluated with respect to different background and attack traffic rates. Since the two datasets used in this chapter are collected at different network entities and contain attacks with different characteristics, evaluation over these datasets allows us to compare the scalability of the proposed NADSs under varying traffic volumes. Detection delay is evaluated separately for high- and low-rate attacks.

Based on our findings, we propose a few promising guidelines to improve the accuracy and scalability of existing and future NADSs. Our results show that the proposed guidelines result in an average detection rate increase of 5% to 10%, while reducing the false alarm rates up to 50%.

BACKGROUND

In order to combat the rapidly-evolving malicious attacks, network intrusion detection methods have also become increasingly sophisticated. Intrusion Detection Systems (IDS) offer techniques for modeling and recognizing normal and abusive system behavior. These have potential to mitigate or prevent malicious attacks, if updated signatures or novel attack recognition and response capabilities are in place. Such methodologies include: statistical models, immune system approaches, protocol verification, file checking, neural networks, whitelisting, expression matching, state transition analysis, dedicated languages, genetic algorithms and burglar alarms. But, by choosing an attack method suitably an attacker has the possibility of escaping the detection of an IDS.

IDS Detection Methods

In broad terms, the field of intrusion detection comprises two types of detection methods: misuse detection (also known as signature detection) and anomaly detection. Misuse detection, the predominant detection method employed in today's anti-virus software, requires a signature of an attack to be known before the attack can be detected. While such signature based detectors can provide 100% detection rates for known attacks, they have an inherent limitation of not being able to detect new or previously-unseen attacks; a 468% increase in previously-unseen attacks was reported over just a six month period in 2007 (Symantec, 2002-2008). Moreover, development and dissemination of attack signatures require human intervention and therefore misuse detectors are finding it difficult to cope with rapidly-evolving network intrusions.

On the other end of the intrusion detection spectrum are Network-based Anomaly Detection Systems (NADSs) which model the benign or normal traffic behavior of a network or host and detect significant deviations from this model to identify anomalies in network traffic. Since NADSs rely on normal traffic behavior for attack detection, they can detect previously unknown attacks. Consequently, significant effort has been focused on development of NADSs in the past few years (WiSNet, 2008).

Anomaly detection systems can further be categorized into either host based systems or network based systems (Khayam, 2006):

1. **Network-based ADS:** Network based systems detect anomalies by analyzing unusual network traffic patterns (WisNet, 2008)
2. **Host based ADS:** Host-based systems detect anomalies by monitoring an endpoints operating system (OS) behavior, for instance by tracking OS audit logs, processes, command-lines or keystrokes (Cui, 2005 - DuMouchel, 1999)

The network-based IDSs can further be either endpoint or perimeter based depending on the traffic analyzed for anomaly identification.

Accuracy Criteria

The accuracy of an intrusion detection system is generally evaluated on two competing criteria:

1. **Detection rate:** What fraction of anomalies are correctly detected by the IDS.
2. **False Alarm rate:** What fraction of the total anomalies detected by the IDS are in fact benign data.

To understand the tradeoff between these accuracy criteria, consider an IDS that classifies all the test data as anomalous. Such an IDS will achieve 100% detection rate, but at the cost of an unacceptable 100% false alarm rate. At the other end of this spectrum, consider an IDS that classifies all of the test data as normal. This IDS will have an attractive 0% false alarm rate, but is useless because it does not detect any anomalies. To evaluate the accuracy of an IDS, detection thresholds of the IDS are tuned and for each threshold value the detection rate is plotted against the false alarm rate. Each point on such a plot, referred to as an ROC curve (Lippmann, 2000), represents performance results for one configuration (or threshold value) whereas the curve represents the behavior for the complete set of configurations.

A receiver operating characteristics (ROC) curve is a technique for visualizing, organizing and selecting classifiers based on their performance (Fawcett, 2004; Fawcett, 2005).

ADS EVALUATION FRAMEWORK

In this section we would give details regarding the evaluated anomaly detection systems and the datasets used for the evaluation. Moreover, characteristic features of the two datasets will also be provided.

Anomaly Detection Algorithms

We will focus on network-based anomaly detectors and compare the anomaly detectors proposed in (Williamson, 2002; Jung, 2004; Schechter, 2004; Mahoney, 2001; Lakhina, 2004; Soule, 2005; Gu, 2005; NIDES). Most of these detectors are quite popular and used frequently for performance comparison and benchmarking in the ID research community. Improvements to these algorithms have also been proposed in (Sellke, 2005), (Weaver, 2004 – Ganger, 2002), (Mahoney, 2002; Mahoney, 2003; Lakhina, 2004; Lakhina, 2005; Zou, 2003; Wong, 2005)[1].

Before briefly describing these detectors, we highlight that some of these detectors are designed specifically for portscan detection, while others are general-purpose network anomaly detectors. The evaluated ADSs range from very simple rule modeling systems like PHAD (Mahoney, 2001) to very complex and theoretically-inclined partially Self-Learning systems like the PCA-based subspace method (Lakhina, 2004) and the Sequential Hypothesis Testing technique (Jung, 2004). This diversity is introduced to achieve the following objectives: a) to correlate the performance of the NADSs with the classes of the taxonomy in which they fall; b) to identify promising traffic features and theoretical frameworks for portscan anomaly detection; c) to investigate the accuracy, and delays of these anomaly detectors under different attack and normal traffic scenarios and at different points of deployment in the network; and d) to identify a set of promising portscan detection guidelines that build on the strengths and avoid the weaknesses of the evaluated anomaly detectors.

We provide brief descriptions of the evaluated algorithms. Majorly we will focus on the algorithm adaptation and parameter tuning for the datasets under consideration. Readers are referred (Williamson, 2002; Jung, 2004; Schechter, 2004; Mahoney, 2001; Lakhina, 2004; Soule, 2005; Gu, 2005; NIDES) for details of the algorithms. For techniques operating on fixed-sized time windows, we use a window of 20 seconds. All other parameters not mentioned in this section are the same as those described in the algorithms' respective papers.

1. **Rate Limiting:** Rate limiting (Williamson, 2002; Twycross, 2003) detects anomalous connection behavior by relying on the premise that an infected host will try to connect to many different machines in a short period of time. Rate limiting detects portscans by putting new connections exceeding a certain threshold in a queue. An alarm is raised when the queue length, η_q, exceeds a threshold. ROCs for endpoints are generated by varying $\eta_q = \mu + k\sigma$, where μ and σ represent the sample mean and sample standard deviation of the connection rates in the training set, and $k = 0, 1, 2, \ldots$ is a positive integer. Large values of k will provide low false alarm and detection rates, while small values will render high false alarm and detection rates. In the LBNL dataset, connection rate variance in the background traffic is more than the variance in the attack traffic. Therefore, to obtain a range of detection and false alarm rates for the LBNL dataset, we use a threshold of $\eta_q = \omega\mu$, with a varying parameter $0 \geq \omega \leq 1$, and the queue is varied between 5 and 100 sessions.

2. **Threshold Random Walk (TRW) Algorithm:** The TRW algorithm (Jung, 2004) detects incoming portscans by noting that the probability of a connection attempt being a success should be much higher for a benign host than for a scanner. To leverage this observation, TRW uses sequential hypothesis testing (i.e., a likelihood ratio test) to classify whether or not a remote host is a scanner. We plot ROCs for this algorithm by setting different values of false alarm and detection rates and computing the likelihood ratio thresholds, η_0 and η_1, using the method described in(Jung, 2004).

3. **TRW with Credit-based Rate Limiting (TRW-CB):** A hybrid solution to leverage the complementary strengths of Rate Limiting and TRW was proposed by Schechter et al. (Schechter, 2004). Reverse TRW is an anomaly detector that limits the rate at which new connections are initiated by applying the sequential hypothesis testing in a reverse chronological order. A credit increase/decrease algorithm is used to slow down hosts that are experiencing unsuccessful connections. We plot ROCs for this technique for varying η_0 and η_1 as in the TRW case.

4. **Maximum Entropy Method:** This detector estimates the benign traffic distribution using maximum entropy estimation (Gu, 2005). Training traffic is divided into 2, 348 packet classes and maximum entropy estimation is then used to develop a baseline benign distribution for each packet class. Packet class distributions observed in real-time windows are then compared with the baseline distribution using the Kullback-Leibler (K-L) divergence measure. An alarm is raised if a packet class' K-L divergence exceeds a threshold, η_k, more than h times in the last W windows of t seconds each. Thus the Maximum Entropy method incurs a detection delay of at least $h \times t$ seconds. ROCs are generated by varying η_k.

5. **Packet Header Anomaly Detection (PHAD):** PHAD learns the normal range of values for all 33 fields in the Ethernet, IP, TCP, UDP and ICMP headers (Mahoney, 2001). A score is assigned to each packet header field in the testing phase and the fields' scores are summed to obtain a packet's aggregate anomaly score. We evaluate PHAD-C32 (Mahoney, 2001) using the following packet header fields: source IP, destination IP, source port, destination port, protocol type and TCP flags. Normal intervals for the six fields are learned from 5 days of training data. In the

test data, fields' values not falling in the learned intervals are flagged as suspect. Then the top n packet score values are termed as anomalous. The value of n is varied over a range to obtain ROC curves.

6. **PCA-based Subspace Method:** The subspace method uses Principal Component Analysis (PCA) to separate a link's traffic measurement space into useful subspaces for analysis, with each subspace representing either benign or anomalous traffic behavior (Lakhina, 2004). The authors proposed to apply PCA for domain reduction of the Origin-Destination (OD) flows in three dimensions: number of bytes, packets, IP-level OD flows. The top k eigenvectors represent normal subspaces. It has been shown that most of the variance in a link's traffic is generally captured by 5 principal components (Lakhina, 2004). A recent study showed that the detection rate of PCA varies with the level and method of aggregation (Ringberg, 2007). It was also concluded in (Ringberg, 2007) that it may be impractical to run a PCA-based anomaly detector over data aggregated at the level of OD flows. We evaluate the subspace method using the number of TCP flows aggregated in 10 minutes intervals. To generate ROC results, we changed the number of normal subspace as $k = 1, 2, \ldots, 15$. Since the principal components capture maximum variance of the data, as we increase k, the dimension of the residual subspace reduces and fewer observations are available for detection. In other words, as more and more principal components are selected as normal subspaces, the detection and false alarm rates decrease proportionally. Since there is no clear detection threshold, we could not obtain the whole range of ROC values for the subspace method. Nevertheless, we evaluate and report the subspace method's accuracy results for varying number of principal components.

7. **Kalman Filter based Detection:** The Kalman filter based detector of (Soule, 2005) first filters out the normal traffic from the aggregate traffic, and then examines the residue for anomalies. In (Soule, 2005), the Kalman Filter operated on SNMP data to detect anomalies traversing multiple links. Since SNMP data was not available to us in either dataset, we model the traffic as a 2-D vector X_t. The first element of X_t is the total number of sessions (in the endpoint dataset) or packets (in the LBNL dataset), while the second element is the total number of distinct remote ports observed in the traffic. We defined a threshold, η_f on the residue value r to obtain ROC curves. Thresholding of r is identical to the rate limiting case. An alarm is raised, if $r < -\eta_f$ or $r > \eta_f$.

8. **Next-Generation Intrusion Detection Expert System (NIDES):** NIDES (NIDES) is a statistical anomaly detector that detects anomalies by comparing a long-term traffic rate profile against a short term, real-time profile. An anomaly is reported if the Q distribution of the real-time profile deviates considerably from the long-term values. After specific intervals, new value of Q are generated by monitoring the new rates and compared against a predefined threshold, η_s. If $\Pr(Q > q) < \eta_s$, an alarm is raised. We vary η_s over a range of values for ROC evaluation.

Evaluation Datasets

We wanted to use real, labeled and public background and attack datasets to measure the accuracy of the evaluated anomaly detectors. Real and labeled data allow realistic and repeatable quantification of an anomaly detector's accuracy, which is a main objective of this chapter. Moreover, as defined before, another objective is to evaluate the accuracy or scalability of the anomaly detectors under different normal and attack traffic rates and at different points of deployment in the network.

Table 1. Background traffic information for the LBNL dataset

Date	Duration(mins)	LBNL Hosts	Remote Hosts	Backgnd Rate (pkt/sec)	Attack Rate (pkt/sec)
10/4/04	10min	4,767	4,342	8.47	0.41
12/15/04	60min	5,761	10,478	3.5	0.061
12/16/04	60min	5,210	7,138	243.83	72

This evaluation objective is somewhat unique to this effort, with (Wong, 2005) being the only other study that provides some insight into host versus edge deployments.

Different network deployment points are responsible for handling traffic from varying number of nodes. For instance, an endpoint requires to cater for only its own traffic, while an edge router needs to monitor and analyze traffic from a variety of hosts in its subnet. In general, as one moves away from the endpoints towards the network core, the number of nodes, and consequently the traffic volume, that a network entity is responsible for increase considerably. We argue that if an algorithm that is designed to detect high- or low-rate attacks at a particular point of deployment, say an edge router, scales to and provides high accuracy at other traffic rates and deployment points, say at endpoints, then such an algorithm is quite valuable because it provides an off-the-shelf deployment option for different network entities. (We show later in this chapter that some existing algorithms are able to achieve this objective.)

To test the anomaly detectors for scalability, we use two real traffic datasets that have been independently-collected at different deployment points. The first dataset is collected at the edge router of the Lawrence Berkeley National Laboratory (LBNL), while the second dataset is collected at network endpoints by our WiSNet research lab[2]. In this section, we describe the data collection setups and the attack and background traffic characteristics of the LBNL and the endpoint datasets.

The LBNL Dataset: This dataset was obtained from two international network locations at the Lawrence Berkeley National Laboratory (LBNL) in USA. Traffic in this dataset comprises packet-level incoming, outgoing and internally-routed traffic streams at the LBNL edge routers. Traffic was anonymized using the tcpmkpub tool; refer to (Pang, 2006) for details of anonymization.

LBNL Background Traffic: LBNL data used in this chapter is collected during three distinct time periods. Some pertinent statistics of the background traffic are given in Table 1. The average remote session rate (i.e., sessions from distinct non-LBNL hosts) is approximately 4 sessions per second. The total TCP and UDP background traffic rate in packets per second is 4. We also wanted to use a traffic dataset collected at a backbone ISP network; such datasets have been used in some prior studies (Lakhina, 2004 – Lakhina, 2005). However, we could not find a publicly available ISP traffic dataset. shown in column 5 of the table. A large variance can be observed in the background traffic rate at different dates. This variance will have an impact on the performance of volumetric anomaly detectors that rely on detecting bursts of normal and malicious traffic. The main applications observed in internal and external traffic are Web (HTTP), Email and Name Services. Some other applications like Windows Services, Network File Services and Backup were being used by internal hosts; details of each service, information of each service's packets and other relevant description are provided in (Pang, 2005).

LBNL Attack Traffic: Attack traffic was isolated by identifying scans in the aggregate traffic

Table 2. Background traffic information for four endpoints with high and low rates

Endpoint ID	Endpoint Type	Duration (months)	Total Sessions	Mean Session Rate(/sec)
3	Home	3	373,009	1.92
4	Home	2	444,345	5.28
6	Univ	9	60,979	0.19
10	Univ	13	152,048	0.21

traces. Scans were identified by flagging those hosts which unsuccessfully probed more than 20 hosts, out of which 16 hosts were probed in ascending or descending order (Pang, 2006). Malicious traffic mostly comprises failed incoming TCP SYN requests; i.e., TCP portscans targeted towards LBNL hosts. However, there are also some outgoing TCP scans in the dataset. Most of the UDP traffic observed in the data (incoming and outgoing) comprises successful connections; i.e., host replies are received for the UDP flows. Table 1 [column 6] shows the attack rate observed in the LBNL dataset. Clearly, the attack rate is significantly lower than the background traffic rate. Thus these attacks can be considered low rate relative to the background traffic rate. (We show later that background and attack traffic at endpoints exhibit the opposite characteristics.) Since most of the anomaly detectors used in this chapter operate on TCP, UDP and/or IP packet features, to maintain fairness we filtered the background data to retain only TCP and UDP traffic. Moreover, since most of the scanners were located outside the LBNL network, to remove any bias we filter out internally-routed traffic. After filtering the datasets, we merged all the background traffic data at different days and ports. Synchronized malicious data chunks were then inserted in the merged background traffic.

Endpoint Dataset: Since no publicly-available endpoint traffic set was available, we spent up to 14 months in collecting our own dataset on a diverse set of 13 endpoints. Complexity and privacy were two main reservations of the participants of the endpoint data collection study. To address these reservations, we developed a custom tool for endpoint data collection. This tool was a multi-threaded MS Windows application developed using the Winpcap API (Winpcap). (Implementation of the tool is available at (WiSNet, 2008).) To reduce the packet logging complexity at the endpoints, we only logged some very elementary session-level information of TCP and UDP packets. Here a *session* corresponds to a bidirectional communication between two IP addresses; communication between the same IP address on different ports is considered part of the same network session. To ensure user privacy, the source IP address (which was fixed/static for a given host) is not logged, and each session entry is indexed by a one-way hash of the destination IP with the hostname. Most of the detectors evaluated in this chapter can operate with this level of data granularity. Statistics of the two highest rate and the two lowest rate endpoints are listed in Table 2[3].

As can be intuitively argued, the traffic rates observed at the endpoints are much lower than those at the LBNL router. In the endpoint context, we observed that home computers generate significantly higher traffic volumes than office and university computers because: 1) they are generally shared between multiple users, and 2) they run peer-to-peer and multimedia applications. The large traffic volumes of home computers are also evident from their high mean number of sessions per second. For this chapter, we use 6 weeks of endpoint traffic data for training and testing. Results for longer time periods were qualitatively similar.

Table 3. Endpoint attack traffic for two high- and two low-rate worms

Malware	Release Date	Avg. Scan Rate(/sec)	Port(s) Used
Dloader-NY	Jul 2005	46.84	TCP 135, 139
Forbot-FU	Sept 2005	32.53	TCP 445
MyDoom-A	Jan 2006	0.14	TCP 3127-3198
Rbot-AQJ	Oct 2005	0.68	TCP 139,769

To generate attack traffic, we infected Virtual Machines (VMs) on the endpoints by the following malware: Zotob.G, Forbot-FU, Sdbot-AFR, Dloader-NY, SoBig.E@mm, MyDoom.A@mm, Blaster, Rbot-AQJ, and RBOT.CCC; details of the malware can be found at (Symantec). These malware have diverse scanning rates and attack ports/applications. Table 3 shows statistics of the highest and lowest scan rate worms; Dloader-NY has the highest scan rate of 46.84 scans per second (sps), while MyDoom-A has the lowest scan rate of 0.14 sps, respectively. For completeness, we also simulated three additional worms that are somewhat different from the ones described above, namely Witty, CodeRedv2 and a fictitious TCP worm with a fixed and unusual source port. Witty and CodeRedv2 were simulated using the scan rates, pseudocode and parameters given in research and commercial literature (Symantec; Shannon, 2004).

Endpoint Background Traffic: The users of these endpoints included home users, research students, and technical/administrative staff. Some endpoints, in particular home computers, were shared among multiple users. The endpoints used in this study were running different types of applications, including peer-to-peer file sharing software, online multimedia applications, network games, SQL/SAS clients etc.

Endpoint Attack Traffic: The attack traffic logged at the endpoints mostly comprises outgoing portscans. Note that this is the opposite of the LBNL dataset, in which most of the attack traffic is inbound. Moreover, the attack traffic rates (Table 3) in the endpoint case are generally much higher than the background traffic rates (Table 2). This characteristic is also the opposite of what was observed in the LBNL dataset. This diversity in attack direction and rates provides us a sound basis for performance comparison of the anomaly detectors evaluated in this chapter (Jung, 2004; Schechter, 2004).

For each malware, attack traffic of 15 minutes duration was inserted in the background traffic of each endpoint at a random time instance. This operation was repeated to insert 100 non-overlapping attacks of each worm inside each endpoint's background traffic.

PERFORMANCE EVALAUTION OF CONTEMPORARY NADSS AND LESSONS LEARNT

In this section, we evaluate the accuracy, scalability and delay of the anomaly detectors described in the last section on the endpoint and router datasets.

Accuracy and Scalability Comparison

We present Receiver Operating Curve (ROC) analysis on the endpoint dataset. The following section explains the scalability experiments in which ROC analysis is performed on the LBNL dataset and the results are compared with the endpoint experiments.

Averaged ROCs for the Endpoint Dataset: Figure 1 provides the averaged ROC analysis of the anomaly detection schemes under consider-

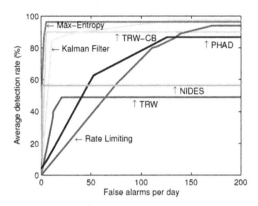

ation. Clearly, the Maximum Entropy detector provides the highest accuracy by achieving near 100%detection rate at a very low false alarm rate of approximately 5 alarms/day. The Maximum Entropy detector is followed closely by the credit-based TRW approach. TRW-CB achieves nearly 90% detection rate at a reasonable false alarm rate of approximately 5 alarms/day. The original TRW algorithm, however, provides very low detection rates for the endpoint dataset. Based on these results, the Maximum Entropy algorithm provides the best accuracy on endpoints, while TRW provides the best detection on LBNL dataset.

The Kalman Filter approach is also quite accurate as it provides up to 85% detection rates at a reasonably low false alarm cost. Rate Limiting, although designed to detect outgoing scanning attacks, provides very poor performance. This result substantiates the results of (Wong, 2005) where very high false positive rates for high detection rates were reported for classical rate limiting. Hence, we also deduce that rate limiting is ineffective for portscan detection at endpoints.

PHAD does not perform well on the endpoint data set. The detection is accompanied with very high false alarm rates. NIDES achieve reasonable detection rates at very low false alarm rates, but is unable to substantially improve its detection

rates afterwards. PHAD relies on previously seen values in the training dataset for anomaly detection. Therefore, if a scanner attacks a commonly-used port/IP then PHAD is unable to detect it. On similar grounds, if the malicious traffic is not bursty enough as compared to background traffic then NIDES will not detect it, irrespective of how much the detection threshold is tuned. Due to the thresholding difficulties for the subspace method, in Figure 2 we report results for this technique for varying values of selected principal components. The highest detection rate of 22% is observed at $k = 2$ principal components. This already low detection rate decreases further at $k = 5$ and drops to 0% at $k = 15$. False alarm rates show the opposite trend. Thus the subspace method fails to give acceptable accuracy on the endpoint dataset.

The ROC results for the endpoint dataset are somewhat surprising because two of the top three detectors are general-purpose anomaly detectors (Maximum Entropy and Kalman Filter), but still outperform other detectors designed specifically for portscan detection, such as the TRW and the Rate Limiting detectors. We, however, note that this analysis is not entirely fair to the TRW algorithm because TRW was designed to detect incoming portscans, whereas our endpoint attack traffic contains mostly outgoing scan packets. The credit-based variant of TRW achieves high accuracy because it leverages outgoing scans for portscan detection. Thus TRW-CB combines the complementary strengths of rate limiting and TRW to provide a practical and accurate portscan detector for endpoints. This result agrees with earlier results in (Wong, 2005).

Averaged ROCs for the LBNL Dataset: Figure 3 shows the ROCs for the LBNL dataset. It reveals that the Maximum Entropy detector is unable to maintain its high accuracy on the LBNL dataset; i.e., the Maximum Entropy algorithm cannot scale to different points of network deployment. TRW's performance improves significantly as it provides a 100% detection rate at a negligible false alarm cost. TRW-CB, on the other hand, achieves a detec-

Figure 2. Detection and false alarm rates for the subspace method

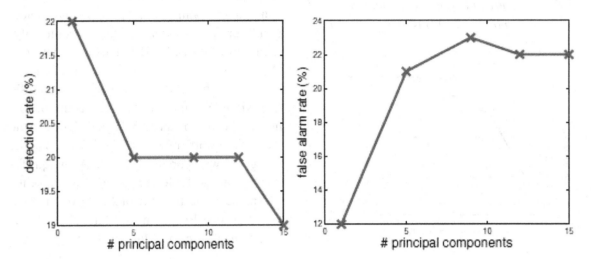

tion rate of approximately 70%. Thus contrary to the endpoint dataset, the original TRW algorithm easily outperforms the TRW-CB algorithm on LBNL traces. As explained, the LBNL attack traffic mostly comprises failed incoming TCP connection requests. TRW's forward sequential hypothesis based portscan detection algorithm is designed to detect such failed incoming connections, and therefore it provides high detection rates. Thus on an edge router, TRW represents a viable deployment option.

Kalman Filter detector's accuracy drops as it is unable to achieve a detection rate above 60%. PHAD provides very high detection rates, albeit

at an unacceptable false alarm rate. Other detectors' results are similar to the endpoint case. It can be observed from Figure 3 that all algorithms except TRW fail to achieve 100% detection rates on the LBNL dataset. This is because these algorithms inherently rely on the high burstiness and volumes of attack traffic. In the LBNL dataset, the attack traffic rate is much lower than the background traffic rate. Consequently, the attack traffic is distributed across multiple time windows, with each window containing very few attack packets. Such low density of attack traffic in the evaluated time-windows remains undetected regardless of how much the detection thresholds are decreased.

Delay Comparison

Table 4 provides the detection delay for each anomaly detector. On the endpoint dataset, delay is reported for the highest and the lowest rate attacks, while on the LBNL dataset this delay is computed for the first attack that is detected by an anomaly detector. A delay value of 1 is listed if an attack is not detected altogether. It can be observed that detection delay is reasonable (less than 1 second) for all the anomaly detectors except

Figure 3. ROC analysis on the LBNL dataset

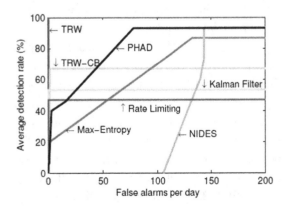

Table 4. Detection delay of the anomaly detectors

	Rate Limiting	TRW	TRW-CB	Max Entropy	NIDES	PHAD	Subspace Method	Kalman Filter
MyDoom (msec)	310	510	40	215000	∞	900	79	377
Dloader-NY (msec)	140	320	20	56000	0.086	990	23	417
LBNL (msec)	660	660	290	86000	330	330	∞	800

the Maximum Entropy detector which incurs very high detection delays. High delays are observed for the Maximum Entropy detector because it waits for perturbations in multiple time windows before raising an alarm. Among other viable alternatives, TRW-CB provides the lowest detection delays for all three experiments. Detection delay for the TRW is also reasonably low.

Lessons Learnt

Here we outline the objectives of the study and the deductions pertaining to these objectives. Moreover, promising portscan detection guidelines are proposed based on the NADS evaluation along with some experimental results, in the form of ROC curves, for the accuracy improvements realized due to the proposed guidelines.

Objectives of the Study: In this study, we evaluated eight prominent network-based anomaly detectors using two portscan traffic datasets having complementary characteristics. These detectors were evaluated on accuracy, scalability and delay criteria. Based on the results of this study, we now rephrase and summarize our deductions pertaining to the main objectives of this study:

- *Which algorithms provide the best accuracy under varying rates of attack and normal traffic and at different points of deployment?* Under the varying attack and background traffic rates observed in the two datasets, a general-purpose Maximum Entropy Detector (Gu, 2005) and variants of the Threshold Random Walk (TRW) al-

gorithm (Jung, 2004; Schechter, 2004) provided the best overall performance under most evaluation criteria. In this context, TRW is suitable for deployment at routers, while TRW-CB and Maximum Entropy are suitable for deployment at endpoints.

- *What are the promising traffic features and theoretical frameworks for portscan anomaly detection?* The Maximum Entropy and TRW detectors use statistical distributions of failed connections, ports and IP addresses. Furthermore, based on the results of the Maximum Entropy detector on endpoints, a histogram-based detection approach, in which baseline frequency profiles of a set of features is compared with real-time feature frequencies, appears very promising.

- *What detection delays are incurred by the anomaly detectors?* If an attack is detected, detection delay is less than 1 second for all anomaly detectors, except the Maximum Entropy Estimation method which incurs very large delays.

- *What are promising portscan detection guidelines that build on the strengths and avoid the weaknesses of the evaluated anomaly detectors?* From the high detection rates of the Maximum Entropy and PHAD detectors, it appears that using a higher dimensional feature space facilitates detection, without compromising complexity. On the other hand, relying on specific traffic features (e.g., rate, connection failures, etc.) can degrade accuracy as the attack and background traffic characteristics change. In summary, a number of statistical features used in an intelligent histogram-based classification framework appear promising for portscan anomaly detection.

Why do Some NADSs Perform Better than Others? In light of the accuracy evaluation results, Maximum Entropy provides best detection and false alarm rates on individual basis because of the following inbuilt characteristics:

- It segregates traffic into multiple packet classes;
- Analyzes a high dimensional feature space;
- Generates an alarm when anomalies span across multiple time windows.

PHAD detector operates on similar principles and thus also provides high detection rates. In all datasets we observe that traffic rates keep changing. While all NADSs apply fixed thresholds to classify anomalies in real-time traffic, an accurate NADS should vary its classification thresholds with respect to the changing patterns in benign traffic.

Promising Guidelines to Improve the Accuracy of Existing and Future NADSs: Based on above discussion, we propose the following guidelines to improve the accuracy of NADSs:

- **Guideline 1:** To reduce the false alarm rates, NADSs should raise an alarm only when they encounter anomalies spanning across multiple time windows.
- **Guideline 2:** To improve the detection rates, NADSs should simultaneously consider multiple packet header fields, e.g. TCP SYN, Ports, Protocol etc.
- **Guideline 3:** To improve detection rates, NADSs should segregate traffic into multiple packet classes before anomaly detection.

- **Guideline 4:** Adaptive thresholding should be introduced to allow the NADSs to dynamically adjust their detection thresholds in accordance with the changing normal traffic characteristics.

Guidelines 1-4 aim at improving the accuracy of the anomaly detection system as well as reduce human intervention in their operation. Following is a detailed description of these guidelines and the accuracy improvements achieved:

Multi-Window Classification (Guideline 1): We have seen in the comparative evaluation study of the NADSs, that most NADSs suffer from high false alarm rates. The problem mainly stems from the fact that most NADSs raise an alarm as soon as the first anomalous time window is identified. We observed that, due to an inherent burstiness present in attack traffic, anomalies tend to sustain across multiple time windows. An example of this behavior is shown in Figure 4. In Figure 4(a), even if a false alarm is generated for a benign traffic window, the false alarm does not span multiple windows. On the other hand, anomalous activity tends to occur in bursts, and therefore multiple successive windows are flagged as anomalous. This difference between NADS classification on malicious and benign traffic can be leveraged to reduce an NADS' false alarm rate. Specifically, an NADS can reduce its false alarms if it raises an alarm only after sufficient number of anomalous time windows have been observed in a given time period. We call this simple existing technique *Multi-Window Classification.*

For accurate multi-window classification, we consider a fixed number of w most recent classifications by an NADS. In the w classifications, a majority vote is taken to classify the current time window as benign or anomalous. It should be highlighted that multi-window classification will introduce detection delays in the NADSs. However, as already shown, detection delays of most existing NADSs are extremely low and hence

Figure 4. An example of multi-window classification: Maximum-entropy detector's output on five LBNL time windows containing benign and malicious traffic

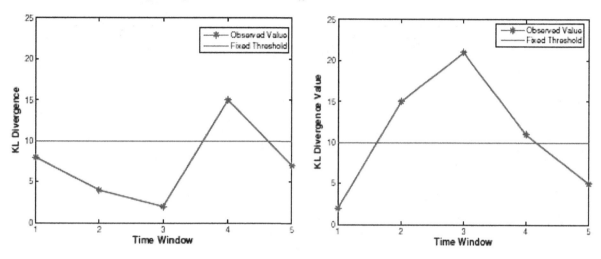

these NADSs can tolerate slightly longer detection delays to achieve higher accuracies.

Feature Space Extension (Guideline 2): We have seen in the comparative performance evaluation that Maximum Entropy and PHAD are the highest accuracy detectors. Both these detectors employ a rich feature space for detection. Thus greater the number of packet fields analyzed for anomaly detection, higher the probability of finding the anomaly. Thus, if within one time window, instead of analyzing a few packet header fields, the maximum available fields are analyzed, its highly probable that the NADS finds an anomaly that perturbs any of the observed packet feature.

Figure 5 shows the distribution of the packet score calculated for each packet based on the packet header fields analyzed. In Figure 5(a) PHAD detector computes the packet score based on a single anomalous packet header field. Figure 5(b) shows the packet score distribution, for PHAD, when multiple packet header fields are simultaneously used for packet score calculation. In Figure. 5(a), since packet score does not exceed the specified threshold value, PHAD detector fails to detect the anomalies which are otherwise detected if diverse packet features are analyzed as shown in Figure. 5(b). Thus, using a rich fea-

ture space assists the detection of anomalies that perturb any network traffic feature resulting in high detection rates for the NADSs.

Traffic Splitting (Guideline 3): Traffic Splitting is also aimed at improving an NADS's detection rate. Our preliminary investigation revealed that much of the malicious traffic is not detected because of an averaging-out effect introduced by relatively large volumes of benign background traffic. More specifically, if the attack traffic rate is comparable to or less than the background traffic rate then background traffic acts like noise during anomaly detection and allows malicious traffic to bypass an NADS.

As an example, note that aggregate traffic routed towards/from a network is a composite of multiple traffic types, such as TCP, UDP, ARP, ICMP traffic etc. Now consider the Witty worm which was a very high-rate UDP-based worm. Since TCP comprises of almost 80% of the traffic seen on the Internet, if an NADS analyzes aggregate network traffic then the attack traffic is overwhelmed by the majority TCP traffic. Such traffic averaging degrades the detection rate of an NADS. Note that in this example traffic other than UDP acts as noise and, depending upon whether the volume of background traffic is substantial,

Figure 5. PHAD detector's output for a single and multiple features analyzed for anomaly detection on LBNL dataset

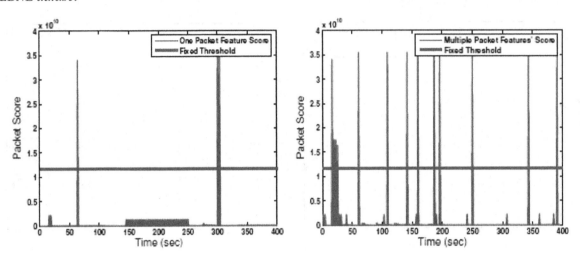

would either delay or prevent the detection of the anomaly. To counter this problem, we propose to perform anomaly detection separately on different types of network traffic. Hence, we use traffic semantics to segregate a single traffic stream into multiple traffic substreams before anomaly detection is performed. Such *traffic splitting* will inherently allow the background traffic to be segregated from the attack traffic, thereby facilitating the anomaly detection phase. After traffic splitting, separate instances of an NADS operate on different substreams in parallel. The outputs of these NADS instances are combined to detect anomalies. Based on the example given above, traffic splitting should, in addition to improving detection rates, reduce detection delays.

As a proof-of-concept, in Figure 6 shows a comparison of aggregate traffic with segregated TCP and UDP traffics. Both of these anomalous windows were observed and analyzed in the Threshold Random Walk Credit Based (TRW-CB) algorithm under RBOT.CCC's and Witty's malicious traffic. TRW-CB calculates the likelihood ratio for detecting anomalies. It is clear from the Figure 6 that when aggregate traffic is analyzed without segregation, the output of the likelihood ratio test does not cross the fixed TRW-CB threshold and the malicious traffic remains undetected for both examples. However, when traffic splitting is employed and TCP and UDP traffic is analyzed separately, the threshold is exceeded many times in the 200 second windows shown in Figure 6(a) and (b). Hence traffic splitting removes the noisy background traffic from malicious traffic and subsequently increases the detection rate of an NADS.

Adaptive Thresholding (Guideline 4): Traffic characteristics vary considerably across different organizations. For instance, traffic characteristics of academic research organizations are quite different from commercial enterprises. Similarly, different network deployment points are responsible for handling traffic from varying number of nodes. For instance, an endpoint requires to cater for only its own traffic, while an edge router needs to monitor and analyze traffic from a variety of hosts in its subnet. Even for the same network entity, traffic characteristics keep changing due to diurnal and other network usage patterns. As an example, consider the LBNL background traffic rates shown in Fig. 7 (solid line). It can be observed that the traffic rates change from approximately 500 pkts/sec to 10,000 pkts/sec within a few seconds. Under such varying traffic

Figure 6. An example of traffic splitting: Segregated and aggregate traffic rates during a TCP and a UDP attack

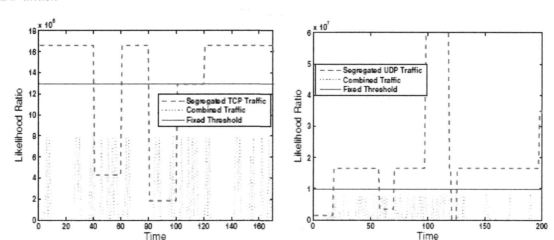

characteristics, existing NADSs require regular manual intervention for accurate operation. More specifically, a system or network administrator is responsible for adjusting the sensitivity of the anomaly detectors when the number of false alarms (i.e., traffic classified as malicious but which is in fact benign) increases. This sensitivity is adjusted using detection thresholds which are used to flag an anomaly. However, this repeated manual input renders an NADS less automated and more prone to configuration errors.

We argue that an effective ADS should automatically detect varying traffic patterns and adjust its detection threshold in accordance with varying traffic characteristics. If accurate, such an adaptive thresholding mechanism can eliminate the need for human threshold tuning, thereby making an NADS more automated. Moreover, as a by-product adaptive thresholding should also improve the accuracy of an NADS by tracking normal traffic patterns. (Here accuracy is defined in terms of detection versus false alarm rates.) In this section, we propose adaptive thresholding techniques that can accurately track the changing behavior of network traffic.

Threshold Prediction: We use adaptive thresholding to track the values of the detection feature(s)

that an NADS is employing. For instance, in the Maximum- Entropy detector, the adaptive thresholding logic will use prior observed values to predict the next K-L divergence values of each traffic class, while in the TRW detector the output of the likelihood ratio test will be tracked by the adaptive thresholding module. Irrespective of the traffic metric being employed by an NADS, a good adaptive thresholding module should be able to predict the next value with high accuracy. To achieve accurate threshold prediction, we used a stochastic algorithm i.e., Kalman filter based detector (Soule, 2005). Kalman filter based prediction is a well known technique and was readily applied for adaptive thresholding. However, we divided the observed metrics/scores into equal sized bins (i.e. ranges). These bins were then predicted using kalman filter. This provides the range of values expected for the next time interval.

Since the main motivation for adaptive thresholding is to reduce human intervention by accurately tracking varying traffic characteristics. As an example, consider Fig. 7 which shows the traffic rates (pkts/sec) observed in a 100 seconds subset of the LBNL dataset and the rates predicted by kalman filter. For prediction, rates were divided into bins of k = 500 packets and predicted on per

Figure 7. Background traffic rate prediction for the LBNL dataset

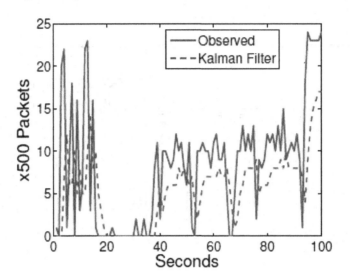

second basis. It can be seen in Figure 7 that kalman predictor follows the observed rate trend.

Similarly, Figure 8 shows the threshold tracking accuracy of the predictor in an anomalous LBNL time window of the Maximum-Entropy detector; the threshold in this case is the K-L divergence of a packet class that has been perturbed by the attack. It can be clearly seen that the kalman predictor estimates the highly-varying K-L divergence values with remarkable accuracy. Furthermore, note in Figure 8 that selecting a fixed threshold may allow a few anomalies to go undetected, especially anomalies which do not cause significant perturbations in the actual network traffic. For instance, in the 60 second output shown in Figure 8 only 10 of these values cross the fixed threshold. In this experiment, the Maximum- Entropy algorithm was detecting an anomaly if 12 or more values in a 60 second window exceed the fixed threshold. Hence, this anomaly will not be detected by a fixed threshold. Adaptive thresholding, on the other hand, accurately predicts the K-L divergence in the next window and the observed (perturbed) divergence exceeds this threshold more than 20 times in a 60 second window, thereby allowing the Maximum- Entropy detector to flag the anomaly. Furthermore, observe from Figure 8 that for many

seconds the observed K-L values drop to 0. These low values give a crafty attacker the leverage to introduce malicious traffic that does not exceed the fixed threshold of [0; 10]. However, an adaptive threshold immediately learns the change and set the threshold to 0, thus ensuring that no room is available for such a mimicry attack.

NADS Performance Improvements Achieved by the Proposed Guidelines: We now argue that the guidelines are complementary to each other. These can be applied simultaneously to achieve higher accuracy while limiting the need for human intervention during NADS operation.

Figure 9 shows a block diagram of an NADS that jointly employs the proposed guidelines. The first thing we note is that none of the guidelines require modifications to the NADS. The Traffic Splitter is working as a pre-NADS phase which is segregating a single stream of traffic into multiple packet classes; these classes can be formed on any basis. The second phase, as shown in Figure 9 is the feature space extension. Once traffic is segregated into multiple packet classes, each packet class is further segregated into multiple packet features to be examined for an anomaly. Each packet feature class is sent to a separate NADS instance which uses the threshold provided by the

Figure 8. Behavior of adaptive and fixed threshold in anomalous window

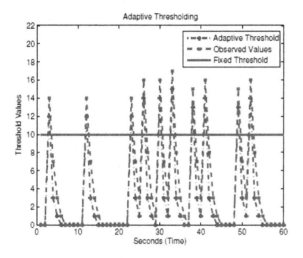

Adaptive Thresholding Module to classify traffic in the observed window as benign or anomalous. Outputs from multiple instances of the NADS, each analyzing a unique packet feature class, are combined into a single result and handed over to the Multi-Window Classifier. The Multi-Window Classifier acting as a post-NADS phase takes the majority vote of prior classification results to decide whether or not an alarm should be raised.

Figure 10 shows the accuracy of five prominent NADSs along with the jointly-improved versions of these detectors after application of the proposed guidelines; all parameters are the same as described in previous sections. Due to a lack of threshold tuning capability, adaptive thresholding only results in a single point on the ROC plane. Figure 10(a) shows the accuracy comparison for the endpoint dataset. Maximum Entropy improves slightly on its already accurate performance. Jointly-improved Kalman Filter detector provides better accuracy than the original algorithm with a detection rates of approximately 96%. TRWCB detector maintains similar accuracy as before, but with the additional advantage of ADS automation. PHAD and TRW detectors show dramatic improvements in accuracies as they achieve detection rate improvements of approximately 45% and 70%, respectively, without compromising their

Figure 9. Block diagram of network-based anomaly detection system that jointly employs the proposed guidelines

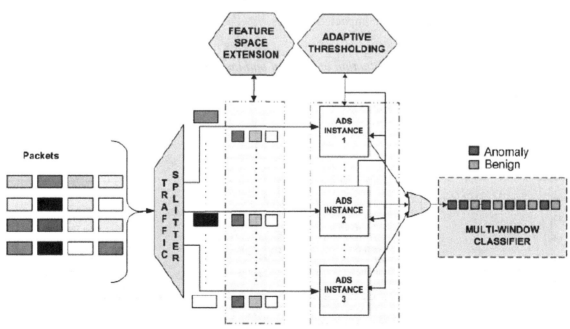

low false alarms rates. Note that although there was a slight degradation in the jointly-improved TRW's accuracy on the LBNL dataset, on the endpoint dataset the proposed techniques provide remarkable accuracy improvements for TRW. Thus the proposed guidelines, in addition to the benefits enumerated above, allow an NADS to scale to different points of deployment in the network.

From Figure 10(b), marked and mostly consistent improvements in all the NADSs' accuracies can be observed on the LBNL dataset. The Maximum-Entropy detector achieves a remarkable 100% detection rate at a reasonable false rate. Kalman Filter based detector's accuracy also improves drastically as its detection rate increases from 54% to 80% with few false alarms. A similar accuracy improvement trend is observed for the PHAD detector. No improvement in detection/false alarm rate is observed in the TRW-CB detector; however, it continues to provide the same detection rates without any human intervention and at an acceptable false alarm rate. The TRW detector is the only exception on the LBNL dataset as it incurs somewhat higher false alarms after using the proposed guidelines.

Evaluating NADSs in space and across multiple time windows might have an impact on

Table 5. Detection delay of the improved variants of maximum entropy and PHAD

	Improved- Max Entropy	Improved- PHAD
MyDoom (msec)	157	900
Dloader-NY (msec)	100	990
LBNL (msec)	333	330

the detection delay of the detectors. So we also perform delay comparison so as to observe the extent of the delay that Guideline-1 can incur. Table 5 provides the detection delay for Maximum Entropy detector and PHAD. It can be observed that the detection delay for the Improved variant of Maximum Entropy detector is dramatically lower than the original algorithm. This is because the Improved variant of the Maximum Entropy detector does not wait for multiple anomalous windows before raising an alarm. For PHAD, the detection delay remains unaltered because the Improved variants simultaneously operates in space and time. In the following section, we highlight the accuracy improvements that can be realized by jointly applying all these guidelines.

Figure 10. ROC-based accuracy evaluation of original and improved NADS algorithms

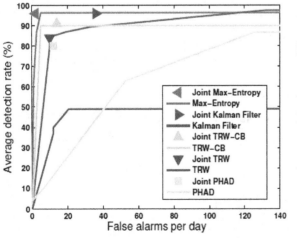
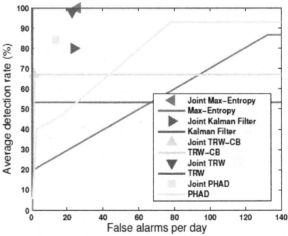

CONCLUSION

The main aim of this chapter was to introduce the readers to the basic building blocks of Network-based Anomaly Detection Systems and to identify the features that distinguish one NADS from the other. We evaluated and compared eight prominent network based anomaly detectors on two independently collected public portscan datasets. These NADSs employed different traffic features and diverse theoretical frameworks for anomaly detection and have been used frequently for performance benchmarking in Intrusion Detection research literature. NADSs were evaluated on three criteria: accuracy, scalability, and detection delay. Accuracy was evaluated by comparing ROC (false alarms per day versus detection rate) characteristics of the NADSs. Scalability was evaluated with respect to different background and attack traffic rates. Since the two datasets used in this chapter were collected at different network entities and contained attacks with different characteristics, evaluation over these datasets allowed us to compare the scalability of the proposed NADSs under varying traffic volumes. Detection delay was evaluated separately for high- and low-rate attacks. Based on our findings, we proposed a few promising portscan detection guidelines to improve the accuracy and scalability of existing and future NADSs. Our experimental results showed that the proposed guidelines resulted in an average detection rate increase of 5% to 10%, while reducing the false alarm rates up to 50%. Thus, the proposed guidelines, while reducing human intervention, provided drastic and consistent improvements in NADSs' accuracies.

REFERENCES

Aguirre, S. J., & Hill, W. H. (1997). *Intrusion detection fly-off: Implications for the United States Navy*. (MITRE Technical Report MTR 97W096).

Arbor Networks. (2010). *Peakflow SP & Peakflow-X*. Retrieved from http://www.arbornetworks.com/peakflowsp, http://www.arbornetworks.com/peakflowx

Chen, S., & Tang, Y. (2004). *Slowing down internet worms*. IEEE ICDCS.

Cisco. (2010). *IOS flexible network flow*. Retrieved from http://www.cisco.com/go/netflow

Cui, W., Katz, R. H., & Tan, W.-T. (2005, April). *BINDER: An extrusion-based break-in detector for personal computers*. Usenix Security Symposium.

Debar, H., Dacier, M., Wespi, A., & Lampart, S. (1998). *A workbench for intrusion detection systems*. IBM Zurich Research Laboratory.

Denmac Systems, Inc. (1999). *Network based intrusion detection: A review of technologies*.

DuMouchel, W. (1999). *Computer intrusion detection based on Bayes factors for comparing command transition probabilities*. Tech. Rep. 91, National Institute of Statistical Sciences.

Durst, R., Champion, T., Witten, B., Miller, E., & Spagnuolo, L. (1999). Testing and evaluating computer intrusion detection systems. *Communications of the ACM, 42*(7), 53–61. doi:10.1145/306549.306571

Fawcett, T. (2004). *ROC graphs: Notes and practical considerations for researchers*. HP Laboratories Technical Report, Palo Alto, USA.

Fawcett, T. (2005). *An introduction to ROC analysis*. Elsevier.

Ganger, G., Economou, G., & Bielski, S. (2002). Self-securing network interfaces: What, why, and how. (Carnegie Mellon University Technical Report, CMU-CS-02-144).

Gu, Y., McCullum, A., & Towsley, D. (2005). *Detecting anomalies in network traffic using maximum entropy estimation*. ACM/Usenix Internet Measurement Conference (IMC).

Ilgun, K., Kemmerer, R. A., & Porras, P. A. (1995, March). State transition analysis: A rulebased intrusion detection approach. *IEEE Transactions on Software Engineering, 21*(3), 181–199. doi:10.1109/32.372146

Ingham, K. L., & Inoue, H. (2007). *Comparing anomaly detection techniques for HTTP*. Symposium on Recent Advances in Intrusion Detection (RAID).

Jung, J., Paxson, V., Berger, A. W., & Balakrishnan, H. (2004). *Fast portscan detection using sequential hypothesis testing*. IEEE Symp Sec and Priv.

Khayam, S. A. (2006). *Wireless channel modeling and malware detection using statistical and information-theoretic tools*. PhD thesis, Michigan State University (MSU), USA.

Lakhina, A., Crovella, M., & Diot, C. (2004). *Characterization of network-wide traffic anomalies in traffic flows*. ACM Internet Measurement Conference (IMC).

Lakhina, A., Crovella, M., & Diot, C. (2004). *Diagnosing network-wide traffic anomalies*. ACM SIGCOMM.

Lakhina, A., Crovella, M., & Diot, C. (2005). *Mining anomalies using traffic feature distributions*. ACM SIGCOMM.

Lazarevic, A., Ertoz, L., Kumar, V., Ozgur, A., & Srivastava, J. (2003). *A comparative study of anomaly detection schemes in network intrusion detection*. SIAM International Conference on Data Mining (SDM).

LBNL/ICSI. (2010). *Enterprise Tracing Project*. Retrieved from http://www.icir.org/enterprise-tracing/download.html

Lincoln Lab, M. I. T. (1998-1999). *DARPA-sponsored IDS evaluation*. Retrieved from www.ll.mit.edu/IST/ideval/data/dataindex.html

Lippmann, R. P., Fried, D. J., Graf, I., Haines, J. W., Kendall, K. R., & McClung, D. … Zissman, M. A. (2000). *Evaluating intrusion detection systems: The 1998 DARPA off-line intrusion detection evaluation*. DISCEX, 2, (pp. 12-26).

Lippmann, R. P., Haines, J. W., Fried, D. J., Korba, J., & Das, K. (2000). The 1999 DARPA offline intrusion detection evaluation. *Computer Networks, 34*(2), 579–595. doi:10.1016/S1389-1286(00)00139-0

Mahoney, M. V., & Chan, P. K. (2001). *PHAD: Packet Header anomaly detection for identifying hostile network traffic*. (Florida Tech technical report CS-2001-4).

Mahoney, M. V., & Chan, P. K. (2002). *Learning models of network traffic for detecting novel attacks*. (Florida Tech, technical report CS-2002-08).

Mahoney, M. V., & Chan, P. K. (2003). *Network traffic anomaly detection based on packet bytes*. ACM SAC.

Mahoney, M. V., & Chan, P. K. (2003). *An analysis of the 1999 DARPA/Lincoln Laboratory evaluation data for network anomaly detection*. Symposium on Recent Advances in Intrusion Detection (RAID).

McAfee Corporation. (2005). McAfee virtual criminology report: North American study into organized crime and the Internet.

McHugh, J. (2000). *The 1998 Lincoln Laboratory IDS evaluation* (a critique). Symposium on Recent Advances in Intrusion Detection (RAID).

Mueller, P., & Shipley, G. (2001, August). Dragon claws its way to the top. *Network Computing*. Retrieved from http://www.networkcomputing.com/1217/1217f2.html

Next-Generation Intrusion Detection Expert System (NIDES). (2010). *NIDES Project*. Retrieved from http://www.csl.sri.com/projects/nides/

Pang, R., Allman, M., Bennett, M., Lee, J., Paxson, V., & Tierney, B. (2005). *A first look at modern enterprise traffic*. ACM/Usenix Internet Measurement Conference (IMC).

Pang, R., Allman, M., Paxson, V., & Lee, J. (2006). The devil and packet trace anonymization. *ACM CCR, 36*(1).

Ptacek, T. H., & Newsham, T. N. (1998). *Insertion, evasion, and denial of service: Eluding network intrusion detection*. Secure Networks, Inc.

Puketza, N., Chung, M., Olsson, R. A., & Mukherjee, B. (1997). A software platform for testing intrusion detection systems. *IEEE Software, 14*(5), 43–51. doi:10.1109/52.605930

Puketza, N. F., Zhang, K., Chung, M., Mukherjee, B., & Olsson, R. A. (1996). A methodology for testing intrusion detection systems. *IEEE Transactions on Software Engineering, 22*(10), 719–729. doi:10.1109/32.544350

Ringberg, H., Rexford, J., Soule, A., & Diot, C. (2007). *Sensitivity of PCA for traffic anomaly detection*. ACM SIGMETRICS.

Roesch, M. (1999). *Snort – Lightweight intrusion detection for networks*. USENIX Large Installation System Administration Conference (LISA).

Schechter, S. E., Jung, J., & Berger, A. W. (2004). *Fast detection of scanning worm infections*. Symposium on Recent Advances in Intrusion Detection (RAID).

Sellke, S., Shroff, N. B., & Bagchi, S. (2005). *Modeling and automated containment of worms*. DSN.

Shannon, C., & Moore, D. (2004). The spread of the Witty worm. *IEEE Security & Privacy, 2*(4), 46–50. doi:10.1109/MSP.2004.59

Shipley, G. (1999). ISS RealSecure pushes past newer IDS players. *Network Computing.* Retrieved from http://www.networkcomputing.com/1010/1010r1.html

Shipley, G. (1999). Intrusion detection, take two. *Network Computing.* Retrieved from http://www.nwc.com/1023/1023f1.html

Soule, A., Salamatian, K., & Taft, N. (2005). *Combining filtering and statistical methods for anomaly detection*. ACM/Usenix Internet Measurement Conference (IMC).

Symantec. (2010). *Security response.* Retrieved from http://securityresponse.symantec.com/avcenter

Symantec Internet Security Statistics. (2008). *Symantec Internet security threat reports I–XI.*

The, N. S. S. Group. (2001). *Intrusion detection systems group test* (2nd ed.). Retrieved from http://nsslabs.com/group-tests/intrusion-detection-systems-ids-group-test-edition-2.html

Twycross, J., & Williamson, M. M. (2003). *Implementing and testing a virus throttle*. Usenix Security.

Weaver, N., Staniford, S., & Paxson, V. (2004). *Very fast containment of scanning worms*. Usenix Security.

Wikipedia. (2010). *Wikipedia main page*. Retrieved from http://en.wikipedia.org/

Williamson, M. M. (2002). *Throttling viruses: Restricting propagation to defeat malicious mobile code*. ACSAC.

Winpcap. (2010). *Winpcap homepage*. Retrieved from http://www.winpcap.org/

WiSNet. (2008). *Bibliography of network-based anomaly detection systems*. Retrieved from http://www.wisnet.seecs.nust.edu.pk/downloads.php

Evaluation of Contemporary Anomaly Detection Systems

WiSNet. (2010). *WiSNet ADS comparison homepage, November 2010*. Retrieved from http://www.wisnet.seecs.nust.edu.pk/projects/adeval/

Wong, C., Bielski, S., Studer, A., & Wang, C. (2005). *Empirical analysis of rate limiting mechanisms*. Symposium on Recent Advances in Intrusion Detection (RAID).

Yocom, B., & Brown, K. (2001). Intrusion battleground evolves. *Network World Fusion*. Retrieved from http://www.nwfusion.com/reviews/2001/1008bg.html

Zou, C. C., Gao, L., Gong, W., & Towsley, D. (2003). *Monitoring and early warning of Internet worms*. ACM Conference on Computer and Communications Security (CCS).

KEY TERMS AND DEFINITIONS

Botnet: Botnet is a collection of software agents, or robots, that run autonomously and automatically (Wikipedia).

Phishing: Phishing is the process of attempting to acquire sensitive information such as usernames, passwords and credit card details by masquerading as a trustworthy entity in an electronic communication (Wikipedia).

Portscan: Portscan is an attack that sends client requests to a range of server port addresses on a host, with the goal of finding an active port and exploiting a known vulnerability of that service (Wikipedia).

ROCs: An ROC curve is a technique for visualizing, organizing and selecting classifiers based on their performance (Fawcett, 2004; Fawcett, 2005).

Spam: Spam is the use of electronic messaging systems to send unsolicited bulk messages indiscriminately (Wikipedia).

Zero Day Attacks: Zero-day attacks are attacks/threats that exploit system vulnerabilities yet unknown to the software developers.

ENDNOTES

[1] Some promising commercial ADSs are also available in the market now (Peakflow; Cisco NetFlow). We did not have access to these ADSs, and therefore these commercial products are not evaluated in this study.

[2] We also wanted to use a traffic dataset collected at a backbone ISP network; such datasets have been used in some prior studies (Lakhina, 2004 – Lakhina, 2005). However, we could not find a publicly available ISP traffic dataset.

[3] The mean session rates in Table II are computed using time-windows containing one or more new sessions. Therefore, dividing total sessions by the duration does not yield the session rate of column 5.

Section 3
Formal Methods and Quantum Computing

Chapter 7
Practical Quantum Key Distribution

Sellami Ali
International Islamic University Malaysia (IIUM), Malaysia

ABSTRACT

We have presented a method to estimate parameters of the decoy state protocol based on one decoy state protocol for both BB84 and SARG04. This method can give different lower bound of the fraction of single-photon counts (y_1), the fraction of two-photon counts (y_2), the upper bound QBER of single-photon pulses (e_1), the upper bound QBER of two-photon pulses (e_2), and the lower bound of key generation rate for both BB84 and SARG04. The effects of statistical fluctuations on some parameters of our QKD system have been presented. We have also performed the optimization on the choice of intensities and percentages of signal state and decoy states which give out the maximum distance and the optimization of the key generation rate. The numerical simulation has shown that the fiber based QKD and free space QKD systems using the proposed method for BB84 are able to achieve both a higher secret key rate and greater secure distance than that of SARG04. Also, it is shown that bidirectional ground to satellite and inter-satellite communications are possible with our protocol. The experiment of decoy state QKD has been demonstrated using ID-3000 commercial QKD system based on a standard 'Plug & Play' set-up. One decoy state QKD has been implemented for both BB84 and SARG04 over different transmission distance of standard telecom fiber.

DOI: 10.4018/978-1-60960-851-4.ch007

INTRODUCTION

The need for highly secure communication systems is quite evident in the world today. Large amounts of information are transferred continuously, whether it be important banking information or a simple phone call. With this growing information exchange, the possibilities for unauthorized reception are also increased. In the classical cryptography a variety of encryption algorithms have been introduced, providing different levels of security. Apart from one, they all have in common that in principle they can be cracked. For example, the RSA cryptosystem, one of the widely used algorithms (e.g. in SSL, SSH), relies on the fact that it is difficult to find the factors of large integers. There are two threats to this method: The first is that more computational power will help to make time-consuming attacks (like brute-force attacks) more convenient. Moreover, someone might even think of an efficient algorithm for factoring integers. The second problem is that quantum computers are in fact already capable of executing the factorization efficiently. Until now, it cannot be done with large integers and it will probably take some time for it to become practical, but for crucial applications "probably secure" is not enough.

On the other hand, there exists a classical, unconditionally secure cryptographic algorithm, but it has a big problem: It requires a random key, which has to be as long as the message itself and this has to be transported securely from one party to the other. This cannot be done classically.

Here, an amazing idea comes into play: Quantum mechanics has the property of hiding some information from us, as expressed in Heisenberg's uncertainty relation. Could this inherent ignorance be used as an advantage over a potential eavesdropper? It turns out, that this is indeed possible and after discussing the essential quantum mechanical properties, it will be introduced a method of establishing a secret key between two parties, which is provably secure. This security is a direct consequence of the fundamental axioms of quantum mechanics. As long as we do not find that we can gain more information on quantum states than described by quantum mechanics, this scheme has to be regarded secure.

Really interesting about this method is that a usually unfavorable property of quantum mechanics is actually employed to achieve something that can't be done outside the quantum world. The fact that two non-commuting observables can only be measured with limited precision allows unconditionally secure key distribution. The whole idea has been named quantum cryptography or quantum key distribution (QKD).

The central objective of this chapter is to study and implement practical systems for quantum cryptography using decoy state protocol. In particular we seek to improve dramatically both the security and the performance of practical QKD system (in terms of substantially higher key generation rate and longer distance). The main objectives of this research are:

1. Presenting a method to estimate parameters of decoy state method based on one decoy state protocol for both BB84 and SARG04.
2. Simulation of fiber-based and free space Decoy State Quantum Key Distribution based on practical decoy state protocols which are mentioned in the first objective for both BB84 and SARG04.
3. Experimental realization of one decoy state protocols which is mentioned in the first objective: one decoy state protocol.

BACKGROUND

Quantum cryptography is based on physical principles which cannot be defeated. This need for secure communications provided the driving force for interest in quantum cryptography, or quantum key distribution in particular. In 1983 Wiesner put forth as idea for counterfeit-proof money by employing single quantum states (Wiesner, S. 1979; Bennett, C.H., Brassard, G., Breidbart, S., and Wiesner, S. 1982). However, storing single quantum states for extended periods of time is difficult in practice, so the idea was treated as an academic curiosity for the most part. In 1984 Bennett and Brassard suggested that instead of using the single quanta states to store information, they could use them to transmit information (Bennett, C.H., Brassard. 1984; Bennett, C.H., Brassard, G. 1984). It took several years to make it into experimental reality, and in 1989 the breakthrough experimental free-space system was demonstrated (Bennett, C.H., Brassard, G. 1989). Other quantum information systems were also spun off, including quantum key distribution with optical fibers (Bennett, C.H. 1982) and the use of Einstein-Podolsky-Rosen entangled pairs (J.D. Franson and H lives. 1994).

Quantum key distribution (QKD) (Ekert, A.K. 1991) was proposed as a method of achieving perfectly secure communications. Any eavesdropping attempt by a third party will necessarily introduce an abnormally high quantum bit error rate in a quantum transmission and thus be caught by the users. With a perfect single photon source, QKD provides proven unconditional security guaranteed by the fundamental laws of quantum physics (Mayers, D. 2001). Most current experimental QKD set-ups are based on attenuated laser pulses which occasionally give out multi-photons. Therefore, any security proofs must take into account the possibility of subtle eavesdropping attacks, including the PNS (photon number splitting) attack (Ma, X., Fung, C.-H. F., Dupuis, F., Chen, K., Tamaki, K., and Lo, H.-K. 2006). A hallmark of those subtle attacks is that they introduce a photon-number dependent attenuation to the signal. Fortunately, it is still possible to obtain unconditionally secure QKD, even with (phase randomized) attenuated laser pulses, as theoretically demonstrated by (Inamori, H., L¨utkenhaus, N., and Mayers, D. 2001). and Gottesman-Lo-L¨utkenhaus-Preskill (GLLP) (Gottesman, D., Lo, H.-K., Lütkenhaus, N., and Preskill, J. 2004). However, one must pay a

steep price by placing severe limits on the distance and the key generation rate (Koashi, M. 2004).

How can one increase the key generation rates and distances of unconditionally secure QKD? A brute force solution to the problem is to develop single photon sources, which is a subject of much recent interest (Keller, M., Held, K., Eyert, V., Vollhardt, D., and Anisimov, V.I. 2004). However, such a brute force approach clearly takes a lot of experimental research efforts. It came as a big surprise that a simple solution—the decoy state method actually exists (Hwang, W.-Y. 2003). Such a simple solution is based on better theory, rather than better experiments. The decoy state method allows us to achieve unconditional security based on quantum mechanics and to improve dramatically the performance of QKD systems.

The decoy state protocol idea is the following: In addition to the usual signal states of average photon number μ, Alice prepares decoy states of various mean photon numbers $\mu_0, \mu_1, \mu_2, \ldots$ (but with the same wavelength, timing, etc.). Alice can achieve this, for instance, via a variable attenuator to modulate the intensity of each signal. It is essential that each signal is chosen randomly to be either a signal state or a decoy state. Both signal states as well as decoy states consist of pulses containing $\{0, 1, 2, \ldots\}$ photons, just with different probabilities. Given a *single i*-photon pulse, the eavesdropper has no means to distinguish whether it originates from a signal state or a decoy state. Hence, the eavesdropper on principle cannot act differently on signal states and on decoy states. Therefore, any attempt to suppress single-photon signals in the signal states will lead also to a suppression of single-photon signals in the decoy states. After Bob's announcement of his detection events, Alice broadcasts which signals were indeed signal states and which signals were decoy states (and which types). Since the signal states and the decoy states are made up of different proportions of single-photon and multi-photon pulses, any photon-number dependent eavesdropping strategy has different effects on the signal states and on the decoy states. By computing the gain (i.e., the ratio of the number of detection events to the number of signals sent by Alice) separately for signal states and each of the decoy states, the legitimate users can with high probability detect any photon-number dependent suppression of signals and thus unveil a PNS attack.

THE PROPOSED DECOY STATE METHOD

In this section, we present a simple method that can study the secure key generation rate when single-photon and two-photon pulses are employed to generate secure key. We present the estimations and perform the optimization of decoy state parameters of one decoy state, and two decoy states protocols for both BB84 and SARG04. This method can estimate the lower bound of the fraction of single-photon counts (y_1), the fraction of two-photon counts (y_2), the upper bound QBER of single-photon pulses (e_1), the upper bound QBER of two-photon pulses (e_2), and to evaluate the lower bound of key generation rate for both BB84 and SARG04. Due to finite data size in real-life experiments, we give the estimation of statistical fluctuations of some parameters such as: the gain and QBER of signal state and the gain and QBER of decoy state which are used in the estimation of the lower bound of key generation rate. We provide equations that give the optimum percentages and intensities of the decoy states and the signal state. Then we can get the maximum and the optimization of the key generation rate.

Here, we propose a method to evaluate the lower bound of the key generation rate for both BB84 and SARG04 by the estimation of the lower bound of fraction of one photon count y_1, two photon counts y_2, upper bound of quantum bit-error rate (QBER) of one-photon e_1 and upper bound of quantum bit-error rate (QBER) of two-photon e_2. It is assumed that Alice can prepare and

emit a weak coherent state $\left| \sqrt{\mu} e^{i\theta} \right\rangle$. Assuming the phase θ of each signal is randomized, the probability distribution for the number of photons of the signal state follows a Poisson distribution with some parameter μ(the intensity of signal states) which is given by $p_i = e^{-\mu} \dfrac{\mu^i}{i!}$, Alice's pulse will contain i-photon. Therefore, it has assumed that any Poissonian mixture of the photon number states can be prepared by Alice. In addition, Alice can vary the intensity for each individual pulse.

Assuming Alice and Bob choose the signal and decoy states with expected photon numbers μ, v_1, v_2, v_3, ..., v_n, they will get the following gains and QBER's for signal state and n-decoy states (Ma, X., Qi, B., Zhao, Y., and Lo, H.-K. 2005):

$$Q_\mu e^\mu = y_0 + \mu y_1 + \sum_{i=2}^{\infty} y_i \frac{\mu^i}{i!}$$

$$Q_\mu = y_0 + 1 - e^{-\eta\mu}$$

$$E_\mu Q_\mu e^\mu = e_0 y_0 + \mu e_1 y_1 + \sum_{i=2}^{\infty} e_i y_i \frac{\mu^i}{i!}$$

$$E_\mu = \frac{1}{Q_\mu} \left(e_0 y_0 + e_{\det ector} \left(1 - e^{-\eta\mu} \right) \right)$$

$$Q_{v_1} e^{v_1} = y_0 + v_1 y_1 + \sum_{i=2}^{\infty} y_i \frac{v_1^i}{i!}$$

$$Q_{v_1} = y_0 + 1 - e^{-\eta v_1}$$

$$E_{v_1} Q_{v_1} e^{v_1} = e_0 y_0 + e_1 v_1 y_1 + \sum_{i=2}^{\infty} e_i y_n \frac{v_1^i}{i!}$$

$$E_{v_1} = \frac{1}{Q_{v_1}} \left(e_0 y_0 + e_{\det ector} \left(1 - e^{-\eta v_1} \right) \right)$$

$$Q_{v_2} e^{v_2} = y_0 + v_2 y_1 + \sum_{i=2}^{\infty} y_i \frac{v_2^i}{i!}$$

$$Q_{v_2} = y_0 + 1 - e^{-\eta v_2}$$

$$E_{v_2} Q_{v_2} e^{v_2} = e_0 y_0 + e_1 v_2 y_1 + \sum_{i=2}^{\infty} e_i y_i \frac{v_2^i}{i!}$$

$$E_{v_2} = \frac{1}{Q_{v_2}}\left(e_0 y_0 + e_{\det ector}\left(1 - e^{-\eta v_2}\right)\right)$$

$$Q_{v_3} e^{v_3} = y_0 + v_3 y_1 + \sum_{i=2}^{\infty} y_i \frac{v_3^i}{i!}$$

$$Q_{v_3} = y_0 + 1 - e^{-\eta v_3}$$

$$E_{v_3} Q_{v_3} e^{v_3} = e_0 y_0 + e_1 v_3 y_1 + \sum_{i=2}^{\infty} e_i y_i \frac{v_3^i}{i!}$$

$$E_{v_3} = \frac{1}{Q_{v_3}}\left(e_0 y_0 + e_{\det ector}\left(1 - e^{-\eta v_3}\right)\right)$$

$$\vdots$$

$$Q_{v_n} e^{v_n} = y_0 + v_n y_1 + \sum_{i=2}^{\infty} y_i \frac{v_n^i}{i!}$$

$$Q_{v_n} = y_0 + 1 - e^{-\eta v_n}$$

$$E_{v_n} Q_{v_n} e^{v_n} = e_0 y_0 + e_1 v_n y_1 + \sum_{i=2}^{\infty} e_i y_i \frac{v_n^i}{i!}$$

$$E_{v_n} = \frac{1}{Q_{v_n}}\left(e_0 y_0 + e_{\det ector}\left(1 - e^{-\eta v_n}\right)\right)$$

$$(1)$$

Where y_i is the conditional probability of a detection event at Bob's side given that Alice sends out an i-photon state which comes from two parts, background (y_0) and true signal. η is the overall transmittance. Also, e_i is the QBER of an i-photon signal, e_0 is the error rate of background, and $e_{detector}$ is the probability that a photon hit the erroneous detector. Assuming Alice and Bob choose signal and decoy state with mean photon number μ, v_1, v_2, v_3, ..., v_n which satisfy these inequalities:

$$0 < \mu \le 1, 0 \le v_1 \le 1, 0 \le v_2 \le 1, ..., 0 \le v_n \le 1,$$
$$v_1 > v_2 \ge v_3 \ge ... \ge v_n$$

$$(2)$$

Where n is number of decoy states.

Here, we present one decoy state, vacuum + one decoy state, two decoy states, and vacuum + two decoy states protocols and show more precisely how it can be used to estimate the lower bound of y_1 and upper bound of e_1 in order to get the final key generation rate of our QKD system for BB84 and to estimate the lower bound of fraction of two photon counts y_2 and upper bound of quantum bit-error rate (QBER) of two-photon e_2 for SARG04. We will introduce two factors x and z which are factors for determining the lower bounds of the fraction of single-photon and two photon counts and the upper bounds of single-photon and two photons QBER.

Case A1 of One Decoy State Protocol for BB84

In this protocol, we should estimate the lower bounds of y_1 and the upper bounds of e_1. Intuitively, only one decoy state is needed for the estimation. Here, we investigate how to use one decoy state to estimate those bounds.

Suppose that Alice randomly changes the intensity of her pump light among 2 values (one decoy state and a signal state) such that the intensity of one mode of the two mode source is randomly changed among v and μ, which satisfy inequalities $0 \le v < \mu \le 1$, $0 < x \le 1$, and $x > \frac{v}{\mu}$. Where, v is the mean photon number of the decoy state and μ is the expected photon number of the signal state.

According to Eq. (1), the gain of signal and one decoy state are given by:

$$Q_\mu e^\mu = y_0 + \mu y_1 + \sum_{i=2}^{\infty} y_i \frac{\mu^i}{i!}$$
$$Q_v e^v = y_0 + v y_1 + \sum_{i=2}^{\infty} y_i \frac{v^i}{i!}$$

$$(3)$$

By using the inequality (8) in (Hwang, 2003), $0 \le v < \mu \le 1$, $0 < x \le 1$, and $x > \frac{v}{\mu}$ we get

$$\frac{\sum_{i=2}^{\infty} P_i(v)y_i}{\sum_{i=2}^{\infty} P_i(\mu)y_i} \le \frac{P_2(v)}{P_2(\mu)} \tag{4}$$

Then,

$$\frac{\sum_{i=2}^{\infty} y_i \frac{v^i}{i!}}{\sum_{i=2}^{\infty} y_i \frac{\mu^i}{i!}} \le \frac{v^2}{\mu^2} \le \frac{1}{x}\frac{v^2}{\mu^2}$$

Multiply both sides by $x\mu^2 \sum_{i=2}^{\infty} y_i \frac{\mu^i}{i!}$ we found

$$x\mu^2 \sum_{i=2}^{\infty} y_i \frac{v^i}{i!} \le v^2 \sum_{i=2}^{\infty} y_i \frac{\mu^i}{i!} \tag{5}$$

Using Eq (3) we found

$$x\mu^2 \left(Q_v e^v - y_0 - v y_1 \right) \le v^2 \left(Q_\mu e^\mu - y_0 - \mu y_1 \right) \tag{6}$$

By solving inequality (6), the lower bound of y_1 is given by

$$y_1 \ge y_1^{L,v} = \frac{1}{\left(x\mu^2 v - v^2 \mu \right)} [x\mu^2 Q_v e^v - v^2 Q_\mu e^\mu \\ - \left(x\mu^2 - v^2 \right) y_0] \tag{7}$$

According to Eq. (1), then the lower bound of the gain of single photon state is given by

$$Q_1^{L,v} = \frac{\mu e^{-\mu}}{\left(x\mu^2 v - v^2 \mu \right)} [x\mu^2 Q_v e^v - v^2 Q_\mu e^\mu \\ - \left(x\mu^2 - v^2 \right) y_0] \tag{8}$$

According to selected values of x we can deduce different lower bounds for the gain of single photon states. For $x = 1$:

$$Q_1^{L,v} = \frac{e^{-\mu}}{\left(\mu v - v^2 \right)} [\mu^2 Q_v e^v - v^2 Q_\mu e^\mu \\ - \left(\mu^2 - v^2 \right) y_0] \tag{9}$$

For $x = \frac{v}{\mu^2}$:

$$Q_1^{L,v} = \frac{\mu e^{-\mu}}{\left(1-\mu \right)} \left[\frac{1}{v} Q_v e^v - Q_\mu e^\mu - \left(\frac{1}{v} - 1 \right) y_0 \right] \tag{10}$$

For $x = \frac{v}{\mu^3}$:

$$Q_1^{L,v} = \frac{\mu e^{-\mu}}{\left(\frac{1}{\mu} - \mu \right)} \left[\frac{1}{v\mu} Q_v e^v - Q_\mu e^\mu - \left(\frac{1}{v\mu} - 1 \right) y_0 \right] \tag{11}$$

For $x = \frac{v}{\mu^4}$:

$$Q_1^{L,v} = \frac{\mu e^{-\mu}}{\left(\frac{1}{\mu^2} - \mu \right)} \left[\frac{1}{v\mu^2} Q_v e^v - Q_\mu e^\mu - \left(\frac{1}{v\mu^2} - 1 \right) y_0 \right] \tag{12}$$

For $x = \frac{v}{\mu^5}$:

$$Q_1^{L,v} = \frac{\mu e^{-\mu}}{\left(\frac{1}{\mu^3} - \mu \right)} \left[\frac{1}{v\mu^3} Q_v e^v - Q_\mu e^\mu - \left(\frac{1}{v\mu^3} - 1 \right) y_0 \right]$$

$$\vdots \tag{13}$$

For $x = \frac{v}{\mu^N}$, $N \ge 2$, and $\mu^N \ge v$ Then:

$$Q_1^{L,v} = \frac{\mu e^{-\mu}}{\left(\dfrac{1}{\mu^{N-2}} - \mu\right)}\left[\frac{1}{v\mu^{N-2}}Q_v e^v - Q_\mu e^\mu - \left(\frac{1}{v\mu^{N-2}} - 1\right)y_0\right]$$

$$(14)$$

N is a positive.

According to Eq (1), the QBER of the signal and one decoy states are given by

$$E_\mu Q_\mu e^\mu = e_0 y_0 + \mu e_1 y_1 + \sum_{i=2}^{\infty} e_i y_i \frac{\mu^i}{i!}$$
$$E_v Q_v e^v = e_0 y_0 + e_1 v y_1 + \sum_{i=2}^{\infty} e_i y_i \frac{v^i}{i!}$$

$$(15)$$

By using Eq (15), $0 \leq v < \overset{\cdot}{\mu} \leq 1$, and we multiply a parameter z to inequality which is $0 \leq z \leq 1$ we get

$$\sum_{i=2}^{\infty} e_i y_i \frac{\mu^i}{i!} \geq \sum_{i=2}^{\infty} e_i y_i \frac{v^i}{i!} \geq z\sum_{i=2}^{\infty} e_i y_i \frac{v^i}{i!}$$

$$(16)$$

Then,

$$E_\mu Q_\mu e^\mu - e_0 y_0 - \mu e_1 y_1 \geq z\left(E_v Q_v e^v - e_0 y_0 - v e_1 y_1\right)$$

$$(17)$$

By solving inequality (17), the upper bound of e_1 is

$$e_1 \leq e_1^{U,v} = \frac{1}{(\mu - zv)y_1^{L,v}}\left[E_\mu Q_\mu e^\mu - zE_v Q_v e^v - (1-z)e_0 y_0\right]$$

$$(18)$$

According to selected values of z we can deduce different upper bounds for e_1. For $z = 0$:

$$e_1^U = \frac{1}{\mu y_1^{L,v}}\left(E_\mu Q_\mu e^\mu - e_0 y_0\right).$$

$$(19)$$

For $z = 1$:

$$e_1^{U,v} = \frac{1}{(\mu - v)y_1^{L,v}}\left(E_\mu Q_\mu e^\mu - E_v Q_v e^v\right).$$

$$(20)$$

For $z = \mu$:

$$e_1^{U,v} = \frac{1}{\mu(1-v)y_1^{L,v}}\left(E_\mu Q_\mu e^\mu - \mu E_v Q_v e^v - (1-\mu)e_0 y_0\right).$$

$$(21)$$

For $z = v$:

$$e_1^{U,v} = \frac{1}{(\mu - v^2)y_1^{L,v}}\left(E_\mu Q_\mu e^\mu - vE_v Q_v e^v - (1-v)e_0 y_0\right).$$

$$(22)$$

For $z = v\mu$:

$$e_1^{U,v} = \frac{1}{\mu(1-v^2)y_1^{L,v}}\left(E_\mu Q_\mu e^\mu - \mu v E_v Q_v e^v - (1-\mu v)e_0 y_0\right).$$

$$(23)$$

Case B1 of One Decoy State Protocol for SARG04

In this protocol, we should estimate the lower bounds of y_2 and the upper bounds of e_2 in order to get the lower bound of key generation rate for SARG04. Intuitively, only one decoy state is needed for the estimation. Here, we investigate how to use one decoy state to estimate those bounds.

Suppose that Alice randomly changes the intensity of her pump light among 2 values (one decoy states and a signal state) such that the intensity of one mode of the two mode source is randomly changed among v and μ, which satisfy inequalities $0 \leq v < \mu \leq 1$,. Where, v is the mean photon number of the decoy state and μ is the expected photon number of the signal state.

According to Eq. (1), the gain of signal and one decoy state are given by:

$$Q_\mu e^\mu = y_0 + \mu y_1 + \frac{\mu^2}{2}y_2 + \sum_{i=3}^{\infty} y_i \frac{\mu^i}{i!}$$
$$Q_v e^v = y_0 + v y_1 + \frac{v^2}{2}y_2 + \sum_{i=3}^{\infty} y_i \frac{v^i}{i!}$$

$$(24)$$

By using Eq (24), $0 \leq v < \mu \leq 1$, and (4) we get

$$\frac{\sum\limits_{i=3}^{\infty} P_i(v) y_i}{\sum\limits_{i=3}^{\infty} P_i(\mu) y_i} \leq \frac{P_3(v)}{P_3(\mu)} \qquad (25)$$

Then,

$$\frac{\sum\limits_{i=3}^{\infty} y_i \frac{v^i}{i!}}{\sum\limits_{i=3}^{\infty} y_i \frac{\mu^i}{i!}} \leq \frac{v^3}{\mu^3} \qquad (26)$$

Multiply both sides by $\mu^3 \sum\limits_{i=3}^{\infty} y_i \frac{\mu^i}{i!}$ we found

$$\mu^3 \sum\limits_{i=3}^{\infty} y_i \frac{v^i}{i!} \leq v^3 \sum\limits_{i=3}^{\infty} y_i \frac{\mu^i}{i!} \qquad (27)$$

Using Eq (2) we found

$$\mu^3 \left(Q_v e^v - y_0 - v y_1 - \frac{v^2}{2} y_2 \right) \leq v^3 \left(Q_\mu e^\mu - y_0 - \mu y_1 - \frac{\mu^2}{2} y_2 \right) \qquad (28)$$

By solving inequality (28), the lower bound of y_2 is given by

$$y_2 \geq y_2^{L,v} = \frac{2}{\left(\mu^3 v^2 - v^3 \mu^2 \right)} \left(\mu^3 Q_v e^v - v^3 Q_\mu e^\mu - (v\mu^3 - v^3\mu) y_1^{L,v} - \left(\mu^3 - v^3 \right) y_0 \right) \qquad (29)$$

According to Eq. (1), then the lower bound of the gain of two photon state is given by

$$Q_2^{L,v} = \frac{\mu^2 e^{-\mu}}{\left(\mu^3 v^2 - v^3 \mu^2 \right)} \left(\mu^3 Q_v e^v - v^3 Q_\mu e^\mu - (v\mu^3 - v^3\mu) y_1^{L,v} - \left(\mu^3 - v^3 \right) y_0 \right) \qquad (30)$$

According to Eq (1), the QBER of the signal and one decoy states are given by

$$E_\mu Q_\mu e^\mu = e_0 y_0 + \mu e_1 y_1 + \frac{\mu^2}{2} e_2 y_2 + \sum\limits_{i=3}^{\infty} e_i y_i \frac{\mu^i}{i!}$$

$$E_v Q_v e^v = e_0 y_0 + v e_1 y_1 + \frac{v^2}{2} e_2 y_2 + \sum\limits_{i=3}^{\infty} e_i y_i \frac{v^i}{i!}$$

$$0 \leq v < \mu \leq 1, \qquad (31)$$

By using Eq (31) we get

$$\sum\limits_{i=3}^{\infty} e_i y_i \frac{\mu^i}{i!} \geq \sum\limits_{i=3}^{\infty} e_i y_i \frac{v^i}{i!} \qquad (32)$$

Then,

$$E_\mu Q_\mu e^\mu - e_0 y_0 - \mu e_1 y_1 - \frac{\mu^2}{2} e_2 y_2 \geq \left(E_v Q_v e^v - e_0 y_0 - v e_1 y_1 - \frac{v^2}{2} e_2 y_2 \right) \qquad (33)$$

By solving inequality (33), the upper bound of e_2 is

$$e_2 \leq e_2^{U,v} = \frac{2}{(\mu^2 - v^2) y_2^{L,v}} \left(E_\mu Q_\mu e^\mu - E_v Q_v e^v - (\mu - v) e_1^{U,v} y_1^{L,v} \right) \qquad (34)$$

After estimating the lower bounds of y_1 and y_2 and the upper bounds of e_1 and e_2 for each decoy state protocol. Then, we can use the following formula to calculate the final key generation rate of our QKD system for both BB84 and SARG04 protocols (Fung, C.-H., Tamaki, K., & Lo, H.-K. 2006):

$$R_{BB84} \geq R_{BB84}^L = q\{-Q_\mu f(E_\mu) H_2(E_\mu) + Q_1^L [1 - H_2(e_1^U)]\} \qquad (35)$$

$$R_{SARG04} \geq R_{SARG04}^L = -Q_\mu f(E_\mu) H_2(E_\mu) + Q_1^L [1 - H_2(e_1^U)] + Q_2^L [1 - H_2(e_2^U)] \qquad (36)$$

where q depends on the implementation (1/2 for the BB84 protocol due to the fact that half of the time Alice and Bob disagree with the bases, and if one uses the efficient BB84 protocol, $q \approx 1$), f(x) is the bi-direction error correction efficiency as a function of error rate, normally $f(x) \geq 1$ with Shannon limit $f(x) = 1$, and $H_2(x)$ is binary Shannon information function having the form $H_2(x) = -x \log2(x) - (1 - x) \log2 (1 - x)$.

THE STATISTICAL FLUCTUATIONS

In real life, we would like to consider a QKD experiment that can be performed within say a few hours or so. This means that our data size is finite. Here, we will see that this type of statistical fluctuations is a rather complex problem. Depending on standard error analysis, we can give the estimation of statistical fluctuations of some parameters such as: the gain and QBER of signal state and the gain and QBER of decoy states which are used in the estimation of the lower bound of fraction of one photon count y_1, two photon counts y_2, upper bound of QBER of one-photon e_1 and upper bound of quantum bit-error rate (QBER) of two-photon e_2. Then, we can estimate the lower bound of key generation rate for both BB84 and SARG04 protocols with the statistical fluctuations. The statistical fluctuations of some parameters are given by:

$$\hat{Q}_{\mu} = Q_{\mu}\left(1 \pm \frac{\sigma}{\sqrt{N_{\mu}Q_{\mu}^2}}\right)$$

$$\hat{E}_{\mu} = E_{\mu}\left(1 \pm \frac{\sigma}{\sqrt{N_{\mu}E_{\mu}^2}}\right)$$

$$\hat{Q}_{v_1} = Q_{v_1}\left(1 \pm \frac{\sigma}{\sqrt{N_{v_1}Q_{v_1}^2}}\right)$$

$$\hat{E}_{v_1} = E_{v_1}\left(1 \pm \frac{\sigma}{\sqrt{N_{v_1}E_{v_1}^2}}\right)$$

$$\hat{Q}_{v_2} = Q_{v_2}\left(1 \pm \frac{\sigma}{\sqrt{N_{v_2}Q_{v_2}^2}}\right)$$

$$\hat{E}_{v_2} = E_{v_2}\left(1 \pm \frac{\sigma}{\sqrt{N_{\mu}E_{v_2}^2}}\right)$$

$$\vdots$$

$$\hat{Q}_{v_n} = Q_{v_n}\left(1 \pm \frac{\sigma}{\sqrt{N_{v_n}Q_{v_n}^2}}\right) \tag{37}$$

$$\hat{E}_{v_n} = E_{v_n}\left(1 \pm \frac{\sigma}{\sqrt{N_{\mu}E_{v_n}^2}}\right)$$

Where, $\hat{Q}_{\mu}, \hat{Q}_{v_1}, \hat{Q}_{v_2}, ..., \hat{Q}_{v_n}$ are gains of $\mu, v_1, v_2, ..., v_n$ respectively with statistical fluctuations. $N_{\mu}, N_{v_1}, N_{v_2}, N_{v_3}, ..., N_{v_n}$ are the numbers of pulses used as signal and decoy states ($\mu, v_1, v_2, ..., v_n$), and σ is standard deviation. Note that the gains of the signal and decoy states tend to decrease exponentially with distance. Therefore, statistical fluctuations tend to become more and more important as the distance of QKD increases. In general, as the distance of QKD increases, large and larger data sizes will be needed for the reliable estimation of Q_1, Q_2, e_1 and e_2 (and hence R_{BB84}^L and R_{SARG04}^L), thus requiring a longer QKD experiment.

The Optimization of the Key Generation Rate for Both BB84 and SARG04

In experiment, it is natural to choose the intensities and percentages of signal state and decoy states which could give out the maximum distance and the optimization of the key generation rate. Denote the number of pulses (sent by Alice) for signal as N_{μ}, and for n- decoy states as $N_{\mu}, N_{v_1}, N_{v_2}, N_{v_3}, ..., N_{v_n}$. Then, the total number of pulses sent by Alice is given by

Box 1.

$$\begin{cases} \dfrac{\partial R_{BB84}^{L,\nu_1,\nu_2,\nu_3,...,\nu_n}}{\partial N_\mu} = \dfrac{\partial R_{BB84}^{L,\nu_1,\nu_2,\nu_3,...,\nu_n}}{\partial N_{\nu_1}} = \dfrac{\partial R_{BB84}^{L,\nu_1,\nu_2,\nu_3,...,\nu_n}}{\partial N_{\nu_2}} = \dfrac{\partial R_{BB84}^{L,\nu_1,\nu_2,\nu_3,...,\nu_n}}{\partial N_{\nu_3}} = ... = \dfrac{\partial R_{BB84}^{L,\nu_1,\nu_2,\nu_3,...,\nu_n}}{\partial N_{\nu_n}} = 0 \\[2ex] \dfrac{\partial R_{BB84}^{L,\nu_1,\nu_2,\nu_3,...,\nu_n}}{\partial \mu} = \dfrac{\partial R_{BB84}^{L,\nu_1,\nu_2,\nu_3,...,\nu_n}}{\partial \nu_1} = \dfrac{\partial R_{BB84}^{L,\nu_1,\nu_2,\nu_3,...,\nu_n}}{\partial \nu_2} = \dfrac{\partial R_{BB84}^{L,\nu_1,\nu_2,\nu_3,...,\nu_n}}{\partial \nu_3} = ... = \dfrac{\partial R_{BB84}^{L,\nu_1,\nu_2,\nu_3,...,\nu_n}}{\partial \nu_n} = 0 \\[2ex] \dfrac{\partial R_{BB84}^{L,\nu_1,\nu_2,\nu_3,...,\nu_n}}{\partial l} = 0 \end{cases} \qquad (39)$$

$$N_T = N_\mu + N_{\nu_1} + N_{\nu_2} + N_{\nu_3} + ... + N_{\nu_n} = const. \qquad (38)$$

To maximize the key generation rate, we need to derive a lower bound of Q_1, Q_2 and an upper bound of e_1, e_2 (as functions of data size $N_\mu, N_{\nu_1}, N_{\nu_2}, N_{\nu_3},..., N_{\nu_n}$ and $\mu, \nu_1, \nu_2, \nu_3, ..., \nu_n$), taking into full account of statistical fluctuations. Then, we substitute those bounds into Eqs. (35,36 to calculate the lower bound of the key generation rate for both BB84 and SARG04 protocols, denoted by $R_{BB84}^{L,\nu_1,\nu_2,\nu_3,...,\nu_n}$ and $R_{SARG04}^{L,\nu_1,\nu_2,\nu_3,...,\nu_n}$. Thus, $R_{BB84}^{L,\nu_1,\nu_2,\nu_3,...,\nu_n}$ and $R_{SARG04}^{L,\nu_1,\nu_2,\nu_3,...,\nu_n}$ are function of $N_\mu, N_{\nu_1}, N_{\nu_2}, N_{\nu_3},..., N_{\nu_n}$, $\mu, \nu_1, \nu_2, \nu_3, ..., \nu_n$, and l and will be maximized when the optimal distribution satisfies: (see Box 1)

And for SARG04: (see Box 2)

Solving Eqs. (37, 39, and 40), we can get values of $N_\mu, N_{\nu_1}, N_{\nu_2}, N_{\nu_3},..., N_{\nu_n}$ and $\mu, \nu_1, \nu_2, \nu_3, ..., \nu_n$ for both BB84 and SARG04 protocols.

THE SIMULATION OF PRACTICAL DECOY QKD SYSTEM: THE SIMULATION OF FIBER-BASED PRACTICAL DECOY QKD SYSTEM

In this section, we discuss and give the simulation of practical decoy state QKD system which is important for setting optimal experimental parameters and choosing the distance to perform certain decoy method protocol. The principle of simulation is that for certain QKD set-up, if the intensities, percentages of signal state and decoy states are known, we could simulate the gains and QBERs of all states. This is the key point in the experiment. More precisely, we evaluate the values of the gain of signal and decoy states ($\hat{Q}_0, \hat{Q}_\mu, \hat{Q}_{\nu_1}$), the overall QBER for signal and decoy states ($\hat{E}_\mu, \hat{E}_{\nu_1}$) and then calculate the lower bound of the single and two photon gains, the upper bound QBER of single and two photon pulses, and then substitute these results into Eqs. (35 and 36 for getting the lower bound of key generation rate for both BB84 and SARG04 protocols.

First, we try to simulate an optical fiber based QKD system using our decoy state method for BB84, the losses in the quantum channel can be derived from the loss coefficient α in dB/km and the length of the fiber l in km. the channel transmittance can be written as $\eta_{AB} = 10^{-\frac{\alpha l}{10}}$, and the overall transmission between Alice and Bob is given by $\eta = \eta_{Bob}\eta_{AB}$, where $\alpha = 0.21 dB/km$ in our set-up is the loss coefficient, η_{Bob} is the transmittance in Bob's side. We choose the detection efficiency of $\eta = 4.5 \times 10^{-2}$, detectors dark count rate of $y_0 = 1.7 \times 10^{-6}$, the probability that a photon hits the erroneous detector ($e_{detector} = 0.033$),

Box 2.

$$\begin{cases} \dfrac{\partial R_{SARG04}^{L,\nu_1,\nu_2,\nu_3,...,\nu_n}}{\partial N_\mu} = \dfrac{\partial R_{SARG04}^{L,\nu_1,\nu_2,\nu_3,...,\nu_n}}{\partial N_{\nu_1}} = \dfrac{\partial R_{SARG04}^{L,\nu_1,\nu_2,\nu_3,...,\nu_n}}{\partial N_{\nu_2}} = \dfrac{\partial R_{SARG04}^{L,\nu_1,\nu_2,\nu_3,...,\nu_n}}{\partial N_{\nu_3}} = ... = \dfrac{\partial R_{SARG04}^{L,\nu_1,\nu_2,\nu_3,...,\nu_n}}{\partial N_{\nu_n}} = 0 \\[3mm] \dfrac{\partial R_{SARG04}^{L,\nu_1,\nu_2,\nu_3,...,\nu_n}}{\partial \mu} = \dfrac{\partial R_{SARG04}^{L,\nu_1,\nu_2,\nu_3,...,\nu_n}}{\partial \nu_1} = \dfrac{\partial R_{SARG04}^{L,\nu_1,\nu_2,\nu_3,...,\nu_n}}{\partial \nu_2} = \dfrac{\partial R_{SARG04}^{L,\nu_1,\nu_2,\nu_3,...,\nu_n}}{\partial \nu_3} = ... = \dfrac{\partial R_{SARG04}^{L,\nu_1,\nu_2,\nu_3,...,\nu_n}}{\partial \nu_n} = 0 \\[3mm] \dfrac{\partial R_{SARG04}^{L,\nu_1,\nu_2,\nu_3,...,\nu_n}}{\partial l} = 0 \end{cases} \quad (40)$$

the wavelength ($\lambda = 1550nm$), the data size is N $= 6 \times 10^9$. These parameters are taken from the GYS experiment (Gobby, C., Yuan, Z., and Shields, A. 2004). We choose the intensities, the percentages of signal state and decoy states which could give out the optimization of key generation rate and the maximum secure distance for the protocols which are proposed. The search for optimal parameters can be obtained by numerical simulation.

Figure 1 illustrates the simulation results of QBER of single photon (e_1) against the secure distance of fiber link for cases ($\mu > v$). The QBER of single photon (e_1) increases by increasing the transmission distance. Note that the previous QBER of single photon (e_1) is higher than the proposed QBER of single photon (e_1) from a distance of around 40 km for both cases. At 140 km, the proposed QBER of single photon (e_1) is around 0.08 and the previous QBER of single photon (e_1) is 0.12. By using the proposed QBER of single photon (e_1) we can increase the transmission distance as seen in Figure 2.

The figure (2) shows the simulation results of the key generation rate against the secure distance of fiber link for one decoy state protocol (with statistical fluctuation) with different values of x when ($\mu > v$). For case ($\mu > v$), it is found that the key generation rate and transmission distance for two cases ($x = \dfrac{v}{\mu^2}$ and $x = \dfrac{v}{\mu^3}$) are higher than the case ($x = 1$).

Case of SARG04

In principle, Alice and Bob can estimate Q_1, Q_2, e_1 and e_2 accurately with the decoy state. Hence, $\mu_{Optimal}$ should maximize the untagged states ratio $\Omega = \dfrac{Q_1}{Q_\mu}$ and $\Omega' = \dfrac{Q_2}{Q_\mu}$. Let us start with a numerical analysis on Eq. (36) directly. For each distance, we determine the optimal μ that maximizes the key generation rate. Now, we would like to do an analytical discussion under some approximations. We take the approximations $y_0 \ll \eta \ll 1$. We have:

$$y_{1,SARG04} \simeq \frac{1}{2}\left(\eta\left(e_{det} + 0.5\right) + y_0\right),$$
$$Q_{1,SARG04} \simeq y_1 \mu e^{-\mu},$$
$$e_{1,SARG04} \simeq \frac{1}{2}\left(\eta e_{det} + 0.5 y_0\right) / y_1,$$
$$y_2 \simeq \frac{1}{2}\left(2\eta\left(e_{det} + 0.5\right) + y_0\right),$$

$$Q_2 \simeq y_2 \frac{\mu^2}{2} e^{-\mu},$$
$$e_2 \simeq \frac{1}{2}\left(2\eta e_{det} + 0.5 y_0\right) / y_2,$$
$$Q_{\mu,SARG04} = \frac{1}{4} y_0 e^{-\eta\mu} + \left(\frac{e_{det\,ector}}{2} + \frac{1}{4}\right)\left(1 - e^{-\eta\mu}\right),$$
$$E_{\mu,SARG04} = \left[\frac{1}{4} y_0 e^{-\eta\mu} + \frac{e_{det\,ector}}{2}\left(1 - e^{-\eta\mu}\right)\right] / Q_{\mu,SARG04}.$$

$$(41)$$

Figure 1. The simulation results of QBER of single photon (e_γ) against the secure distance of fiber link when ($\mu > v$)

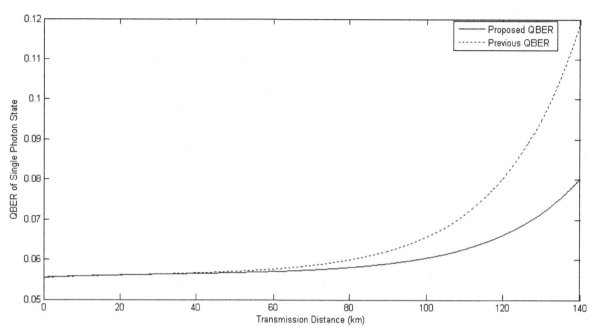

Figure 2. The simulation results of the key generation rate against the secure distance of fiber link for different values of x when ($\mu > v$)

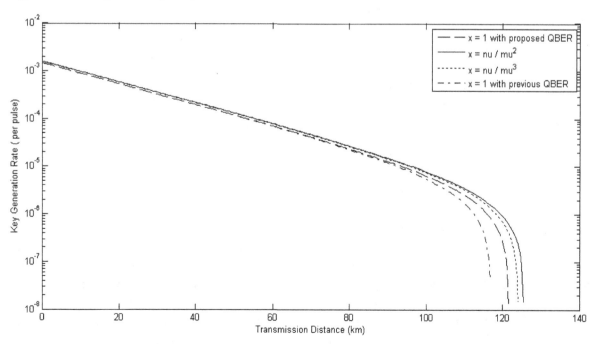

By substituting these formula into Eq. (36) the key generation rate for SARG04 with both single and two photon contributions is given by:

$$R^L_{SARG04} = -Q_\mu f(E_\mu) H_2(E_\mu) + Q_1^L[1 - H_2(e_1^U)] + Q_2^L[1 - H_2(e_2^U)]$$

(42)

The optimum choice of μ which maximize the lower bound of key generation rate R^L_{SARG04}, we have solved the following equation:

$$\frac{\partial R^L_{SARG04}}{\partial \mu} = 0.$$

(43)

By using the data which is taken from an experiment (Gobby, C., Yuan, Z., & Shields, A. 2004). We have obtained that $\mu_{Optimal} \approx 0.221$ with only single photon contributions and $\mu_{Optimal} \approx 0.212$ with both single and two photon contributions. We have also confirmed the optimum choice of μ using simulation as seen in Figure 3. By increasing the distance we found that the optimal mean photon number is constant until we reach the maximal secure distance (approximately zero key generation rate).

Second, we try to simulate an optical fiber based QKD system using our decoy state method for SARG04, the losses in the quantum channel can be derived from the loss coefficient α in dB/km and the length of the fiber l in km. the channel transmittance can be written as $\eta_{AB} = 10^{-\frac{\alpha l}{10}}$, and the overall transmission between Alice and Bob is given by $\eta = \eta_{Bob}\eta_{AB}$, where $\alpha = 0.21 dB/km$ in our set-up is the loss coefficient, η_{Bob} is the transmittance in Bob's side. We choose the detection efficiency of $\eta = 4.5 \times 10^{-2}$, detectors dark count rate of $y_0 = 1.7 \times 10^{-6}$, the probability that a photon hits the erroneous detector ($e_{detector} = 0.033$), the wavelength ($\lambda = 1550nm$), the data size is $N = 6 \times 10^9$. These parameters are taken from the GYS experiment (Gobby, C., Yuan, Z., and Shields, A. 2004).

Figure 4 illustrates the simulation results of the key generation rate against the distance of fiber link for different decoy state protocols. Curve (a) is for both single and two photons contributions (with infinite number of decoy states) for SARG04. Curve (b) is for only single photon contributions (with infinite number of decoy states) for SARG04. Curve (c) shows one decoy state when ($\mu > v$) with statistical fluctuation. The maximal secure distances of the four curves are 97 km, 93 km, and 71 km.

4.2 Free space simulation: Next, we draw the attention to simulate a free space QKD system using our decoy state method for both SARG04 and BB84. We assume that conventional telescope architectures, like the Cassegrain type, are used both in the transmitting and receiving sides. They are reflective telescopes, in which the secondary mirror produces a central obscuration. Moreover, their finite dimensions and the distance between them are responsible of the beam diffraction. The attenuation due to beam diffraction and obscuration can be expressed as

$$\eta_{diff} = \eta_{diff_t}\eta_{diff_r},$$

$$\eta_{diff_t} = \exp\left[-\frac{2\left(D_{M2_t}\right)^2}{w^2}\right] - \exp\left[-\frac{2\left(D_{M1_t}\right)^2}{w^2}\right],$$

$$\eta_{diff_r} = \exp\left[-\frac{2\left(D_{M2_r}\right)^2}{w^2}\right] - \exp\left[-\frac{2\left(D_{M1_r}\right)^2}{w^2}\right],$$

$$w \approx \frac{\lambda L}{\pi w_0}$$

(44)

where the subscript t refers to the transmit telescope and r to the receive one. λ is the wavelength, and D_{M1} and D_{M2} are the radius of the primary and secondary mirrors, respectively. w is the waist radius of the Gaussian beam and L is the distance between the telescopes.

Figure 3. The simulation results of the key generation rate against the signal mean photon number (μ) for SARG04 with only single photon and with both single + two photon contributions. (a) For both single and two photons contributions. (b) For only single photon contributions.

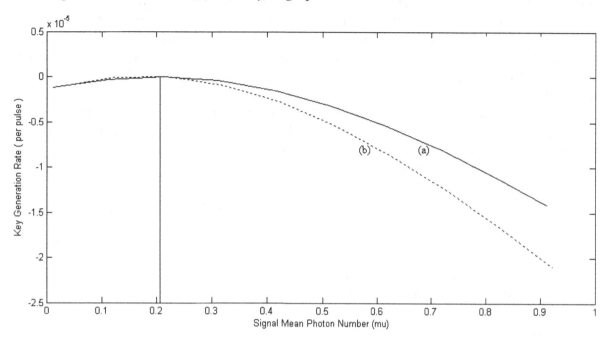

Figure 4. The simulation results of the key generation rate against the distance of fiber link for different decoy state protocols. (a) For both single and two photons contributions. (b) For only single photon contributions. (c) One decoy state when (μ > v).

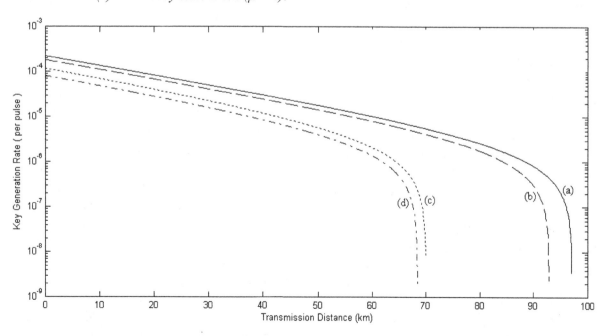

Since the atmospheric attenuation (η_{atm}) is produced by three phenomena: scattering, absorption and turbulence, it can be expressed as $\eta_{atm} = \eta_{scatt}\eta_{abs}\eta_{turb}$. The light is absorbed and scattered by the gas molecules and the aerosols when it passes through the atmosphere. However, the most relevant contribution to the atmospheric attenuation is caused by the turbulence, which is due to thermal fluctuations that produce refractive index variations. The turbulence depends basically on the atmospheric conditions and the position of the ground station. Finally, the total channel attenuation can be written as

$$\eta = \eta_{diff}\eta_{atm}\eta_{det} \tag{45}$$

The assumed link parameters are the wavelength $\lambda = 650nm$ corresponds to an absorption window and the 0.65 efficiency peak of the chosen detector (an SPCM-AQR-15 commercial silicon avalanche photodiode detector) with 1.7×10^{-6} counts/pulse dark counts. The satellite telescopes radius of the primary and secondary mirrors are 15 cm and 1cm, respectively. The ground telescopes radius of the primary and secondary mirrors are 50 cm and 5cm, respectively. The values of telescopes radii have been obtained from the SILEX Experiment and the Tenerife's telescope. The uplink attenuation due to turbulence has been computed considering the Tenerife's telescope (⊔3km above sea level) for two conditions: 1 hour before sunset ($\eta_{turb} = 5dB$) and a typical clear summer day ($\eta_{turb} = 11dB$). The turbulence effect on the downlink is negligible. The scattering attenuation is evaluated using a model of Clear Standard Atmosphere, which results in $\eta_{scatt} = 1dB$.

By simulating the different scenarios, we found the curves with similar shapes. They illustrate the simulation results of the key generation rate against the transmission distance for both BB84 and SARG04 protocols as shown in Figure 5, Figure 6, Figure 7, and Figure 8. The distances in the downlink are significantly larger compared

to the uplink thanks to the lack of turbulence attenuation. In fact, medium earth orbit (MEO) satellite downlink communication using our estimations is possible. This increase in distance is not achieved in the inter-satellite link due to the reduced telescope dimensions. The most relevant parameters that influence the critical distance are the turbulence attenuation and the telescopes dimensions. Therefore, bidirectional ground-to-low earth orbit (LEO) satellite communication is possible with our estimations.

EXPERIMENTAL SET-UP

Before experiment, we have performed the numerical simulation which is important for setting optimal experimental parameters and choosing the distance to perform certain decoy state protocol. Then, we can perform the experiment and observe the values of $\hat{Q}_0, \hat{Q}_\mu, \hat{Q}_{\nu_1}$ and $\hat{E}_\mu, \hat{E}_{\nu_1}$ (these parameters with statistical fluctuations) and then deduce the optimization of the lower bound of fraction of single-photon and two photon counts and upper bound QBER of single-photon and two photon pulses. Existing commercial QKD systems are bi-directional. To show conceptually how simple it is to apply the decoy state idea to a commercial QKD system, we chose ID-3000 commercial Quantum Key Distribution system manufactured by id Quantique. The id 3000 Clavis system consists of two stations controlled by one or two external computers. A comprehensive software suite implements automated hardware operation and complete key distillation. Two quantum cryptography protocols are implemented (BB84 and SARG04 protocols). The exchanged keys can be used in an encrypted file transfer application, which allows secure communications between two stations.

The prototype of this QKD system is described in (Gobby, C., Yuan, Z., and Shields, A. 2004). Here we describe it briefly: This QKD system

Figure 5. A satellite-ground downlink. The key generation rate against the transmission distance link (km). (a) The asymptotic decoy state method (with infinite number of decoy states) for BB84. (b) The key generation rate of one decoy state protocol with the statistical fluctuations (BB84) when $x = \dfrac{v}{\mu^2}$. (c) The key generation rate of one decoy state protocol with the statistical fluctuations (BB84) when $x = \dfrac{v}{\mu^3}$. (d) The key generation rate of one decoy state protocol with the statistical fluctuations (BB84) when $x = 1$. (e) The asymptotic decoy state method (with infinite number of decoy states) for both single and two photons contributions (SARG04).

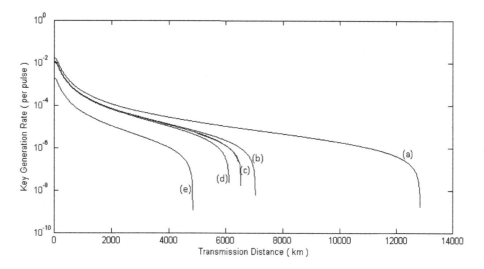

is called p and p auto-compensating set- up, where the key is encoded in the phase between two pulses traveling from Bob to Alice and back (see Figure 1). A strong laser pulse (at 1550 nm) emitted at Bob is separated at a first 50/50 beam splitter (BS), after having traveled through a short arm and a long arm, including a phase modulator (PMb) and a 50 ns delay line (DL), respectively. All fibers and optical elements at Bob are polarization maintaining. The linear polarization is turned by 90 degree in the short arm, therefore the two pulses exit Bob's step-up by the same port of the PBS. The pulses travel down to Alice, are reflected on a Fraday mirror, attenuated and come back orthogonally polarized. In turn, both pulses now take the other path at Bob and arrive at the same time at BS where they interfere. Then, they are detected either in D1, or after passing through the circulator (C_1) in D2. Since the two pulses take

the same path, inside Bob in reversed other, this interferometer is auto-compensated.

For implementation of one decoy state protocol, we modulate the pulses amplitude by these levels: μ, v. In our implementations, the attenuation is done by placing a VOA (variable optical attenuator) in Alice's side.

Figure 9 illustrates the schematic of the optical and electric layouts in our system. The commercial QKD system by id Quantique consists of Bob and "Jr. Alice". In our decoy state experiment, the actual (sender's) system is called "Alice". It consists of "Jr. Alice" and four new optical and electronics components added by us. More concretely, for our decoy state protocol, we place the Intensity Modulator IM right in front of Jr. Alice. Its "idle state" is set to maximum transmittance. When the frame comes from Bob, the IM is in the idle state. After the first pulse reaches coupler C2,

Figure 6. An inter-satellite link. The key generation rate against the transmission distance link (km). (a) The asymptotic decoy state method (with infinite number of decoy states) for BB84. (b) The key generation rate of one decoy state protocol with the statistical fluctuations (BB84) when $x = \dfrac{v}{\mu^2}$. (c) The key generation rate of one decoy state protocol with the statistical fluctuations (BB84) when $x = \dfrac{v}{\mu^3}$. (d) The key generation rate of one decoy state protocol with the statistical fluctuations (BB84) when $x = 1$.

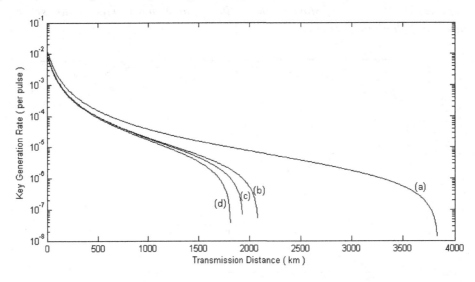

it will be detected by the classical detector and a synchronization signal will be output to trigger the Decoy Generator. The Decoy Generator (DG in Figure 9), being triggered, will hold a delay time td before outputting NP modulation voltages driving the Decoy IM to attenuate the intensity of each the NP signals to be either that of signal state or decoy state dynamically, according to the Decoy Profile. The Decoy Profile is generated before the experiment and loaded from computer to the Decoy Generator as an "Arbitary Waveform". For preparing the Decoy Profile, we generate a sequence of integers $\{1 \le n_i \le 100\}$ which is equal to the pulses number of each frame. Depending on the optimum pulses distribution, some of the i positions will be assigned as signal state and the rest will be assigned as decoy state. In our experiment, a frame of NP pulses (NP = 624) is generated from Bob and sent to Alice. Within a frame, the time interval between signals is 200ns.

The next frame will not be generated until the whole frame has returned to Bob. The long delay line inside Jr. Alice promises that the incoming signal and returning signal will not overlap in the channel between Bob and Jr. Alice so as to avoid Rayleigh Scattering.

RESULTS AND DISCUSSION

The numerical simulation has been performed to find out the optimal parameters. For BB84 with one decoy state and vacuum + one decoy state protocols, we set $\mu = 0.48$ and $v = 0.13$. The numbers of pulses used for one decoy state protocol as signal state, and decoy state are $N_\mu = 0.67N$, and $N_v = 0.33N$ respectively. For SARG04 with one decoy state protocol, we set $\mu = 0.22$ and $v = 0.14$. The numbers of pulses used for one decoy state protocol as signal state, and decoy state are

Figure 7. A ground-satellite uplink 1 hour before sunset (η_{turb} = 5dB). The key generation rate against the transmission distance link (km). (a) The asymptotic decoy state method (with infinite number of decoy states) for BB84. (b) The key generation rate of one decoy state protocol with the statistical fluctuations (BB84) when $x = \dfrac{v}{\mu^2}$. (c) The key generation rate of one decoy state protocol with the statistical fluctuations (BB84) when $x = \dfrac{v}{\mu^3}$. (d) The key generation rate of one decoy state protocol with the statistical fluctuations (BB84) when $x = 1$.

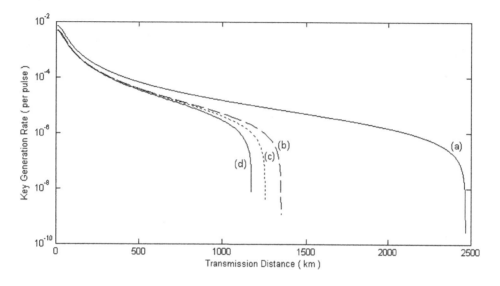

$N_\mu = 0.65N$, and $N_v = 0.35N$ respectively. Where $N = 100 \times 10^6$ is the total number of pulses sent by Alice in this experiment. After the transmission of all the N signals, Alice broadcasted to Bob the distribution of decoy states as well as basis information. Bob then announced which signals he had actually received in correct basis. We assume Alice and Bob announced the measurement outcomes of all decoy states as well as a subset of the signal states.

The Experimental Results

Table 1 and Table 2 are the results of experiment. With the experiment results, and using the above equations, we can get $Q_1^L, e_1^U, Q_2^L, e_2^U, R_{BB84}^L$ and R_{SARG04}^L.

Alice and Bob have to derive a lower bound on the key generation rate, R^L for BB84 and SARG04 by applying the theory of one decoy state to their experimental data. The transmittance/gain of the decoy state Q_v and its error rate E_v could also be acquired directly from experiments. The experimental results are shown in Table 3 and Table 4. Note that the gain of vacuum state is indeed very close to the dark count rate, therefore the vacuum state in our experiment is quite "vacuum". By taking statistical fluctuations into account, we could estimate $Q_1^L, e_1^U, Q_2^L, e_2^U, R_{BB84}^L$ and R_{SARG04}^L by plugging these experimental results into their Equations. In our analysis of experimental data, we estimated Q_1^L, e_1^U, Q_2^L, and e_2^U very conservatively as within 10 standard deviations (i.e., $u_a = 10$).

Tables (1-4) show the experimental results. The experimental results are in excellent agreement with simulation results. The results show that the key generation rate decreases by increas-

Figure 8. A ground-satellite uplink during a typical clear summer day (η_{turb} = 11dB). The key generation rate against the transmission distance link (km). (a) The asymptotic decoy state method (with infinite number of decoy states) for BB84. (b) The key generation rate of one decoy state protocol with the statistical fluctuations (BB84) when $x = \dfrac{v}{\mu^2}$. (c) The key generation rate of one decoy state protocol with the statistical fluctuations (BB84) when $x = \dfrac{v}{\mu^3}$. (d) The key generation rate of one decoy state protocol with the statistical fluctuations (BB84) when $x = 1$.

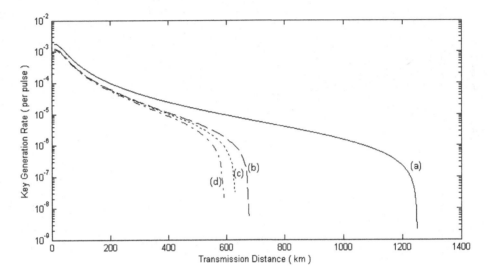

Figure 9. Schematic of the experimental set-up in our system. Inside Bob/Jr. Alice: components in Bob/ Alice's package of ID-3000 QKD system. Our modifications: IM: Intensity Modulator; DG: Decoy Generator. Components of original ID-3000 QKD system: LD: laser diode; APD: avalanche photon diode; Ci: fiber coupler; Φ_i: phase modulator; PBS: polarization beam splitter; PD: classical photo detector; FM: faraday mirror. Solid line: SMF28 single mode optical fiber; dashed line: electric signal.

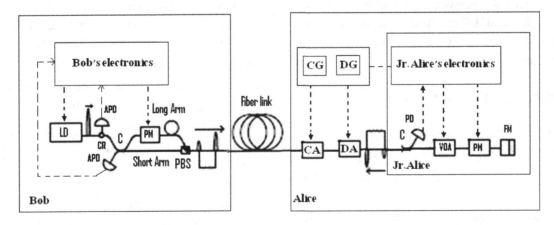

Table 1. The experimental results of one decoy state protocol for BB84. The length of fiber, gains of μ laser pulse Q_μ, QBER of key generated from μ laser pulse E_μ, gains of v laser pulse Q_v and QBER of key generated from v laser pulse E_v. These values are all measured directly from experiment.

Length (km)	Q_μ(BB84)	Q_v(BB84)	E_μ(BB84)	E_v(BB84)
10	0.009	0.0025	0.0119	0.0171
30	0.0035	9.65 E-04	0.0151	0.0282
60	8.40 E-04	2.54 E-04	0.0309	0.0791

Table 2. The experimental results of one decoy state protocol for SARG04. The length of fiber, gains of μ laser pulse Q_μ, QBER of key generated from μ laser pulse E_μ, gains of v laser pulse Q_v and QBER of key generated from v laser pulse E_v. These values are all measured directly from experiment.

Length (km)	Q_μ(BB84)	Q_v(BB84)	E_μ(BB84)	E_v(BB84)
10	0.0011	7.20 E-04	0.0689	0.0728

Table 3. The length of fiber, gain of single photon laser pulse Q_1^L, QBER of key generated from single laser photon pulse e_1^U, rate of generating secure key R_{BB84}^L. These values are all calculated through the above equations with parameters from Table 1. These are parameters of one decoy state protocol.

Length (km)	Q_1^L(BB84)	e_1^U(BB84)	R_{BB84}^L
10	0.0051	0.0212	0.0015
30	0.0019	0.028	4.58 E-04
60	3.90 E-04	0.0664	2.16 E-05

Table 4. The length of fiber, gain of single and two photons laser pulse Q_1^L, Q_2^L, QBER of key generated from single and two photon laser pulse e_1^U, e_2^U rate of generating secure key R_{SARG04}^L. These values are all calculated through above equations with parameters from Table 2.

Length (km)	Q_1^L(SARG04)	e_1^U(SARG04)	Q_2^L(SARG04)	e_2^U(SARG04)	R_{SARG04}^L
10	8.12 E-04	0.1163	2.80 E-04	0.1464	7.94 E-06

ing the transmission distance. Comparing these results, it can be seen that the fiber based QKD system using decoy method for BB84 is able to achieve both a higher secret key rate and greater secure distance than SARG04. This lead to say that the two-photon part has a small contribution to the key generation rates at all distances. By using decoy state method, higher key generation rate and longer secure distance can be achieved.

FUTURE RESEARCH DIRECTIONS

Further improvements, both in key rate and secure transmission distance, are required for some applications. Another crucial point is that, in real life, one needs to consider some extra disturbances (e.g., quantum signals may share the channel with regular classical signals). The final goal is to achieve a customer friendly QKD system that can be easily integrated with the Internet. Statistical fluctuations need to be considered in QKD with a finite key length. There is some work on this topic recently (e.g., by Renner) One interesting topic is to apply Koashi's complementary idea to finite key QKD and compare it with prior results. To achieve a higher QKD key rate, one can consider other QKD protocols. Continuous variable QKD is proposed to achieve a higher key rate in the short and medium transmission distance. One open question is the security of continuous variable QKD. This is an appealing topic in the field. Modeling and simulations for continuous variable QKD are also interesting. To achieve an intercontinental transmission distance, ground-satellite QKD is a promising proposal. One interesting project is to test the feasibility of ground-satellite QKD. In Chapter, we have preliminarily studied the feasibility of ground-satellite QKD using the proposed decoy state method. A study of the disturbance of atmosphere is needed to develop a more realistic model for the ground-satellite channel. By modeling and simulating, one can investigate the requirement for QKD components. For example, what efficiency and noise level of single photon detectors are required and how large the telescope is needed. Meanwhile, it is interesting to explore good QKD schemes for ground-satellite QKD.

CONCLUSION

One of the major problems in a practical QKD system is that a single photon source is difficult to obtain with current technology. In 2003, Hwang came with a simple solution which is called the decoy state method. Such a simple solution is based on better theory, rather than better experiments. The decoy state method allows us to achieve unconditional security based on quantum mechanics and to improve dramatically the performance of QKD systems.

We have presented a decoy state method which can estimate parameters of one decoy state protocol for both BB84 and SARG04. It can also give us different lower bounds of the fraction of single-photon and two-photon counts and upper bounds of single-photon and two-photon QBER for each decoy state protocol. Due to finite data size in real-life experiments, the issue of statistical fluctuations has been discussed. We provide a rough estimation on the effects of statistical fluctuations in practical implementations. The optimum pulses distribution of data, mean photon number of signal and decoy states, the maximum distance and the optimization of the key generation rate have been performed by numerical simula-

tion. Our results show that the fiber based QKD and free space QKD systems using the proposed method for BB84 are able to achieve both a higher secret key rate and greater secure distance than that of BB84. Hence, the two-photon part has a small contribution to the key generation rates at all distances. Also, our results show that bidirectional ground to satellite and inter-satellite communications are possible using our protocol.

The practical one decoy state QKD system using commercial QKD system has been implemented over different transmission distance of standard telecom fiber using ID-3000 commercial QKD system. The experimental results are in excellent agreement with simulation results. For both the experimental and simulation results, we have found that fiber based QKD system using the presented method for BB84 is able to achieve both a higher secret key rate and greater secure distance than BB84. This further lead to say that the two-photon part has a small contribution to the key generation rates at all distances.

REFERENCES

Bennett, C. H. (1992). Quantum cryptography using any two nonorthogonal states. *Physical Review Letters*, *68*(21), 3121–3124. doi:10.1103/PhysRevLett.68.3121

Bennett, C. H., Bessette, F., Brassard, G., Salvail, L., & Smolin, J. (1992). Experimental quantum cryptography. *Journal of Cryptology*, *5*(1), 3–28. doi:10.1007/BF00191318

Bennett, C. H., & Brassard, G. (1984). Quantum cryptography: Public key distribution and coin tossing. *Proceedings of IEEE International Conference on Computers, Systems, and Signal Processing, Bangalore* (p. 175). New York, NY: IEEE.

Bennett, C. H., & Brassard, G. (1989). The dawn of a new era for quantum cryptography: The experimental prototype is working. *SIGACT News, 20*(4), 78. doi:10.1145/74074.74087

Bennett, C. H., Brassard, G., Breidbart, S., & Wiesner, S. (1982). *Quantum cryptography or unforgettable subway tokens. Advances in Cryptography: Proceeding of Crypto '82* (pp. 267–275). New York, NY: Plenum.

Bennett, C. H., Brassard, G., Crépeau, C., & Maurer, U. M. (1995). Generalized privacy amplification. *IEEE Transactions on Information Theory, 41*(6), 1915. doi:10.1109/18.476316

Bennett, C. H., Brassard, G., & Robert, J.-M. (1988). Privacy amplification by public discussion. *Society for Industrial and Applied Mathematics Journal on Computing, 17*(2), 210–229.

Bennett, C. H., Mor, T., & Smolin, J. A. (1996). The parity bit in quantum cryptography. *Physical Review A., 54*(4), 2675–2684. doi:10.1103/PhysRevA.54.2675

Fung, C.-H., Tamaki, K., & Lo, H.-K. (2006). Performance of two quantum key distribution protocols. *Physical Review A., 73*(1), 012337. doi:10.1103/PhysRevA.73.012337

Gobby, C., Yuan, Z., & Shields, A. (2004). Quantum key distribution over 122 km of standard telecom fiber. *Physical Review Letters, 84*(19), 3762–3764.

Gottesman, D., Lo, H.-K., Lütkenhaus, N., & Preskill, J. (2004). Security of quantum key distribution with imperfect devices. *Quantum Information and Computation, 4*(5), 325–360.

Hwang, W.-Y. (2003). Quantum key distribution with high loss: Toward global secure communication. *Physical Review Letters, 91*(5), 057901. doi:10.1103/PhysRevLett.91.057901

Inamori, H., Lutkenhaus, N., & Mayers, D. (2001). *Unconditional security of practical quantum key distribution.*

Keller, M., Held, K., Eyert, V., Vollhardt, D., & Anisimov, V. I. (2004). Continuous generation of single photons with controlled waveform in an ion-trap cavity system. *Nature, 431*(7012), 1075–1078. doi:10.1038/nature02961

Koashi, M. (2004). Unconditional security of coherent-state quantum key distribution with a strong phase-reference pulse. *Physical Review Letters, 93*(12), 120501. doi:10.1103/PhysRevLett.93.120501

Ma, X., Fung, C.-H. F., Dupuis, F., Chen, K., Tamaki, K., & Lo, H.-K. (2006). Decoy-state quantum key distribution with two-way classical post-processing. *Physical Review A., 74*(3), 032330. doi:10.1103/PhysRevA.74.032330

Ma, X., Qi, B., Zhao, Y., & Lo, H.-K. (2005). Practical decoy state for quantum key distribution. *Physical Review A., 72*(1), 012326. doi:10.1103/PhysRevA.72.012326

Mayers, D. (2001). Unconditional security in quantum cryptography. *Journal of Association for Computing Machinery, 48*(3), 351–406.

Wiesner, S. (1983). Conjugate coding. *SIGACT News, 15*(1), 78-88.

ADDITIONAL READING

Koashi, M. (2004). Unconditional security of coherent-state quantum key distribution with a strong phase-reference pulse. *Physical Review Letters, 93*(12), 120501. doi:10.1103/PhysRevLett.93.120501

Koashi, M. (2006). Efficient quantum key distribution with practical sources and detectors. *arXiv e-printsquant–ph*/0609180.

Kraus, B., Branciard, C., & Renner, R. (2007). Security of quantum-key-distribution protocols using two-way classical communication or weak coherent pulses. *Physical Review A.*, *75*(1), 012316. doi:10.1103/PhysRevA.75.012316

Kraus, B., Gisin, N., & Renner, R. (2005). Lower and upper bounds on the secret-key rate for quantum key distribution protocols using one-way classical communication. *Physical Review Letters*, *95*(8), 080501. doi:10.1103/PhysRevLett.95.080501

Kurtsiefer, C., Zarda, P., Halder, M., & Gorman, P. M. (2002). Long distance free space quantum cryptography. *Proceedings of the Society for Photo-Instrumentation Engineers*, *4917*, 25–31.

Kurtsiefer, C., Zarda, P., Mayer, S., & Weinfurter, H. (2001). The breakdown flash of silicon avalanche photodiodes backdoor for eavesdropper attacks? *Journal of Modern Optics*, *48*(13), 2039–2047. doi:10.1080/09500340108240905

Lo, H.-K. (2003). Method for decoupling error correction from privacy amplification. *New Journal of Physics 5* (1), 36.1–36.24.

Lo, H.-K. (2005). Higher-security thresholds for quantum key distribution by improved analysis of dark counts. *Physical Review A.*, *72*(3), 032321. doi:10.1103/PhysRevA.72.032321

Lo, H.-K., & Chau, H. F. (1999). Unconditional security of quantum key distribution over arbitrarily long distances. *Science*, *283*(5410), 2050–2056. doi:10.1126/science.283.5410.2050

Lo, H.-K., Chau, H. F., & Ardehali, M. (2005). Efficient quantum key distribution scheme and a proof of its unconditional security. *Journal of Cryptology*, *18*(2), 133–165. doi:10.1007/s00145-004-0142-y

Lo, H.-K., Ma, X., & Chen, K. (2005). Decoy state quantum key distribution. *Physical Review Letters*, *94*(23), 230504. doi:10.1103/PhysRevLett.94.230504

Lütkenhaus, N. (1999). Estimates for practical quantum cryptography. *Physical Review A.*, *59*(5), 3301–3319. doi:10.1103/PhysRevA.59.3301

Lütkenhaus, N. (2000). Security against individual attacks for realistic quantum key distribution. *Physical Review A.*, *61*(5), 052304. doi:10.1103/PhysRevA.61.052304

L˝utkenhaus, N., & Jahma, M. (2002). Quantum key distribution with realistic states: photon number statistics in the photon number splitting attack. *New Journal of Physics 4* (1), 44.1-44.9

Ma, X. (2005). Security of quantum key distribution with realistic devices. *arXiv e-printsquant–ph/*0503057.

Ma, X., Fung, C.-H. F., Dupuis, F., Chen, K., Tamaki, K., & Lo, H.-K. (2006). Decoy-state quantum key distribution with two-way classical post-processing. *Physical Review A.*, *74*(3), 032330. doi:10.1103/PhysRevA.74.032330

Ma, X., Qi, B., Zhao, Y., & Lo, H.-K. (2005). Practical decoy state for quantum key distribution. *Physical Review A.*, *72*(1), 012326. doi:10.1103/PhysRevA.72.012326

Makarov, V., Anisimov, A., & Skaar, J. (2006). Effects of detector efficiency mismatch on security of quantum cryptosystems. *Physical Review A.*, *74*(2), 022313. doi:10.1103/PhysRevA.74.022313

Mayers, D. (2001). Unconditional security in quantum cryptography. *Journal of Association for Computing Machinery*, *48*(3), 351–406.

Morgan, G. L., Nordholt, J. E., Peterson, C. G., & Simmons, C. M. (1998). Free-space quantum-key distribution. *Physical Review A.*, *57*(4), 2379. doi:10.1103/PhysRevA.57.2379

Muller, A., Greguet, J., & Gisin, N. (1993). Experimental demonstration of quantum cryptography using polarized photons in optical fibre over more than 1 km. *Europhysics Letters*, *23*(6), 383–388. doi:10.1209/0295-5075/23/6/001

Muller, A., Zbinden, H., & Gisin, N. (1996). Quantum cryptography over 23 km in installed under-lake telecom fibre. *Europhysics Letters*, *33*(5), 335–339. doi:10.1209/epl/i1996-00343-4

Nogues, G., Rauschenbeutel, A., Osnaghi, S., Brune, M., Raimond, J. M., & Haroche, S. (1999). Seeing a single photon without destroying it. *Nature*, *400*(6741), 239–242. doi:10.1038/22275

Pearson, D. (2004). High-speed QKD reconciliation using forward error correction. *In: The 7th International Conference on Quantum Communications, Measurement, and Computing*, 299–302.

Rarity, J. G., Gorman, P. M., & Tapster, P. R. (2000). Free-space quantum cryptography and satellite key uploading. *in IQEC, International Quantum Electronics Conference Proceedings*.

Rarity, J. G., Gorman, P. M., & Tapster, P. R. (2001). Secure key exchange over 1.9 km free-space range using quantum cryptography. *Electronics Letters*, *37*(8), 512–514. doi:10.1049/el:20010334

Rarity, J. G., Tapster, P. R., Gorman, P. M., & Knight, P. (2002). Ground to satellite secure key exchange using quantum cryptography. *New Journal of Physics*, *4*(1), 82. doi:10.1088/1367-2630/4/1/382

Renner, R., Gisin, N., & Kraus, B. (2005). Information-theoretic security proof for quantum-key-distribution protocols. *Physical Review A.*, *72*(1), 012332. doi:10.1103/PhysRevA.72.012332

Scarani, V., Acın, A., Ribordy, G., & Gisin, N. (2004). Quantum cryptography protocols robust against photon number splitting attacks for weak laser pulses implementations. *Physical Review Letters*, *92*(5), 057901. doi:10.1103/PhysRevLett.92.057901

Shannon, C. E. (1949). Communication theory for secrecy systems. *The Bell System Technical Journal*, *28*(4), 656–715.

KEY TERMS AND DEFINITIONS

BB84: The QKD protocol presented by Bennett and Brassard in 1984

DSP: Decoy State Protocol

EDP: Entanglement distillation protocol

EPR pair: A maximally entangled photon pair that originated from the Einstein- Podolsky-Rosen paradox

GLLP: The security proof of QKD with imperfect devices proposed by Gottesman,Lo, L¨utkenhaus, and Preskill

LOCC: Local operations and classical communication; 1-LOCC: local operations and one-way classical communication; 2-LOCC: local operations and two-way classical communication

PNS: Photon Number Splitting

QKD: Quantum Key Distribution

SARG04: The QKD protocol presented by Scarani-Acin-Ribordy-Gisin 2004

Chapter 8
Automated Formal Methods for Security Protocol Engineering

Alfredo Pironti
Politecnico di Torino, Italy

Davide Pozza
Politecnico di Torino, Italy

Riccardo Sisto
Politecnico di Torino, Italy

ABSTRACT

Designing and implementing security protocols are known to be error-prone tasks. Recent research progress in the field of formal methods applied to security protocols has enabled the use of these techniques in practice. The objective of this chapter is to give a circumstantial account of the state-of-the-art reached in this field, showing how formal methods can help in improving quality. Since automation is a key factor for the acceptability of these techniques in the engineering practice, the chapter focuses on automated techniques and illustrates in particular how high-level protocol models in the Dolev-Yao style can be automatically analyzed and how it is possible to automatically enforce formal correspondence between an abstract high-level model and an implementation.

DOI: 10.4018/978-1-60960-851-4.ch008

INTRODUCTION

Security protocols enable distributed interactions to occur securely even over insecure networks. Well known examples are the protocols for secure authentication or key exchange that we use daily. With the growth of connectivity over the Internet, there is an increasing demand for secure distributed ICT systems, which in turn is rapidly widening the spread and scope of security protocols. Web services, grid computing, electronic commerce and SCADA systems for remote control are just few examples of the many emerging distributed applications that need security. In addition to the bare data secrecy and authenticity goals, which characterize the most classical protocols, new different goals such as non-repudiation or secure transactions in electronic commerce systems have recently started to be considered as desirable, with several new protocols being proposed. The role of standards is fundamental in this field, because distributed applications rely on interoperability. However, the variegated needs of applications may sometimes call for proprietary solutions as well, when standards do not (yet) cover needs adequately. So, tasks such as designing and implementing security protocols are becoming less esoteric and more common, either as part of new standards development or as part of new products development.

These tasks are generally quite critical, because of the delicate role security protocols normally play in protecting valuable assets. Furthermore, despite their apparent simplicity, security protocols are very difficult to get right, even when developed and reviewed by experts, because they add the difficulty of taking into account all the possible operations of malicious parties to the ones of concurrent operation in a distributed environment. It is then widely recognized that the rigorous approach of formal methods plays a key role in developing security protocol designs and implementations at the desired quality level.

Although using formal methods is still considered difficult and requires expertise, research on formal methods in general, and on their application to security protocols in particular, has recently made much progress. Therefore, difficulty is progressively mitigated by the greater automation level and user friendliness that can be achieved. This progress is also being acknowledged by development process standards and evaluation standards, such as the Common Criteria for Information Technology Security Evaluation (2009), which prescribe the use of formal methods for attaining the highest assurance level, required for the most critical system components. It can be expected that in the near future the role of these more rigorous practices will further increase, as the demand for critical components increases.

The objective of this chapter is to give a circumstantial account of the state-of-the-art formal techniques that can help in improving the quality of security protocol designs and implementations in practice. The chapter aims to show what can still be done in practice, using the most promising available research results that do not require excessive expertise from users, thus being affordable. The intended focus is then on those techniques that have already been studied in depth and that can offer acceptable user-friendly automated tool support, demonstrated by research prototype tools. The newest theoretical research trends will just be mentioned, in order to show how the research in this field is moving on.

BACKGROUND

A security protocol can be defined as a communication protocol aimed at reaching a goal in a distributed environment even in the presence of hostile agents that have access to the network. Examples of security goals are user authentication (that is, proving a user's identity to another remote user) and secrecy in data exchange (that is, transferring data in such a way that only the intended recipients can read transmitted data).

Like any other communication protocol, a security protocol involves a set of actors, also called principals or agents, each one playing a protocol role and exchanging protocol messages with the other protocol actors. However, differently from normal communication protocols, security protocols are designed in order to reach their goals even in the presence of hostile actors who can eavesdrop and interfere with the communication of honest agents. For example, an attacker agent is normally assumed to be able to intercept and record protocol messages (passive attacker), and even alter, delete, insert, redirect, reorder, and reuse intercepted protocol messages, as well as freshly create and inject new messages (active attacker). The goals of the protocols are normally reached by using cryptography, which is why these protocols are also named cryptographic protocols.

The logic of a cryptographic protocol is often described abstractly and informally without getting into the details of cryptography. This informal description is also called the "Alice and Bob notation", because protocol roles are usually identified by different uppercase letters and are associated to agent identities with evocative names in function of their roles, such as for example (A)lice for the first protocol participant, (B)ob for the second one, (E)ve for an eavesdropper and (M)allory for a malicious active attacker.

For example, the core part of the Needham & Schroeder (1978) public key mutual authentication protocol can be described in Alice and Bob notation as

1: A→B: {A,NA}KBpub
2: B→A: {NA,NB}KApub
3: A→B: {NB}KBpub

This protocol became notorious because of a flaw that was discovered by Lowe (1996) several years after its publication. The protocol aims at guaranteeing each participant about the identity of the other participant and at establishing a pair of shared secrets between them. A protocol description in Alice and Bob notation is a sequence of rules, each one describing a protocol message exchange in the form X→Y: M where X is the sender, Y is the intended recipient and M is the message. For example, the first rule specifies that agent Alice (A) sends to agent Bob (B) message {A,NA}KBpub. This writing stands for an encrypted pair where the components of the pair are Alice's identity A and a freshly generated nonce NA. The pair is encrypted with KBpub, that is Bob's public key. The (unreached) goal is that, after having completed the message exchange, Alice and Bob are certain about each other's identity, and the nonces NA and NB have been shared between each other, but have been kept secret to anyone else.

Another semi-formal notation often used to represent the logic of security protocols is UML sequence diagrams. For example, the Needham & Schroeder (1978) protocol described above can be equivalently represented by the UML

Figure 1. Needham-Schroeder public key protocol

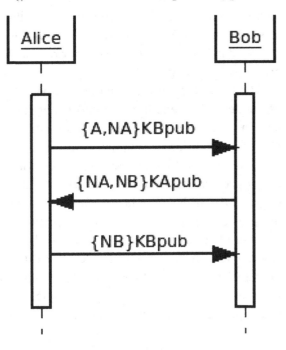

Figure 2. An attack on the Needham-Schroeder public key protocol

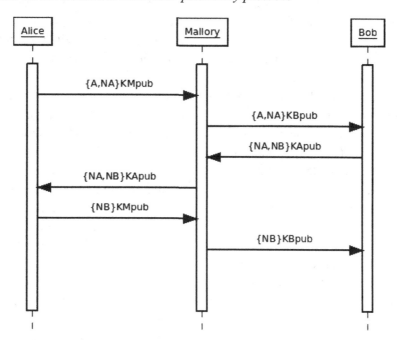

sequence diagram of Figure 1. Each actor has a vertical lifeline that extends from top to bottom, and exchanged messages are represented by arrows, whose caption is the content of the message. Both "Alice and Bob" notation and UML sequence diagrams are effective in representing a typical protocol scenario, while error handling or conditional execution are better represented by more formal and refined languages, such as the ones described in the rest of this chapter.

An attack on a security protocol is a protocol run scenario where the protocol does not reach the intended goal because of the hostile activity of an attacker. For example, if the protocol has been designed to ensure the secrecy of a secret datum D, an attack on the protocol is a protocol run in which an attacker gets the datum D (or partial knowledge on it). An attack is relevant only if it may occur with a non-negligible probability and using realistic resources. For example, the probability that an attacker who does not know a key guesses the value of the key is normally negligible because of the key length and because of its pseudo-random nature. The word "attack"

often implicitly refers to run scenarios that may occur with non-negligible probability and using realistic resources.

Some attacks on security protocols exploit errors in protocol logic and are independent of details such as cryptographic algorithms or message encoding. These attacks can be described in terms of the abstract protocol descriptions shown above. For example, the attack discovered on the Needham-Schroeder protocol (Lowe, 1996) can be represented via the UML sequence diagram of Figure 2. The attack works out when a malicious agent Mallory (M) can convince Alice to exchange a nonce with him, so that he can use the messages from Alice to talk with Bob, while making Bob think that he is talking with Alice. Hence, Mallory is able to obtain Bob's "secret" nonce that was intended for Alice.

Other attacks cannot be described abstractly in this way, because they depend on details or interactions of particular cryptosystems.

Attacks on security protocols can be categorized according to the protocol properties they break (e.g. secrecy, authentication). Moreover, in a more technical way they can be categorized by the categorization of the kinds of weaknesses or flaws they exploit (Gritzalis, Spinellis & Sa, 1997 and Carlsen, 1994). According to the latter, the main classes can be described as follows.

Attacks based on Cryptographic Flaws exploit weaknesses in the cryptographic algorithms, by means of cryptanalysis, in order to break ideal cryptographic properties (e.g. determining the key used to encrypt a message from the analysis of some encrypted messages).

Attacks based on Cryptosystem-Related Flaws exploit protocol flaws that arise from the bad interaction between the protocol logic and specific properties of the chosen cryptographic algorithm. An example can be found in the Three-Pass protocol (Shamir, Rivest & Adleman, 1978) which requires the use of a commutative function (such as the XOR function) to perform encryption. Because of the reversible nature of the XOR function and of the way this function is used to encrypt the messages of the protocol, it is possible for an attacker to decrypt some encrypted data by XORing intercepted encrypted messages of the protocol session. Another example can be found in some implementations of the widely deployed SSH protocol (Ylonen, 1996), where some bits of the encrypted plaintext can be recovered by an attacker, by injecting maliciously crafted packets when encryption is in CBC mode (Albrecht, Paterson & Watson, 2009).

Attacks based on Elementary Flaws exploit protocol weaknesses that are considered elementary in the sense that the protocol completely disregards some kind of protection. For example, the attack described in Burrows, Abadi, & Needham (1990) on the CCITT X.509 protocol (Marschke, 1988) can be classified as an attack of this kind. Here, a message is encrypted and then a signature is applied to the encrypted part. Since the signature itself is not protected in any way, the attacker can simply replace it with the attacker's signature in order to appear as the originator of the message to the sender.

Attacks based on Freshness Flaws (or Replay Attacks) arise when one or more protocol participants cannot distinguish between a freshly generated message and an old one that is being reused. Thus, the attacker can simply replay an old message making the victim believe that it is a newly generated one. An example of a protocol containing this kind of flaw is the Needham & Schroeder (1978) secret key protocol, where the third message of the protocol can be replayed by an attacker, so that an old key (possibly compromised) is reused for the communication.

Guessing Attacks concern protocols that use messages containing predictable information encrypted with weak keys, either because poorly chosen (e.g. obtained by user passwords) or because generated by weak random number generators. These flaws can be exploited by analyzing old sessions of protocol runs in order to gain knowledge on the characteristics and on the internal status of pseudo-random generators. Another way to exploit these vulnerabilities is by performing dictionary-based attacks in order to guess keys, when the key space can be determined a priori (i.e. the most-likely combinations of bits forming the key can be determined). An example of a guessing attack is possible on the Needham & Schroeder (1978) secret key protocol, in addition to the reply attack explained above. The guessing attack can occur because keys are obtained from user-chosen passwords

Attacks based on Internal Action Flaws exploit protocol flaws that occur when an agent is unable to or misses to perform the appropriate actions required to securely process, receive, or send a message. Examples of such actions are: performing some required computation (such as a hash), performing checks aimed at verifying the integrity, freshness or authenticity of a received message, or providing required fields (such as a digest) inside a message. Often, these flaws are due to incomplete or wrong protocol specifications. An example of this flaw can be found in the Three-Pass protocol (Shamir, Rivest & Adleman,

1978) because, in the third step, the check that the received message must be encrypted is missing.

Oracle Attacks happen when an attacker can use protocol participants as "oracles", in order to gain knowledge of some secret data, or in order to induce them to generate some data that the attacker could not generate on his own. Note that such data could be obtained by the attacker by interacting with one or more protocol sessions, even in parallel, while impersonating several agents. It is worth noting that these attacks may be possible because of the simultaneous presence of multiple protocols with unforeseen dependencies. Even if each protocol is safe, it may be that their combination is flawed because it enables some oracle attack. This may happen, for example, when the same keys are used by different protocols. For example, the Three-Pass protocol (Shamir, Rivest & Adleman, 1978 and Carlsen, 1994) is subject to this kind of attack in addition to the attack mentioned above.

Type Flaw Attacks happen when an attacker cheats a protocol agent by sending him a message of a type different than the expected one, and the receiver agent does not detect the type mismatch and uses message data in an unexpected way. An example of this attack is possible on the Otway-Rees protocol (Otway & Rees, 1987), where an attacker can reply parts of the first protocol message so that they are interpreted as a legitimate field of the last protocol message and in this way cheat Alice by inducing her to believe to have exchanged a secret key with Bob while in fact she has not.

It is also possible to have attacks that exploit bugs in protocol implementations rather than bugs on protocols. For example, this occurs when an attacker exploits a divergence between the behavior of the implementation and the behavior prescribed by the protocol.

Attacks can furthermore be divided into two other broad categories: the attacks that can be performed by a passive attacker; and the attacks that require an active attacker. An attack performed by a passive attacker can be carried out without altering message exchange, simply by eavesdropping the exchanged messages. With this respect the Needham-Schroeder attack is an active attack, because the attacker must interact with the protocol agents by placing himself between the two. The most common forms of active attacks are the replay attack and the man in the middle (MITM) attack. In the former, the attacker replays an old message to an honest protocol actor that cannot distinguish between a freshly generated message and the old one. In the latter, the attacker intercepts all the messages exchanged by protocol actors (i.e. the attacker is in the middle of the communication), and relays intercepted messages and/or fabricates and injects new ones. In this way, actors are induced to believe that they are directly talking to each other, while, in the reality, the attacker is successfully impersonating the various protocol actors to the satisfaction of the other actors.

Security protocols normally reach their goals after a few message exchanges. However, despite this apparent simplicity, their logic flaws can be subtle and difficult to discover and to avoid during design. The difficulty comes not only from the bare use of cryptography, which is common to other cryptography applications. The extra complexity of security protocols comes from the unbounded number of different possible scenarios that arise from the uncontrolled behavior of dishonest agents, who are not constrained to behave according to the protocol rules, combined with the possibility to have concurrent protocol sessions with interleaved messages.

Without rigorous protocol models and automated tools for analyzing them it is difficult to consider all the possible attack scenarios of a given protocol. This has been demonstrated by the case of protocols that were designed by hand and discovered to be faulty only years after their publication, as it happened with the Needham-Schroeder authentication protocol. It is particularly significant that the attack on this protocol was discovered with the help of formal modeling and automated analysis (Lowe, 1996).

A rigorous, mathematically-based approach to modeling, analyzing and developing applications is called a formal method. The mathematical basis of formal methods opens the possibility to even prove facts about models. For example, a formal model of a security protocol and its environment can be mathematically proved to fulfill a given property, such as the inability of attackers to learn the protocol secret data.

Of course, the results about protocol models are as significant as the model is. When a proof of correctness is obtained on a very abstract model, where many low-level details are abstracted away, attacks that rely on such low-level aspects cannot be excluded. On a more refined model, where such low-level details are taken into account, a proof of correctness can show those attacks are impossible. Unfortunately, as the complexity of models increases, a fully formal model and a proof of correctness become more difficult to achieve, and in any case a gap remains between formal models on one side and real protocols with real actors implemented in usual programming languages on the other side.

Formal methods can be supported by software tools. For example, tools can be available for searching possible attacks in protocol models or for building correctness proofs about models. When a formal method is supported by automatic tools, it is said to be an automated formal method.

Having automated formal methods is normally considered to be a must for formal method acceptability in production environments, because of the prohibitive level of expertise that is normally needed for using non-automated formal methods. One of the problems with automation is that as the complexity of models increases beyond a very abstract level, all the main questions about protocol correctness become undecidable, which prevents tools from always being able to come out with a proof of correctness automatically.

Traditionally, there have been two different approaches to rigorously model and analyze security protocols. On one hand are those models that use an algebraic view of cryptographic primitives, often referred to as "formal models"; on the other hand are those models that use a computational view of such primitives, generally referred to as "computational models".

The algebraic view of cryptography is based on perfect encryption axioms: (1) The only way to decrypt encrypted data is to know the corresponding key; (2) Encrypted data do not reveal the key that was used to encrypt them; (3) There is sufficient redundancy in encrypted data, so that the decryption algorithm can detect whether a ciphertext was encrypted with the expected key; (4) There is no way to obtain original data from hashed data; (5) Different data are always hashed to different values; (6) Freshly generated data are always different from any existing data and not guessable (with non-negligible probability); (7) A private (resp. public) key does not reveal its public (resp. private) part.

Under these assumptions, cryptography can be modeled as an equational algebraic system, where terms represent data, constructors represent different encryption or data construction mechanisms, and destructors represent the corresponding decryption or data extraction mechanisms. For example, the constructor symEnc(M,k), the destructor symDec(X,k) and the equation symDec(symEnc(M,k),k) = M represent an algebraic system for symmetric encryption. As another example, the constructor H(M) represents hashing. The absence of a corresponding destructor represents non-invertibility of the cryptographic hash function.

Formal models allow simple and efficient reasoning about security protocol properties, because of their high level view on cryptography. However, there are two main drawbacks. One is that some cryptographic functions, mostly relying on bitwise operations, like for example XOR functions, are difficult to be represented in an equational algebraic model, or they could lead to undecidable models. The second one is that, because of the high abstraction level, there are several possible flaws that may be present in the protocol implementation, but that are not caught in the formal model. For example, this happens because the algorithms implementing a particular cryptographic function do not satisfy some of the ideal assumptions made: as an instance, any function generating n bit nonces cannot satisfy assumption (6) after 2^n runs.

Computational models, in contrast, represent data as bit strings and use a probabilistic approach to allow some of the perfect encryption assumptions to be dropped. Assuming a bounded computational power (usually polynomial) for an attacker, the aim is to show that, under some constraints, the probability of an assumption being violated is negligible, that is, it is under an acceptable threshold. Technically, this is achieved by showing that an attacker cannot distinguish between encrypted data and true random data. Computational models can be used to deal with more cryptographic primitives, and to model more low level issues than formal models. However, they require more resources during protocol analysis, and usually the proofs are more difficult to be automated.

Historically, formal and computational models have evolved separately: the former focusing on the usage of basic cryptographic functions, and working at a higher level; the latter considering more implementation details and possible issues. Recent ongoing work starting from the seminal research of Abadi & Rogaway (2002), is trying to reconcile the two views and to relate them.

STATE OF THE ART

Security Protocol Engineering Issues

This subsection briefly accounts, categorizes and discusses the main issues that can lead to get flawed security protocols, starting from their design phase down to the implementation and application deployment phases. As shown below, flaws are constantly discovered, even in the recent past, which advocates for the use of more reliable engineering methodologies for security protocols. The next subsections present the state of the art of such methodologies based on automatic formal methods.

When a new security protocol is being developed, design is the first phase where flaws can be introduced. Regardless of the severity of weaknesses that they can cause, these flaws are in general very critical, because they will apply to all deployed implementations. The use of formal modeling and formal verification is an effective way to mitigate this issue, because it improves the understanding of the protocol and guarantees its correctness, up to the detail level that is captured by the formal model. Although there is evidence that the use of formal methods improves quality of the outcome artifact, the cost-effectiveness of their adoption, especially when used only once in the design phase, is still uncertain (Woodcock, Larsen, Bicarregui & Fitzgerald, 2009). For this reason, best practices and design guidelines that protocol experts have defined after a careful analysis of the most common mistakes made in designing security protocols (e.g. Abadi & Needham, 1996 and Yafen, Wuu, & Ching-Wei, 2004) are another important resource for protocol designers.

Implementing a security protocol is another development phase where flaws can be introduced, due to divergences between the protocol specification and its implementing code. Such divergences are often caused by programming mistakes (e.g. OpenSSL Team, 2009) or by unfortunate interpretations of an ambiguous specification (e.g. Albrecht et al., 2009). Again, formally specifying the security protocol avoids interpretation errors, and in principle enables implementations to be (semi-automatically) derived, thus reducing the probability of introducing mistakes.

Other programming mistakes introduce so-called vulnerabilities. They are security problems that may affect any software that receives data from a public channel, not just security protocols. They derive from unhandled or unforeseen input data that may cause the protocol implementation to crash or to produce nasty effects on the host where the protocol implementation is running. Notable examples are stack overflows that can be exploited in order to run arbitrary code on the host where the software runs. Vulnerabilities do not directly imply a failure of reaching the protocol goals, but they can be exploited for violating other security policies or for compromising the whole host.

Automating Formal Protocol Analysis

When done by hand, formal analysis of security protocol models can be an error prone task, as often the security proofs require a large number of steps that are difficult to track manually.

The final goal of automating such techniques is to give formal evidence (i.e. a mathematical proof) of the fact that a protocol model satisfies or does not satisfy certain security properties under certain assumptions. The mathematics and technicalities of these techniques require specific expertise which may not be part of the background knowledge of security experts. Then, automation and user-friendliness of such techniques and tools are key issues in making them acceptable and useable in practice.

Research in this field has always paid highest attention to these issues. For example, as highlighted by Woodcock et al. (2009), automation in formal methods has recently improved so much that in 2006 the effort of automating the proof of correctness for the Mondex project, a smartcard-based electronic cash system, was just 10% of the effort that would have been required in 1999. In fact, in 1999 the system was proven correct by hand; in 2006 eight independent research groups

were able to get automatic proofs for the same system.

Several different automation techniques have been explored, depending on the form of the input model. In the next subsections, the most common forms used to express security protocols models and properties are introduced, and their related verification techniques are explained.

Logics of Beliefs (BAN Logic)

Logics of beliefs (e.g. Burrows, Abadi, & Needham, 1990) are very high-level models for reasoning on security protocols where perfect cryptography is assumed, and only some logical properties are tracked. Technically, they are modal logic systems designed to represent the beliefs of protocol actors during protocol executions. For example, the formula "P believes X" means that actor P believes that predicate X is true, in the sense that P has enough elements to rightly conclude that X is true. Thus, P may behave like X was true. Another formula is "fresh(X)", which means X is fresh data, that is it has not been previously used in the protocol (not even in previous sessions). If X is a newly created nonce, fresh(X) is assumed to hold just after its creation and the actor who just created the nonce believes it fresh (P believes fresh(X)). When a protocol session executes and messages are exchanged, the set of beliefs and other predicates for each actor updates accordingly. This is described in belief logics by a set of inference rules that can be used to deduce legitimate beliefs. Security properties can then be expressed by some predicates on actors' beliefs that must hold at the end of a protocol session.

More specifically, a protocol is described by using the Alice and Bob notation, and assumptions about initial beliefs of each actor are stated. For example, before protocol execution, Alice may already trust a particular server, or be known to be the legitimate owner of a particular key pair. Then, protocol execution is analyzed, so that beliefs of actors are updated after every message is exchanged. For example, after A→B: M has been executed, "A believes A said M" is true, where "A said M" means that A has sent a message including M. The BAN logic inference rules also allow new facts to be inferred from those that are already known. At the end of the protocol, actors' beliefs are compared with the expected ones: if they do not match, then the desired property is not satisfied.

Note that BAN logic can be very useful in protocol comparisons. Indeed, it is possible to compare the initial assumptions required by different protocols that achieve the same security goals. Moreover, it may be possible to find redundancies in the protocol, for example when an actor is induced by a received message to believe a fact that the actor already knows.

A BAN logic model can be verified by means of theorem proving. The theorem proving approach consists of building a mathematical proof in a formal deduction system in order to show that a desired security property holds in the given model. Since manually building formal proofs is a difficult and error-prone task, automation can be particularly effective. Some proof assistants, called theorem provers, can automatically solve simple lemmas, and they also interactively help the user in searching for the complete proof. Some of them, called automatic theorem provers, can even find complete proofs automatically.

Using theorem proving with belief logics is straightforward, because these logics are natively defined as propositional formal systems. However, using the bare logic is not so user-friendly and easy for a non-expert: the protocol, the assumptions made and the desired properties must all be expressed in the belief logic language; then, a proof of the desired properties must be found.

In order to simplify the use of belief logics, researchers have developed tools that automatically translate simple user-friendly descriptions of protocols (in Alice and Bob notation) and their initial assumptions and desired properties into expressions in the belief logic language

(Brackin, 1998). Moreover, as it has been shown by Monniaux (1999), belief logics, such as BAN and GNY, are decidable, i.e. it is possible to build an algorithm that automatically decides, in finite time and space, if a proof for a given proposition exists and, in positive case, finds it. In conclusion, the whole process of translating user-friendly descriptions into a belief logic such as BAN, finding out if the desired properties can be proved and, in positive case, delivering a proof can be automated. In addition, this task is computationally feasible and takes seconds for typical protocols (Monniaux, 1999).

Of course, belief logics such as BAN and GNY have several limitations, because they only apply to authentication properties and they do not catch some kinds of flaws, such as exposure to attacks based on oracles. Nevertheless, experimental studies conducted by Brackin (1998) on the Clark & Jacob (1997) collection of authentication protocols have shown that only a small fraction of known flaws on the high-level descriptions of those protocols are not caught by this approach. Then, this is a fast mechanized analysis that can detect several logical bugs related to authentication in high-level protocol descriptions. It can be used as a preliminary low-cost analysis, before conducting other more expensive and more accurate analyses.

Belief logics have been extensively developed in the past and are now considered mature, so recent works mainly focus on their application (e.g. Qingling, Yiju & Yonghua, 2008) rather than on their development.

Dolev-Yao Models

The Dolev & Yao (1983) model of security protocols is currently widely used in many research works (e.g. Hui & Lowe, 2001, Abadi & Gordon, 1998, Bengtson, Bhargavan, Fournet, Gordon, & Maffeis, 2008, Fábrega, Herzog, & Guttman, 1999, Durgin, Lincoln, & Mitchell, 2004, Chen, Su, Liu, Xiao, 2010) and implemented in many protocol verification tools (e.g. Durante, Sisto, &

Valenzano, 2003, Viganò, 2006, Mödersheim & Viganò, 2009, Blanchet, 2001). Since its introduction, it has gained popularity because it is a simple, high level modeling framework, yet effective in modeling common protocol features and reasoning about many common security properties.

Like logics of beliefs this way of modeling protocols stems from an abstract algebraic view of cryptography, but it is more accurate because it tracks exchanged messages rather than beliefs. In the Dolev-Yao model, a protocol is described by a discrete state-transition system made of communicating parallel sub-systems representing protocol actors. The transition system of each actor describes the actor behavior in terms of sent and received messages. For honest agents this is the behavior prescribed by the protocol, while for attacker agents it can be any behavior.

Many network models with apparently different features can be considered, but in general they can be shown to be equivalent, because one system can be encoded, or simulated, by the others. For example, one possible network model proposed by Schneider (1996) considers the network and the attacker as separate sub-systems, where the attacker is a protocol participant that has special actions, such as forging and eavesdropping messages. Other models (Ryan & Schneider, 2000) instead consider the intruder as the medium itself. Finally, association models (Voydock & Kent, 1983) group all securely connected actors into one "super-actor", leading back to the basic idea of just having "super-actors" communicating only through an untrusted network. Usually, one chooses the network model that will make proving a particular security property as easy as possible.

While Dolev-Yao models can be formalized in different ways, from process calculi, to graphs and automata, to refinement types, the ideas and assumptions of the underlying model are always the same. Normally, protocol actors do not communicate directly over private channels, as this would make security protocols useless; instead, they communicate over the shared untrusted network. Exceptions to this can be modeled, and in this case it is said that two or more actors share a private secure channel, to which the attacker has no access. As an algebraic model of cryptography is considered, many models have a set of data types and a set of constructors, destructors and equations that represent cryptographic functions and their properties. Some models come with a fixed set of cryptographic primitives and associated semantics, while others are extensible, thus enabling a wide range of protocols to be modeled. Being algebraic models, all of them can only represent the ideal properties of cryptographic primitives, so that, for example, cryptographic flaw attacks cannot be represented in these models. Moreover, being an active attacker always able to drop any message, it turns out that liveness properties, such as "an acknowledgment is eventually received", cannot be checked within Dolev-Yao models. This is not a big issue after all, since many common security properties, such as secrecy and authentication, can be defined as safety properties, and thus fully handled in the Dolev-Yao models.

Summing up, the general features of Dolev-Yao models make them amenable to represent protocol flaws based on wrong usage of cryptographic primitives that are independent of the particular cryptosystems used, while such models are not tailored to spotting other protocol flaws or flaws in the cryptosystems themselves. The power of the intruder is believed to be enough to express its worst behavior, under the assumptions of perfect cryptography (for example, it can never guess nonces or keys, nor even partially recover a key from a given ciphertext). Moreover, it is worth pointing out that many other implementation details are usually not captured by Dolev-Yao models, so protocol flaws that may arise because of these details cannot be caught too. For instance, side channels are usually not modeled. For example, one attacker could infer some information by looking at power consumption of certain devices during computation, or data transmitted over a secured channel could be inferred by looking at the data rate at which they are sent.

Table 1. Applied pi calculus terms

M, N::=	Terms
a, b, c	name
x, y, z	variable
$f(M_1, M_2, ..., M_n)$	function application

Representing Dolev-Yao Models as Process Calculi

Among the different formalisms that have been developed to specify security protocols at the Dolev-Yao level, process calculi are among the most used ones, hence they are taken as an example here. Specifically, a variant of the applied pi calculus, which is one of the most user-friendly process calculi, is shown as an example.

Process calculi are algebraic systems designed to represent communicating processes and their exchanged data, with a well-defined formal semantics. Because of their abstraction level, they are a good tool for formally describing communication protocols in the Dolev-Yao style.

For example, Spi calculus is a process calculus for security protocols (Abadi & Gordon, 1998) that has been designed as a security-aware extension of the pi-calculus (Milner, 1999). It is close to a programming language, in that it enables explicit representation of input/output operations as well as checks on received messages. This is amenable to the derivation of implementations, since operations in the specification can be mapped into corresponding operations in the implementation.

The applied pi calculus (Abadi & Fournet, 2001) is similar to the Spi calculus but it is based on an equational system where constructors, destructors and equations can themselves be specified, making the language easily extensible. In this chapter, the slightly extended and machine readable version of the applied pi calculus as it is accepted by a popular verification tool (Blanchet, 2009) is presented as an example. From now on, in this chapter the expression "applied pi calculus"

will refer to this extended and machine readable version.

The applied pi calculus syntax is composed of terms, formally defined in Table 1, and processes, formally defined in Table 2. A term can be an atomic name (e.g. 'a'), a variable (e.g. 'x') that can be bound to any other term once, or a (constructor) function application $f(M_1, M_2, ..., M_n)$. For each constructor, corresponding destructor functions and equations can be defined separately, so as to specify an equational system that models the properties of cryptographic operations. For convenience, a syntactic sugar is introduced for tuples of terms, denoted by $(M_1, M_2, ..., M_n)$, which can be encoded within the standard syntax by corresponding constructor and destructor functions.

The semantics of processes can be described as follows. The null process '0' does nothing. The parallel process P|Q executes P and Q in parallel, while the replication process !P behaves as an unbounded number of instances of P running in parallel. The restriction process 'new a; P' creates a fresh name 'a', that is a name not known to anyone else, including the attacker. The conditional process 'if M = N then P else Q' behaves like P if M and N are the same term (modulo the equational theory), otherwise it behaves like Q; if Q is '0' the else branch can be omitted. The destructor application process 'let x = $g(M_1, M_2, ..., M_n)$ in P else Q' tries to compute the result of the application of the destructor function. If this result can be computed (i.e. an equation can be applied), the result is stored into variable 'x' and the process behaves like P, else it behaves like Q; again the else branch can be omitted if Q is '0'. With the tuples syntactic sugar, the destructor application process can also be used in a compact form of tuple-splitting process 'let $(x_1, x_2, ..., x_n)$ = M in P else Q'. The input process in(c,x); P receives a message from channel 'c' and stores it into variable 'x'. The output process out(c,M); P outputs the message M on channel 'c', then behaves like P. Finally, the auxiliary process 'event $f(M_1, M_2, ..., M_n)$; P' emits special events needed to estab-

Table 2. Applied pi calculus processes

P, Q::=	Processes
0	null process
P | Q	parallel composition
!P	replication
new a; P	restriction
if M = N then P else Q	conditional
let x = g(M_1, M_2, ..., M_n) in P else Q	destructor application
in(c,x); P	message input
out(c,M); P	message output
event f(M_1, M_2, ..., M_n); P	auxiliary authenticity event

lish correspondence properties such as authentication (more on this later).

A typical applied pi calculus protocol specification defines one process for each agent, and a "protocol instantiation" process, describing how protocol agents interact with each other in a protocol run. In such models, security properties can be specified as predicates that must hold for all the runs of a particular protocol. For example, secrecy can be defined as a reachability property, asking whether there exists one run where the attacker can get to know some data D that should be kept secret. The special correspondence events mentioned above enable reasoning about authentication properties. Suppose Alice wants to authenticate to Bob, meaning that at the end of a protocol run Bob can be sure he has been talking with Alice. This can be modeled by the following property: "Each time Bob ends a protocol session apparently with Alice, agreeing upon some session data D, Alice had previously started a protocol session with Bob, agreeing upon the same session data D." This is achieved by defining two events, namely *running* and *finished*. Bob emits a finished(D) event after the protocol run and Alice emits a running(D) event as soon as the session is started and the relevant session data D are available. The authentication property is then expressed requiring that in each trace of the protocol each time a finished(D) event occurs, a corresponding running(D) event (referencing the same data D) has taken place in the past.

Communicating Sequential Processes (CSP) is another process calculus that has been used to model security protocols (Ryan & Schneider, 2000). Each process models a protocol actor and is described by the events it will emit on a particular communication channel. Essentially, message exchange is performed by honest agents by emitting send.A.B.M events, meaning that actor A sends message M apparently to B, and receive.B.A.M events, meaning that actor B receives message M apparently from A.

Differently from the applied pi calculus, in CSP the checks performed on the received data are always implicitly represented in the input operation. When emitting the receive.B.A.M event, one agent is willing to receive a message only if the received data pattern-match against M. This means that, during message reception, it is implicitly assumed by the CSP model that "all possible checks" will be performed on the received data (Ryan & Schneider, 2000). While this behavior is acceptable at an algebraic level, because pattern matching can be implemented by syntactic matching, it becomes non trivial to preserve the same semantics down to executable implementations of CSP processes, which makes this modeling framework not so amenable to deal with implementations of security protocols.

Automated Verification of Dolev-Yao Models by Theorem Proving

Security protocols expressed as Dolev-Yao models can be verified by theorem proving. Essentially, the protocol specification is translated into a logic system where facts such as "message M has been transmitted" or "the attacker may know message M" are represented. Therefore, proving that a security property holds amounts to proving that a particular assertion (for example, "the attacker may know secret S") cannot be derived in the formal system. However, due to the undecidability of security properties such as secrecy and authentication in Dolev-Yao models (Comon & Shmatikov, 2002), it is not possible to develop an automatic procedure that in finite time and space always decides correctly whether or not a security property holds for any given protocol model.

Three main possible ways to cope with this undecidability problem have been explored. One is restricting the model (e.g. by bounding the number of parallel sessions), so as to make it decidable. This approach, which has been extensively used for state exploration techniques, has the drawback of reducing the generality of the results. A second possibility is to make the verification process interactive, i.e. not fully automatic. This is the approach taken for example by Paulson (1998). Here the obvious drawback is that, although libraries of reusable theorems can reduce the degree of interactivity, user expertise in using a theorem prover is needed. Moreover, there is no guarantee of eventually getting a result. A third possibility, that suffers from the same latter limitation, is using semi-decision procedures, which are automatic but may not terminate, or may terminate without giving a result, or may give an uncertain result. This approach has been adopted, for example, by Song, Berezin, & Perrig (2001) and Blanchet (2001). In particular, the ProVerif tool (Blanchet, 2001, Blanchet, 2009) is also publicly available and is one of the most used tools in the class of automatic theorem provers for Dolev-Yao models. It is based on a Prolog engine and accepts protocol descriptions expressed either directly by means of Prolog rules that are added to the ProVerif formal system, or in the more user-friendly applied pi calculus described in Table 1 and Table 2, which is automatically translated into Prolog rules. ProVerif does not terminate in some cases. When it terminates, different outcomes are possible. ProVerif may come up with a proof of correctness, in which case the result is not affected by uncertainty, i.e. the protocol model has been proved correct under the assumptions made. ProVerif may sometimes terminate without being able to prove anything. In this case, however, it is possible that ProVerif indicates potential attacks on the protocol. This ability is particularly useful to understand why the protocol is (possibly) flawed and is generally not provided by other theorem provers. Note however that the attacks produced by ProVerif may be false positives, because of some approximations it uses. That said, on most protocols the tool terminates giving useful results, which makes it one of the most used automated tools now available for verifying security protocols.

As an example, the Needham-Schroeder protocol specified in the applied pi calculus, as accepted by ProVerif, is shown in Box 1.

As usual, the two protocol actors are described by two separate processes, A and B, while a third process called Inst models the protocol sessions, by specifying concurrent execution of an unbounded number of instances of A and B processes.

In the example, role A is parameterized by a key pair KA, containing its public and private keys (denoted Pub(KA) and Pri(KA) respectively), by KBPub, i.e. B's public key, and by AID, i.e. A's identifier. At line 2a, A creates the nonce NA and, at line 3a, AID and NA are sent to B, encrypted under B's public key, over channel cAB. At line 4a A receives on channel cAB the response from B and stores it in the *resp* variable, which is then decrypted at line 5a. Since *resp* is supposed to be an encryption made with A's public key, it is decrypted with A's private key, and the result of decryption is stored in the *resp_decr* variable. At line 6a, *resp_decr* is split into two parts that are stored in variables xNA and xNB: the former should store A's nonce, while the latter should store B's nonce. Since A's nonce is known, at line 7a it is checked that the received value xNA matches with the original NA value. If this is the case, at line 8a A sends the received B's nonce encrypted with B's public key over channel cAB.

In applied pi calculus, fresh data (that is data created with the "new" operator) are neither

Box 1.

```
1a: A(KA,KBPub,AID):=
2a:         new NA;
3a:         out(cAB, pubenc((AID,NA), KBPub);
4a:         in(cAB, resp);
5a:         let resp_decr = pridec(resp, Pri(KA)) in
6a:         let (xNA,xNB) = resp_decr in
7a:         if xNA = NA then
8a:         out(cAB, pubenc(xNB, KBPub));
9a:         0
1b: B(KB,KAPub,AID):=
2b:         in(cAB, init);
3b:         let init_decr = pridec(init, Pri(KB)) in
4b:         let (xAID, xNA) = init_decr in
5b:         if xAID = AID then
6b:         new NB;
7b:         out(cAB, pubenc((xNA,NB), KAPub);
8b:         in(cAB, resp);
9b:         let xNB = pridec(resp, Pri(KB)) in
10b:         if xNB = NB then
11b:         0
1i: Inst():= new KA; new KB; out(cAB, (Pub(KA), Pub(KB))); (
2i:             !A(KA,Pub(KB),AID) | !B(KB,Pub(KA),AID)
3i:         )
```

known nor guessable by the attacker, while global data (such as AID or the communication channel cAB) are assumed to be known by the attacker. In particular this means that the attacker can actively or passively control the communication channel cAB, or try to cheat B sending him A's identity; however, the attacker does not know agents' private keys (while the public ones are known because they are sent in clear over the public channel before starting the protocol, at line 1i).

In applied pi calculus, the attacker is the environment, i.e. it is not modeled explicitly, but it is assumed that the attacker can be any applied pi calculus process running in parallel with Inst().

As explained above, the Needham-Schroeder protocol should ensure that at the end of a session A and B are mutually authenticated. In particular,

authentication of A to B is the property that does not hold in the protocol. In order to express this property, so that it can be verified by the ProVerif tool, the specification must be enriched with the special *running* and *finished* events. Authentication of A to B can be expressed by adding an *event running(AID, NA, XNB, Pub(KA), KBPub)* statement in the A process, just before the third message is sent, that is between lines 7a and 8a. The corresponding *event finished(AID, xNA, NB, KAPub,Pub(KB))* statement is added to the B process at the end of the session, that is between lines 10b and 11b.

When ProVerif analyzes the enriched specification, it can automatically state that the authentication property is false. Moreover, an attack trace is returned, showing how the attacker can in fact

Figure 3. (a) Model extraction and (b) code generation approaches

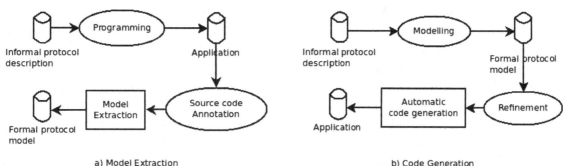

a) Model Extraction   b) Code Generation

break the property. The returned attack trace is essentially the same as the one shown in Figure 3.

Conversely, the authentication of B to A holds. When this property is expressed by properly enriching the specification with the *running* and *finished* events, ProVerif can prove that such property is true.

Automated Verification of Dolev-Yao Models by State Exploration

Another available technique is state exploration, which works by extensively analyzing all possible protocol runs. Then, rather than looking for a correctness proof, the analysis looks for violations of the desired security properties in the model runs. If a run of the model is found in which one of the desired security properties is violated, it can be concluded that the protocol does not satisfy that property; furthermore, the run that leads to the violation constitutes an attack on the protocol. For instance, let us assume a desired property of a protocol is the inability of the attacker to learn a certain secret. If a run of the model is found leading to a state in which the attacker knows the secret, then an attack has been found, which also shows by a counterexample that the desired property does not hold. If instead the model runs are exhaustively searched without finding any violation of the desired properties, it can be concluded that the model satisfies these properties. This conclusion is in principle equivalent

to a proof of correctness like the one that can be obtained by a theorem prover. In practice, however, the aforementioned undecidability issue prevents the analysis from always getting to a proof of correctness. Indeed, Dolev-Yao models cannot be searched exhaustively by naïve state exploration because they are infinite, which is their main source of undecidability. The usual approach followed by state exploration tools is to bound the model so as to turn it into a finite one, which can be searched exhaustively. In this way, the analysis always terminates, either finding out one or more counterexamples, or without finding any flaw. In the second case, no full correctness proof has been reached, because the model had been simplified, but nonetheless something new is known: no flaws are present in the reduced model. This increases the confidence in the protocol correctness with respect to what was known before running the analysis. Some researchers have found that if a protocol satisfies some particular conditions, even a non-exhaustive finite search can be enough to give a correctness proof (e.g. Lowe, 1998, Arapinis, Delaune & Kremer, 2008). Unfortunately, real protocols not always meet such conditions. Another approach to get to a full security proof, used for example in the Maude-NPA by Escobar, Meadows, & Meseguer (2009), is to combine state exploration with inductive theorem proving techniques.

Although state exploration cannot always get to a proof of correctness, its main values are that it can be fully automated and that, on finite models, it always terminates with some useful information, either of correctness or with a counterexample. Moreover, its ability to find attacks is very important because it lets the user diagnose why a protocol is faulty. In contrast, with theorem proving tools, it may happen that a proof is not found but at the same time no hint about possible flaws in the protocol is given.

State exploration analysis for security protocols can be implemented in several different ways. Some researchers have built prototype tools specifically tailored for the analysis of security protocols, such as the NRL Protocol Analyzer (Meadows, 1996) and its next-generation Maude-NPA (Escobar et al., 2009), OFMC (Basin, Mödersheim, & Viganò, 2005) and its homonymous successor (Mödersheim, & Viganò, 2009), S3A (Durante et al., 2003) and many others. Other researchers instead have shown how general-purpose state exploration tools such as model checkers can be used for the same purpose. Among the model checkers that have been experimented for analyzing security protocols, we can mention FDR (Lowe, 1996), and Spin (Maggi & Sisto, 2002).

The first attempts at state exploration worked with strictly finite models, obtained by imposing a double restriction: on one hand a bounded number of protocol sessions, on the other hand a bounded message complexity (obtained, for example, by assuming the maximum number of operations an attacker applies to build messages is bounded). Later on, it was discovered that it is possible to relax the second restriction, i.e. the one on message complexity, without losing decidability. Of course, relaxing this restriction leads to infinite-state models, because each time one of the protocol agents inputs some data, the attacker can send to that agent one of infinitely many different messages (all the ones the attacker can build using its current knowledge, which are infinite if no bound is put on message complexity). Nevertheless, the infinite number of states and transitions can be partitioned into a finite

number of equivalence classes. Each class can be described using free variables, each of which can be instantiated into infinitely many different terms. The key point is that the analysis can be conducted without instantiating variables immediately, so that classes of states and of transitions are represented symbolically in the analysis by means of symbolic entities that include uninstantiated variables. This technique, initially introduced by Huima (1999), has led to the construction of state exploration tools that can successfully analyze protocol models with the only restriction of having a bounded number of sessions. Some tools, such as OFMC (Mödersheim, & Viganò, 2009), offer the user the possibility of avoiding to introduce an a-priori bound on the number of sessions and, using a lazy evaluation approach, they can effectively search the state space even in this case. Of course, because of undecidability, the search may not terminate if the number of sessions is left unbounded.

One problem that still remains with all state exploration tools is state explosion: the number of states and state paths to be explored increases exponentially with the number of protocol sessions. Therefore, it is typically practical to analyze models with only few sessions.

The different features of state exploration and theorem proving tools, which are somewhat complementary, suggest that good results can be obtained by a combined use of the two. For instance, a state exploration tool can be used initially, because of its ability to report attacks. When some confidence in the protocol correctness has been achieved, it is then possible to switch to a theorem prover, which can provide the final correctness proof without any limitation on the number of sessions.

Among the efforts towards the possibility of integrated use of different analysis tools, the most relevant one started with the AVISPA project (Viganò, 2006), followed by the AVANTSSAR project, aiming at the specification and verification of security-aware systems by means of state-of-the-art state exploration tools.

Automated Verification of Dolev-Yao Models by Type Checking

A novel technique, that complements security protocol specifications described by means of process calculi with refinement type systems, is implemented in the F7 framework (Bengtson et al., 2008, Bhargavan, Fournet, & Gordon, 2010). A refinement type is denoted by $\{x:T|C(x)\}$, where x is a variable, T is a type name, and C(x) is a logic formula that can depend on x itself. The refinement type $\{x:T|C(x)\}$ is a subtype of the classical type $\{x:T\}$; a value M of $\{x:T|C(x)\}$ is such that M is a value for $\{x:T\}$, and C(M) is true.

For example, the type $\{k:Key \mid MayMAC(k)\}$ is the type of cryptographic keys that can be used to perform MAC operations over protocol data.

In F7, a protocol is specified by using a concurrent lambda-calculus, which is then annotated with refinement types. The used lambda-calculus has no embedded primitives for cryptography; instead they are provided as a library that implements a symbolic, algebraic model of such primitives, thus behaving like a Dolev-Yao model. Moreover, the lambda-calculus has special "assume C(x)" and "assert C(x)" expressions, that can be used by honest agents to specify authentication properties. Given a value M, the "assume C(M)" expression means that the proposition C(M) is true, while the "assert C(M)" can be used to test whether the fact C(M) can be derived during a protocol run.

In order to describe the attacker, a universal type Un is defined. This type can be subtype or supertype of any other type, and represents data known by the attacker. Then, the specification of an attacker is any process A typed as Un. When Un is used as a subtype of another type T, then T is said to be of tainted kind, meaning that values of T may come from the attacker; when Un is used as a supertype of T, then T is said to be of

public kind, meaning that values of T may be sent to the attacker.

A specification is safe if no assertion can ever fail at run-time, despite the best effort of the attacker to let an assertion fail. In order to check whether a specification is safe, standard type checking and partial type inference algorithms can be used. Because of undecidability issues, it may be impossible to find a typing even for a correct protocol, and hence to find a proof of correctness.

Automatic Verification of Computational Models

As explained in section 2, computational models are more refined than the abstract formal models described above, because they take cryptanalysis issues into account. As a consequence, formal automatic verification of such models is more difficult. Two strategies have been essentially investigated in order to prove security properties on computational models. On one hand, the "indirect" strategy consists of proving the security properties on a more abstract formal model, and then to show that a corresponding computationally sound model is implied to be secure too. On the other hand, the "direct" strategy consists of proving the security properties directly in the computationally sound environment.

For the indirect approach, existing tools in the formal model domain can be re-used, although, in order to be able to prove the computational soundness of a formal model, the latter often needs to be enriched by many details that usually harden verification. Furthermore, once the formal model has been proven secure, it is still needed to show that it is computationally sound. Such computational soundness proof has usually to be developed manually for each protocol model and each security property, although recent research by Comon-Lundh & Cortier (2008) aims at providing some general results that can be applied on certain classes of security properties.

For the direct approach, some first attempts at applying automated theorem proving to computational models have recently been documented. The most relevant work is the one by Blanchet (2008), who has built and made available a prototype prover called CryptoVerif that is sound in the computational model. The tool accepts a process calculus inspired by the applied pi calculus. However, some significant semantic differences exist between the CryptoVerif input language and the applied pi calculus, so that it is currently not possible to feed both ProVerif and CryptoVerif with the same models. The CryptoVerif tool operates by interpreting the model as a "game", where the protocol is secure when the attacker has negligible probability of winning the game (that is, of breaking the security property). This tool can find proofs automatically in some cases, but undecidability prevents it from always deciding in finite time if a proof exists. With respect to ProVerif and other tools that operate on Dolev-Yao models and that have been proved useful in practice, this one is newer, so that no enough experience reports are currently available to shed light on its practical applicability.

Formally Linking Protocol Specification and Implementation

Up until now, the chapter mainly focused on formal, abstract specifications of protocols and their verification. However, real implementations of security protocols, implemented in a programming language, may significantly differ from the verified formal specification, so that the real behavior of the protocol differs from the abstractly modeled and verified one, possibly enabling attacks that are not possible according to the formal specification.

In order to ensure that the formal model is correctly refined by the implementation, two development methodologies can be used, namely model extraction (Bhargavan, Fournet, Gordon,

& Tse, 2006, Jürjens, 2005, Goubault-Larrecq & Parrennes, 2005) and code generation (Pozza, Sisto & Durante, 2004, Pironti & Sisto, 2007, Tobler & Hutchison, 2004, Jeon, Kim, & Choi, 2005). These approaches are depicted in Figure 3 and detailed in the next subsections.

The Model Extraction Approach

In the model extraction approach depicted in Figure 3(a), one starts by manually developing a full blown implementation of a security protocol from its specification, and enriches the source code with annotations about its intended semantics. This enriched code is then used to automatically extract an abstract formal model. The extracted formal model can then be verified (not depicted), in order to check the desired security properties, by one of the techniques presented in the previous sections. This approach has the advantage of allowing existing implementations to be verified without changing the way applications are currently written, except when annotations in the source code are required, in order to specify the link between implementation data and abstract terms. Usually, a full model of the protocol implementation is too complex to be handled. Therefore, to make verification feasible, many approaches extract an over-approximated model, where some details are soundly abstracted away, and only the relevant protocol logic parts are represented. These over-approximations could lead the analysis to report false positives, when the abstract model is flawed, but that flaw is ruled out in the code, by some implementation details that are abstracted in the formal model. However, when the over-approximations are sound, it is ensured that any flaw in the code is still present in the abstract model, and can thus be found (in other words, no flaw is missed when extracting the model).

In the work by Bhargavan, Fournet, Gordon, & Tse (2006), applications are written in F#, a dialect of the ML functional language. Then the fs2pv tool translates the F# program into a ProVerif model, that can be checked for security properties. The translation function implemented by fs2pv is proven to be sound under a Dolev-Yao attacker, meaning that the extracted ProVerif model preserves all the secrecy and authentication faults of the F# code, when a Dolev-Yao attacker is assumed. Actually, not all the F# code that constitutes the implementation of the security protocol is translated into the ProVerif model. Indeed, the F# cryptographic libraries are assumed to be correct, and are symbolically represented as Dolev-Yao constructors and destructors in the abstract model.

By using the fs2pv model extraction tool, Bhargavan, Fournet, & Gordon (2006) developed a provably correct reference implementation for WS-Security. Although this case study showed how the tool could be used in practice, it also showed some major drawbacks of this methodology. Functional languages such as ML (or its dialect F#) are not very common in the programming practice; furthermore, some constraints on the input F# code actually only allowed newly written code to be verified, instead of existing applications. Moreover, small changes in the F# code lead to different ProVerif models, some of which can easily be verified, while for others the verification process may diverge, requiring fine tuning of the original F# code, in order to enable verification. Nevertheless, the outcome of this case study is a fully functional provably correct implementation of the WS-Security standard, that can be used as a reference implementation, or even directly reused by other applications.

In the work by Goubault-Larrecq & Parrennes (2005) a similar approach is developed, but the source code of the implementation is the popular C language. In order to link the C data structures to symbolic Dolev-Yao terms, the user is required to annotate the source code with trust assertions. Then, a simplified control flow graph is extracted from the annotated C source code, and translated into a set of first-order logic axioms. The obtained axioms, together with a logical formalization of the requested security properties, are finally checked with an automated theorem prover. Since a full operational model of a C program would be too complex to be handled, some sound over approximations are made by the tool. This means that security faults will be caught, but some false positives can arise.

The Code Generation Approach

In the code generation approach depicted in Figure 3(b), one starts by deriving an abstract formal model from the informal protocol description, and refines such high-level formal model with low-level implementation details that would be not captured otherwise. The abstract model and its refinement information are then used to automatically generate the final implementation code. Also (not depicted), the abstract formal model can be used to check the desired security properties on the protocol.

In general, abstract models dealing with Dolev-Yao attackers use symbolic representations of terms, meaning that data encoding as bit strings is usually abstracted away. Moreover, since perfect encryption is assumed, the cryptographic algorithms are usually not represented. However, the code generation approach should allow the developer to specify these details, in order to generate interoperable applications that can conform to existing standards or specifications.

In this approach, once the formal model has been verified, tool automation is rather important in order to avoid manually introduced errors during the refinement phase form the formal model to the derived implementation. Like with the model extraction approach, tools should be trusted or verifiable too. Even when some implementation code must be manually written, it is important to ensure that this manually written code cannot introduce security faults. It must be pointed out that the code generation approach only allows new applications to be generated, and cannot deal with existing ones, thus not stimulating software reuse (only the general purpose libraries and the models can be reused).

Several attempts have been made in this field. For example, two independent works both named spi2java (Pozza et al. 2004, Tobler & Hutchison, 2004) allow the programmer to start from a verified spi calculus specification, and to get the Java code that implements it. On one hand, the framework by Tobler & Hutchison (2004) uses Prolog to implement the Spi to Java translator, thus facilitating the verification of the translator correctness. On the other hand, the framework by Pozza et al. (2004) comes with a formal definition of the Spi to Java translation (Pironti & Sisto, 2010), and enables interoperability of the generated applications (Pironti & Sisto, 2007), also giving sufficient conditions under which some manually written parts of the implementation are safe.

The spi2java tool by Pozza et al. (2004) has been used to develop an SSH Transport Layer Protocol (TLP) client (Pironti & Sisto, 2007). The client has been tested against third party servers, thus showing that an implementation adhering to the standard can be obtained. Although showing that the approach is practically useful, the case study also stressed some of its shortcomings. For example, half of the code composing the SSH TLP client was manually written. Although there exist sufficient conditions stating that no flaws can arise from that code, the manual effort to derive the application was still considerable. Moreover, the code is not as efficient as some other popular SSH TLP implementations, and the developer has no way to modify the generated code to improve code efficiency, without losing the guarantees about its correctness.

Another tool for security protocol code generation is AGC-C# (Jeon et al., 2005), which automatically generates C# code from a verified CASPER script. Unlike other works, this tool does not support interoperability of the generated code. Moreover, it accepts scripts that are slightly different from the verified Casper scripts. Manual

modifications of the formal model are error prone, and the generated code starts from a model that is not the verified one.

Discussion

Both model extraction and code generation approaches present a trade-off between the ability of proving security properties, and the possibility of writing applications in the way they are commonly written. In the model extraction approach, a functional language with formal semantics (like for example ML) is much simpler to reason about than an imperative language without formal semantics (like for example C); in the code generation approach, code optimizations are not allowed, in favor of achieving higher confidence about the correctness of the generated code. Note that, in principle, the code generation approach can ensure by construction that the automatically generated applications are also free from low-level errors like buffer overflows or integer overflows while the model extraction approach cannot.

It is finally worth pointing out that the tools described in these sections are research prototype tools, which aim is to show the feasibility of an approach. As also stated by Woodcock et al. (2009), industrial adoption of these techniques could make them better engineered, i.e. more usable and efficient.

FUTURE RESEARCH DIRECTIONS

The pervasiveness of networks made security protocols so widespread and tailored to the different applications that some of them cannot be adequately modeled and checked within the Dolev-Yao and BAN frameworks. For example, popular applications, like e-commerce, may require security goals that are not safety properties and thus cannot be checked in the presence of an active Dolev-Yao attacker. For example, in an e-commerce protocol, the attacker may cheat in completing a purchase, thus gaining by paying less than agreed with the merchant. It seems that these scenarios are better modeled with a game-theoretical approach (Gu, Shen, & Xue, 2009): each protocol actor is a potential attacker, that tries to cheat to maximize its profit (or, to "win" the game). Then, a security protocol is fair, if there exists no winning strategy for any player, meaning that at the end of the game every actor ended with a fair, agreed profit.

As hinted above, basic Dolev-Yao models have no concept of timing, nor of other side-channel information, such as power consumption or resource usage. In order to solve this issue, more refined models should be considered. However, this would both increase the complexity of specifications, making them harder to understand and write, and the complexity of verification. Again, a compositional approach could mitigate this problem. Note that being able to model and trace resource usage could also mitigate denial of service (DoS) attacks: if a security protocol is designed such that, during a DoS attack session, the attacked agent uses less resources than the attacker, it becomes unworthy for the attacker to complete its job (Meadows, 2001). Unfortunately, this does not hold for distributed DoS, where the attacker controls different machines, thus having much more computational power than the attacked agent. Finally, it must be noted that resource usage can be implementation dependent, making it non-trivial to model this aspect in an abstract and generic way.

Dolev-Yao models assume perfect cryptography, meaning that all possible bad interactions between the protocol and the cryptographic algorithms are not considered. Since recent works provide correctness proofs for some cryptographic algorithms (e.g. Bresson, Chevassut, & Pointcheval, 2007) (which also highlight their limitations), the next foreseeable step in this direction is to merge the two worlds, providing models and correctness proofs of security protocols, down to the cryptographic algorithm level.

Two indicators of field maturity show that there is still some research work to be done. The first indicator is the presence of standard frameworks or methodologies. As a matter of fact, no commonly agreed standard exists in protocol specification or verification: each problem stated above is solved with special approaches and tools, and their interoperability is quite limited. Indeed, very few de-facto standards for generic security protocols exist; the ISO/IEC CD 29128 (2010) standard is currently under development, but it is not trivial to foresee whether it will be widely adopted or not.

The second indicator is the usage of formal methods in the release of a security protocol standard. As the tool support is often not completely automatic and user-friendly, and it requires some expertise and implies a steep learning curve, formal methods are usually deemed too expensive for the average security protocol standard. The result is that often standards are released without the support of formal methods, and the latter are applied after the standard is published (see the AVISPA project, Viganò, 2006), making it hard to fix issues highlighted by their application. It is expected that as soon as more automatic and user-friendly tools will emerge, and the presence of networks of computers will become even more pervasive and dependable, formal methods will be adopted, in order to fulfill the call for some form of certification of correctness.

In turn, this will require that automatic formal methods will be able to scale to handle large protocols, and even full security-aware applications, that make use of different protocols simultaneously. Unfortunately, composition of security protocols is not linear (Cremers, 2006), meaning that combining two protocols does not guarantee that the outcome protocol preserves the security properties of the two. Indeed, combining protocols may have a disruptive effect, actually even breaking some of the expected security properties. As a practical example, an e-commerce website may wish to use SSL/TLS in order to setup a secure channel with the customer, and then use some electronic payment protocol (EPP) to redirect the customer to the bank website, in order to perform the purchase. Although each protocol could be proven secure in isolation, flaws may be found when using them together. When dealing with protocol composition, one (negative) result is already available: for each security protocol, a made-up attack-protocol can be found, which breaks security of the original protocol (Kelsey, Schneier, & Wagner, 1997). In principle, this means that it is not possible to check the interaction of one protocol with any other protocol, because it would be always possible to find a corresponding attack-protocol. Nevertheless, it is still meaningful to select a group of interacting protocols (SSL/TLS and EPP in the example) and check their interactions. Combining protocols greatly increases their complexity, making formal verification harder to apply, because of the required resources. Since this issue has a practical impact, it is believable that some research will be motivated in finding some compositional properties for security protocols, or some methodologies that would allow modular verification of security protocols. For example, Cortier, & Delaune (2009) propose to tag security protocols that share the same secrets, so that they execute like each protocol is running in isolation, because their messages cannot be interchanged. This approach does not apply to existing protocols, but it could be taken into account in the design of new protocols.

As an example of new aspects of security protocols that researchers are trying to include in formal analysis tools, we can mention open-ended protocols. Usually, security protocols have a fixed number of participants and a fixed message structure; only the number of sessions and the steps made by the attacker to create a message can be unbounded. However, there exist protocols, such as group key exchange protocols, where the number of participants is unbounded, or protocols where the message exchange sequence

may contain loops with an unbounded number of cycles. These protocols are known as open-ended protocols. For example, any protocol dealing with certificate chains is an open-ended protocol, because it faces a potentially unbounded number of certificate checks to be performed, each involving message exchanges in order to check the certificate revocation lists. Few works (e.g. Küsters, 2005) have explicitly addressed this problem, probably because classic protocols were deemed more urgent to address. Nevertheless, the increasing number of Internet-connected mobile devices is rising the need of open-ended protocols, making if foreseeable that more research work dealing with open-ended protocols verification will be developed.

CONCLUSION

This chapter has introduced the main problems that have to be addressed for engineering security protocols and how formal methods and related automated tools can now help protocol designers and implementers to improve quality. The chapter has stressed the progress that has been made in this field in the last years. While in the past formal security proofs required so high levels of expertise that only few researchers and field experts could develop them, the availability of fully automated tools has now enabled a wider number of protocol developers to get advantage of formal methods for security protocols. Given the vast scope of available solutions, attention has been focused just on the most popular and most representative ones, without exhaustiveness claims. The chapter has covered not just the formal protocol design techniques, but also the techniques that can be used in order to enforce strict correspondence between formal protocol specifications and their implementations.

REFERENCES

Abadi, M., & Fournet, C. (2001). *Mobile values, new names, and secure communication*. In Symposium on Principles of Programming Languages (pp. 104-115).

Abadi, M., & Gordon, A. D. (1998). A calculus for cryptographic protocols: The Spi calculus. *Research Report 149*.

Abadi, M., & Needham, R. (1996). Prudent engineering practice for cryptographic protocols. *IEEE Transactions on Software Engineering, 22*, 122–136. doi:10.1109/32.481513

Abadi, M., & Rogaway, P. (2002). Reconciling two views of cryptography (The computational soundness of formal encryption). *Journal of Cryptology, 15*(2), 103–127.

Albrecht, M. R., Watson, G. J., & Paterson, K. G. (2009). *Plaintext recovery attacks against SSH*. In IEEE Symposium on Security and Privacy (pp. 16-26).

Arapinis, M., Delaune, S., & Kremer, S. (2008). From one session to many: Dynamic tags for security protocols . In *Logic for Programming* (pp. 128–142). Artificial Intelligence, and Reasoning.

Basin, D. A., Mödersheim, S., & Viganò, L. (2005). OFMC: A symbolic model checker for security protocols. *International Journal of Information Security, 4*(3), 181–208. doi:10.1007/s10207-004-0055-7

Bengtson, J., Bhargavan, K., Fournet, C., Gordon, A. D., & Maffeis, S. (2008). *Refinement types for secure implementations*. In IEEE Computer Security Foundations Symposium (pp. 17-32).

Bhargavan, K., Fournet, C., & Gordon, A. D. (2006). *Verified reference implementations of WS-Security protocols*. In Web Services and Formal Methods (pp. 88-106).

Bhargavan, K., Fournet, C., & Gordon, A. D. (2010). *Modular verification of security protocol code by typing*. In Symposium on Principles of Programming Languages (pp. 445-456).

Bhargavan, K., Fournet, C., Gordon, A. D., & Tse, S. (2006). *Verified interoperable implementations of security protocols*. In Computer Security Foundations Workshop (pp. 139-152).

Blanchet, B. (2001). *An efficient cryptographic protocol verifier based on prolog rules*. In IEEE Computer Security Foundations Workshop (pp. 82-96).

Blanchet, B. (2008). A computationally sound mechanized prover for security protocols. *IEEE Transactions on Dependable and Secure Computing, 5*(4), 193–207. doi:10.1109/TDSC.2007.1005

Blanchet, B. (2009). Automatic verification of correspondences for security protocols. *Journal of Computer Security, 17*(4), 363–434.

Brackin, S. (1998). *Evaluating and improving protocol analysis by automatic proof.* In IEEE Computer Security Foundations Workshop (pp. 138-152).

Bresson, E., Chevassut, O., & Pointcheval, D. (2007). Provably secure authenticated group Diffie-Hellman key exchange. [TISSEC]. *ACM Transactions on Information and System Security, 10*(3). doi:10.1145/1266977.1266979

Burrows, M., Abadi, M., & Needham, R. (1990). A logic of authentication. *ACM Transactions on Computer Systems, 8*(1), 18–36. doi:10.1145/77648.77649

Carlsen, U. (1994). *Cryptographic protocol flaws: Know your enemy*. In IEEE Computer Security Foundations Workshop (pp. 192-200).

Chen, Q., Su, K., Liu, C., & Xiao, Y. (2010). *Automatic verification of web service protocols for epistemic specifications under Dolev-Yao model*. In International Conference on Service Sciences (pp. 49-54).

Clark, J., & Jacob, J. (1997). *A survey of authentication protocol literature: Version 1.0* (Technical Report).

Common Criteria. (2009). *Information Technology security evaluation and the common methodology for Information Technology security evaluation*. Retrieved from http://ww.commoncriteriaportal.org/index.html

Comon, H., & Shmatikov, V. (2002). Is it possible to decide whether a cryptographic protocol is secure or not? *Journal of Telecommunications and Information Technology, 4*, 5–15.

Comon-Lundh, H., & Cortier, V. (2008). *Computational soundness of observational equivalence*. In ACM Conference on Computer and Communications Security (pp. 109-118).

Cortier, V., & Delaune, S. (2009). Safely composing security protocols. *Formal Methods in System Design, 34*(1), 1–36. doi:10.1007/s10703-008-0059-4

Cremers, C. J. F. (2006). *Feasibility of multi-protocol attacks* (pp. 287–294). In Availability, Reliability and Security.

Dolev, D., & Yao, A. C.-C. (1983). On the security of public key protocols. *IEEE Transactions on Information Theory, 29*(2), 198–207. doi:10.1109/TIT.1983.1056650

Durante, L., Sisto, R., & Valenzano, A. (2003). Automatic testing equivalence verification of Spi calculus specifications. *ACM Transactions on Software Engineering and Methodology, 12*(2), 222–284. doi:10.1145/941566.941570

Durgin, N. A., Lincoln, P., & Mitchell, J. C. (2004). Multiset rewriting and the complexity of bounded security protocols. *Journal of Computer Security, 12*(2), 247–311.

Escobar, S., Meadows, C., & Meseguer, J. (2009). *Maude-NPA: cryptographic protocol analysis modulo equational properties*. In Foundations of Security Analysis and Design (pp. 1-50).

Fábrega, F. J. T., Herzog, J. C., & Guttman, J. D. (1999). Strand spaces: Proving security protocols correct. *Journal of Computer Security, 7*(2/3), 191–230.

Goubault-Larrecq, J., & Parrennes, F. (2005). *Cryptographic protocol analysis on Real C Code* (pp. 363–379). In Verification, Model Checking, and Abstract Interpretation.

Gritzalis, S., Spinellis, D., & Sa, S. (1997). *Cryptographic protocols over open distributed systems: A taxonomy of flaws and related protocol analysis tools*. In International Conference on Computer Safety, Reliability and Security (pp. 123-137).

Gu, Y., Shen, Z., & Xue, D. (2009). *A game-theoretic model for analyzing fair exchange protocols*. In International Symposium on Electronic Commerce and Security (pp. 509-513).

Hui, M. L., & Lowe, G. (2001). Fault-preserving simplifying transformations for security protocols. *Journal of Computer Security, 9*(1/2), 3–46.

Huima, A. (1999). *Efficient infinite-state analysis of security protocols*. In Workshop on Formal Methods and Security Protocols.

ISO/IEC CD 29128. (2010). *Verification of cryptographic protocols*. Under development.

Jeon, C.-W., Kim, I.-G., & Choi, J.-Y. (2005). *Automatic generation of the C# Code for security protocols verified with Casper/FDR*. In International Conference on Advanced Information Networking and Applications (pp. 507-510).

Jürjens, J. (2005). *Verification of low-level crypto-protocol implementations using automated theorem proving*. In Formal Methods and Models for Co-Design (pp. 89-98).

Kelsey, J., Schneier, B., & Wagner, D. (1997). *Protocol interactions and the chosen protocol attack*. In Security Protocols Workshop (pp. 91-104).

Küsters, R. (2005). On the decidability of cryptographic protocols with open-ended data structures. *International Journal of Information Security*, *4*(1-2), 49–70. doi:10.1007/s10207-004-0050-z

Lowe, G. (1996). Breaking and fixing the Needham-Schroeder public-key protocol using FDR. *Software - Concepts and Tools, 17*(3), 93-102.

Lowe, G. (1998). *Towards a completeness result for model checking of security protocols*. In IEEE Computer Security Foundations Workshop (pp. 96-105).

Maggi, P., & Sisto, R. (2002). *Using SPIN to verify security properties of cryptographic protocols*. In SPIN Workshop on Model Checking of Software (pp. 187-204).

Marschke, G. (1988). *The directory authentication framework. (. CCITT Recommendation, X*, 509.

Meadows, C. A. (1996). The NRL protocol analyzer: An overview. *The Journal of Logic Programming, 26*(2), 113–131. doi:10.1016/0743-1066(95)00095-X

Meadows, C. A. (2001). A cost-based framework for analysis of denial of service in networks. *Journal of Computer Security, 9*(1), 143–164.

Milner, R. (1999). *Communicating and mobile systems: The Pi-Calculus*. Cambridge University Press.

Mödersheim, S., & Viganò, L. (2009). *The open-source fixed-point model checker for symbolic analysis of security protocols*. In Foundations of Security Analysis and Design (pp. 166-194).

Monniaux, D. (1999). *Decision procedures for the analysis of cryptographic protocols by logics of belief*. In IEEE Computer Security Foundations Workshop (pp. 44-54).

Needham, R., & Schroeder, M. (1978). Using encryption for authentication in large networks of computers. *Communications of the ACM, 21*(12), 993–999. doi:10.1145/359657.359659

OpenSSL Team. (2009). *OpenSSL security advisor*. Retrieved from http://www.openssl.org/news/secadv_20090107.txt

Otway, D., & Rees, O. (1987). Efficient and timely mutual authentication. *Operating Systems Review, 21*(1), 8–10. doi:10.1145/24592.24594

Paulson, L. (1998). The inductive approach to verifying cryptographic protocols. *Journal of Computer Security, 6*(1-2), 85–128.

Pironti, A., & Sisto, R. (2007). *An experiment in interoperable cryptographic protocol implementation using automatic code generation*. In IEEE Symposium on Computers and Communications (pp. 839-844).

Pironti, A., & Sisto, R. (2010). Provably correct Java implementations of Spi calculus security protocols specifications. *Computers & Security, 29*(3), 302–314. doi:10.1016/j.cose.2009.08.001

Pozza, D., Sisto, R., & Durante, L. (2004). *Spi-2Java: Automatic cryptographic protocol Java code generation from Spi calculus*. In Advanced Information Networking and Applications (pp. 400-405).

Qingling, C., Yiju, Z., & Yonghua, W. (2008). A minimalist mutual authentication protocol for RFID system & BAN logic analysis . In *International Colloquium on Computing* (pp. 449–453). Communication, Control, and Management. doi:10.1109/CCCM.2008.305

Ryan, P., & Schneider, S. (2000). *The modelling and analysis of security protocols: The CSP approach*. Addison-Wesley Professional.

Schneider, S. (1996). *Security properties and CSP*. In IEEE Symposium on Security and Privacy (pp. 174-187).

Shamir, A., Rivest, R., & Adleman, L. (1978). *Mental poker (Technical Report)*. Massachusetts Institute of Technology.

Song, D. X., Berezin, S., & Perrig, A. (2001). Athena: A novel approach to efficient automatic security protocol analysis. *Journal of Computer Security, 9*(1/2), 47–74.

Tobler, B., & Hutchison, A. (2004). *Generating network security protocol implementations from formal specifications*. In Certification and Security in Inter-Organizational E-Services. Toulouse, France.

Viganò, L. (2006). Automated security protocol analysis with the AVISPA tool. *Electronic Notes in Theoretical Computer Science, 155*, 61–86. doi:10.1016/j.entcs.2005.11.052

Voydock, V. L., & Kent, S. T. (1983). Security mechanisms in high-level network protocols. *ACM Computing Surveys, 15*(2), 135–171. doi:10.1145/356909.356913

Woodcock, J., Larsen, P. G., Bicarregui, J., & Fitzgerald, J. (2009). Formal methods: Practice and experience. *ACM Computing Surveys, 41*(4), 1–36. doi:10.1145/1592434.1592436

Yafen, L., Wuu, Y., & Ching-Wei, H. (2004). *Preventing type flaw attacks on security protocols with a simplified tagging scheme*. In Symposium on Information and Communication Technologies (pp. 244-249).

Ylonen, T. (1996). *SSH - Secure login connections over the internet*. In USENIX Security Symposium (pp. 37-42).

ADDITIONAL READING

Abadi, M. (1999). Secrecy by typing in security protocols. *Journal of the ACM, 46*(5), 749–786. doi:10.1145/324133.324266

Abadi, M. (2000). Security protocols and their properties. In *Foundations of Secure Computation* (pp. 39-60).

Abadi, M., & Blanchet, B. (2002). Analyzing security protocols with secrecy types and logic programs. *ACM SIGPLAN Notices, 37*(1), 33–44. doi:10.1145/565816.503277

Aura, T. (1997). Strategies against replay attacks. In *IEEE Computer Security Foundations Workshop* (pp. 59-68).

Bodei, C., Buchholtz, M., Degano, P., Nielson, F., & Nielson, H. R. (2005). Static validation of security protocols. *Computers & Security, 13*(3), 347–390.

Bugliesi, M., Focardi, R., & Maffei, M. (2007). Dynamic types for authentication. *Journal of Computer Security, 15*(6), 563–617.

Carlsen, U. (1994, Jun). Cryptographic protocol flaws: know your enemy. In *Computer Security Foundations Workshop* (pp. 192-200).

Clarke, E. M., Jha, S., & Marrero, W. (2000). Verifying security protocols with Brutus. *ACM Transactions on Software Engineering and Methodology, 9*(4), 443–487. doi:10.1145/363516.363528

Coffey, T. (2009). A Formal Verification Centred Development Process for Security Protocols . In Gupta, J. N. D., & Sharma, S. (Eds.), *Handbook of Research on Information Security and Assurance* (pp. 165–178). IGI Global.

Crazzolara, F., & Winskel, G. (2002). Composing Strand Spaces. In *Foundations of Software Technology and Theoretical Computer Science* (pp. 97-108).

Denker, G., & Millen, J. (2000). CAPSL integrated protocol environment. In *DARPA Information Survivability Conference and Exposition* (pp. 207-221).

Donovan, B., Norris, P., & Lowe, G. (1999). Analyzing a library of security protocols using Casper and FDR. In *Workshop on Formal Methods and Security Protocols*.

Durgin, N. A., & Mitchell, J. C. (1999). Analysis of Security Protocols. In *Calculational System Design* (pp. 369-395).

Gong, L. (1995). Fail-stop protocols: An approach to designing secure protocols. In *Dependable Computing for Critical Applications* (pp. 44-55).

Gordon, A. D., Hüttel, H., & Hansen, R. R. (2008). Type inference for correspondence types. In *Security Issues in Concurrency* (pp. 21-36).

Gordon, A. D., & Jeffrey, A. (2003). Authenticity by Typing for Security Protocols. *Journal of Computer Security, 11*(4), 451–521.

Haack, C., & Jeffrey, A. (2006). Pattern-matching spi-calculus. *Information and Computation, 204*(8), 1195–1263. doi:10.1016/j.ic.2006.04.004

Hubbers, E., Oostdijk, M., & Poll, E. (2003). Implementing a Formally Verifiable Security Protocol in Java Card. In *Security in Pervasive Computing* (pp. 213-226).

ISO/IEC 15408 - Security techniques - Evaluation criteria for IT security. (2005).

Jürjens, J. (2002). UMLsec: Extending UML for Secure Systems Development. In *The Unified Modeling Language* (pp. 412-425).

Kocher, P. C. Ja_e, J., & Jun, B. (1999). Differential power analysis. In *Advances in Cryptology - CRYPTO* (pp. 388-397).

Lodderstedt, T., Basin, D. A., & Doser, J. (2002). A UML-Based Modeling Language for Model-Driven Security . In *The Unified Modeling Language* (pp. 426–441). SecureUML. doi:10.1007/3-540-45800-X_33

Lowe, G. (1997). A hierarchy of authentication specifications. In *Computer Security Foundations Workshop* (pp. 31-43).

Luo, J.-N., Shieh, S.-P., & Shen, J.-C. (2006). Secure Authentication Protocols Resistant to Guessing Attacks. *Journal of Information Science and Engineering, 22*(5), 1125–1143.

Marschke, G. (1988). The Directory Authentication Framework. *CCITT Recommendation, X*, 509.

Meadows, C. (2003). Formal Methods for Cryptographic Protocol Analysis: Emerging Issues and Trends. (Technical Report).

Meadows, C. (2004). Ordering from Satan's menu: a survey of requirements specification for formal analysis of cryptographic protocols. *Science of Computer Programming, 50*(1-3), 3–22. doi:10.1016/j.scico.2003.12.001

Mitchell, J. C., Mitchell, M., & Stern, U. (1997, May). Automated analysis of cryptographic protocols using MurΦ. In *IEEE Symposium on Security and Privacy* (pp. 141-151).

Pironti, A., & Sisto, R. (2008a). Formally Sound Refinement of Spi Calculus Protocol Specifications into Java Code. In *IEEE High Assurance Systems Engineering Symposium* (pp. 241-250).

Pironti, A., & Sisto, R. (2008b). *Soundness Conditions for Message Encoding Abstractions in Formal Security Protocol Models* (pp. 72–79). Availability, Reliability and Security.

Roscoe, A. W., Hoare, C. A. R., & Bird, R. (1997). *The theory and practice of concurrency*. Prentice Hall PTR.

Ryan, P., Schneider, S., Goldsmith, M., Lowe, G., & Roscoe, B. (Eds.). (2001). *The Modelling and Analysis of Security Protocols*. Addison-Wesley.

Stoller, S. D. (2001). A Bound on Attacks on Payment Protocols. In *IEEE Symposium on Logic in Computer Science* (p. 61).

Wen, H.-A., Lin, C.-L., & Hwang, T. (2006). Provably secure authenticated key exchange protocols for low power computing clients. *Journal of Computer Security, 25*(2), 106–113. doi:10.1016/j.cose.2005.09.010

Woo, T. Y. C., & Lam, S. S. (1993). A Semantic Model for Authentication Protocols. In *IEEE Symposium on Security and Privacy* (pp. 178-194).

Xiaodong, S. D., David, W., & Xuqing, T. (2001). Timing analysis of keystrokes and timing attacks on SSH. In *USENIX Security Symposium* (pp. 25-25).

KEY TERMS AND DEFINITIONS

Code Generation: Technique for automatically refining a formal model into an implementation.

Formal Method: Mathematically-based method for specifying and analyzing systems.

Formal Model: Description of a system with unambiguous, mathematically defined semantics.

Formal Verification: Providing evidence (by a mathematical proof) of a property holding on a formal model.

Model Extraction: Technique for automatically extracting a formal model from an implementation.

Security Protocol: Communication protocol aimed at achieving a goal over an unsecure network.

State Space Exploration: Formal verification technique based on exploration of all the possible behaviors of a model.

Theorem Proving: Formal verification technique based on direct building of mathematical proofs.

Section 4
Embedded Systems and SCADA Security

Chapter 9
Fault Tolerant Remote Terminal Units (RTUs) in SCADA Systems

Syed Misbahuddin
Sir Syed University of Engineering and Technology, Pakistan

Nizar Al-Holou
University of Detroit Mercy, USA

ABSTRACT

A Supervisory Control and Data Acquisition (SCADA) system is composed of number of remote terminal units (RTUs) for collecting field data. These RTUs send the data back to a master station, via a communication link. The master station displays the acquired data and allows the operator to perform remote control tasks. An RTU is a microprocessor based standalone data acquisition control unit. As the RTUs work in harsh environment, the processor inside the RTU is susceptible to random faults. If the processor fails, the equipment or process being monitored will become inaccessible. This chapter proposes a fault tolerant scheme to untangle the RTU's failure issues. According to the scheme, every RTU will have at least two processing elements. In case of either processor's failure, the surviving processor will take over the tasks of the failed processor to perform its tasks. With this approach, an RTU can remain functional despite the failure of the processor inside the RTU. Reliability and availability modeling of the proposed fault tolerant scheme have been presented. Moreover, cyber security for SCADA system and recommendations for the mitigation of these issues have been discussed.

DOI: 10.4018/978-1-60960-851-4.ch009

INTRODUCTION

Supervisory Control and Data Acquisition (SCADA) systems have been designed to monitor and control the plants or equipment used in industrial applications. Some example industries in which SCADA systems are used are: telecommunications applications, water and waste control, energy sector including oil, gas refining and transportation applications etc. (IEEE) (ANS/IEEE, 1987). The SCADA systems transfer data between a SCADA central host computer and Remote Terminal Units (RTUs). The information exchange is also carried out between Programmable Logic Controllers (PLCs) and SCADA master units (IEEE, 2000). The SCADA systems' application can be very simple or complex. For example, a simple SCADA system can be used to observe the environmental conditions of a small building and another SCADA system can be employed to examine the critical activities inside a nuclear power plant.

SCADA's central station dynamically sends the configuration and control programs to RTUs. In some situations, the local programming units are also used to configure remote RTUs. Depending upon the requirement, the RTUs can directly communicate with other RTUs on peer-to-peer basis. One of the RTU in SCADA system can perform the role of relay station to another RTU. A relay RTU provides store and forward action facility.

SCADA SYSTEM ARCHITECTURE

A SCADA system consists of a Master Terminal Unit (MTU), communication equipment, and geographically distributed Remote Terminal Units (RTUs), as in Figure 1. The RTUs are linked with MTU via communication link as shown below:

The RTUs collect data and send it to the SCADA's host computers located at some central position. Generally, a SCADA system may be

Figure 1. Typical SCADA system with master unit connected with RTU

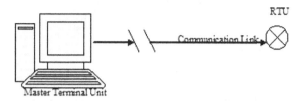

associated with several of I/O points for data collection. An operator can decide polling rate for field data collection. The polling rate is influenced by several parameters such as number of sites, the required amount of data at each site, the available maximum bandwidth of the communication channel and the minimum required display and control time (Scadalink, 2010).

Arguably, it can be stated that the SCADA system's rationale and objective depend upon the proper functioning of a remote terminal unit. The failure of one or more RTUs is therefore detrimental. In this chapter we have investigated a mechanism which will guarantee the service availability of RTU despite its failures. The Reliability and Availability analysis of the proposed scheme is discussed and the discussion of results is presented later in the chapter.

SMART SENSORS

The sensors normally work under the control of a microprocessor or microcontroller. The host processor is responsible for initiating the data sampling and collecting the digital output of the physical parameter the sensor is sensing. In smart sensors, the intelligence is delegated to the sensor unit itself. A smart sensor contains a Microcontroller (μC), a signal conditioning unit, an Analog-to-Digital Controller (A/D) and the interface (Alba, 1988). The microcontroller makes the sensor capable of distributed processing, compensation, self calibrating and so on. Figure 2 shows the elements of smart sensor.

Figure 2. Smart sensor

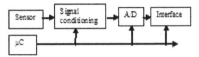

Figure 3. Block diagram of FTRTU

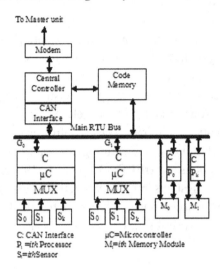

The sensed data is signal conditioned and converted into digital form under the control of a microcontroller. The interface unit inside the smart sensor places the converted data onto the communication bus. Controller Area Network (CAN) communication protocol may be used to send the sensor data the in the form of CAN messages (Bosch, 1991). Transmitted sensor data encapsulated in CAN message format can be read by any CAN-enabled processing node connected to the bus. The application of smart sensors will mitigate the host processor from directly controlling the sensors.

FAULT TOLERANT REMOTE TERMINAL UNIT

In SCADA system, the telemetry is used to send commands and programs to remote terminal units (RTUs) located at remote locations. Also, the telemetry is used to receive monitoring information from them (IEEE, 2000), (Smith and Block, 1993). As the remote terminal units work in harsh environment,, the processing elements inside RTUs are also subjected to intermittent or permanent failures (Breuer, 1973). If the processing unit inside an RTU becomes faulty, the whole RTU becomes unavailable and no data can be accessed from the sensors under RTU's control. The service availability of RTU can be maintained by introducing fault tolerant features within RTU. Different RTU manufactures have suggested various fault tolerant schemes. In one of the approach, a redundant RTU has been used to withstand the faults in RTU (Iclink, 2010). In

case of either RTU's failure, the surviving RTU can continue providing the required services. In another solution, CPU and I/O units are used in fully triple redundant (TMR) to fulfill the reliability requirements (Woodward, 2010).

In this chapter, a software based fault tolerant scheme is proposed. In this scheme, a RTU contains at least two processing elements or microcontrollers and a central control unit (CCU). All processing elements (PEs) within the RTU are connected to a communication bus. The data communication over this bus is according to Controller Area Network (CAN) protocol. All the sensors in the RTU are grouped into multiple sensor groups. Each sensor group is monitored by one microcontroller unit (μC) through a multiplexer (MUX) as shown Figure 3. All μC reads the sensor data and pass it to the CAN interface unit, which will send it to the main RTU bus in the CAN message format. The CCU reads the related CAN message and passes the sensor data to the remote central monitoring unit in the SCADA system. All PEs maintains the sensor data's history in its local memory. This data history is passed to the central controller periodically.

Figure 4. CAN Version 2.0A and 2.0B

SOF	11 Bits Identifier	RTR	Control Field	0 to 8 Bytes	EOF

CAN Version 2.0A

SOF	11 Bits Identifier	SRR	IDE	18 Bits Identifier	Control Field	0 to 8 Bytes	EOF

CAN Version 2.0B

CAN PROTOCOL

The CAN protocol developed by Robert Bosch has been specially designed for real time networks. It is becoming de-facto standard for connecting the electronic control units in various real time applications (Gupta, 1995). There are two versions of CAN protocols in use called CAN version 2.0A and 2.0B. The main difference between these versions is the length of message identifier. Version 2.0A and version 2.0B have 11 and 29 bits message identifier respectively, as shown in Figure 4.

We have selected CAN version 2.0A for our proposed scheme of transferring sensor data from RTU to the MTU. The 11-bits message ID field of CAN messages can be manipulated to represent different types of messages. For example, the first three bits ($m_0 m_1 m_2$) can be used to represent the RTU number. Next three bits $m_3 m_4 m_5$ represent the message type. The bits m_6 and m_7 represent the sensor group number (SGN). Finally, the last 3 bits of message represent sensor ID (SID) in a sensor group. The sensor data will be sent in payload of the CAN message. The messaging scheme is illustrated by following example.

Example: Assume temperature information from the RTU number 0 is to be sent to the master unit from a sensor number 0 in the group 0. If the code for temperature information is 000, the CAN message ID is shown below Figure 5.

FAULT TOLERANT SCHEME

The central control unit determines every processor's state by sending periodic diagnostic messages to each processing element inside the RTU. All active processors will respond to the CCU by sending the acknowledgment messages. If the central control unit does not receive an acknowledgment message from a processor within a predefined time interval, then it will mark it as faulty processor. The central control unit transfers the code of the failed node stored in code memory to the local memory of the surviving processor. The central control unit will then assign the tasks of the failed processor to the surviving processor. The assigned processor can access the sensor group attached to the failed processor through CAN bus inside the RTU. The assigned processor will continue its original tasks in addition to its assigned tasks on time sharing basis. According to the proposed fault tolerant scheme, every processing unit in the RTU has the potential to execute the tasks of any other processor. Consequently, if half of the processor in RTU failed then with surviving processor in the RTU can continue providing its services to the master unit.

Like any other processor, the central control unit inside TRU is also vulnerable to intermittent or permanent failures. The central control unit's failure is catastrophic because in case of its failure, no sensor data will be accessible inside the RTU. In order to avoid such a situation, a single line called Central Controller's Active line (CCA) can be introduced as proposed by Vishnubhtla and Mahmud (Serma, 1988). In this scheme the controller's active line remains at high logic as long as the central control unit is functioning. On the other hand, if the central control becomes faulty, its active line will reset to low logic. The low logic on CCU's active line will trigger a watchdog timer.

Figure 5. CAN message for Temperature information from sensor # 0 in sensor group # 0 in RTU # 0

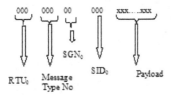

Figure 6. Parallel configuration for reliability calculation

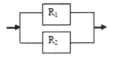

If the central control active line does not return to high logic within a specified time window, the watchdog timer output will interrupt any processor inside RTU to take the responsibility of the central control unit. The emulating processor will continue its original tasks along with the tasks of failed central control unit on time sharing basis.

In order to handle the tasks of the failed processor, every processor inside RTU works in multiprogramming mode. In a single-processor multiprogramming system, two processes (one process related to the surviving processor and second process related to the failed processor) reside in the surviving processor's local memory and share the single processor, which executes one of these processes on time sharing basis.

RELIABILITY MODELING

Reliability is defined as the probability a system is functioning accurately for a period of length time *t* (Trividi, 1990). In this section, the reliability modeling for the proposed fault tolerant RTU is presented. Since every processing element in RTU is capable of performing the tasks of another failing processor, a parallel configuration shown in Figure 6 can be considered for the reliability estimation for the proposed fault tolerant RTU. In Figure 6, R_1 and R_2 are considered as reliabilities of two processing elements having potential of taking over the job of each other.

If R_c and F_c are the cumulative reliability and unreliability of the module respectively, then the

unreliability of the processor module can be calculated as follows:

$$F_c = (1-R_1)(1-R_2) \tag{1}$$

The reliability of the processor module is calculated as:

$$R_c = 1-F = 1-(1-R_1)(1-R_2) \tag{2}$$

We assume that the processor's failure is exponentially distributed with failure rate μ. If the reliabilities of both processors are same inside the RTU, then we can say:

$$R_1 = R_2 = e^{-\mu t} \tag{3}$$

With equal reliabilities for the processing units, we can determine the reliability of the module as:

$$R_c = 2e^{-\mu t} - e^{-2\mu t} \tag{4}$$

The reliability of the complete RTU includes the reliability of the central control unit as well. Therefore, we can say RTU's reliability is:

$$R_{rtu} = (R_c)(R_{ccu}) \tag{5}$$

The RTU's reliability is computed for a typical failure rate as shown below in table 1. Second column is the RTU reliability of single processing unit. The third column is the reliability of the module in which a surviving processor takes the tasks of the failed processing unit within the RTU. The comparison shows that the proposed fault tolerant scheme improves the RTU reliability.

Table 1. Reliability comparison

Time	R_{nft}	R_{wft}
0	1	1
100	0.318	0.5347
300	0.03225	0.0634

Figure 7. Markov model of a processor in RTU

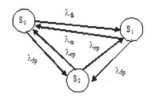

AVAILABILITY MODELING OF A PROCESSING NODE IN FTRTU

Availability is an important metric that is commonly used along with other metrics to evaluate a fault tolerant computer system. Availability may be defined as the probability that the system is operating correctly and is available to perform its intended jobs at an instant of time (t)(Salim, 1991). A Markov model can be developed to model a processing node's availability in the RTU (Misbahuddin, 2006).

A processor that performs the tasks of another processor is called a "primary" processing node (PPN). A processor whose tasks are performed by the primary processor is called the "secondary" processing node (SPN). Considering this scheme, three states can be defined for every primary processor in proposed system. Figure 7 depicts the Markov model that shows these three states.

The states shown in Figure 7 are defined as below (Misbahuddin, 2006):

- S_0: Single operational state: The state in which the processing node is performing its own tasks only.
- S_1: Dual operational state: The state in which a primary processing node executes the tasks of other processing node that has become faulty. The primary processing node performs the tasks of the secondary processing node in addition to PPN's own tasks on time sharing basis.
- S_2: Faulty state: The state in which processing node is not available due to a fault.

The state transition probabilities for the Markov model are defined as follows:

- λ_{fs}: Dual task rate: The rate at which a primary processing node switches from S_0 to S_1 due to fault in the secondary processing node.
- λ_{rs}: Dual task recovery rate: The rate at which the primary processor switches from S_1 to S_0 when the faulty secondary processing node recovers from its fault.
- λ_{fp}: Failure rate: The rate at which a primary processor gets faulty.
- λ_{rp}: Recovery rate: The rate at which a primary processor recovers from a fault.

A stochastic transitional matrix (S) can be generated from the Markov model shown in Box 1.

State probabilities of the processing node are the unique non-negative solution of the following equations.

$$P(S_j) = \sum_i P(S_i)\lambda_{ij} \qquad (6)$$

$$\sum_j P(S_j) = 1 \qquad (7)$$

In (6) and (7), the parameter λ_{ij} may be defined as the transition rate from *ith* state to *jth* state and $P(S_j)$ is considered as the limiting probability of the *jth* state. The probability of a single operational state (S_0) of the processor can be derived from the matrix S, equations (6) and (7) and the result is:

Box 1.

		S_0	S_1	S_2
	S_0	$1-(\lambda_{fs}+\lambda_{fp})$	λ_{fs}	λ_{fp}
S=	S_1	λ_{rs}	$1-(\lambda_{rs}+\lambda_{fp})$	λ_{fp}
	S_2	λ_{rp}	λ_{rp}	$1-2\lambda_{rp}$

$$P(S_0) = \frac{\lambda_{rp}(2\lambda_{rs} + \lambda_{fp})}{(2\lambda_{rp} + \lambda_{fp})(\lambda_{rs} + \lambda_{fs} + \lambda_{fp})} \quad (8)$$

Similarly, the probability of the processing node in the dual operational mode (S1) is calculated and the result is:

$$P(S_1) = \frac{2\lambda_{fs}\lambda_{rp} + \lambda_{fp}\lambda_{rp}}{(\lambda_{ro} + \lambda_{fs} + \lambda_{fp})(2\lambda_{rp} + \lambda_{fp})} \quad (9)$$

$P(S_1)$ can be used to compute the availability of the tasks of the faulty processing node. A primary processing node may be considered as "available" to perform its tasks as long as it is in state S_0 or in S_1. Therefore, the processor's availability can be defined as follows:

$$A=P(S_0)+P(S_1) \quad (10)$$

Substituting equations (8) and (9) in (10), we obtain the processor's availability in terms of the processor's failure and recovery rates as shown below:

$$A = \frac{2\lambda_{rp}}{2\lambda_{rp} + \lambda_{fp}} \quad (11)$$

In order to compare the availability of the proposed system with a similar system without fault tolerant capability, a simple Markov model of a processing node is developed. The simple Markov model is for the system which does not have any fault tolerant capability. Therefore, the Markov states will have two states namely, single

Figure 8. Markov model for a processor without fault tolerance

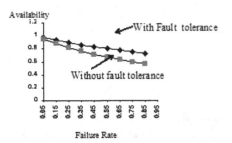

operational state (S0) and the failure state (S2). This Markov model is shown in Figure 8.

λ_{fp} and λ_{rp} in Figure 8 represent failure and repair rates of the processing node in a system that does not have fault tolerant capability. In this case, the processor is available only when it is in S_0. The processor's availability is derived as:

$$P(S_0) = \frac{\lambda_{rp}}{\lambda_{rp} + \lambda_{fp}} \quad (12)$$

If A_{woft} represents the Availability of the processor without fault-tolerance, then we can say that A_{woft} is equal to $P(S_0)$:

$$A_{woft} = P(S_0) \quad (13)$$

DISCUSSION OF THE RESULT

To evaluate the fault-tolerance capability of the proposed architecture, another metric is used which is called the Availability Improvement Factor (AIF). AIF is defined as (Harri, 1991):

$$AIF = \frac{A - A_{woft}}{A_{woft}} \quad (14)$$

AIF indicates the improvement in availability in the proposed system compared with an architecture that has no fault-tolerance capability.

Table 2. Failure rate vs. availability

λ_{fp}	A	A_{woft}	AIF(%)
5.0 E-05	9.779736E-01	9.568965E-01	2.202
1.5E-04	9.367089E-01	8.809524E-01	6.329
2.5E-04	8.987854E-01	8.161765E-01	10.121
3.5E-04	8.638132E-01	7.602740E-01	13.618
4.5E-04	8.314607E-01	7.115384E-01	16.853
5.5E-04	8.014441E-01	6.686747E-01	19.855
6.5E-04	7.735192E-01	6.306818E-01	22.648
7.5E-04	7.474747E-01	5.967742E-01	25.252
8.5E-04	7.231270E-01	5.663265E-01	27.687
9.5E-04	7.003155E-01	5.388349E-01	29.968
1.05E-03	6.788991E-01	5.138889E-01	32.110
1.15E-03	6.587537E-01	4.911504E-01	34.124
1.25E-03	6.397695E-01	4.703390E-01	36.023
1.35E-03	6.218488E-01	4.512195E-01	37.815

Availability (A) of a processor in RTU is calculated for different failure rates and compared with Awoft. The result is shown in Table 2, which also shows AIF as a function of the failure rate. It is clear from the Table 2 that the processing node's availability is more than that of the system that is without fault tolerant capability. Table 2 shows that AIF increases as the failure rate increases. Figure 9 shows a comparison between A and Awoft for the same failure rates. Clearly, availability of the processors in the proposed system is higher than that of similar RTU without fault-tolerance capability. Figure 10 shows AIF as a function of the failure rate. This result indicates that the AIF increases as the failure rate increases. This means that as the working conditions are worsened, the availability in the proposed system is improved. Therefore, the proposed architecture has a good potential for the SCADA systems.

Figure 9. Processing node availability as a function of failure rate

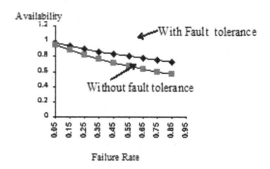

Figure 10. AIF vs processor's failure rate

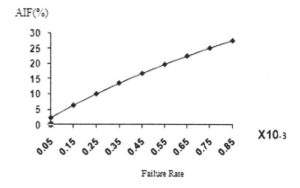

CYBER SECURITY AND VULNERABILITY FOR SCADA SYSTEMS

In SCADA systems, vulnerabilities can impact three main components namely Master Station (Computer), remote terminal unit (RTU) and Communication Networks (Ten, 2007), (Brown, 2007), (NERC, 2006), (Berg, 2005), (Falco, 2002). Since RTUs are spreading out over large areas, they are more vulnerable than others and are at higher security risks. The vulnerability of Internet and TCP/IP protocol can be extended to SCADA systems. As a result, SCADA systems are subjected to cyber attacks with major consequences. These cyber attacks can come from internal employee or external hackers. The most commonly used attacks are discussed briefly below (Ten, 2007):

1. Packet Sniffing: a hacker or an employee can install sniffer software to sniff packets and may modify them in the network to control different components of the systems like the RTU.
2. Access the system through its open ports and other vulnerabilities and send undesired control signals to trigger harmful actions.
3. Denial of Service (DOS) attack: The concept of this attack is to flood the SCADA system in order to exhaust its resources and disrupt its services to legitimate users.
4. Spoofing attack where a hacker imitates another user by changing data and thereby gaining illegitimate access.

CYBER SECURITY MITIGATION

The new generation of SCADA systems uses transmission control protocol/Internet (TCP/IP) protocol, with which the hackers are familiar. Moreover, there are different hacking tools and resources to hack the systems that use the standard TCP/IP protocol. The common solutions for TCP/IP security threats might not be sufficient for some complicated systems such as SCADA. To protect SCADA systems from unauthorized access, the following minimum steps should be followed (Ten, 2007), (Falco, 2002), (Permann, 2010):

1. Work with other countries and professional/standard organizations such as IEEE, NERC to develop and implement security standards.
2. Follow NERC guidelines for authentication, data flow, segmented network, and dedicated/isolated hosts (NERC 2006).
3. Perform vulnerability evaluation and penetration testing periodically using well-known techniques and tools such as IP scanning and port scanning. Hackers use IP scanning first to gather information about the SCADA network infrastructure. Then, the hackers use the port scanning to search for open ports, as

each open port is associated with a service that can be exploited to gain access to the SCADA components and network.
4. Use Firewalls, routers, and other Intrusion Detection Systems (IDS) at different interface points between various components such as computer, RTU and communication networks to limit the access to a specific component and thereby reduce its potential risk and vulnerability impact. This will form a Virtual Private Network (VPN) over the Internet (Ten, 2007).
5. Use electronic defense-in-depth concept, which includes multiple layers of protective shields, as one layer is penetrated another layer is revealed (ESIAC, 2010).
6. Perform backup and restart major components of the SCADA system periodically.

CONCLUSION

A SCADA system monitors the remote processes or equipment via state-of-the art communication links. In SCADA systems, the data measurement at the remote side is under the control of a remote terminal unit (RTU). If the processor used inside RTU becomes faulty, then the remote data monitoring will be become unavailable. There is no way for the master unit in SCADA to fix RTU until and unless physical maintenance is performed for the failed RTU. In this chapter, we have proposed a fault tolerant scheme for the RTU. This scheme allows a RTU keep functioning as long as one of the two processing units is in working condition. We have also suggested that sensors can be grouped according to their types. Each processor in an RTU can access its corresponding sensor group via RTU main bus. This scheme allows every processor to access the sensor data related to another processor through the local bus. Analysis shows that the Reliability and Availability of the RTU are improved due to the proposed fault tolerant methodology. Finally, the issue of cyber security related to SCADA systems has been addressed.

REFERENCES

Alba, M. (1988). *A system approach to smart sensors and smart actuator design.* (SAE paper 880554).

ANS/IEEE, C37.1. (1987). Definition, specification, and analysis of systems used for supervisory control and data acquisition, and automatic control.

Berg, M., & Stamp, J. (2005). *A reference model for control and automation systems in electric power.* Sandia National Laboratories. Retrieved from http://www.sandia.gov/scada/documents/sand_2005_1000C.pdf

Breuer, M. A. (1973, March). Testing for intermittent faults in digital circuits. *IEEE Transactions on Computers, 22*(3), 241–246. doi:10.1109/T-C.1973.223701

Brown, T. (2005, Jun./Jul.). Security in SCADA systems: How to handle the growing menace to process automation. *IEE Comp. and Control Eng., 16*(3), 42–47. doi:10.1049/cce:20050306

ESISAC. (2010). *Electronic security guide.* Retrieved from http://www.esisac.com/publicdocs/Guides/SecGuide_ElectronicSec_BOTapprvd-3may05.pdf

Falco, J., Stouffer, S., Wavering, A., & Proctor, F. (2002). *IT security for industrial control.* MD: Gaithersburg.

Gupta, S. (1995). *CAN facilities in vehicle networking* (pp. 9-16). (SAE paper 900695).

Hariri, S. (1991, May). A hierarchical modeling of availability in distributed systems. *Proceedings International Conference on Distributed Systems,* (pp. 190-197).

Iclink. (2010). *Products.* Retrieved from http://www.iclinks.com/Products/Rtu/ICL4150.html

IEEE. (1987). *Fundamentals of supervisory systems.* (IEEE Tutorial No. 91 EH-03376PWR).

IEEE. (2000). *IEEE recommended practice for data communications between remote terminal units and intelligent electronic devices in a substation.* (IEEE Std 1379-2000. Revision of IEEE Std 1379-1997).

Misbahuddin, S. (2006). A performance model of highly available multicomputer systems. *International Journal of Simulation and Modeling, 26*(2), 112–120.

NERC. (2006). *Cyber security standards.* Retrieved from http://www.nerc.com/~filez/standards/Cyber-Security-Permanent.html

Permann, R. M., & Rohde, K. (2005). *Cyber assessment methods for SCADA security.* Retrieved from http://www.inl.gov/scada/publications/d/cyber_assessment_methods_for_scada_security.pdf

Robert Bosch. (1991). *CANS specification, ver. 2.0.* Stuttgart, Germany: Robert Bosch GmbH.

Scadalink. (2010). *Support.* Retrieved from http://www.scadalink.com/support/scada.html

Smith, H. L., & Block, W. R. (1993, January). RTUs slave for supervisory systems. *Computer Applications in Power, 6,* 27–32. doi:10.1109/67.180433

Ten, C., Govindarasu, M., & Liu, C. C. (2007, October). *Cyber security for electric power control and automation systems* (pp. 29-34).

Trividi, K. (1990, July). Reliability evaluation of fault tolerant systems. *IEEE Transactions on Reliability, 44*(4), 52–61.

Vishnubhtla, S. R., & Mahmud, S. M. (1988). *A centralized multiprocessor based control to optimize performance in vehicles.* IEEE Workshop on Automotive Applications of Electronics, Detroit, MI.

Woodward. (2010). *Document*. Retrieved from http://www.woodward.com/pdf/ic/85578.pdf

KEY TERMS AND DEFINITIONS

Availability: Availability may be defined as the probability that the system is operating correctly and is available to perform its intended jobs at an instant of time (t)

CAN Protocol: Controller Area Network protocol originally designed for Automotive application, which allows data communication is form of short messages over a serial bus.

Denial of Service (DOS): The concept of this attack is to flood Computer system in order to exhaust its resources and disrupt its services to legitimate users.

Reliability: Reliability is defined as the probability a system is functioning accurately for a period of length time t.

Remote Terminal Units: A processor based unit to access data and send control units in SCADA System

SCADA: Supervisory Control and Data Acquisition System used in industries for remote information gathering via Remote Terminal Units (RTU)

Smart Sensor: A sensor unit with processing capability

Chapter 10
Embedded Systems Security

Muhammad Farooq-i-Azam
COMSATS Institute of Information Technology, Pakistan

Muhammad Naeem Ayyaz
University of Engineering and Technology, Pakistan

ABSTRACT

Not long ago, it was thought that only software applications and general purpose digital systems i.e. computers were prone to various types of attacks against their security. The underlying hardware, hardware implementations of these software applications, embedded systems, and hardware devices were considered to be secure and out of reach of these attacks. However, during the previous few years, it has been demonstrated that novel attacks against the hardware and embedded systems can also be mounted. Not only viruses, but worms and Trojan horses have been developed for them, and they have also been demonstrated to be effective. Whereas a lot of research has already been done in the area of security of general purpose computers and software applications, hardware and embedded systems security is a relatively new and emerging area of research. This chapter provides details of various types of existing attacks against hardware devices and embedded systems, analyzes existing design methodologies for their vulnerability to new types of attacks, and along the way describes solutions and countermeasures against them for the design and development of secure systems.

DOI: 10.4018/978-1-60960-851-4.ch010

INTRODUCTION

A few years ago almost all electronic equipment was built using analog components and devices. However, after the advent of microprocessors and microcontrollers majority of electronic equipment developed today uses digital components for design implementation. Embedded systems are finding their use in diverse applications ranging from complicated defense systems to home gadgets. Smart cards, debit and credit cards, DVD players, cell phones and PDAs are just a few examples of embedded systems that we use in our daily lives.

Under certain circumstances and conditions, a larger digital system is usually dependent upon the functions of smaller component embedded systems for its function and operation. For example, a general purpose computer houses many smaller embedded systems. A hard disk, a network interface card, CD-ROM drive are examples of embedded systems used by a computer system for its operation. In addition to this, large industrial plants, nuclear power plants, passenger and fighter aircrafts, weapons systems, etc. are a few of many places where embedded systems are part of a bigger system.

With this increased usage of embedded systems in our daily lives, it is not unusual that bad guys and criminals try to take advantage of weak links in their security. Specially, the embedded systems used in financial institutions, battlefield equipment, fighter planes and industrial and nuclear plants may become targets of attack due to the importance of functions performed by them. Therefore, it is essential that these systems and the components used in them are highly dependable and their security is not compromised.

A number of security incidents related to embedded systems have been reported in the literature. For example, in 2001, Shipley and Garfinkel found an unprotected modem line to a computer system which was being used to control a high voltage power transmission line (Koopman, 2004). In another incident, a disgruntled employee

in Australia released almost 250 million tons of raw sewage by causing failure of control system of a waste treatment plant through a remote attack (IET, 2005).

It is pertinent to mention here that the organizations which become target of attack may not like to publicize the incident due to various reasons. For example, it may disclose a vulnerable area of their systems or it may cause them a bad name and raise questions against security of their other assets. Furthermore, security threats against embedded systems do not propagate as rapidly as those against a standard operating system or software application. This is because majority of personal computer systems is similar and it is easier for any security threat to replicate from one system to the other. On the other hand, each embedded device is unique and it is almost impossible for a security threat to propagate from one device to the other. Moreover, a security threat against an embedded device is generally initiated at any one of the design stages before the device is built. Security threats against a software system may be programmed at any time after they have been developed and deployed. These are a few of the many reasons that we do not come to see as many security incidents reported against embedded systems as against software applications. Despite this fact, security incidents have been reported against hardware devices and embedded systems, a couple of which have been cited above and a few more will be mentioned later in this chapter.

BACKGROUND

Embedded systems security is a new and emerging area of research. It is meeting point of many disciplines such as electronics, logic design, embedded systems, signal processing and cryptography. It is closely related to the area of information and software systems security because software is an integral component of any embedded system.

First microprocessor was developed around 1971 and later innovations in this field resulted in the development of computer systems and embedded devices. Software is an integral component of the both. In particular, every desktop computer carries a critical piece of software called the operating system. It manages the hardware resources and makes it possible for an end user to operate the computer. Other software applications in a computer run on top of the operating system.

It was the software component of digital systems which was first subjected to different types of security threats and attacks and many security incidents were reported against different operating systems and software applications. This started in 1970s and continues to date. However, embedded systems security gained importance in 1990s, specially, after side channel attacks were shown to be successful against smart cards. Later, emergence of networked embedded systems highlighted this area of research as the embedded devices could now be subjected to remote attacks.

Many of the methods and techniques used in the attacks against software applications can also be used against embedded devices, specially, in the firmware component. However, a few considerations involving the security of an embedded system are different from those of a general purpose digital system. To get a better perspective, it would help to look at the traits of embedded systems security which are different from those of software security.

Embedded Systems Security Parameters

An embedded system is a digital device that does a specific focused job as compared to a general purpose digital system such as a personal computer. Whereas a general purpose digital system can be used for a variety of tasks by installing new software, the software for an embedded system is generally fixed and has limited flexibility in allowing user programs to run. For example, an operating system in a desktop computer allows user to perform a variety of tasks by installing appropriate software. The software can later be un-installed, modified or updated without much of a hassle. However, in the case of an embedded system, this is not the case. A traffic light controller, for example, is a dedicated system performing a specific function. The software in such a digital system has limited flexibility and usually does not allow user to install new software on top of the base software. Also modification and up-gradation of software is not as easy as in the case of desktop computer. The software for such a system normally resides in Electrically Erasable and Programmable Read Only Memory (EEPROM) which has to be re-programmed using EEPROM programmers. In the context of security, it has an important implication i.e. if software in an embedded system is compromised, it will be lot more difficult to replace or upgrade as compared to software in a general purpose digital system. There are usually no software upgrades and patches for bugs as far as embedded devices are concerned.

Embedded systems have limited resources e.g. small memory, no secondary storage device and small input and output devices. These limitations provide an avenue of attack in that a software virus or a hardware Trojan horse can cause denial of service by consuming any of these resources. For example, many of the embedded systems have energy constraints and are often battery powered. These may have to operate over battery over an extended period of time and the power consumption has to be very low. By seeking to drain the battery, an attacker can cause the system failure even when breaking into the system is impossible.

Embedded systems generally carry out tasks that have timing deadlines. Missing these timing deadlines may cause loss of property or even life. Again this is a unique attack vector against embedded systems. By simply, adding some sort of delay in the execution of an instruction or a series of instructions, the attacker can achieve the objective of the attack.

Figure 1. Layers of abstraction in an FPGA based design

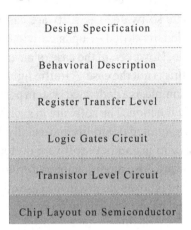

| Design Specification |
| Behavioral Description |
| Register Transfer Level |
| Logic Gates Circuit |
| Transistor Level Circuit |
| Chip Layout on Semiconductor |

While desktop systems and other similar equipment may operate in an environment where temperature and environment conditions are controlled to meet the requirements of the equipment installed, some of the embedded systems usually operate under extreme environment conditions, e.g. high temperature, humidity and even radiation. Causing any of these environment parameters to change can also affect the performance of embedded systems.

General purpose computers usually employ a popular brand of processors. Whereas, in the case of embedded systems there is a lot of variation in processors and operating systems. This provides for an inherent security against the propagation of attacks and security threats from one device to the other.

Embedded systems might operate unattended without the need of a system administrator. Therefore, there is usually no reporting mechanism on the attacks being carried out against the device similar to those reported by an antivirus or firewall in the case of traditional computer systems.

Construction of embedded systems invariably depends upon hardware devices and components such as Integrated Circuits (ICs). There is a broad array of attacks which can be mounted against an embedded system either at the level of firmware or at the level of circuit. Further, circuit level

attacks may exist either at the level of discrete components or hidden in an integrated circuit. In other words, security issues in an embedded system do not confine themselves to a single layer of abstraction but rather span across various layers of abstraction from tiny hardware components to firmware and software. In addition, the discrete components or the integrated circuit may or may not be part of an embedded system.

SECURITY ISSUES IN EMBEDDED SYSTEMS

A system is secure if it could be used only for the purpose for which it is intended and only by the prescribed and authorized user and is available to provide service at any time. This statement is also true for embedded systems in general.

Before we discuss the types of attacks and security issues, it is imperative to understand the lifecycle and design and development methodologies related to hardware devices and embedded systems.

Hardware devices and embedded systems can be implemented in a number of ways depending upon the application of the particular system under development. For example, we can develop a typical embedded system using an appropriate microcontroller and peripheral components. Similarly, for some other embedded system, an implementation using a Field Programmable Gate Array (FPGA) may be more appropriate. Whatever strategy for implementation of the embedded system we may choose, there are various stages involved from design to implementation. Figure 1 below shows various stages or layers of abstraction from design to implementation for an embedded system using an FPGA.

A security loophole may be present at any of these layers and detection becomes more and more difficult as we move from top to bottom layer. This fact is shown with increasing level of gray from the top layer to the bottom layer.

Types of Attacks

Attacks on embedded systems can be broadly categorized as:

- Design and algorithmic attacks
- Side channel attacks

As the name suggests, a design and algorithmic attack exploits weakness inherent in the design and algorithm of the embedded system whereas a side channel attack attempts to exploit weakness in the implementation of the design. It is pertinent to point out that the bug may be left un-intentionally which is seldom the case or intentionally by the designer(s) involved at various stages of the implementation of the design.

Design and algorithmic attacks rely on the bug left in the device during the design stage in any of the layers of abstraction of the embedded system. For example, in the case of an FPGA based system, the bug may be left in the program code of the system which is usually written using a Hardware Description Language (HDL). It may also be planted intentionally by the designer after the HDL code synthesis at the logic gate level. Such a bug exists in the embedded system in the shape of tangible hardware and is commonly known as hardware Trojan horse. In a similar fashion, the bug may be planted at the transistor level design or indeed at the level of semiconductor in the case of an integrated circuit. In the case of a microcontroller and microprocessor based embedded system, the bug may be planted in the control program of the microcontroller. Though the bug exists in the software code, it may still be called hardware Trojan horse as it alters the designated behavior of the embedded system to achieve hidden objectives.

In the case of side channel attacks, the attacker treats the embedded system as a black box and analyzes the inside of the system by feeding it various types of inputs and then observing the behavior of the system and its output. These types of attacks are normally used to extract some secret information from the embedded system.

Hardware Trojan Horses

Consider the case of standalone embedded systems i.e. an embedded system that is not part of any network. As the embedded device does not interact with any external network, it may be thought that no attacks can be mounted against the device. However, it is still possible for a malicious design engineer to leave a malignant hole i.e. a Trojan horse in the system. For example, a design engineer could program an embedded device to run correctly for all operations except, say, #2600th, or program it in such a way to behave erratically after certain number of operations or under a certain critical condition. If the device is part of a critical safety system in, say, an industrial process plant, the consequences may have a devastating effect on the plant operation. The result may be degraded performance, partial shutdown of the process or even complete failure of the entire plant.

The designer could also leave a hardware Trojan horse that can be controlled remotely, possibly using a radio channel, in an otherwise standalone embedded system. It may be noted that the Trojan horse may be part of an embedded system in the shape of discrete components or at the level of transistors in an integrated circuit. In the first case, the Trojan horse may be present on a circuit board of the embedded system, and in the second case, it may be present inside an integrated circuit in the shape of transistors.

It would be interesting to cite just two instances where hardware Trojan horses were detected and found spying on unauthorized information. In the first instance, Seagate external hard drives were found to have a hardware Trojan horse that transmitted user information to a remote entity (Farrell, 2007). In the second instance, Prevelakis and Spinellis (2007) report that, in 2006, Vodafone routers installed in Greece were altered in such a manner so as to allow eavesdropping phone conversation of the prime minister and many other officials.

As discussed earlier, the hardware Trojan horse may be implanted in the hardware device or embedded system at any of the various stages from design to implementation including plantation. This includes the possibility of implant by the designer at the level of behavioral description, by a third party synthesis tool or by the fabrication facility.

Alkabani and Koushanfar (2008) describe a method by which a designer could leave a Trojan horse in the pre-synthesis stage which after going through the rest of stages of implementation becomes part of the circuit. The designer first completes a high level description of the system to arrive at the Finite State Machine (FSM) of the design. It is at this stage that the designer manipulates the FSM by introducing more states into it such that the state transitions and their inputs can be controlled by a hidden input which may be used to trigger a hidden function in the system. As FSM is typically used to specify control part of the design, it occupies a very small fraction to the scale of only 1% of the total area and power consumption of the complete design. Therefore, even if the designer wishes to insert a large number of states which is two or three times of the original number, it is still only a small part of the complete system allowing it be hidden from detection.

Potkonjak, Nahapetian, Nelson and Massey (2009) in their paper describe a hardware Trojan horse meant for a cell phone. The Trojan triggers on the reception of a call from a certain caller ID. The Trojan can either conference call a third party so as to leak all the conversation or it can even render the phone useless.

Clark, Leblanc and Knight (in press) describe a novel hardware Trojan horse which exploits unintended channels in the Universal Serial Bus (USB) protocol to form a covert channel with a device to which it is connected. USB protocol is used to interface a multitude of devices to embedded and computer systems. Keyboard, mouse and speakers are a few of the many devices which use USB interface to connect to a digital system. USB uses two communication channels to interface a keyboard to a digital system. One channel, which is the data channel and is unidirectional, transmits key strokes to the digital systems and the other channel, which is a control channel and is bidirectional, transmits and receives control information, e.g. CAPS lock, NUM lock and SCROLL lock keys to and from the digital system. These are the intended uses of the channels and these channels are not meant to be used for the transmission and reception of other information. Similarly, USB allows interfacing audio speakers to a digital system using control and data channels like those used for keyboard. J. Clark et al. modified the standard use of these channels so as to form a covert channel to transmit and receive information other than meant to be communicated by these channels. Using these primitives, a standard USB keyboard can house additional components so as to also function as a hardware Trojan horse that utilizes the covert channels described above. If such a keyboard is connected to a digital system such as a computer, the security system at the computer will not object to the legitimacy of the USB device as it presents itself as a keyboard to the computer system. After it interfaces to the computer system, it can behave as a standard keyboard and in addition also log sensitive information such as username and password of an important resource such as the computer system itself. Using the username and password, the USB-based hardware Trojan horse can then upload malicious software application such as a software Trojan horse at any time of its convenience. An illustrative representation of such a hardware Trojan horse employing covert USB channels is shown in the Figure 2.

While a few hardware Trojan horse implementation mechanisms have been suggested, examples of which are given above, some detection mech-

Figure 2. USB-based hardware Trojan Horse using covert channels

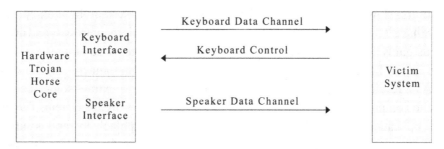

anisms for the hardware Trojan horses have also been proposed. It may be noted that complexity of design and implementation mechanisms adds to the difficulty of detecting a hardware Trojan horse.

Modern hardware devices and circuits contain a large number of gates, transistors, I/O pins. In addition to this, there is a large variety of components in a single hardware device or integrated circuit and a hardware Trojan horse can be implemented in a number of ways. All this added together makes the detection of hardware Trojan horse difficult and specialized task.

Potkonjak, Nahapetian, Nelson, and Massey (2009) have proposed a hardware Trojan horse detection mechanism for an integrated circuit using gate-level characterization. The technique makes non-destructive measurements of certain characteristics of gates in the Integrated Circuits (ICs). These characteristics include timing delay, power consumption and leakage current. Temperature and radiation can also be considered for this purpose. This measurement helps approximating the scaling factor of most of the gates in the integrated circuit. Further, a programming model comprising a linear system of equations is constructed and a statistical analysis helps determine the presence and even location of the hardware Trojan horse. However, this detection technique is limiting in cases where the added gate has the same inputs as a gate of the same type in the original design. Therefore, an attacker can circumvent this detection technique by developing a Trojan logic in

which all the gates in the Trojan circuitry have the same number of inputs as similar gates in the original design which is not something difficult to achieve.

Another mechanism to detect hardware Trojan horse in an integrated circuit, proposed by Jin and Makris (2008) computes a fingerprint of path delays in the integrated circuit by performing measurements on some random samples of normal ICs. The path delays of the suspect chip are also measured and compared against the standard fingerprint. If the results do not match and variation in the path delays of the IC under test is beyond a certain threshold, the IC is marked to have a hardware Trojan horse.

While we are on the topic of hardware Trojan horse, it would be pertinent to mention BIOS virus. BIOS (Basic Input Output System) is the piece of software which resides in the motherboard Read Only Memory (ROM). A few years back, one needed to adopt elaborate procedures using EEPROM programmers to update the software in the ROM. One needed to remove the EEPROM from the motherboard, put it into an EEPROM programmer, and only then one could burn new BIOS program into it. For all this, one needed physical access to the computer system. However, with the emergence of flash ROMs, which is a particular type of EEPROM, the BIOS firmware can be updated without having it to remove from the motherboard. One can now update the firmware in the flash ROM by running a program on the computer where it is installed. It is an advantage and has made life simple for the hardware developers and end users. However, it has also made possible what we have termed as BIOS virus. Once a computer virus gains access to a computer, it can update and infect the firmware in the flash ROM as well. As a result, a remote attacker can gain access to the computer by exploiting some weakness in the application software or the operating system. Once the attacker has gained access to the computer, it can run a piece of software to change the BIOS program in the flash ROM, say, to install a BIOS level rootkit.

A BIOS virus is a piece of malicious software that infects the computer BIOS and resides in the system ROM along with regular BIOS. If a virus infects a certain application or operating system, normally a simple virus scan with antivirus software with updated virus definitions is enough to detect and remove it. However, if a virus is able to infect the BIOS, even the detection becomes difficult. For the removal also, one has to adopt special procedures apart from using regular antivirus software. This includes downloading of new BIOS and all drivers from the manufacturer's website on a clean machine, then booting the infected machine using a clean media e.g. a bootable CD/DVD ROM, porting the downloaded BIOS and drivers to the infected system using a read-only CD or USB followed by their installation on the infected machine.

Side Channel Attacks

Design and algorithmic attacks discussed above usually implant a Trojan horse in the system so that the system can perform a certain hidden action on a trigger. To be more elaborate, a hardware Trojan horse may, for example, be used to send all the records and data of the system to an unauthorized entity over a covert channel or it may be used to allow remote control of the system by an unauthorized entity. For these attacks to be effective, a certain malicious circuitry is usually part of the entire digital system, be it an embedded system based upon microcontrollers and microprocessors or be it an integrated circuit.

Side channel attacks, on the other hand, are usually used to extract some secret information stored inside a digital system. The digital system is treated as a black box and is subjected to various tests by applying different sets of stimuli to its input and noting the output behavior against every input. By comparing the output results against various inputs, an attacker tries to infer the design of the digital system and secret information stored inside it. In other words, side channel attacks exploit weakness of the implementation of the algorithm as compared to algorithmic attacks which exploit weakness in the algorithm itself.

Generally, side channel attacks are mounted against hardware implementations of various encryption algorithms so as to infer the secret key stored inside the hardware security modules. In many cases, the hardware security module under attack is a smart card which is normally used to perform encryption or decryption using the secret key stored inside it. Smart cards have found use in many applications including credit cards, payphone, GSM cell phone SIM card, etc. By seeking to extract the secret key stored inside in any of these cards, the attacker can make a duplicate or clone of the original card thus allowing him or her to use the services provided by it without the knowledge of the legitimate owner of the card. Obviously the attacker will need to have physical access to the card to perform a side channel attack on it.

Kocher (1996) is credited with the development of first side channel attack i.e. timing analysis attack and co-development of power analysis attack (Kocher, Jeffe & Jun, 1999). These attacks laid the foundation of further research leading to the development of more side channel attacks.

There are four broad categories of side channel exploits:

- Time analysis
- Error analysis
- Power analysis
- Electromagnetic Radiation Analysis

Time Analysis

In a side channel attack based on time analysis, the attacker tries to infer protected information by comparing time delays in processing of various forms of information.

For example, take the case of implementation of RSA (Rivest, Shamir, Adleman) public key encryption algorithm in a hardware security module. An attacker can encrypt a few thousand plain text samples and note the time it takes each time. With the analysis of this timing information, the attacker can infer the private key stored in the hardware module. Schmeh (2003) proclaims that in the case of a smart card, only a few hours are needed to extract the key.

Timing analysis was first of the side channel attacks and was developed by Kocher. In his article (Kocher, 1996), he has described timing analysis attacks on implementations of Diffie-Hellman, RSA, DSS (Digital Signature Standard) and other crypto systems. By modeling the attack as a signal detection problem, he is able to show how computationally inexpensive the attack can be. The attack is dependent on the fact that digital systems require different amounts of time to process different inputs and similarly the times vary for different types of steps in a given program. For example, the steps involved in branching and conditional statements and processor instructions for multiplication, division or shift operations each require different amounts of time. By making timing measurements, the attacker can infer

the step being executed and also the type of data being processed.

To further elaborate the timing attack, consider the RSA decryption operations to compute a plaintext message m from cipher text c using private key (d,n) where d is the secret exponent and n is the modulus. The computation required to extract message m is given below:

$$m = c^d \bmod n$$

An attacker can get samples of cipher text c by passively eavesdropping on a target system and n can be inferred from the public key (e,n). By making timing measurements on multiple decrypted computations of the form given above, the perpetrator of the attack can then infer the secret exponent d, thereby enabling him or her to find the secret key (d,n). For timing analysis to work, the attacker must also know the encryption algorithm being used by the victim.

Error Analysis

Error analysis attack is also referred to as fault analysis attack. It was pioneered by Boneh, De-Millo and Lipton (1997) and later developed by Biham and Shamir (1997). In an error analysis side channel attack, the hardware module under attack is falsely activated or damaged and output pattern for a given input is obtained. For example, a smart card is damaged either mechanically or through heat. Output for the same input from a healthy module is also obtained. By comparing the correct and false results, the private key can be reconstructed.

Boneh et al. developed mathematical model of the fault analysis attack based upon transient faults i.e. faults which occur only for a short duration of time and then are gone. For example, flipping of a single bit in a hardware module for a few micro seconds is an example of transient fault. The attacker can also induce the transient faults into a system. Effectiveness of the attack is dependent upon the implementation of the crypto system. For example, for an RSA implementation based upon Chinese remainder theorem, Boneh et al. showed that the modulus can be factored with a very high probability by using a single faulty RSA signature.

The initial fault analysis attack developed by Boneh et al. works against public key crypto systems only and is not feasible against secret key encryption schemes. The attack is based upon algebraic properties of modular arithmetic used in public key encryption algorithms and therefore does not work against secret key encryption algorithms which use bit manipulations instead of arithmetic operations to perform encryption and decryption. Biham and Shamir taking the work further developed differential fault analysis attack which works against both public and secret key encryption schemes. They implemented the attack against an implementation of Data Encryption Standard (DES) and demonstrated that they can extract the DES secret key stored inside a tamper resistant DES hardware encryption device with 50 to 200 known cipher text samples. Even if the DES is replaced by 3DES, the attack can still extract the secret key with the same number of cipher text samples. In the case of encryption algorithms that compute S-boxes as a function of the key, the S-boxes can themselves be extracted.

In addition to these attacks which were developed a few years ago, Takahashi and Fukunaga (2010) demonstrated a successful attack against Advanced Encryption Standard (AES) with 192 and 256-bit keys using C code and a simple personal computer as recent as January 2010. They were able to successfully recover the original 192-bit key using 3 pairs of correct and faulty cipher texts within 5 minutes, and 256-bit key using 2 pairs of correct and faulty cipher texts and 2 pairs of correct and faulty plaintexts within 10 minutes.

Power Analysis

In this type of side channel attack, the attacker feeds different inputs to the embedded system and then observes the power consumed. The attacker then draws conclusions about the stored information by measuring and comparing fluctuations in power consumption. For example, DES key embedded in hardware security module can be inferred after about 100,000 encryption operations (Schmeh, 2003).

Like other side channel attacks, the power analysis attack can either be a simple power analysis attack or differential power analysis (DPA) attack. In the case of simple power analysis, the attacker draws conclusion about the operation being performed by observing the amount of power being consumed. For example, different instructions of a microprocessor take different amounts of time to execute and hence consume different amounts of power while they are being executed. Similarly, different stages of an encryption algorithm take different amount of time and power to execute. Some stages may be more computationally extensive and hence require more amount of power to execute and some other stages may require less amount of power to execute. As a result, by observing the power being consumed at a particular instant of time, the attacker can infer information about the stage of the encryption algorithm being executed and also the data upon which the operation is being performed. In other words, a simple power analysis can reveal the sequence of instructions being executed by the system under attack. Cryptosystems in which the path of execution depends upon the type of data being processed can be broken using this knowledge gained about the sequence of instructions being executed.

In the case of differential power analysis, the attacker not only makes observations of power consumed but also a statistical analysis of the data is carried out to infer the data value and the operation being performed on it. As stated earlier, there can be power variations due to various stages of an encryption algorithm being executed. In addition to this, there will also be power variations due to data values being operated upon in a particular stage. However, power variations due to later are much smaller than those due to the former reasons. These smaller variations are usually lost due to error measurements and other reasons. In these cases, a statistical power model, particularly developed for a target algorithm under test, correlating power consumption due to various stages and different types of data values can be applied to infer the secret values. In the first stage, observations on the power being consumed are made and in the second stage this data is fed to a statistical model. Error correction procedures are also applied to gain more accurate picture of the operations being performed by the system under attack. Typically a cryptographic algorithm uses only parts of the secret key, called sub keys, at certain stages. Instead of running the full blown algorithm, the attacker can write program to simulate selected part of the algorithm where computations involving sub keys are made. The attacker then calculates the intermediate values of that particular stage for all possible sub key guesses. The calculated intermediate values are fed to the statistical power model to predict the power consumption for that computation and hence the corresponding sub key. Then the attacker runs the real cryptosystem under attack with the same input data and makes an observation of the power consumed. The observed power consumption value is compared with the values obtained from the statistical model. All the power consumption values obtained from the statistical model that do not match with the real power consumption value are derived from wrong key guesses. However, matching power consumption value from the statistical model is derived from the correct sub key guess. As a result, the attacker is able to isolate correct sub key guesses from the wrong ones. In this way, by comparing the real power

consumption values with those obtained from the statistical model, the secret key can be inferred.

Differential power analysis attack was initially suggested by Kocher, Jaffe and Jun (1999). Later, Messerges, Dabbish and Sloan (2002) extended the research and provided experimental data and attack details on a smart card. Brier, Clavier and Oliver (2004) further investigated the DPA attack and used classical model for the power consumption of cryptographic devices. The model is based on the Hamming distance of the data handled with regard to an unknown but constant reference state. Once the model is validated, it allows to mount an optimal attack called Correlation Power Analysis (CPA). This attack is similar to the one described earlier except the fact that the power model used as a reference is different from the statistical model.

In addition to the above attacks on crypto systems based on smart cards, the DPA attacks have been shown to be successful on ASIC (Application Specific Integrated Circuit) and FPGA implementations of various encryption algorithms. In particular, Standaert, Ors, Quisquater and Prencel (2004) demonstrated a successful attack against an FPGA implementation of the DES and Ors, Gurkaynak, Oswald and Prencel (2004) demonstrated a successful attack against an ASIC implementation of the AES. Lately, AES encryption algorithm and its implementations have been subjected to various types of tests and attacks. Han, Zou, Liu and Chen (2008) and Kamoun, Bossuet and Ghazel (2009) have independently developed experimental attacks against various types of hardware implementations of this algorithm.

Differential power analysis is one of the most popular side channel attacks because it is easier to conduct and can be repeated without damaging the object under analysis. In particular, smart cards, which typically consist of an 8-bit processor, EEPROM, small amount of RAM and a small operating system have been a particular target of DPA attacks.

Electromagnetic Radiation Analysis

Even if an embedded system does not house a Trojan horse, or is not prone to timing, power or error analysis, it is still possible to breach its security by other means. In an attack based on electromagnetic radiation (EMR) analysis, the attacker captures and reconstructs the signal leaked through the electromagnetic radiation from the target equipment.

It is well known that the US government has been well aware of attacks based on analysis of electromagnetic radiation since 1950s and that display screen of video display units could be reconstructed after capturing their EMR. Standards were developed for the protection against this attack and were called TEMPEST which is an acronym for Telecommunications Electronics Material Protected from Emanating Spurious Transmissions. Partial details of TEMPEST are also available at the Internet. TEMPEST certification for private organizations is very expensive and therefore another standard called ZONE has been developed which is less secure but costs less than TEMPEST. There are three classes of TEMPEST standard: class 1 has the highest level of security and is available only to US government and approved contractors; class 2 is less secure and is again meant for use of US government; class 3 is available for general and commercial purposes.

In his landmark paper, Van Eck (1985) showed that display screen of even standalone systems could be reconstructed within a distance of 2 km by collecting and processing electromagnetic radiation of the display. Van Eck was able to capture the display screen of a computer using a normal TV receiver and a piece of small extension equipment costing only US$ 15.

EMR analysis attack is particularly dangerous against digital signals. If the digital signals of data being processed by a device can be reconstructed remotely, this can reveal the data. For example, hard disk stores information in binary form and when the data is read from or written to the hard disk, the digital signals are generated during these operations. If these signals are strong enough to be reconstructed remotely, the data being read from or written to the hard disk can be seen by the attacker.

Wright (1987), who was a senior intelligence officer in the British Intelligence MI5, revealed in his book, Spycatcher – The Candid Autobiography of a Senior Intelligence Officer, how he was able to reconstruct the messages sent by the French diplomats. At first, he tried to break the cipher but failed. However, Wright and his assistant noticed that the encrypted traffic carried a faint secondary signal. Further analysis revealed that it was the electromagnetic radiation of the encryption machine and signal reconstruction provided them the plain text without having to break the cipher.

EMR analysis attack has also been shown to work against hardware implementations of encryption algorithms. De Mulder et al. (2005) have demonstrated that a simple EMR analysis attack against elliptic curve cryptosystem is able to find all the key bits with a single measurement. Similarly, a differential EMR analysis attack against an improved implementation of the same cryptosystem requires approximately 1000 measurements to find the key bits.

In addition to the four different types of side channel attacks discussed above, there may be attacks which are indirect attacks on embedded systems security. For example, networked embedded systems typically use TCP/IP suite of protocols to communicate with each other and a central processor. There are many proven flaws in TCP/IP suite of protocols which are inherent to the design of these protocols. In addition, there are other vulnerabilities in the implementation of these protocols which an attacker can target to breach the security of an embedded system. All these flaws can be used to exploit and bug the networked embedded systems themselves or communication amongst them.

Countermeasures Against Side Channel Attacks

Development of attacks against hardware and embedded systems has prompted researchers to design appropriate countermeasures against each of these types of attacks.

A countermeasure suggested against timing and power analysis is the insertion of random delays at various stages of the data processing. The delay insertion may be possible at any layer of abstraction. After the delays have been added in a random manner, it will become difficult for the attacker to guess the nature of operations being performed or the data being processed. Similarly, the introduction of delay will also result in change of power profile of the device increasing the complexity of power analysis attack. It may be noted that adding a number of delays will also result in slowing down of the crypto system. Further, adding delay will not significantly reduce the probability of a successful attack and will only increase the complexity of a feasible attack on the system. For example, the attacker will now have to make some more measurements and arrive at some more precise modeling to infer the secret information stored in the hardware device.

It is intuitive to think that an improved and better prevention mechanism against timing analysis would be to make all computation operations to take the same amount of time. However, it is difficult to implement and will render the system too slow to be usable. Instead, a better alternative would be to take out frequently used operations, say, multiplication, division, exponentiation, and then make them execute in a fixed time. In other words, instead of having all instructions to execute in a fixed time, we take out only the frequently used instructions and then make them execute in fixed time. In this way, majority of the operations in the digital system are executed in a fixed time and this significantly increases the complexity of guessing the operation being performed or inference of information stored in the digital system.

A countermeasure against the fault analysis attack would be to run the encryption algorithm twice and then compare the results. The computation is considered valid only if the two results match (Potkonjak, Nahapetian, Nelson, & Massey, 2009). However, this will significantly increase the computation time of the algorithm. Further, the fault analysis attack is still not impossible to mount and only the number of computations required by the attack increase so as to increase the level of complexity of the attack.

As power analysis attacks are more common, there are a number of countermeasures suggested against these types of attacks. For example, Tiri and Verbauwhede (2004) have suggested using Simple Dynamic Differential Logic (SDDL) and Wave Dynamic Differential Logic (WDDL) to build basic gates all of which consume the same amount of power. Any logic implemented with these gates will then have constant power consumption. Similarly, dummy gates and logic can be inserted in a circuit so that the power consumed becomes equal in all operations. Further, by avoiding branching, conditional jumps, etc. many power analytic characteristics of the system can be masked. Another countermeasure suggested against power analysis attacks is the addition of random calculations so as to add dummy peaks in the power model constructed by the attacker.

Primary means of protection against EMR analysis is the use of shields (Faraday cages) in the equipment which is to be protected. In addition to this, the equipment which is to be protected against EMR analysis uses components that have low EMR.

SECURITY OF CELL PHONES

Cell phones, which are a particular category of embedded systems, have specially been a target of various types of attacks ranging from malformed SMS (Short Message Service) text messages and bluetooth packets to cloned SIMs. Our discussion of embedded systems security will not be complete without mentioning issues related to the security of cell phones.

Today's cell phones and PDAs are complex and complicated embedded systems with powerful options. If someone can remotely take control of a cell phone, it could, for example, send SMS messages to the contacts stored in the cell phone or other numbers without knowledge of the owner. It could also send a busy tone to a caller when the phone is in fact not busy or it could be calling the numbers at random. Even it can turn on the microphone in the cell phone and eavesdrop on any conversation going on in the vicinity of the cell phone. In fact, it has been revealed that a cell phone can be used to eavesdrop on conversation even when it is turned off as powering off may only cut off power to the LCD display while the internal circuitry remains operational. McCullagh and Broache (2006) disclosed that FBI has been using cell phones in this way for surveillance of criminals.

Attacks on cell phones can usually be mounted in any of the following ways:

- Attacks using the bluetooth communication protocols
- Attacks using text messages
- Attacks on the SIM card for GSM and CDMA cell phones

Bluetooth is a wireless communication protocol operating at 2.4 GHz for short range communications and one of its objectives is to replace cables and wires connecting peripheral devices. Cell phones and PDAs have a bluetooth interface for a remote headset and also to facilitate communication with other cell phones. However, this also makes it possible to mount remote attacks on the cell phone by exploiting weaknesses in the bluetooth protocol.

First step in an attack against a bluetooth device is building of a malformed object i.e. a legitimate file with invalid contents arranged in such a manner to break the target system. The object is then sent to the victim causing the receiving device to behave as programmed in the malformed object which is usually to allow the attacker to take control of the device.

There are many forms of attack that can be launched using the bluetooth protocol thereby giving rise to a plethora of jargon like bluejacking, bluesnarfing, bluebugging, bluedumping, bluesmack, bluespoofing, etc. Bluejacking is a technique whereby the attacker sends a malformed vCard with message in the name field and exploits OBject EXchange (OBEX) protocol. Bluesnarfing works by using the OBEX push profile to connect to bluetooth device which is in discovery mode. With this attack, the attacker can extract important information from the cell phone e.g. phonebook. Bluebugging is a form of attack that exploits the victim's AT command parser to allowing the attacker to take complete control of victim's cell phone. After taking control, the attacker can virtually make any use of victim cell phone like placing of calls, sending and receiving of text messages, change phone and service settings. Both free and commercial tools are available to exploit the bluetooth protocol. These include Blooover [sic], BTCrack, Bluesnarfer, BTClass, carwhisper, BT Audit, Blueprint, etc.

In an attack exploiting vulnerability in the SMS text message module of the cell phone, the attacker crafts a special SMS message which the victim cell phone is unable to handle so as to cause a crash or cause the execution of payload so as to return control of the victim phone to the attacker. The attacker must know the particular layout of the SMS that will cause the desired behavior on the victim cell phone. To find out such an SMS layout, the attacker may test the particular model of the victim cell phone by fuzzing. Mulliner and Miller (2009) presented a fuzzing methodology for smart cell phones in an information security event. They proposed techniques which would allow a researcher to inject SMS messages into smart phones without using the carrier i.e. the phone service provider. They also demonstrated how they were able to discover a flaw in Apple's iPhone so that it could be hacked using a single SMS message.

Another possible attack on GSM (Global System for Mobile Communication) and CDMA (Code Division Multiple Access) cell phones is the cloning of the Subscriber Identification Module i.e. the SIM card. A SIM card is smart card which contains information, such as the serial number, International Mobile Subscriber Information (IMSI), the cryptographic algorithms A3 and A8, secret key Ki, two passwords i.e. PIN which is for usual use and PUK (PIN Unlock Key) for unlocking the phone and Kc which is derived from Ki during the encryption process. If an attacker gets hold of a victim's SIM card and is able to read the data on the SIM card using a SIM card reader, then she can prepare a duplicate (clone) of the SIM using a SIM card writer. The cell phone holding the cloned SIM can authenticate and communicate with the cell phone service like the original cell phone. However, the attack is not as easy as the above description has presented it. The real problem faced by the attacker is the extraction of secret information from the SIM which is tamper resistant. The GSM cell phones use an algorithm called COMP128 for authentication and derivation of keys. This algorithm was used only to serve as an example by the GSM standard. The mobile operators were supposed to choose a better algorithm replacing COMP128. However, majority of mobile operators went along using COMP128. Later on many weaknesses were discovered in the COMP128 algorithm which allowed an attacker having physical access to a SIM card to exploit the weakness in COMP128 and retrieve the information stored inside a SIM card. This allowed the attacker to prepare a duplicate SIM using the SIM card writer as described above. This remained a major problem for some time until new revisions of COMP128 algorithm were developed. The initial version of COMP128 is now referred to as COMP128-I and subsequent versions are referred to as COMP128-2, COMP128-3 and COMP128-4. Later versions are secure and there are no known attacks against them as yet. As a result, copying of information from a SIM card is only possible in case of old SIM cards employing COMP128-1. Newer SIMs employing later versions of the algorithm are not susceptible to any known attacks and do not reveal stored information and hence do not permit their duplication.

FUTURE RESEARCH DIRECTIONS

As embedded systems security is an emerging area of research, the hardware security research community is expected to discover and develop new forms of attacks on the hardware devices and embedded systems. This will further fuel the research on the countermeasures and protection schemes against these attacks. As a result, there may be a paradigm shift in the design of hardware devices and embedded systems particularly those used in defense applications. For example, design and implementation of an IC may go through fundamental changes from an abstract level description to semiconductor level fabrication so as to incorporate new security measures. For this to happen, the research community needs to come up with reliable and robust techniques which can be implemented at every layer of abstraction.

Embedded systems security shares a few common traits with software security. Therefore, in these common areas existing security techniques and methods may be applied. However, a few of the traits of embedded systems security are different from those of software security. Therefore, new algorithms and techniques will need to be developed for these areas. For example, research community will need to build secure operating systems which can be deployed in embedded systems which are usually resource constrained. This will include implementing security in all the critical functions performed by an operating system.

In many instances, attacks on embedded devices are possible only if physical security of the device is compromised. For example, in the case of side channel attacks on smart card, the attacker first needs to get a copy of the smart card which she intends to attack. Therefore, new security techniques will need to be developed which can prevent physical tampering of the device and ensure that the information stored in it remains secure.

Embedded devices are usually limiting in resources and most of the existing cryptographic algorithms are computation intensive. Implementation of security with the heavy algorithms results in performance degradation. Therefore, lightweight cryptographic algorithms and protocols are needed which are tailored to run on embedded devices with limited resources.

CONCLUSION

Embedded systems are finding widespread uses in every sphere of our lives and their security has become an important research issue. In this chapter, we have discussed the background and current state of research on the threats and attacks being developed against embedded systems. The hardware attacks can be mounted at any of the layers of abstraction involved in the fabrication of the device with varying degrees of success. We have also discussed various countermeasures against these attacks.

REFERENCES

Alkabani, Y., & Koushanfar, F. (2008, July). Extended abstract: Designer's hardware trojan horse. In *Proceedings of IEEE International Workshop on Hardware-Oriented Security and Trust*, HOST 2008, (pp. 82-83). Washington, DC: IEEE Computer Society.

Biham, E., & Shamir, A. (1997). Differential fault analysis of secret key cryptosystems. In *Proceedings of the 17th Annual International Cryptology Conference on Advances in Cryptology, 1294*, (pp. 513-525). London, UK: Springer-Verlag.

Boneh, D., DeMillo, R. A., & Lipton, R. J. (1997). On the importance of checking cryptographic protocols for faults. In *Proceedings of the 16th Annual International Conference on Theory and Application of Cryptographic Techniques*, (pp. 37-51). Berlin, Germany: Springer-Verlag.

Brier, E., Clavier, C., & Oliver, F. (2004). Correlation power analysis with a leakage model. In *Proceedings of Cryptographic Hardware and Embedded Systems –LNCS 3156*, (pp. 135-152). Springer-Verlag.

Clark, J., Leblanc, S., & Knight, S. (in press). Compromise through USB-based hardware trojan horse device. *International Journal of Future Generation Computer Systems, 27*(5). Elsevier B.V.

De Mulder, E., Buysschaert, P., Ors, S. B., Delmotte, P., Preneel, B., Vandenbosch, G., & Verbauwhede, I. (2005). Electromagnetic analysis attack on an FPGA implementation of an elliptic curve cryptosystem. In *Proceedings of the IEEE International Conference on Computer as a Tool*. EUROCON 2005, (pp. 1879-1882).

Farrell, N. (2007, November). Seagate hard drives turn into spy machines. *The Inquirer*.

Han, Y., Zou, X., Liu, Z., & Chen, Y. (2008). Efficient DPA attacks on AES hardware implementations. *International Journal of Communications . Network and System Sciences, 1*, 1–103.

IET. (2005). The celebrated maroochy water attack. *Computing & Control Engineering Journal, 16*(6), 24–25.

Jin, Y., & Makris, Y. (2008). Hardware trojan detection using path delay fingerprint. In *Proceedings of IEEE International Workshop on Hardware-Oriented Security and Trust*, HOST 2008, (pp. 51-57). Washington, DC: IEEE Computer Society.

Kamoun, N., Bossuet, L., & Ghazel, A. (2009). Experimental implementation of DPA attacks on AES design with Flash-based FPGA technology. In *Proceedings of 6th IEEE International Multi-Conference on Systems, Signals and Devices*, SSD'09, Djerba.

Kocher, P. (1996). Timing attacks on implementations of Diffie-Hellman, RSA, DSS and other systems. In N. Koblitz (Ed.), *Proceedings of Annual International Conference on Advances in Cryptology, LNCS 1109*, (pp. 104–113). Springer-Verlag.

Kocher, P., Jaffe, J., & Jun, B. (1999). Differential power analysis. In *Proceedings of the 19th Annual International Cryptology Conference on Advances in Cryptology, LNCS 1666*, (pp. 388–397). Heidelberg, Germany: Springer-Verlag.

Koopman, P. (2004, July). Embedded system security. *IEEE Computer Magazine*, 37(7).

McCullagh, D., & Broache, A. (2006). *FBI taps cell phone mic as eavesdropping tool*. CNET News.

Messerges, T. S., Dabbish, E. A., & Sloan, R. H. (2002, May). Examining smart-card security under the threat of power analysis attacks. [IEEE Computer Society.]. *IEEE Transactions on Computers*, 51(5), 541–552. doi:10.1109/TC.2002.1004593

Mulliner, C., & Miller, C. (2009, July). *Fuzzing the phone in your phone*. Las Vegas, NV: Black Hat.

Ors, S. B., Gurkaynak, F., Oswald, E., & Prencel, B. (2004). Power analysis attack on an ASIC AES implementation. In *Proceedings of the International Conference on Information Technology: Coding and Computing*, ITCC'04, Las Vegas, NV, Vol. 2 (p. 546). Washington, DC: IEEE Computer Society.

Potkonjak, M., Nahapetian, A., Nelson, M., & Massey, T. (2009). Hardware trojan horse detection using gate-level characterization. In *Proceedings of the 46th Annual ACM IEEE Design Automation Conference*, CA, ACM.

Prevelakis, V., & Spinellis, D. (2007, July). The Athens affair. *IEEE Spectrum*, 44(7), 26–33. doi:10.1109/MSPEC.2007.376605

Schmeh, K. (2003). *Cryptography and public key infrastructure on the internet*. West Sussex, England: John Wiley & Sons.

Standaert, F. X., Ors, S. B., Quisquater, J. J., & Prencel, B. (2004). Power analysis attacks against FPGA implementations of the DES. In *Proceedings of the International Conference on Field-Programmable Logic and its Applications (FPL), LNCS 3203*, (pp. 84-94). Heidelberg, Germany: Springer-Verlag.

Takahashi, J., & Fukunaga, T. (2010, January). Differential fault analysis on AES with 192 and 256-bit keys. In *Proceedings of Symposium on Cryptography and Information Security*. SCIS, Japan, IACR e-print archive.

Tiri, K., & Verbauwhede, I. (2004). A logic level design methodology for a secure DPA resistant ASIC or FPGA implementation. In *Proceedings of the Conference on Design, Automation and Test*. IEEE Computer Society.

Van Eck, W. (1985). Electromagnetic radiation from video display units: An eavesdropping risk. [Oxford, UK: Elsevier Advanced Technology Publications.]. *Computers & Security*, 4(4), 269–286. doi:10.1016/0167-4048(85)90046-X

Wright, P. (1987). *Spycatcher – The candid autobiography of a senior intelligence officer*. Australia: William Heinemann.

ADDITIONAL READING

Alkabani, Y., & Koushanfar, F. (2008, July). Extended Abstract: Designer's Hardware Trojan Horse. In *Proceedings of IEEE International Workshop on Hardware-Oriented Security and Trust*, HOST 2008, pp. 82-83, Washington DC, IEEE Computer Society.

Anderson, R. (2001). *Security Engineering: A Guide to Building Dependable Distributed Systems*. England: John Wiley & Sons.

Biham, E., & Shamir, A. (1997). Differential Fault Analysis of Secret Key Cryptosystems. In *Proceedings of the 17th Annual International Cryptology Conference on Advances in Cryptology*, Vol. 1294, pp. 513-525, Springer-Verlag, London, UK.

Boneh, D., DeMillo, R. A., & Lipton, R. J. (1997). On the Importance of Checking Cryptographic Protocols for Faults. *In Proceedings of the 16th Annual International Conference on Theory and Application of Cryptographic Techniques*, pp. 37-51, Berlin, Springer-Verlag.

Debbabi, M., Saleh, M., Talhi, C., & Zhioua, S. (2006). *Embedded Java Security: Security for Mobile Devices*. Springer.

Gebotys, C. H. (2009). *Security in Embedded Devices (Embedded Systems)*. Springer.

Hailes, S., & Seleznyov, A. (2007). *Security in Networked Embedded Systems*. Springer.

Han, Y., Zou, X., Liu, Z., & Chen, Y. (2008). Efficient DPA Attacks on AES Hardware Implementations. *International Journal of Communications . Network and System Sciences*, *1*, 1–103.

Koc, K. C., & Paar, C. (1999). *Proceedings of Cryptographic Hardware and Embedded Systems: First International Workshop*, CHES'99 Worcester, MA, USA, Springer-Verlag.

Kocher, P. (1996). Timing Attacks on Implementations of Diffie-Hellman, RSA, DSS and Other Systems. In: N. Koblitz (Ed.), *Proceedings of Annual International Conference on Advances in Cryptology*, CRYPTO'96, vol. 1109 of LNCS, pp. 104–113, Springer-Verlag.

Kocher, P., Jaffe, J., & Jun, B. (1999). Differential Power Analysis. In *Proceedings of the 19th Annual International Cryptology Conference on Advances in Cryptology*, CRYPTO 99, Vol. 1666, pp. 388–397, Heidelberg, Germany, Springer-Verlag.

Lemke, K., Paar, C., & Wolf, M. (2010). *Embedded Security in Cars: Securing Current and Future Automotive IT Applications*. Springer.

Lessner, D. (2009). *Network Security for Embedded Systems: A feasibility study of crypto algorithms on embedded platforms*. LAP Lambert Academic Publishing.

Mangard, S., Oswald, E., & Popp, T. (2007). *Power Analysis Attacks: Revealing the Secrets of Smart Cards (Advances in Information Security)*. Springer.

Messerges, T. S., Dabbish, E. A., & Sloan, R. H. (2002, May). Examining Smart-Card Security under the Threat of Power Analysis Attacks. [IEEE Computer Society.]. *IEEE Transactions on Computers*, *51*(5), 541–552. doi:10.1109/TC.2002.1004593

Mulliner, C., & Miller, C. (2009, July). Fuzzing the Phone in Your Phone. Black Hat, Las Vegas, NV.

Mustard, S. (2006, January). Security of Distributed Control Systems: The concern increases. [UK, IET.]. *IEEE Computing and Control Engineering Journal*, *16*(Issue 6), 19–25. doi:10.1049/cce:20050605

Nedjah, N., & Mourelle, D. (Eds.). (2004). *Embedded Cryptographic Hardware: Methodologies & Architectures*. Nova Science Publishers.

Nedjah, N., & Mourelle, D. (Eds.). (2006). *Embedded Cryptographic Hardware: Design & Security*. Nova Science Publishers.

Parameswaran, R. G. R. S. (2008). *Microarchitectural Support for Security and Reliability: An Embedded Systems Perspective*. VDM Verlag.

Ray, J., & Koopman, P. (2009, July). Data Management Mechanisms for Embedded System Gateways. In *Proceedings of IEEE International Conference on Dependable Systems and Networks*, DSN'09, pp. 175-184.

Stapko, T. (2007). *Practical Embedded Security: Building Secure Resource-Constrained Systems (Embedded Technology)*. England: Newnes.

U.S.-Canada Power System Outage Task Force, (2004, April). *Final Report on the August 14th, 2003 Blackout in the United States and Canada: Causes and Recommendations*. US-Canada Power System Outage Task Force, The North-American Electricity Reliability Council, USA.

Van Eck, W. (1985). Electromagnetic Radiation from Video Display Units: An Eavesdropping Risk. [Oxford, UK, Elsevier Advanced Technology Publications.]. *Computers & Security*, *4*(4), 269–286. doi:10.1016/0167-4048(85)90046-X

Verbauwhede, I. M. R. (Ed.). (2010). *Secure Integrated Circuits and Systems*. Springer.

Zurawski, R. (2006, July). *Embedded Systems Handbook*. Taylor and Francis Group LLC.

KEY TERMS AND DEFINITIONS

Covert Channel: is a hidden communication channel between a malicious entity and a victim system which is conventionally not used for transfer of information.

Electrically Erasable Programmable Read-Only Memory (EEPROM): is a type of Read Only Memory (ROM) which is used in embedded systems and computers to store data or boot program which must not be destroyed when power is turned off. The data or program can only be erased or programmed electrically.

Embedded System: is a digital system which is designed to perform a specific task or set of tasks as compared to a general purpose computer which allows user to perform various types of tasks by installing new software on top of its operating system.

Field Programmable Gate Array (FPGA): is a type of integrated circuit which can be programmed by the design engineer to implement a particular logic at the hardware level. An HDL is used to program an FPGA.

Finite State Machine (FSM): is an abstract mathematical and behavioral model of a system consisting of a number of finite states that the system may switch to and a finite number of inputs that cause the transition from one state to the other. An FSM is also commonly known as finite state automation or simply state machine.

Fuzz Test: or fuzzing is a testing technique in which the system is provided with various combinations of invalid input and behavior of the system is observed.

Hardware Description Language (HDL): is a computer programming language which is used to describe the logic and flow of an electronic circuit. Examples of HDL are VHDL and Verilog.

Hardware Trojan Horse: is a bug or backdoor in the form of a tangible circuit or software piece of code in the control program of an electronic system. It may allow an unauthorized user to communicate with the system and control it.

S-Box: is an acronym for Substitution-Box and is a type of lookup table which is used in a symmetric key encryption algorithm to perform substitution operation on a given plain text. The box receives m number of input bits and according to some lookup function, translates them to an n number of output bits.

Side Channel Attack: is a type of attack on an embedded system which treats the embedded system as a black box and tries to infer hidden information by observing the behavior (timing, power consumed, etc.) and output of the system by feeding it various types of inputs.

Smart Card: is a small pocket-sized plastic card which has an integrated circuit (usually an embedded processor) inside it.

Subscriber Identification Module (SIM): is a smart card used in GSM and CDMA based cellular telephones to allow users to switch phones by simply switching the SIM.

Section 5
Industrial and Applications Security

Chapter 11
Cyber Security in Liquid Petroleum Pipelines

Morgan Henrie
MH Consulting, Inc., USA

ABSTRACT

The world's critical infrastructure includes entities such as the water, waste water, electrical utilities, and the oil and gas industry. In many cases, these rely on pipelines that are controlled by supervisory control and data acquisition (SCADA) systems. SCADA systems have evolved to highly networked, common platform systems. This evolutionary process creates expanding and changing cyber security risks. The need to address this risk profile is mandated from the highest government level. This chapter discusses the various processes, standards, and industry based best practices that are directed towards minimizing these risks.

INTRODUCTION

This chapter provides practitioners, researchers and those interested in critical infrastructure cyber security concerns a sound foundation on cyber security for crude oil transportation critical infrastructure SCADA systems. Understanding how evolutionary processes have changed this infrastructure control system landscape and how industry is responding to ever increasing cyber security threats is essential for anyone who interacts with these systems at any level.

This chapter's objective is to provide the SCADA system practitioner, manager, engineer, researcher and interested parties an overview of today's SCADA cyber security systems how they came to be, the challenges facing the owner/ operator, a review of current industry standards

DOI: 10.4018/978-1-60960-851-4.ch011

and regulatory landscape as well as examples of how some entities are securing their SCADA networks. This information source provides all interested parties sufficient information to allow them to take the next steps in enhancing their system's cyber security posture.

To this end, the chapter is organized in a progressive manner with each section building on the next in following the following sequence.

- Critical infrastructure – what is it? A discussion on critical infrastructure and its background
- SCADA Systems; a review of how SCADA systems have evolved to the current cyber risk state
- A review of the SCADA Cyber security standards
- Resiliency of SCADA systems are secure SCADA Systems
- Defense in depth Cyber security concepts and applications
- SCADA Cyber Security Environmental Uniqueness
- The management structure required to support the system

CRITICAL INFRASTRUCTURE: WHAT IS IT?

Oil and gas transportation systems are identified as national level critical infrastructures. These infrastructures are essential to every nation's safety, defense, private industry commerce, business operations, and normal life. At some level, every nation's electrical grid, commercial enterprises, military facilities, businesses and homes are dependent on the safe, highly available, and reliable delivery of oil and gas liquids. Historical evidence, such as the recent earthquakes and hurricane events, clearly show that if the oil and gas infrastructures are no longer available, the ability to provide essential services is severely constrained or even prevented.

Transporting liquids from point A to point B has a rich historical background. Using pipelines to move liquid is traced back to at least the tenth century B.C. Around 691 B.C., the first water aqueduct was built in Assyria (BookRags, 2010) while later "The first aqueduct built to supply Rome … was constructed about 312 B. C. and had a length of about 11 miles" (Turneaure et al. 1916). Since these early water transportation efforts, utilization of pipeline systems to move water and other liquid and slurry commodities continues to increase. As an example, the United States (US) Department of Transportation (DOT), Pipeline and Hazardous Materials Safety Administration (PHMSA) Office of Pipeline Safety website identifies that within the United States, 168,900 miles of onshore and offshore hazardous crude oil liquid pipelines are in service. Overall, the "…energy transportation network of the United States consists of over 2.5 million miles of pipelines. That's enough to circle the earth about 100 times" (PHMSA, 2010).

These 168,900 miles of hazardous crude oil liquid pipelines are monitored and controlled by supervisory control and data acquisition (SCADA) systems. Crude oil SCADA systems provide critical status, alarm and process information back to the central operator stations while transferring controls commands and setpoint changes from the central operator station to the remote location. SCADA systems provide the ability to monitor and control thousands of miles of pipeline safely, efficiently and effectively as the infrastructure transports this hazardous material through major cities, environmentally sensitive terrain, under major water ways, and through your local neighborhood day-in and day-out. Without modern SCADA systems it is nearly impossible to safely operate and control these critical infrastructures.

To achieve this capability safely, the hazardous liquid pipeline SCADA system is dependent on telecommunication systems, remote terminal devices, computers, servers, routers, etc. to link field devices, such as a relay status, to the control room operator human machine interface (HMI). The remoteness associated with these systems, numerous physical connections, and ever expanding interconnectivity to other systems is raising crude oil SCADA cyber security vulnerability.

This increased SCADA vulnerability is a derivative of all these factors combined within a system. As an example, systems that are interconnected such as the remote terminal device, the host computer and the internet provides a physical connection from literally anywhere in the world to the remote terminal unit. Common computer operating systems also contribute to increasing vulnerability as more people have greater knowledge and increased skills on common platforms, such asWindows©. Thus, there are more people who can potentially become cyber system attackers. So, as systems become interconnected, on a broader scale, and utilize common equipment the vulnerability increases as well. This chapter presents how cyber security applies to this specific domain within the realm of a resilient system concept.

Within the developed global community, day-in and day-out social interactions, business, construction and industry require fresh water supply, sewer and waste transportation/disposal, telecommunications, and electricity. To a varying degree these infrastructures rely on oil and gas systems as their primary energy source. It is recognized that these systems are so critical that any long term disruption will have cascading negative impacts on national safety and security, public health, as well as local, national and global economic conditions. Due to the potential catastrophic impact many nations have classified or identified these as 'critical infrastructures.'

Preventing any debilitating critical infrastructure impact, as in the form of a cyber security attack, is identified at national government levels as a grave and essential requirement. Ensuring that these systems are always available is vital

but challenged due to a variety of factors. For the oil transportation system, key challenges include diversity and number of facilities required to effectively transport the oil as well as the remote locations where facilities are often placed. Another factor compounding the challenge to ensuring a high level of cyber security is that these critical infrastructures are owned and operated by a variety of private, public or government agencies. Due to the diversity of ownership and lack of interaction or sharing of data and knowledge, a lack of a clear risk domain picture and best practices occurs. SCADA systems are core systems required to support the ability to monitor, operate and safely control these systems.

The critical nature of these systems has been and continues to be the focus of many entities. In the United states, at the federal level there is a strong, if young, effort in process to assist industry and government entities in having the most current information that will assist them in developing resilient control systems. Table 1 is from the Department of Homeland Security (DHS) *Strategy for Securing Control Systems* (DHS, 2009). While Table 1 is a United States (US) centric, listing it provides an excellent example of the various policies and federal level initiatives which have been applied to this process.

As the Table 1 timeline shows, several major events have transpired since 2003. Each step along the line is directed towards providing safe, secure critical infrastructure control systems. Securing these critical infrastructure control systems are nationally and internationally recognized essential functions.

In summary, critical infrastructures are those systems that any long term disruption will have severe impacts to those living within the specific area of occurrence. The negative system impacts can quickly cascade from a local event to a national and even global incident. Further, many critical infrastructures require highly technical, integrated, and complex SCADA systems.

Table 1. Timeline of policies, advisories, and plans supporting control systems security (DHS, 2009, p. 6)

Document	Author	Released Date	Type	Summary
National Strategy to Secure Cyberspace	Presidential Directive	2003	Policy	Provides policy direction to DHS and federal agencies on cybersecurity, including control systems. Indentifies DHS as the lead agency in this effort.
HSPD-7	Presidential Directive	2003	Policy	Directs DHS, in coordination with other sector-specific agencies, to prepare a national plan to protect the infrastructure to include coordination and participation with the private sector.
Critical Infrastructure Protection" Challenges and Efforts to secure Control Systems	GAP	2004	Advisory	Recommends DHS develop and implement a strategy to coordinate efforts to meet challenges associated with security control systems and current efforts for both the federal and private sector
National Infrastructure Protection Plan	DHS	2006	Plan	Provides the overarching planning process and structure for security partnerships and federal/private sector response to protect critical infrastructure.
Sector Specific Plans	SSA	2007	Plan	All Sector Specific Agencies (SSAs) in coordination with SCCs were directed to complete plans within the NIPP partnership framework by 2006. These provide high level assessment, goals, and objectives for infrastructure protection.
Critical Infrastructure Protection: Multiple Efforts to Secure Control Systems Are Under Way, but Challenges Remain	GAO	2007	Advisory	Recommends DHS develop a coordination strategy for public and private sectors and process for improving information sharing
Academic: Toward a Safer and More Secure Cyberspace	NRC	2007	Advisory	The National Research Council (NRC) conducted a study on research priorities for security cyberspace. Control systems issues were included in their scope.
Sector-Specific Roadmaps/ Strategies: Energy Sector Roadmap Chemical Cyber Security Guidance for Addressing Cyber Security in the Chemical industry Water Sector Roadmap	DOE/SCC ACC/SCC ACC/SCC DHS/SCC	2006 2006 2006 2008	Plan Strategy Advisory Plan	Roadmaps provide detailed assessment of where the sector currently stands on initiatives for cybersecurity of control systems, and a plan for reaching an end state that provides for prevention, detection, and mitigation of attacks on these systems.
NSPD-54/HSPD-23	Presidential Directive	2008	Police	Mandatory intrusion detection requirements for federal facilities.

SCADA SYSTEMS

There are several definitions of what is a SCADA system. IEEE Standard, C37.1-1994 defines Supervisory Control and Data Acquisition (SCADA) as "... a system operating with coded signals over communication channels as to provide control of RTU [Remote Terminal Unit] equipment" (IEEE, 1994). The American Petroleum Institute (API) recommended practice, RP 1113, defines SCADA as:

"... a computer based system in which the data Acquisition function includes gathering real-time data through a communication network and control functions include controlling field devices," (API, 2007, p.)

A broader definition, which we will use in this chapter, is that a SCADA system is a software based system or systems used to remotely monitor and control industrial processes from a central facility As this definition states, SCADA is a software based system or set of systems which provides a central facility the ability to monitor industrial process system status, alarms, and other data as well as the ability to generate remote control functions. SCADA systems rely on a variety of intelligent devices to include general purpose computers, special purpose computers such as a programmable logic controller (PLC) or dedicated intelligent systems such as a flow computer.

Essential to modern SCADA systems is the graphical user interface (GUI). The GUI provides the pipeline operator, or as sometimes referenced controller, the ability to monitor and interact with the SCADA system. The remote field data is displayed on the GUI and operator initiated process control changes occur through the GUI. As complex as today's sophisticated SCADA system is, its origins date almost a hundred years ago to the Chicago power company.

Around 1912, the Chicago power industry merged a centrally located control room operator, a remote process control system, a telecommunication interface (also known as the telephone system) and humans on each end into the basics of a SCADA system. This rudimentary SCADA system, was able to obtain remote power station status information and to direct control functions using basic telephone lines and voice communications. By integrating the telephone system, as a means to connect the central control room to the field locations, this early day SCADA structure enhanced the system's effective and efficient operations capabilities (Stouffer, 2005). The power company could ensure a better performing electrical system by operating the system in a near real time basis. This technology advancement was not possible before the integration of the major components into a holistic system.

From these humble beginnings, SCADA systems have evolved into sophisticated technology enablers which allow operation of virtually every type of process control system. SCADA systems now ensure a steady source of critical infrastructure functions such as reliable electrical power, reliable gas supply to factories and homes, and enhanced liquid pipeline monitoring and control. Modern critical infrastructure SCADA systems provide the capability to monitor and control these systems at an effective, safe, and efficient operational level never achieved before. Over time, SCADA systems have become critical technology enabling systems which assist companies to safely and effectively operate remote or distributed systems.

Evolutionary Change

Modern day, highly advanced, technology based SCADA systems are the result of evolutionary change. As the previous section outlines, original SCADA systems linked remote site operational personnel to the central station operator using regular phone lines. This basic network allowed the remote location the ability to pass on what they were observing to the control room operator and take action based on the control room operator commands. This was a very rudimentary but effective system for its time.

The next generation SCADA system involved removal of the remote site individual by increasing the system's automatic capabilities. This automation step involved several major advancements. First, the field system device capabilities were advanced to be able to remotely identify when system states changed. As an example, field systems incorporated relays which identified if a system was operating or was it off line or if a valve position was in either the open or closed position.

To take advantage of these 'new' remote capabilities, some device had to exist which would gather and communicate a set of remote device status information. This advancement involved the development of 'dumb' remote terminal units. These units were basic remote site data concentrators which allowed multiple field status and alarm information to be hardwired into a single device. The various remote device information states were then available to the central site from a single device.

Figure 1. SCADA evolution time line

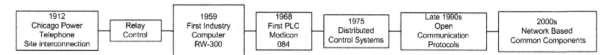

The ability to remotely access the concentrated field information step involved development of the central host system. The central host system retrieved the remote data using a poll – response communication scheme and presented the remote data to the control room operator. Transfer of the information to the control room operator, involved changing local relay states which turned lights on and off on wall size mimic panels. These mimic panels depicted the process and the light's color and status indicated the field device state.

These early systems were designed and implemented by a variety of companies, including pipeline owners and operators. Consistent across the evolving SCADA landscape was the fact that these systems were based on proprietary process and communication methods. Further these systems were standalone entities which were not linked to internal or external networks or business systems.

Evolution continued with the advancement of the field systems into semi-automatic and finally fully automatic systems. This evolutionary step is characterized by the development of programmable logic controllers (PLC) as well as distributed control systems.

PLCs are dedicated computer systems which allow the SCADA system engineer greater capabilities in what could be achieved at the local site level as well as the different type of information which could be transmitted to the central site. Providing local intelligence provides a broad capability depth and enhanced communications. Supporting and contributing to these new system capabilities were advances in the central computing system and GUI capabilities.

Evolution has taken the basic island based proprietary SCADA system to a network based system. This network based system leverages common operating systems, standard communication protocols, and interconnectivity to local systems, business systems, and internet based systems. No longer is the SCADA system an oblique, stand alone island with an inherent level of security based on obscurity. It is a network system based on various standard or commonly available software/hardware systems.

The move from an isolated system to a network based system changes the cyber security risk and vulnerability maps. These changes are driven by the fact that many network and software experts exist. As stated earlier, the more people who have the knowledge and skills to work with these systems increases the potential sources of individuals who could become cyber system attackers.

In summary, this evolutionary advancement transitioned SCADA from the humble 1912 voice control process through an era of limited, proprietary electronic controls operating over dedicated telecommunication systems to today's highly sophisticated and advanced process control network based environment. Each evolutionary step enabled greater process control capabilities and enhanced business opportunities which support modern life styles and world needs (Figure 1). Evolutionary change has also brought forward different levels of associated risk and vulnerabilities that can produce catastrophic consequences.

CYBER SECURITY STANDARDS

Today's modern SCADA system cyber security threats and vulnerabilities and how to minimize them are this chapter's topics. Specifically, the threats this chapter discusses are associated with SCADA systems that are now based on common computer operating systems, common communication networks, standard telecommunication equipment, universal technology standards and firms' greater need to share data across business units and even with other firms. The duality of effectively and efficiently operating SCADA systems, based on common computer operating systems and technology standards, and the increased need to share SCADA based data creates the cyber security challenge. This dichotomous challenge involves protecting the SCADA system from purposeful or accidental cyber security threats on one hand, while providing for a free flow of data to other entities, which provides a competitive business advantage, on the other.

The dual conflict risk is an escalating issue driven not only by employment of widely known and standardized technology solutions which contain known vulnerabilities and susceptibilities but changing global threats and threat levels.

The increasing risk landscape merges with the accepted reality in most major developed nations. As an example, within the United States the federal government has publically stated that "… (1) cybersecurity is now a major national security problem …, (2) decisions and actions must respect privacy and civil liberties, and (3) only a comprehensive national security strategy that embraces both the domestic and international aspects of cyber security will make us more secure" (CSIS, 2008, p. 1). At the international level, the increasing awareness and concern is highlighted by the various international conferences such as the African ICT Best Practices Forum 200" and the 2010 "International Conference on Cyber Security." The common theme is the world is facing an escalating cyber security threat level and planned preventative and response capabilities are required. One way to achieve this is through the development of and deployment of cyber security standards.

As a partial response to the changing risk landscape, within the US, various documents have been issued that are intended to assist the asset owner/operator in reducing their vulnerabilities. If the organization's vulnerabilities can be reduced, it has the cascading effect of reducing the organization's risk map.

These various documents originate from a broad organizational set which include:

- American Petroleum Institute (API)
- Process Control Security Requirements Forum (PCSRF)
- National Institute of Standards and Technology (NIST)
- Industrial Control Systems (ICS)
- System Protection Profile (SPP)
- Instrumentation, Systems and Automation Society (ISA)

Depending of the issuing organization, the available documents are described as standards, recommended practices, best practices, guidelines or technical reports. Regardless of naming convention "…when followed, [they] can provide increased security to control systems" (INL, 2005, p. 1). Table 2 provides an overview of the various SCADA system cyber security related documents.

A review of Table 2 documents identifies the lack of any government regulations, regulated standards, guidelines or recommended best practices (here foreword identified as standards). Table 1 identifies documents associated with various non-government organizations (NGO) cyber security standards. No federal or state regulation is identified.

The key distinction between industry standards and government regulations can be described as the difference between consensus and legality. Industry standards are derived by the collective members and provided as ways to address the item of interest. Use and application of industry standards, by themselves, are voluntary based. Any industry entity can elect to use the standard or not.

Table 2. SCADA security documents

Organization	Documentation Number	Document Purpose	Crude Pipeline Specific
API	API-1164 – "Pipeline SCADA Security"	… provides the high-level view of holistic security practices… (API$_2$, 2007, p. 1)	Yes
PCSRF	SPP – "Security Capabilities Profile for Industrial Control Systems"	…to formally state security requirements associated with industrial control systems (INL, 2005)	Yes
ISA	SP-99 – "Manufacturing and Control System Security Standard"	… to improve the confidentiality, integrity, and availability of components or systems used for manufacturing or control and provided criteria for procuring and implementing secure control systems..(INL, 2005, p. 6)	No
ISA	SP -99-1 – "Concepts, Models and Terminology"	Provides definitions of manufacturing and control system security terms, terminology and a common security model.	No
ISA	SP-99-2 –"Retrofit link encryption for asynchronous serial communications	Manufacturing and control system security program	No
ISO/IEC	17799 "Information Technology – Code of Practice for Information Security Management"	Gives recommendations for information security management. It is high level, broad in scope, conceptual in nature, and intended to provide a basis for an organization to develop its own organizational security standards…."..(INL, 2005, p. 4)	No
IEC	62443-3 "Security for industrial-process measurement and control – Network and systems security	Establishes a framework for securing information and communication technology aspects of industrial process measurement and control systems including its networks and devices on those networks, during the operational phase of the plant's life cycle. It provides guidance on a plant's operational security requirements and is primarily intended for automation system owners/operators (responsible for ICS operation).	No
NERC	CIP-007-1 "Cyber Security – Systems Security Management"	Standard CIP-007 requires Responsible Entities to define methods, processes, and procedures for securing those systems determined to be Critical Cyber Assets, as well as the non-critical Cyber Assets within the Electronic Security Perimeter(s). Standard CIP-007 should be read as part of a group of standards numbered Standards CIP-002 through CIP-009.	No
NIST	800-82 "Guide to Supervisory Control and Data Acquisition (SCADA) and Industrial Control Systems Security"	Guide to Supervisory Control and Data Acquisition (SCADA) and Industrial Control Systems Security (NIST, 2008)	No (Note: This document is in draft form only at the time this document was created)

continued on following page

Table 2. Continued

Organization	Documentation Number	Document Purpose	Crude Pipeline Specific
AGA (American Gas Association)	Report Number 12 – "Cryptographic Protection of SCADA Communications"	• AGA 12, Part 1: Cryptographic Protection of SCADA Communications: Background, Policies & Test Plan • AGA 12, Part 2: Cryptographic Protection of SCADA Communications: Retrofit Link Encryption for Asynchronous Serial Communications • AGA 12, Part 3: Cryptographic Protection of SCADA Communications: Protection of Networked Systems • AGA 12, Part 4: Cryptographic Protection of SCADA Communications: Protection Embedded in SCADA Components How to Read AGA 12, Part 1 AGA 12, Part 1 is intended to serve as a guideline for voluntary implementation of a comprehensive cyber security posture. It focuses on providing background information for improved assessment of a company's cyber security posture, suggesting policies for a comprehensive (AGA, 2006, p. ii)	No
CSA	Z246.1 – "Security Management for Petroleum and Natural Gas Industry Systems" Canadian Standards Association	The premise of this Standard is that security risks should be managed using risk-based and performance-based management processes. … A governance framework for a security management program begins with an awareness of what is serves to protect. (CSA, 2008)	No

Government regulations, on the other hand, are backed by the power of law. Failure to comply with a government regulation can result in penalties such as monetary fines, prison sentences or a combination of both. Compliance with government regulations is mandatory! Occasionally, government regulations will reference an industry standard and based on how the industry standard is written that standard can then become a regulated compliance requirement.

At the time this chapter was written, within the United States, no SCADA cyber security regulation has been issued. This regulatory state of affairs is always subject to change and must be closely followed. As an example, in 2008 the Transportation Security Administration (TSA) issued for comment the "Pipeline Security Guidelines." Draft Rev. 2a. APL September 26, 2008. Contained within this document is direct reference to industry standards such as API-1164. When the TSA document is released, depending on the specific pipeline regulatory oversight agency, this government document may make compliance with

API-1164 mandatory. Ultimately, whether this document becomes a regulation or is a recommended best practice is dependent on how the document is issued and how the local regulatory authority, as well as the legal system, interprets the final state. The key points are that SCADA cyber security regulations are in flux and subject to continuous change and that the pipeline industry standards and recommended practices are much greater than government regulations.

A key example of the pipeline industry cyber security standard maturity is the American Petroleum Institute Pipeline security standard, API-1164. API-1164 is a pipeline industry voluntary standard. As a voluntary standard, each pipeline owner/operator has the liberty to utilize, or not, any and all of this document within their SCADA system.

The foundation for this document originated in the API cybernetics security working group 2002 general meeting. At that meeting it was identified that evolving common technology based SCADA systems were increasingly exposed to both internal and external cyber threats. These threats, coupled with changing and increasing vulnerabilities and susceptibilities posed greater risks to the critical infrastructure than in the era of proprietary based, island configured, SCADA infrastructures.

The Cyber Security meeting requested research and development of a new pipeline SCADA security standard. Over the next year-plus API 1164, edition #1, was developed, reviewed, approved and released for general utilization. The intent of API 1164 is to provide the oil and gas liquid pipeline owner/operator the ability to:

... control the pipeline in such a way that there are no adverse effects on employees, the environment, the public, or the customers as a result of the pipeline company's action or actions from other parties.

This SCADA security program provides a means to improve the security of pipeline SCADA operation by:

- Listing the processes used to identify and analyze the SCADA system vulnerabilities…
- Providing a comprehensive list of practices to harden the core architecture.
- Providing examples of industry best practices. (API$_2$, 2009, p. 1)

In 2004, API-1164, ed. 1, was issued and subsequently well received by the industry and broadly adopted.

In the course of doing business and to ensure that the standards remain current, API normally initiates a standard review cycle every five years. Due to rapid technology changes, improved industry best practices, research outcomes and changing and increasing threats, in 2008, API requested that API-1164 be reviewed and if required updated. On June 4, 2009 API-1164 second edition was formally released.

This second edition has sweeping changes based on new technology developments, industry best practices and research identified capabilities advancement. Ultimately, the revision team strived to develop a holistic system view document that provides the owner/operator a standard which brings together the best and most current practices, processes and capabilities within this domain.

To achieve this higher level standard output, the revision team focused their process on the key philosophical approach of Defense in Depth, Multi-Layer Security (D2MLS) as well as merging the human aspect of the security system with the technology, i.e. a socio-technical approach.

D2MLS leverages the concept that access to the core SCADA system is only achieved once the external source has successfully transitioned through at least two, and preferably three, different levels of technology and processes. As an example, an individual external to the organization must (1) first obtain access to the corporate local area network (LAN) via the use of an authorized password and telecommunication interface. Once the external entity has obtained access to the internal LAN the individual must then (2) transition through a dematerialized zone (DMZ) firewall. The DMZ provides physical and logical separation between the SCADA system and the corporate network. Transitioning or penetrating the DMZ requires a different set of authentication than the corporate network access required.

Assuming the external entity did successfully penetrate the SCADA system DMZ, they then need to (3) obtain access to the actual SCADA network by transitioning through the SCADA side of the DMZ firewall. To obtain authorization through the SCADA DMZ firewall requires a different set of authentication than the earlier systems.

At this point the individual would be on the SCADA internal network but depending on the SCADA system, the corporate cyber security policies, procedures and rules, the individual may still not have access to the actual SCADA system. Depending on the organization to obtain direct access to the various SCADA systems device may involve (4) yet another set of authentication and authorized communication connects.

This example identifies that before allowing direct access to any SCADA device, a properly implemented D2MLS requires multiple authorization levels or extensive knowledge of that specific system's processes. This is defense in depth multi-layer security, D2MLS.

As identified in the previous section, API-1164 second edition incorporated a socio-technical view. This view merges the human aspect of security with the various hardware and software components into a higher level, holistic, socio-technical system of systems.

Achieving the socio-technical system of systems capability occurs by including the need for fully developed corporate cyber security policies, supporting procedures, personnel roles and responsibilities, and technology as part of the overall standard. This new system of systems reduces the organization's SCADA system vulnerabilities as a socio-technical system of systems output exceeds any individual system capability. The system of systems approach builds in and encompasses the D2MLS philosophical view and provides the owner/operator a firm foundation to adapt the standard to their unique environment.

API-1164 is also aligned with Table 1 documents as well as other industry cyber security standards. This alignment was a designed in attributes that the revision team adopted early in the revision process. The team reviewed all available SCADA and process control cyber security documents to ensure that API-1164 was in alignment with these other standards and no inherent conflict would occur.

API-1164 is the sole oil and gas liquid industry specific SCADA system cyber security standard. The 2009 revision provides an in depth, socio-technical, system of systems approach to this complex entity. The standard is rich and comprehensive in its ability to be adopted across the breadth of unique industry environments, regulatory landscapes and corporate philosophies.

RESILIENT SCADA SYSTEMS ARE CYBER SECURE SYSTEMS

SCADA system engineers, analysts, owners and operators often describe, design and engineer SCADA systems to be:

- Highly available systems
- Highly reliable systems
- Redundant systems
- Robust systems

These descriptive terms are intended to identify that due to SCADA systems' essential nature and capabilities, the systems must work correctly each and every time, all the time. System outages, failures, or unknown states are not permissible in critical infrastructure SCADA systems. The owner/operator must have the highest level of assurance that the process is in control. In reality these systems must be resilient systems.

Resilience is "… the ability of organizational, hardware and software systems to mitigate the severity and likelihood of failures or losses, to adapt to changing conditions, and to respond appropriately after the fact….It is an infrastructure wide topic…" (ICOSE, 2010). A resilient system operates correctly each and every time while adapting to changing conditions and providing highly effective and efficient means to recover from an abnormal state. These are required attributes of a critical infrastructure SCADA system. A resilient SCADA system requires that the cyber security component of the system is addressed.

Addressing the SCADA system cyber security ideally starts at the system design and carries forward through the system life cycle. This process involves the systems view that analyzes how the corporate policies, procedures, roles and responsibilities, network topology, telecommunication network, software and hardware combine to form the resilient system.

Beginning at the system design, phase provides the opportunity to design into the system the ability of the system to prevent, where possible, and to mitigate and respond, as necessary, to system failures and losses that might arise from a cyber attack. The essential point of a resilient system design is recognition that it is probably impossible to ensure that any system is perfectly protected from a cyber attack. There is the fact that if a system is operating, a determined adversary can, eventually be successful in their attempts. A resilient system design counters this fact by having a design that mitigates this reality through early detection of an event, effective and rapid transition to a safe state – such as a predetermined failsafe position, and rapid system restore. One way to look at this is the system is able to absorb, contain and dissipate the attacker's shock wave.

The exact process for developing a resilient SCADA system is dependent on the organization and system environment. Yet the following commonalities exist across all domains:

1. Ensure the company has a specific cyber security policy – This establishes the guiding principles for all other steps.
2. Ensure the company has specific cyber security procedures– These are based on the company's policy statement.
3. Ensure that the company has specific cyber security roles and responsibilities written down.
4. Systematically design and engineer the system in compliance to industry standards within the company's policy and procedure requirements.
5. Conduct a peer based system design and engineer review- peer reviewers must be someone other than those directly involved in the design and engineering effort.

6. Development of material procurement specifications that include cyber security requirements.
7. Development and implementation of cyber specific system testing protocols.
8. Development and implementation of SCADA system change control processes.
9. Development and implementation of recurring system analysis processes.

Development of a cyber secure resilient system is multidisciplinary, involving the systems of systems. Design, engineering, implementation as well as operation and maintenance of a cyber secure resilient SCADA system results in the:

… ability of organizational, hardware and software systems to mitigate the severity and likelihood of failures or losses, to adapt to changing conditions, and to respond appropriately after the fact. The study of system resilience includes the creation of a robust infrastructure that designs, builds, tests, maintains, and operates the system. The scope is larger than design, reliability, human factors or system safety. It is an infrastructure wide topic to include customers, developers, suppliers, and all other stakeholders. System resilience has a large interest in cultural, sociological and psychological causes of human-made disasters. Hence, it is truly multidisciplinary. (INCOSE, 2010)

An essential view of a resilient cyber secure SCADA system is acknowledgement that no single technology, process, function or system design can ensure an absolute secure system. New threats continue to occur, new vulnerabilities are identified, new systems create different susceptibility/vulnerability landscapes and organizational cultures form the foundation of the corporate view. To maintain a resilient system requires the continual monitoring of the types of threats, establishment of organizational policies and procedures that maintain the future look of the system and identification and allocation of specific roles and responsibilities to ensure the system's resilient future state. An organizational culture which supports a resilient system philosophy is paramount to the overall system success.

DEFENSE IN DEPTH

Defense in depth was partially covered earlier in this chapter. From a philosophical perspective, a defense in depth objective is to place many different types of roadblocks, between the adversary and the SCADA system. The logic behind placing an array of roadblocks is that an adversary must have extensive knowledge, skills and capabilities to successfully penetrate the system. Therefore, adding technology layers supports the first premise that a defense in depth approach not only provides numerous roadblocks but it also increases the probability that the cyber attacker will be detected.

Figure 2 is a general view of how an enterprise and SCADA network may be configured. This figure serves as a visual for the following defense in depth discussion.

For an external threat, defense in depth starts with the interface between the corporate initial firewall and the World Wide Web (WWW) connection. At this initial point, the firewall has been configured to disable all non-used services and connections. Disabling these features limits the number of access points and methods that would otherwise exist. The firewall rule set is also configured specific to the corporate policy and procedural requirements. These rules inspect each incoming and outgoing message to ensure that they meet the established rule sets. If the message fails these tests, it is rejected and a level of threat is eliminated, the first line of defense.

The second defense line involves the intrusion detection system (IDS). IDSs actively monitor the network for a series of attributes such as policy violations and malicious activities that indicate abnormal events, such as a cyber attack, may be in process. IDSs may generate an alarm indicating an abnormal event is in process while also creating a log of these events. In the case of an intrusion detection and prevention system (IDPS), these systems take the next step and actively block a detected abnormal event as it occurs. IDS/IDPS systems are the second defense layer.

The next security layer involves the antivirus software. Antivirus software checks for known

Figure 2. Generic enterprise/SCADA system

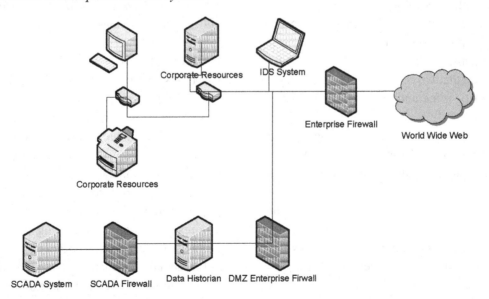

threats and takes appropriate action such as deleting the associated data packet, putting the data packet in quarantine or some other established rule. Antivirus software protects the system from known threats but is not effective for new, never before detected situations. Antivirus software is the next level of a defense in depth, resilient system.

Assuming that the external threat is able to make its way past the initial firewall, the IDS/ IDPS and antivirus software, the attacker must then transition past the network routing rules. Except for the very smallest of networks, most organizations utilize routers to interconnect and route data around the Intranet. Most routers have the ability to be configured for a resilient cyber system which incorporates detailed routing tables. These tables define specifically how data will be transmitted through the network and what connection is allowed between various entities. If an unauthorized data route is attempted, the router will deny the data transfer. In this situation, any attempt to obtain access to the SCADA network must originate from pre-authorized locations over pre-approved routes, as defined in the routing table.

At this network point, the adversary has to have the knowledge, skills and capabilities to transition past four different types of enterprise security defenses. This is before they even approach the SCADA network defensive perimeter of the demilitarized zone (DMZ).

The SCADA DMZ is a physical concept that isolates the SCADA network from all others through a set of firewalls. AS API-1164 defines it, "A DMZ is an intermediary zone between trusted and untrusted networks, providing monitored and controlled access and data transfer" (API$_2$, 2009, p. 2). On one side of the DMZ is the enterprise SCADA DMZ firewall. This firewall is configured to severely limit what services and connections are allowed. The rule sets also limit what types of data requests are allowed through it to any device contained within the DMZ. As an example, the DMZ firewall rule may state that only data read requests are allowed through. This rule precludes

or prevents the transfer of data packets that could write data to the SCADA system or generate control functions to field devices. Further, it is not uncommon that this DMZ firewall is a different manufacturer than the WWW firewall. The different firewall manufacturers force the attacker to know multiple firewalls at a very detailed level. This process reduces the external threat further as the number of people who have this level of knowledge and skill is much lower than those who know and understand single firewall capabilities.

If the intruder has been successful in penetrating all the way to the SCADA DMZ, they must then make it past the SCADA DMZ firewall. The SCADA DMZ firewall should be configured to limit the number of connections and services to an absolute minimum. The SCADA DMZ rule sets should also be established so that the SCADA network can only write data to the devices within the DMZ and not receive data from the DMZ.

Another way to look at this is the SCADA DMZ firewall is a one-way street that allows data out of the SCADA network. At the same time, the SCADA DMZ firewall is a one-way street that only allows data from the DMZ to the system, never from the system to the SCADA DMZ. These one-way restrictions provide a significant road block to any adversary.

Throughout the various security defense in depth locations, additional protection occurs by the utilization and application of strong passwords. Strong passwords are "a combination of upper and lowercase letters, numbers, and special symbols in a non-predictable order" (API$_2$, 2009, p. 8). Passwords are required to acquire access to the various devices along the way, such as the firewalls and routers.

Defense in depth is "A best practice where multiple layers and types of defense strategies are implemented throughout the SCADA system, which may address personnel, technology, and operations throughout the system lifecycle" (API$_2$, 2009, p. 2). A properly designed, configured, operated and maintained resilient, defense in depth protected SCADA system significantly improves the organizational security posture and is good business practice.

SCADA CYBER SECURITY ENVIRONMENTAL UNIQUENESS

Early in this chapter it was identified that many of today's cyber security vulnerabilities and increasing risks are associated with the SCADA system evolution. As outlined, SCADA systems have evolved from rudimentary systems where people communicated between sites over a phone line, to proprietary automated technology islands to highly networked systems based on common operating systems. The current evolutionary path alters the system susceptibility/vulnerability landscape to a much broader threat base and adversary regime.

This increased threat base coincides with common telecommunication hardware, software and firmware platforms, common computing hardware, software and firmware platforms as well as a much broader technology understanding knowledge base. The proprietary island SCADA system is fast disappearing as these common hardware and software based systems are implemented across the oil and gas liquid industry.

What is meant by common systems is that the various devices used in the SCADA system can be and are found in many other disciplines such as the information technology discipline and telecommunication industry discipline. These various disciplines are all network based infrastructures that rely on routers, servers and common operating software.

Network based infrastructures provide an array of system capabilities and opportunities. The increased capabilities are fundamental reasons for application of the technology. As an example, SCADA discipline systems are no longer constrained to a master-slave relationship; they can utilize different topologies such as the distributed control network.

Distributed control capabilities capitalize on the network topology to move the decision applications to where the decision is required. This results in faster response times, greater control capability and improved system efficiency and effectiveness. The down side of distributed control is that a central control center continues to exist. This central control center is chartered to ensure that the system is operated safely, securely, and efficiently. To achieve this visibility requires that data from throughout the system must eventually end up at the central location.

This visibility requirement becomes an issue if the network is lost and the control center can no longer see what is remotely occurring. While the distributed control system is intended to ensure safe operation, many organizations have adopted a corporate policy of shutting the system down during communication outages. While the system may be in a safe state, operation is interrupted until communication is restored.

The distributed control system has another distinct vulnerability issue of multiple points of network access. In the SCADA network island proprietary software era, the master-slave configuration ensured that field data acquisition and control processes did not occur unless initiated by the master. Someone who wanted to initiate a cyber attack had to obtain physical access, duplicate the master and in some cases disable the 'true' master system. These requirements limited the threat to a small number of people with the appropriate skills, hardware, software and system access that could replicate the master system.

In the distributed network the threat level is greater than the island era system. This increased threat is a result of any site being able to initiate control, sending data to other locations and requesting data from other locations. This network capability broadens the number of physical cyber attack locations significantly, and as the remote systems are based on a very common infrastructure, the number of individuals who have in depth knowledge and skills is very large.

The need to manage cyber security vulnerabilities, threats and resulting risk is consistent across the disciplines, be it information technology (IT) or SCADA. Yet, it is incorrect to think that the resulting risks are addressed in identically the same way across the disciplines. Correctly addressing discipline specific cyber security threats is grounded on the dual attributes of system criticality and consequences. This distinction is discussed in the next section.

COMPARISON BETWEEN SCADA AND IT SYSTEMS

The same analogy, in the previous sections, occurs if one analyzes a potential cyber security attack on the company accounting system. In this situation, the loss of confidential data may occur, the ability to generate invoices, receive payments, take orders, etc may also be disabled. Here, the firm may experience negative financial impacts but, again, no life safety or negative environmental impact will occur. IT based cyber security attacks affect the firm's bottom line but do not impact life safety or the environment.

SCADA system based cyber security attacks, on the other hand, have the very real possibility of impacting life safety, the environment and organizational survival. In a worst case scenario, say a SCADA system cyber attack successfully penetrates a refinery system. In this scenario, the attacker alters some critical data to reflect a safe condition while blocking the ability to generate essential safety control commands. In this situation, the process could easily exceed a safe limit, an explosion and fire could occur which not only costs the loss of life but also destroys the firms basic process infrastructure. The refinery could go out of business! SCADA system cyber security attacks can have a much greater impact on the organization than an IT cyber security attack.

Another reason IT cyber security processes cannot be directly applied to the SCADA system is associated with how the systems must operate, i.e. system availability. SCADA systems must operate 24X7X365 where system outages and interruptions are not tolerated. This is a different environment than IT systems where planned system outages or unavailable times can be planned and do occur. A prime example of how the different availability technology requirements impact cyber security approach is highlighted with operating system updates.

Most, if not all, computer operating systems vendors routinely transmit or notify the end user that software updates are available for their system. These updates may address newly identified cyber security issues or software bugs. For single system owners, implementing an update maybe as simple as agreeing to the update and the operating system performs all functions. For other organizations the IT department may have update policies and procedures that define how updates are implemented and how the system will be returned to a known, good, state in case an issue with the update occurs.

As an example, an IT group may require that all operating system updates occur between the hours of midnight and 3 a.m. This time frame is selected as most people are not on their computer during those hours. The time also allows the IT group sufficient time to restore the system to a pre-update state if a problem develops during the changes. While the intent of the operating system update policies and procedures is to minimize end user impact, it does not state that the system will not be in service at all times. In fact, very often a part or most of the entire network is not in service during major operating system modifications. Acknowledging and accepting that enterprise systems or applications may experience outages, for some period of time, is often a normal organizational operating state.

With SCADA systems it is not business as usual if the system is not operating 24X7X365. The control room operator cannot monitor and control critical field processes if the SCADA system is not in service. The need to have the SCADA system always in operation requires a different system update and modification policy and procedure than what and how the enterprise system performs its updates.

Another area where IT cyber security practices are not directly transferrable to the SCADA world is in the area of intrusion detection and prevention systems (IDPS). As API-1164 states:

Due to the nature of SCADA traffic (which is generally considered to be different from more traditional business systems), and unique protocols that may be implemented, the use of the IDPS should be carefully examined to ensure that safe and reliable operation of the system being controlled is not compromised by automated action of the IDPS. (API$_2$, 2009, p. 23)

Within the enterprise IT domain, the use of an IDPS is fairly common and adds another layer of cyber security. Yet, as stated above, SCADA systems sometimes utilize unique protocols which are not supported by today's IDPSs and the available IDPSs rule sets are not fully applicable to the SCADA environment. As this technology matures, its acceptance within the SCADA domain will probably increase. In the interim, directly applying an enterprise IT based IDPS within the SCADA system may generate issues rather than enhance cyber security.

Network monitoring is another distinct domain difference that has not matured to a degree that the IT based systems can be easily applied to the SCADA network. Again, at the writing of this chapter, various SCADA cyber security sources, such as API-1164, identify that '...no universally accepted best practices exist for network monitoring in a SCADA or control system...The aggregation and correlation of information from multiple sources, and the necessity to present it in a meaningful manner can be an onerous task and can be assisted by appropriate tools" (API$_2$, 2009, p. 23). This is a different landscape than the IT enterprise system which has a suite of various

network monitoring systems that can be and are deployed.

SCADA systems cyber security challenges are also slightly different than enterprise systems in the areas of vendor certifications, antivirus software verifications and password rules as well.

Vendor supplied SCADA applications function within the operating system. The vendors provide extensive testing and validation that their SCADA system will perform as designed with a specific computer operating system. This is very much the same as many enterprise software applications. The difference comes about in how fast, if ever, that the software vendor provides certification that its SCADA system will operate correctly with the latest set of updates or the next operating system version. It is not uncommon to find some SCADA vendors are extremely slow in providing validation or that they will never validate that their older systems are capable of operating correctly with a newly released operating system.

SCADA vendor validation that their systems correctly work with most antivirus software is an area that is lacking across many vendor systems. While the enterprise IT department deploys antivirus software and updates the virus definition files on a routine basis, SCADA systems often cannot follow this same process. This limitation is directly tied to the SCADA software vendor's ability to verify that their system will correctly operate with the antivirus software and all the new virus definitions that are supplied. Typically SCADA vendors are smaller organizations that lack sufficient staff resources to keep up with this rapidly advancing field. Due to vendor resource constraints, SCADA system end users are often faced with the internal decision to self verify that their network will work with antivirus software or forgo utilizing these applications.

SCADA systems, especially control room operators, also differ in how system password protection is applied. Within the enterprise world it is a common password practice that user specific passwords are required and these must be changed on a routine basis, such as every 180 days. Within the SCADA control room environment, individual passwords and frequently changing passwords are generally not deployed. This difference is derived from the fact that these systems must operate continuously and cannot be shutdown just to allow the next shift control room operator to sign on to the system with their unique password. In this situation, either no password is used or a common password is used for all operators.

As these examples highlight, different policies and procedures are required for enterprise IT systems and SCADA systems. These differences are driven by how the systems must function, within their unique environment and vendor support constraints. While both technology domains utilize common hardware and software platforms, specific applications, cultures and environments drive the need for different policies, procedures and processes.

OPERATING SYSTEM UPDATE APPROACHES

Several operating system update approaches are present within the SCADA discipline. Some firms take the position that they will not update their SCADA operating system unless required by the SCADA vendor. In this situation, the SCADA computer operating system falls further and further behind the original vendor supplied system. A second approach is that on a planned schedule all updates are first tested on an offline SCADA system. If the testing indicates that the updates will not adversely affect the network, these changes are loaded into one computer at a time and system normal operation is verified prior to implementing the changes on any other site.

A third approach is a slight modification of the second approach. This approach still validates that the operating software updates will not affect the offline system. Once this is validated, the operating system updates are loaded into the backup,

offline, SCADA system. The backup system is monitored for some time to ensure no adverse impacts are noted. Once a level of confidence is obtained, the backup system is transitioned to prime and operation is closely monitored.

Once a review of the 'now prime' operating system validates normal operation, the operating system updates are loaded on the 'now backup' SCADA systems. The backup system is then forced to primary state and system operation monitored. At any time, during this process, if an abnormal operating state occurs, the old operating system can be quickly restored by just falling back to the pre-update system.

Utilizing the backup system for all testing and validation provides a multi- step safety process. Step one is validation that in an offline system the updates appear to operate correctly. Step two verifies that in the backup mode all operating system modifications appear to function correctly. Step three verifies that the operating system updates provide a safe on line system operation while providing a quick step four of being able to return to the earlier and presumably correctly operating system by just falling back to the previous network configuration.

MANAGEMENT INFRASTRUCTURE

"Quality is everyone's responsibility"
W. Edwards Deming

When Deming made the lead-in quote, SCADA system cyber security was not on the organization or international radar screen, yet there was a concern about quality and providing value to the end customer. In today's environment, quality must and does include a continuous improvement quality function. Cyber security can accurately be described and linked to the realm of quality and the need for continuous improvement. To this end due diligence in understanding the new and emerging threats, new vulnerabilities/ susceptibilities, and organizational risks and then taking proactive steps to address the evolving landscape is required. This continuous improvement process starts and ends with the organization's management infrastructure. Edwards Deming identifies that a successful quality program is 85% management structure. The same is valid for an effective and efficient SCADA cyber security program.

Several cyber security standards support the context that organizational management is an essential element of the overall system. Such references include:

Security governance involves setting organization-wide policies and procedures that define how the security management program (SMP) should be appropriately integrated into the company's overall management system. Security governance includes management commitment and accountability. Organizational policies and procedures provide clear direction, commitment, responsibility, and oversight and define the security environment for the owner/operator. (CSA, 2008, p. 8)

The Vendor shall, within their own organization, practice and maintain policies, standards and procedures which are compliant with the requirements specified in this document (IIUA, 2010, p. 9)

The operator shall develop a SCADA security management program system with defined policies and procedures that complements and works with the pipeline security plan developed under the guidance of the API's Security Guidelines for the Petroleum Industry. (API$_2$, 2009, p. 11)

These standards clearly identify that cyber security requires a governance system. This organizational cyber security governance system starts with the policy statement. A policy statement is that formal, written, reviewed and updated statement which outlines the ways the organization will conduct its cyber security program and how it will respond to cyber security threats and subsequent risks. Stated another way policies are principles, rules, and guidelines formulated or adopted by an organization to reach its long-term goals.

The company cyber security policy establishes the foundation from which specific procedures will be developed. The procedures provide the day-to-day methods on how the various personnel associated with the SCADA system will perform their duties. As an example, specific procedures will provide a design basis so engineers and software analysts will have specific objectives and requirements for the design, engineerimg, procurement and implementation of a new system.

Specific procedures will also identify how modifications and changes are handled. The procedure will explicitly identify how modifications and changes are validated before being installed on an active system, how system restoration will occur, and who must approve of the change. Disaster recovery plans are also part of the specific procedures which are developed to support the policy statement.

The management infrastructure can be summarized as:

- Company SCADA cyber security system policy statement
- Procedures which establish the following within the organizational context;
  ◦ Roles, responsibilities and authority levels
  ◦ System design basis
  ◦ How SCADA and enterprise system interconnections occur
  ◦ How SCADA and 3rd party interconnections occur
  ◦ How wireless interconnections are applied and secured
  ◦ How SCADA and service provider interconnections occur
  ◦ How SCADA data is classified, handled and stored
  ◦ Physical access control rules and procedures

- ○ How system modifications and changes are performed
- ○ How system testing is performed
- ○ Training requirements
- ○ Disaster recovery plans

The management system develops, promotes, and continuously supports a sustainable cyber security position.

FUTURE RESEARCH DIRECTIONS

SCADA cyber security research is an expanding topic area. Academia, national laboratories, and vendors are all seeking ways to increase critical infrastructure control system security posture. These efforts are funded by both private and public organizations.

At the present time, most of this research is in the area of software and hardware technology. The objective is how to prevent someone from obtaining unauthorized access and implementing changes. These are all worthy research areas. Yet, two areas of future research is required. Specifically, the area of resilient SCADA system design and the design of an holistic SCADA cyber security program are essential elements to ensuring a secure critical infrastructure.

As discussed earlier in this chapter, one must always assume that SCADA system unauthorized access will happen. Within this context, how is the system designed to respond? This is the foundational resilient system question. Can the affected system mitigate the negative consequences and provide means to rapidly restore the system to a known, safe, and operational state? These questions need further funded research.

To develop a resilient system requires a holistic systems approach. Acknowledging that the final system will be entity specific, this research should develop an overarching approach and recommended best practices. Very much like the various industry standards of today the final

research objective is not to develop a one-size-fits all holistic, resilient system but to develop the framework, guiding principles and identification of best practices. The research objective then forms the foundation documentation from which each organization can proceed forward in the development of their specific system design, engineering, implementation, operation and maintenance program.

CONCLUSION

SCADA systems continue to evolve to meet the changing demands of advancing technology, user needs and regulatory requirements. With evolving and expanding usage comes additional security treats. Computer system hackers are found in many industries throughout the world. Keeping oil and gas pipeline infrastructure process capability running smoothly is essential. Therefore, minimizing cyber system vulnerability and increasing system resilience is essential.

The Center for Strategic and International Studies *Securing the Cyberspace for the 44th Presidency* report succinctly states that "Cybersecurity is among the most serious economic and national security challenges we face in the twenty-first century… As one general officer put it in his briefing to us: "In cyberspace, the war has begun." (CISI, 2008, p. 77). This war can have drastic negative impact on the life, safety and economic well being of every civilized society. To this end a continuously improving, resilient cyber security system must be implemented.

Implementation of a resilient system is specific to each owner/operator's unique environment. Various industry standards, recommended best practices, and guidelines exist. These various documents provide each owner/operator a place to start, questions to ask, and best practices which may apply. The documents are just an initial start; the owner/operator must make the cyber security program their own.

The full security management governance program begins with the company policy from which specific procedures are developed. Organizational specific roles and responsibilities are developed so personnel can then be assigned and trained to fulfill these roles and responsibilities.

The resilient cyber system accepts that negative system impacts can and may happen. Yet, the system is designed, operated and maintained in such a state that a cyber attack is either prevented or negative consequences are severely limited. The resilient system provides a highly available system but it also provides a system that mitigates the negative potential while providing rapid restoration capabilities.

Resilience is a requirement, not a 'nice to have,' capability. A presentation at the Institute for Information Infrastructure Protection (I3P) *I3P Security Forum: Connecting the Business and Control System Networks* contends that resilience is achieved by;

- Addressing security in layers, such as
- Data
- Applications
- Platforms and operating systems
- Networks and communications systems
- Boundary systems
- Control systems
- Physical access
- Implementing;
- Best Practices [such as];
- Awareness
- Define the boundaries – understand operational requirements and risk
- Defining roles and responsibilities
- Life-cycle approach
- Tools and technologies
- Methodologies / processes and procedures
- Metrics (McIntyre, et al., 2008)

SCADA cyber security must be designed into the system as early as possible. Key to ensuring that the proper level of security is achieved requires a strong management structure and acceptance of on various industry standards.

REFERENCES

American Gas Association (AGA). (2006). *Cryptographic protection of SCADA communications part 1: Background, policies and test plan (AGA12, Part1).* Retrieved from http://www.aga.org/NR/rdonlyres/B797B50B-616B-46A4-9E0F-5DC877563A0F/0/0603AGAREPORT12.PDF

American Petroleum Institute. (API). (2007). *Developing a pipeline supervisory control center.* (API Publication No. RP 1113). Washington, DC: American Petroleum Institute.

American Petroleum Institute. (API). (2009). *Pipeline SCADA security.* (API Publication No. API-1164). Washington, DC: American Petroleum Institute.

BookRags. (2010). *Research.* Retrieved January 12, 2010, from http://www.bookrags.com/research/aqueduct-woi/

Canadian Standards Association (CSA). (2008). *Security management for petroleum and natural gas industry systems, Z246.1.* Retrieved from http://www.shopcsa.ca/onlinestore/GetCatalogDrillDown.asp?Parent=4937

Center for Strategic and International Studies (CSIS). (2008). *Securing cyberspace for the 44th presidency: A report of the CSIS Commission on Cybersecurity for the 44th Presidency.* Washington, DC: Government Printing Office.

Department of Homeland Security (DHS). (2009). *Strategy for securing control systems: Coordinating and guiding federal, state and private sector initiatives.* Retrieved from http://www.us-cert.gov/control_systems/pdf/Strategy%20for%20Securing%20Control%20Systems.pdf

Idaho National Laboratory (INL). (2005), *A comparison of cross-sector cyber security standards*, Robert P. Evans. (Report No. INL/EXT-05-00656). Idaho Falls, ID.

Institute of Electrical and Electronics Engineering (IEEE). (1994). *IEEE standard definition: Specification, and analysis of systems used for supervisory control, data acquisition, and automatic control – Description*. Washington, DC: IEEE Standards Association.

International Council of System Engineering (INCOSE). (2010). *International Council on Systems Engineering*. Retrieved from http://www.incose.org/

International Instrument Users' Associations – EWE (IIUA). (2010). *Process control domain-security requirements for vendors*, (Report M 2784-X-10). Kent, United Kingdom: International Instrument Users' Associations – EWE.

McIntyre, A., Stamp, J., Richardson, B., & Parks, R. (2008). *I3P Security Forum: Connecting the business and control system networks*. Albuquerque, NM: Sandia National Lab.

National Transportation Safety Board (NSTB). (2005). *Supervisory Control and Data Acquisition (SCADA) in liquid pipeline safety study*. (Report No. NTSB/SS-05/02, PB2005-917005). Retrieved from http://www.ntsb.gov/publictn/2005/ss0502.pdf

Pipeline and Hazardous Material Safety Administration (PHMSA). (2010). *Pipeline basics*. Retrieved from http://primis.phmsa.dot.gov/comm/PipelineBasics.htm?nocache=5000

Stouffer, K., Falco, J., & Scarfone, K. (2008). *Guide to Industrial Control Systems (ICS) security*. (Report No. NIST SP 800-82). Retrieved from http://www.nist.gov

Transportation Security Administration (TSA). (2008). *Transportation Security Administration: Pipeline security guidelines, rev. 2a*. Washington, DC: TSA.

Turneaure, F. E., & Russell, H. L. (1916). *Public water-supplies – Requirements, resources, and the construction of works*. New York, NY: John Wiley & Sons, Inc.

Turner, N. C. (1991, September). *Hardware and software techniques for pipeline integrity and leak detection monitoring*. Society of Petroleum Engineers, Inc. Paper presented at meeting of the Offshore Europe Conference, Aberdeen, Scotland.

ADDITIONAL READINGS

Fink, R. K., Spencer, D. F., & Wells, R. A. (2006). *Lessons Learned fro Cyber Security Assessments of SCADA and Energy Management Systems*. U. S. Department of Energy Office of Electricity Delivery and Energy Reliability.

Henrie, M., & Carpenter, P. S. (2006, Apri-May). *Process Control Cyber-Security: A Case Study. IEEE* Paper Presented at the I&CPS Technical Conference, April 20 – May 3, Detroit, MI.

Henrie, M., & Liddell, P. J. (2008). *Quantifying Cyber Security Risk: Part 1* (*Vol. 55*, p. 3). Control Engineering.

Henrie, M., & Liddell, P. J. (2008). *Quantifying Cyber Security Risk: Part 2* (*Vol. 55*, p. 5). Control Engineering.

Hollnagel, E. Woods, D.D, & Leveson, N., (2006), *Resilience Engineering: Concepts and Prec*epts, Burlington, VT: Ashgate.

McIntyre, A. (2009). Final institute report refines, forecasts cyber-security issues . *Oil & Gas Journal, 107*(43).

McIntyre, A., Stampe, J., Cook, B., & Lanzone, A. (2006). Workshops identify threats to process control systems Vulnerabilities in Current Process Control Systems. *Oil & Gas Journal, 104*(38).

Shaw, W. T. (2009). *Cybersecurity for SCADA Systems*. Tulsa, OK: PennWell Books.

Stamp, J., Dillinger, J., & Young, W. (2003). *Common Vulnerabilities in Critical Infrastructure Control systems*. Albuquerque, NM: Sandia National Laboratories.

KEY TERMS AND DEFINITIONS

Defense in Depth: using multiple layers of technology and process to achieve higher levels of security.

External Cyber Attack: an entity, external to the organization internal network trying to obtain unauthorized access to the internal resources.

Holistic SCADA System: full encompassing system that includes software, hardware, telecommunications, policies, procedures, roles and responsibilities.

Internal Cyber Attack: an entity, internal to the organization network trying to obtain unauthorized access to the internal resources.

Management security system: the combination of security policy, procedures, roles and responsibilities that establish the company direction, actual processes and identifies what position performs the exact activities and their subsequent responsibilities.

Resilient SCADA System: a SCADA system that reduces risks as much as practical but provides processes to mitigate and minimize adverse impacts of a negative event.

SCADA Cyber Security: the process of providing a secure, safe, effective and efficient SCADA system against computer software based attacks.

Chapter 12
Application of Cyber Security in Emerging C4ISR Systems

Ashfaq Ahmad Malik
National University of Sciences & Technology, Pakistan

Athar Mahboob
National University of Sciences & Technology, Pakistan

Adil Khan
National University of Sciences & Technology, Pakistan

Junaid Zubairi
State University of New York at Fredonia, USA

ABSTRACT

C4ISR stands for Command, Control, Communications, Computers, Intelligence, Surveillance & Reconnaissance. C4ISR systems are primarily used by organizations in the defense sector. However, they are also increasingly being used by civil sector organizations such as railways, airports, oil, and gas exploration departments. The C4ISR system is a system of systems and it can also be termed as network of networks and works on similar principles as the Internet. Hence it is vulnerable to similar attacks called cyber attacks and warrants appropriate security measures to save it from these attacks or to recover if the attack succeeds. All of the measures put in place to achieve this are called cyber security of C4ISR systems. This chapter gives an overview of C4ISR systems focusing on the perspective of cyber security warranting information assurance.

DOI: 10.4018/978-1-60960-851-4.ch012

Figure 1. The concept of C4ISR (Stokes, 2010)

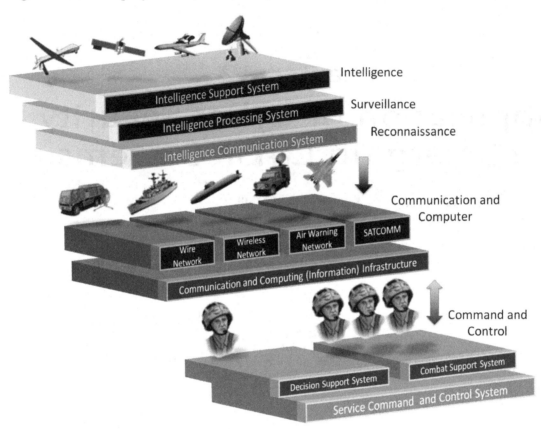

INTRODUCTION TO THE C4ISR SYSTEMS

C4ISR is the abbreviation of Command, Control, Communications, Computers, Intelligence, Surveillance & Reconnaissance (Figure 1). The C4ISR system is the central nervous system of military organizations. There is an increase in requirement and usage of these systems even by civil organizations such as railways, airports, oil and gas exploration departments, etc., hence C4I systems are a source of growing attraction for various people and organizations. The primary objective of a C4ISR system is to present the overall scenario and picture of the area of interest (such as a battlefield, operation area of ships/forces in sea/land/air or a disaster area, etc.). This allows a clear situational awareness for better decision making by the mission commanders to achieve their missions. A comprehensive and better situational awareness of the battlefield helps the commander in making of effective and timely decisions which in turn helps in effective control of the situation through an advance planning and efficient utilization of the available resources. Figure 1 shows the overall concept of C4ISR systems.

Historically, C4ISR systems have followed an evolutionary path in their development. The terminology of C4ISR is used by the military organizations, specially by US-DoD, to mean the use of organizational setup utilized by military forces for carrying out a mission. The first C of C4ISR stands for command which means authority over subordinates with responsibility. Second C stands for control which means exercising authority over subordinates. These are the aspects of leadership and are commonly known as C2. The facilities used by commanders and leaders in carrying out their assigned missions are largely dependent on communication and computers hence terms C3 and C4 are well known and accepted. The I of C4ISR represents Intelligence, i.e. the collecting of information which is required by leaders/commanders to carry out a mission. Hence the terms C3I and C4I started coming into use over a period of time. The information is gathered through intelligence, surveillance and reconnaissance which is the reason for the ISR part. The systematic observation of certain things is called surveillance whereas observations on specific occasions is defined as reconnaissance. Hence, the systems are now collectively termed as C4ISR systems (Anthony, 2002).

The overall purpose of a modern C4ISR System is to achieve a better Command & Control of a situation (i.e. in the battlefield, at sea, disaster management, etc.) through good and updated ISR functions and using the latest computer and communication technologies effectively. A very brief and comprehensive C2 model which has been basically derived from tactical level but also fits in higher more strategic levels is described as bottom up approach for design of C2 systems (Anthony, 2002) (Stanton, et. al., 2008):

It is proposed that the command and control activities are triggered by events such as the receipt of orders or information, which provide a mission and a description of the current situation of events in the field. The gap between the mission and the current situation lead the command system to determine the effects that narrow that gap. This in turn requires the analysis of the resources and constraints in the given situation. From these activities, plans are developed, evaluated and selected. The chosen plans are then rehearsed before being communicated to agents in the field. As the plan is enacted, feedback from the field is sought to check that events are unfolding as expected. Changes in the mission or the events in the field

may require the plan to be updated or revised. When the mission has achieved the required effects the current set of command and control activities come to an end. The model distinguishes between 'command' activities and 'control' activities. Command comprises proactive, mission-driven, planning and co-ordination activities. Control comprises reactive, event-driven monitoring and communication activities. The former implies the transmission of mission intent whereas the latter implies reactions to specific situations.

Nowadays the trend of using the information, communication and computer technologies has increased manifolds. Their use in medical, defense, banking, education, research etc., or we can say that in every walk of life has quite obviously increased. The use of PDAs, laptops, mobile phones, ipods, gaming and communication devices in our day to day life has increased tremendously. Everyone is on-line and connected together through a network of computers. The use of similar technologies in defense sector has also increased in order to get the benefit of improvement in operational capabilities at less cost. Hence the information is shared with all stakeholders in the military chain of command through networking of equipment/systems of decision makers, their implementers/effectors and having information sources. There are different network oriented defense terminologies in use such as Network-Centric Warfare (NCW) by the US-DoD (US-DoD, 2005), Network Enabled Capability (NEC) by the UK (MoD, 2004) and Network-Based Defense (NBD) by the Swedish Military (Nilsson, 2003), for example. These terms are also similar to C4ISR. Figure 2 shows the network oriented defense concept in which the decision makers, the effectors and information sources are interconnected in a common network. The services on the network are used by all stakeholders. C4ISR works on a similar concept.

Despite the fact that C4ISR systems have their origins in security centric organizations like the military, cyber security of these systems, for

Figure 2. Network oriented structure: NEC/NCW/NBD (Ericsson, 2006)

various reasons discussed later in this chapter, is still an open question and an area which is keenly being researched. In this chapter we shall provide an overview of the current state of cyber security of C4ISR systems. We shall provide references to additional material which the reader may access to get further details. Now we provide information on the organization of the remainder of our chapter.

After this introduction, section 2 goes into more details of the C4ISR system themselves. This should provide sufficient frame of reference for a reader not already familiar with the C4ISR systems. In section 3 we provide the cyber security requirements of C4ISR systems and the threats to which these systems are exposed. In section 4 we provide various case studies of reported cyber security breaches in C4ISR systems. The sample of reported cases which we present should justify the relevance and importance of the cyber security requirements of C4ISR systems. In section 5 we discuss the cyber security aspects of the standardized C4ISR architectures. Here we primarily focus on the DoDAF, a well accepted C4ISR architectural framework. In section 6 we discuss the security aspects of the TCP/IP proto-

col suite. TCP/IP development was also initiated and supported by the US-DoD. TCP/IP forms the foundation of all modern network applications and C4ISR systems are no exception. An appreciation of security vulnerabilities inherent in original TCP/IP protocols will put forward many cyber security considerations for the C4ISR system design and uses. In section 7 we discuss the cyber security of various of C4ISR components including the operating systems, Electronic Mail systems, Communication Systems from the end to end perspective, communication data links and Identity and Access Management Systems. In section 8 we provide examples of many of the success stories and best practices for cyber security of C4ISR system components. We emphasize on current trends and approaches and, wherever possible, we provide examples of noteworthy projects and initiatives. In section 9 we discuss the increasing use of open source information processing modules as building blocks for C4ISR systems.

Finally, we conclude our chapter by summarizing the findings presented in the entire chapter and highlight some directions for future research in cyber security of C4ISR systems.

Figure 3. Generalized view of Naval C4ISR system (NAP, 2006)

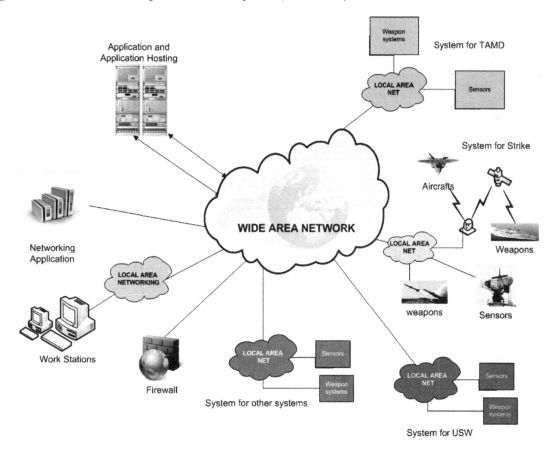

GENERALIZED VIEW OF A C4ISR SYSTEM

C4ISR system is a system of systems. It can also be called a distributed system using a common communication or the network infrastructure. The US Navy, Army and Air Force are working under the umbrella of the US-DoD. They consider C4ISR as a unified, mission-driven organization for achieving the idea and vision of network-centric operations (NCO). Its working is like that of the Internet where information sources from different communities of interest such as strike forces, Theater Air and Missile Defense (TAMD), Undersea Warfare (USW) work as separate user enclaves. These are, however, connected to the same network and to one another through agreed working protocols and similar type of technology.

Various services are provided to the end users through design of a service-oriented architecture of systems. Figure 3 presents a general view of a naval C4ISR architecture.

To develop a clear idea of C4ISR systems, their various components will be discussed in parts in the following sub-sections.

Command-and-Control (C2) Systems

C2 systems include software, methods, and procedures that enable commanders to make decisions and control their forces (Rand, 2009). The United States is a leader in development of defense technologies in general, and C2 systems in particular. Various C2 systems developed by USA are C2P/CDLMS, GCCS-J, GCCS-M, etc. among others. These systems are generally based

Figure 4. Systems View of GCCS-M (NAP, 2006)

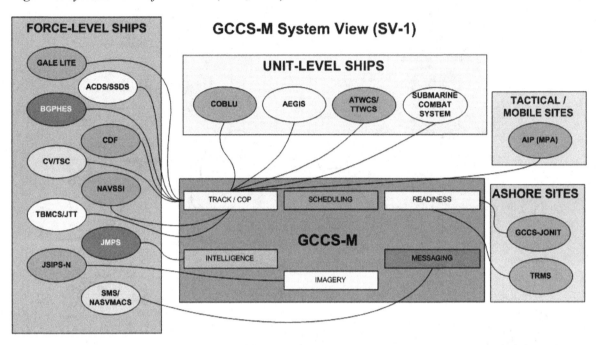

on the Internet Protocol (IP), Service Oriented Architecture (SOA), Global Information Grid (GIG) so as to provide C4ISR capabilities to their defense forces. As the maritime war theater is the most complex one, covering the four dimensions of land, air, sea-level and under the sea-level, it is apt to discuss C4ISR systems for this environment. To gauge an idea how GCCS-M, a naval C4ISR system, looks like its systems view is depicted in figure 4. In the interest of avoiding repetition the acronyms in the figure are defined at the end of the chapter along with other acronyms and keywords.

The GCCS-M means the maritime component of the Global Command and Control System (GCCS) family of systems (FOS). The GCCS-M is installed on board approximately 325 United States Navy (USN) ships and submarines and at 65 ashore and tactical mobile sites. The functional components of the system are linked to a variety of inputs and outputs. Hence alignment of interface requirements and matching the pro-

tocols for seamless integration of variety of systems is a primary concern. As so many systems are being integrated, security aspects of the system without compromising the performance/interoperability of the system, is another major concern. Once a new input or output is required to be interfaced with the system, the interface requirements of complete system are required to be looked into. The Joint Command and Control (JC2) program is intended to replace the entire GCCS FOS.

Another recent development in C2 systems is the Deployable Joint Command and Control System (Navsea, 2007), commonly known as DJC2. It is an integrated command and control headquarters system which enables a commander to set up a self-contained, self-powered, computer network-enabled temporary headquarters facility anywhere in the world within 6-24 hours of arrival at a location. The DJC2 command and control architecture is an open architecture based

Figure 5. Key US Navy communications systems (NAP, 2006)(NAP, 1999)

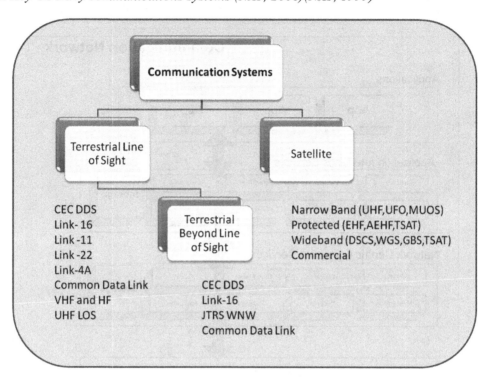

on Service Oriented Architecture principles. The architecture utilizes several technologies – including Internet Protocol Convergence (IPC) and virtualization – to reconcile the DJC2 system's robust IT requirements (i.e., five different networks, C2 and collaboration software applications, and communications) with its stringent deployability and rapid set-up requirements. The DJC2 system is a fully tested, fully certified U.S. military system. Its certifications include Transportability through air/sea/road/rail, Information Assurance, Joint Interoperability, Authority to Operate.

Communications and Computer

Effective and secure communications is the backbone of a military organization and especially the Navy. Its importance cannot be ruled out for a flexible C4ISR systems (Figure 5). The operations in sea require robust and reliable communication amongst various platforms such as surface ships, submarines, aircraft and establishments ashore.

The diversified functions of C4ISR require reliable and secure links among various platforms to cater for the many applications which includes C2, exchanging tactical/common pictures, sharing sensor data, engaging time critical targets etc. US Navy has the most versatile and diversified communication infrastructure. Figure 6 shows important data links which include satellite, terrestrial line-of-sight (LOS) and beyond-line-of-sight (BLOS) communication facilities. In the interest of avoiding repetition the acronyms in the figure are defined at the end of the chapter along with other acronyms and keywords.

In C4ISR scenario the global Internet-like military communication system is referred to as the Global Information Grid (GIG). The communication infrastructure of GIG consists of air platforms, satellite, radio, land lines i.e. optical fiber. It has four tiers. Tier 1 is ground based coverage which includes GIG-BE and JTRS. Tier 2 is the coverage provided by AAV/UAVs. Tier 3 is Wide Area Coverage provided by LEOS (Low

Figure 6. A concept of integration of applications, services and data assets using the GIG communication infrastructure (NAP, 2006)

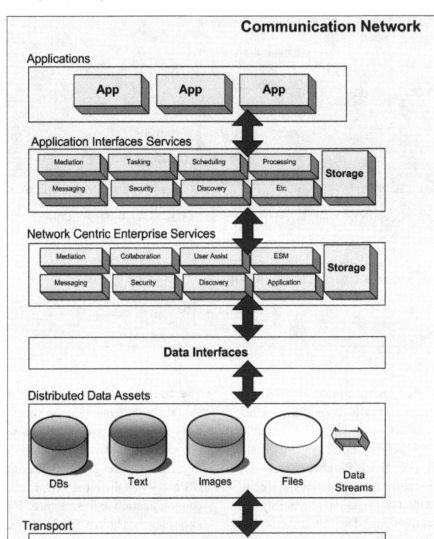

Earth Orbiting Satellites) and Tier 4 is Global Area Coverage provided by GEOS (Geosynchronous Earth Orbiting Satellites). In addition to being a communication network, the GIG also provides the network services, storage for data along with user friendly application interfaces for usability of the available data. There is a shared, fiber-based, terrestrial communications network having quasi infinite bandwidth. Information Assurance is achieved in GIG through application of HAIPE (High Assurance Internet Protocol Encryptor). The Enterprise System Management (ESM) Services, Messaging Services, Discovery (search) Services, Mediation Services, Collaboration Services, Assistance Services, Information Assurance/Security Services, Storage Services, Application Services are the various GIG Enterprise Services (GES). Figure 6 shows the integration of applications, services and data assets using the GIG communication infrastructure.

ISR

The purpose of ISR as part of C4ISR is initially to find, then to fix and, finally, to keep a track both friend and foe forces. The damage assessment of a particular area or target belonging to friendly or enemy forces is another aspect. During peace time Signal Intelligence (SIGINT) is carried out and enemy's sensors data is analyzed. The same is then used in case of war. There are technologically advanced and powerful space-based image intelligence (IMINT), signals intelligence (SIGINT) and measurement and signatures intelligence (MASINT) collection systems. The data is to be effectively utilized in case of war. It is essential that forces have access to data from these capabilities and that they are able to task the capabilities. The situational picture is to great extent improved with the help of using sensors data from UAVs (such as Global Hawk and Predator), new Multi-mission Maritime Aircrafts including MPAs (Maritime Patrol Crafts) and AWACS such as E-2C aircraft and fixed land radars/sensors etc. The data is transferred through links hence the security of data and its proper usability is a primary concern; as an intruder may modify the data or deny the data resulting in denial of service (DoS).

C4ISR Architectures

Due to inherent complexity of C4ISR systems their design is based on formal standards specifying the architectures. Architecture is the structure of components, their relationships, and the principles and guidelines governing their design and evolution over time (US-DoD, 1995). An architecture is the fundamental organization of a system embodied in its components, their relationships to each other, and to the environment, and the principles guiding its design and evolution (ISO/IEC, 2007). There are two types

of architectures. The Program Level or Solutions Architecture is the first and most traditional type. This architecture has been required, defined, and supported by major US-DoD processes for solution, evaluation, interoperability, and resource allocation. The second type of architecture is Enterprise Architecture which provides a complete road-map that how and where the programs or the projects fit in the organizations. Department of Defense Architecture Framework (DODAF) (US-DoD, 1997), (US-DoD, 2007) (US-DoD, 2009), Ministry of Defense Architecture Framework (MODAF)(MOD, 2005a), (MOD, 2005b) and NATO Architecture (NAF) (NATO, 2007) are landmarks in the development of C4I systems or any other defense related information system. However, MODAF and NAF have been derived from DODAF being pioneer in enterprise architecture development. The evolution of C4ISRAF to DoDAF is shown in figure 7.

DODAF

DoDAF does not prescribe any particular models, but instead concentrates on data as the necessary ingredient for architecture development. DoDAF is the structure for organizing architecture concepts, principles, assumptions, and terminology about operations and solutions into meaningful patterns to satisfy specific DoD purposes. The US-DoD has taken lead and necessary steps to cater to advancement in the field of IT for modern warfare. NCW makes essential information available to authenticated and authorized users when and where they need it to carryout Net-Centric Operations (NCO). The models described by DoDAF can have seven viewpoints i.e. All Viewpoint (AV), Capability Viewpoint (CV), Data and Information Viewpoint (DIV), Operational Viewpoint (OV), Project Viewpoint (PV), Services Viewpoint (SvcV), Standard Viewpoint (StdV), Systems Viewpoint (SV). These viewpoints are further divided into two AVs, seven CVs, three DIVs, six OVs, three PVs, ten ScvVs, two StdVs

Figure 7. Evolution of DODAF (US-DoD, 2007)

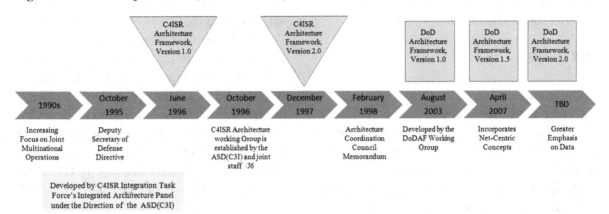

and ten SVs making it all together 43 viewpoints to comprehensively define or architect a C4ISR enterprise system. However, choice of a particular viewpoint is dependent on the architect. The systems view of GCCS-M was shown in figure 4.

MoDAF

MoDAF has been derived from DoDAF V1.0 (US-DoD, 2009). The viewpoints of MoDAF are Acquisition View (AcV), Technical View (TV), System View (SV), Operational View (OV), Strategic View (StV) and All View (AV). A total of 38 views are available in MoDAF categorized in aforesaid six Viewpoints. Some of these views are used to provide high-level summary information of C4ISR enterprise architecture, some provide specific aspects, and the remaining show interrelationship between each other. MoDAF has utilized two additional viewpoints i.e. acquisition and capability views. Most recently, DoDAF V2.0 has also utilized the data elements related to acquisition and capability viewpoints of MoDAF.

NAF

NATO Architecture Framework (NAF) is used by NATO in support of its organizational goals. NAF has also been derived from DoDAF. How-

ever, the latest version of NAF has been made by incorporating the experiences of different nations (including the US and the UK), the industry and the academia. As in case of other architectures there are seven different viewpoints or views i.e. NATO All View (NAV), NATO Capability View (NCV), NATO Programme View (NPV), NATO Operational View (NOV), NATO Systems View (NSV), NATO Service-Oriented View (NSOV) and NATO Technical View (NTV).

Analysis of Architectures

A study was conducted to analyze using Analytic Hierarchy Process (AHP) by Alghamdi. The results of this study proved that MoDAF is leading to DoDAF in case of interoperability, governance, practice and adoptability wise. While DODAF is leading to MODAF in case of scalability, tool support, taxonomy, process completeness, maturity and partitioning wise. In case of NAF to MODAF and DODAF, the NAF has a secondary position. After comparative analysis of results it has been found that MODAF is ranked as first, DODAF as second and NAF as third in AHP assessment methodology (Alghamdi, 2009).

IMPORTANCE OF CYBER SECURITY IN C4ISR SYSTEMS

Nowadays there is an increase in reliance on information, computer and communication technologies for conduct of military operations. This factor has made the IT infrastructure a hot target for the adversaries. C4ISR is all about integration, interoperability and networking of many systems making it a large single system as such we can call it a "system of systems". Hence the opponents have more and more opportunity to attack it. This forces designers of C4ISR systems to take extra measures against attack by a clever and determined enemy for making the system to be secure against these types of attacks.

Security in C4ISR systems is a two dimensional problem. Firstly, it means the physical security of the facilities where different components/parts of the larger system of systems are installed. No one can do this better than the military. However, the second part which is more demanding and challenging is the information security (INFOSEC) which may be called as cyber security; as it is not clearly understood at all the levels.

The world has become more unpredictable and unstable, and new risks have emerged, in particular computer attacks. Cyber security issues are arising out of digital information, worldwide networks and application interconnection as well as the speeding-up of data dissemination. Paperless documentation and exchange automation are radically changing the economic, social and political environment of nations, making them more vulnerable.

Definitions Related to Cyber Security

As per Thales cyber security is defined as "the coordinated actions in order to prevent, analyze and react in case of cyber attacks. The main goals are to protect in a permanent way and to provide customer with a timely and relevant measures to deal with the risks targeting the Information systems" (Thales, 2010). As per Merriam Websters Dictionary definition of cyber security is the "measures taken to protect a computer or computer system (as on the Internet) against unauthorized access or attack" (Merriam-Webster, 2010).

Recently, a more comprehensive and closely related term that is being used is Information Assurance (IA). IA is defined as measures that protect and defend information and information systems by ensuring their availability, integrity, authentication, confidentiality, and non-repudiation (CNSS, 2010). Information assurance field has been developed from the practice of information security. Information Security focuses on CIA Triad i.e. Confidentiality, Integrity and Availability. Information security has grown from practices and procedures of computer security.

Generic Vulnerabilities and Security Requirements and Services of C4ISR Systems

Any computer network or information system is vulnerable to two types of attacks i.e. passive attacks and active attacks. The passive attacks can be traffic analysis and release of message contents. Passive attacks are generally very difficult to detect, however, encryption is a common technique to prevent passive attacks. Active attacks involve modification of data streams or the creation of false streams. These types of attacks fall into four categories i.e. masquerade, replay, modification of messages and denial of service (DoS) (Stallings, 2003). Appropriate security mechanisms are designed and used to detect, prevent, or recover from a security attack. Various security mechanisms are encipherment, digital signatures, access control, data integrity, authentication exchange, traffic padding, routing control, notarization, trusted functionality, security label, event detection, auditing, recovery, etc.

There are four general vulnerabilities that can be experienced in C4ISR systems. Those are unauthorized access to data, clandestine alteration of data, identity fraud and denial of service (DoS). All of these vulnerabilities may have the catastrophic effects on national interests of a country. For example, unauthorized access to data on a C4I computer may result in inflicting severe damage to a nation by obtaining and using classified or unclassified sensitive information by an adversary. Similarly, military planning may be severely affected if clandestine alteration of data on a C4I computer is done by the enemy. The identity fraud may result in modification of situational awareness through insertion of unwanted/changed information, issuing of fake orders, etc. All these will affect the morale and effective working of the defense forces. By application of DoS on a C4I system, the time critical operational planning and completion of tasks may be affected.

The C4ISR systems require appropriate measures and requirements for the vulnerabilities discussed above for achieving confidentiality, integrity and availability of data and maintaining system configuration through elaborate security guidelines and accountability of personnel authorized to access the information sources. Following security services are required to cater the security requirements (Stallings, 2003):

- **Authentication:** ascertaining the user identity through various means such as passwords, fingerprints, digital certificates, etc.
- **Access Control:** Permission or authority to perform specified actions as authorized in policy guidelines.
- **Data Confidentiality:** protection of data against unauthorized disclosure.
- **Data Integrity:** The assurance that data received and is same as transmitted by authorized user.
- Non-repudiation: Providing protection against denial by participants once participated in communication.

- **Availability:** Ensuring availability of a capability or system at all times or whenever desired/required.

Enforcement of Cyber Security Measures and Mechanisms

As we have seen in our previous discussion the infrastructure or architecture of C4ISR systems is Network Centric and it has an Internet like core. Hence it is vulnerable to cyber attacks and demands necessary security measures to protect the network and the data. Every organization has its own security policies and especially the defense sector, where security of information is their bread and butter, has stringent security policies. The C4ISR whether developed or procured should be able to implement the security policies of the organization receiving it. As the technical security solutions are made in light of the guiding policies, therefore, the security objectives are related to authority, identity and authenticity for controlling access to a system by authorized users. Other security aspects are protection of data and resources against intrusion and attacks, keeping confidentiality, integrity, privacy and non repudiation of data.

The number and level of security requirements is worked out against the demand of the situation. Depending on the operational scenario, a balance between security and other system performance measures is to be kept through risk management. The security measures and solutions can be classification of information, defining isolated zones of security and user roles with appropriate level of access and authority. The technical security measures can be logging, digital certificates, encryption, firewalls, digital signatures, smartcards, etc. Physical measures may include "only authorized entry". Another physical measure can be use of physically separated access equipment, which is used with different layers of virtual networks with different classifications, with physically common network. Last, but not the least, there is a requirement of a "reaction force" or in the "Network Operations Center" to tackle potential harm which can be caused by an intruder (Ericsson, 2006).

CASE STUDIES MANIFESTING THE IMPORTANCE OF CYBER SECURITY

In this section some of the historical events with respect to cyber warfare and cyber breaches have been mentioned to further highlight the importance and application of cyber security in C4ISR systems. These events have been selected from different books, papers, and news papers as indicated.

Eligible Receiver

Realizing the developing threat of cyber security to C4ISR systems as far back as 1997, the Eligible Receiver 97 was the first large-scale no-notice DoD exercise which was conducted in the summer of 1997 on directions of Chairman of the Joint Chiefs of Staff. The purpose was to test the ability of the United States to respond to cyber attacks on the DoD and U.S. national IT infrastructure. Simulated attacks were conducted on power/communications systems and information systems at the Pentagon, defense support agencies, and in combatant commands. Various types of vulnerabilities were exploited such as bad or easily guessed passwords, operating system deficiencies, and improper system configuration control, sensitive site-related information posted on open Web pages, inadequate user awareness of operational security, and poor operator training. The exercise provided real evidence of the vulnerabilities in DoD information systems and deficiencies in the ability of the United States to respond effectively (Robinson, 2002).

Solar Sunrise

In February 1998, many cyber attacks were experienced on US Navy, Marines and Air Force computers. These were mainly of the DoS variety. These attacks exploited the vulnerability of Solaris OS which was used in many of the C4ISR systems. A patch to address some of the vulnerabilities was released after one month. Considering possible Middle East War a large scale joint investigation namely 'Solar Sunrise' (Robinson, 2002) was conducted by the Air Force, Navy, Army, NASA, the NSA, the Department of Justice, the CIA and FBI.

An 18-year old Israeli and two California teenagers were eventually concluded to be the culprits.

Recent Rise in Cyber Attacks on US Information Systems

Though determining exact statistics about US Information Systems would be unrealistic. However, rise in number of attacks has been observed (Wortzel, 2009). A 20% rise in attacks against US-DoD information systems was measured from 2007 to 2008 when the number of attacks rose from 43,880 to 54,640. Based on trends of the first half of 2009 it was estimated that there is 60% increase in attacks as compared to 2008 i.e. a total of approximately 87,570 (USCESRC, 2009). Other US Government agencies also experienced similar rise in cyber attacks (US-CERT, 2009). These attacks involved penetration in system security, extracting critical data, navigation and mapping of cyber systems, etc. The results may be very alarming if malicious software is embedded which may destroy the system resources. Hence necessary counter measures especially in C4ISR systems are very vital for success of military forces.

Wikileaks

Recently, a large number (approximately 91,000) of US classified military records in Afghanistan War have been leaked and published on a website http://wikileaks.org/. This is one of the largest unauthorized disclosures in military history (ABC, 2010). The White House has attacked the on-line whistle-blowing site Wikileaks after it published some 200,000 pages of secret American military files about the war in Afghanistan (CBS, 2010). The event manifests the requirement of enforcing appropriate cyber security measures on defence related information systems including C4ISR systems.

Stuxnet Worm

Stuxnet worm is a virus which damages and disrupts the working of industrial computer aided controls also known as SCADA. The Bushehr nuclear power plant has been attacked along with other 30,000 IP addresses in Iran (Saenz, 2010), (AFP, 2010), (Reuters, 2010a). As per Symantec and Kaspersky Lab it is a Cyber Warfare type of attack on Iran's Nuclear ambitions (Reuters, 2010b). This is one of the latest signs now that the digital dominion will be the battle field in conflicts of the world in future. As per Kaspersky Lab, Stuxnet is a working and fearsome prototype of a cyber-weapon that will lead to the creation of a new arms race in the world (Reuters, 2010b).

The closest technical perspective mentioning intricacies of Stuxnet's attack strategy are discussed in ensuing sentences. Stuxnet worm exploits the weaknesses of the Operating System i.e. it steals authentication certificates and upgrades from peer to peer. It monitors the supervisory control and data acquisition (SCADA) systems and analyzes the configuration running on SCADA systems. After certain period of time it takes over the control and disrupts or shuts down the industrial systems inflicting heavy losses in terms of down time and its cost effects or even in complete disaster of the system. The SCADA system used with Iranian nuclear facility is that of Siemens which utilizes the Windows OS. The complexity of Stuxnet worm indicates that it is a nation-grade cyber warfare. The fallouts and effects of Stuxnet worm may envelope the power plants, other local factories, etc. which may directly effect the general public (Langer, 2010).

The case studies and examples cited in this section bring forth the importance and requirements of Cyber Warfare. US-DoD has rightly analyzed and understood the requirement and recently a separate command has been formed in USN, namely CYBERCOM, to address the cyber warfare.

There are other departments such as Department of Homeland Security, National Security Agency, etc., which are looking after the broad spectrum of cyber security.

CYBER SECURITY IN STANDARDIZED C4ISR ARCHITECTURES

In this section we discuss the cyber security aspects of different architectures (DoDAF, NAF and MoDAF) in relation to the best practices of cyber security. The capabilities of C4ISR may experience various types of attacks and are vulnerable to integrity, availability, and confidentiality with respect to operation of the system. These attacks may result in failures of the system or equipment, gaining unauthorized access to the services and data of the system and, finally, resulting in undermining the functions of a C4ISR system. Hence there is a requirement of identification of all possible threats and applying necessary security measures which reduce the known and potential vulnerabilities to an acceptable level. Moreover, we have to strike a balance between the ease of use of system and the desired level of security. However, higher is the security, lesser the ease of use of the system and vice versa.

Figure 8. Usability versus security

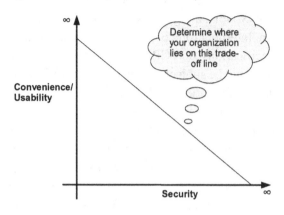

The same is shown in figure 8. Hence system designers and owners have to make a compromise between usability and security.

DoDAF V2.0

In DoDAF V2.0 the different cyber security measures against potential vulnerabilities have been described. These include physical measures (e.g. applying guards, locks, fences, CCTVs, etc.), procedural measures (i.e. defining procedures for accessing the data by trustworthy and reliable personnel), Communication Security (COM-SEC) measures, Information Security measures (INFOSEC) and Transient Electromagnetic Pulse Emanation Standard (TEMPEST).

DoDAF also acknowledges the fact that the measures adopted and implemented to protect any capability or system may have an undesirable affect on the capability. Hence the employed security measure should be in proportion to the value of the asset. A risk management approach in this regard is recommended to be applied considering the analysis of the asset. The characteristics that are considered during risk assessment are the environment in which it is deployed (friendly/hostile), value of the asset itself, the criticality factor (i.e. how important is that asset in carrying out the desired activities by the end user to achieve a goal) and the trust-worthiness (Personnel Clearance) of the operator/user. Similarly, the same security aspects/areas are covered by MODAF.

NAF

According to the NAF perspective C4ISR system being a distributed system has number of stakeholders. The stakeholders are required to collaborate amongst each other for Communities of Interest (CoIs) to achieve common goals and missions. Security is one of the CoIs which has been catered in NAF. NAF has defined and identified the security related stakeholders and CoIs. The security CoI of NAF caters for and provides key and security management. It also provides secure end-to-end information processing and exchange services through detailed architectural planning, implementation of secure services and secure service delivery management while applying NAF. The stakeholders involved in security CoI are IC (Infrastructure Committee), NC3A (NATO Consultation, Command and Control Agency) and the NCSA (NATO Communication and Information Systems (CIS) Services Agency).

Application of Best Practices of Cyber Security in C4ISR Architectures

C4ISR systems are combination of a variety of technologies and systems. Efforts have been made to standardize the C4ISR architectures. The DoDAF, MoDAF, NAF, SOA, etc. have been referred to in our discussion. However, these architectures do not give detailed view of Cyber Security aspects. There are other organizations which are carrying out detailed studies in the fields of Cyber Security and Information Assurance such as the NIST, NSA, CNSS, ISO/IEC, the Information Assurance Technical Framework Forum (IATFF), DISA, Department of Homeland Security (DHS), Information Assurance Technology Analysis Center (IATAC) etc. The standards and the procedures thus evolved by these reputed organizations can be regarded as the best practices in relevant areas. C4I system design from a cyber security perspective involves a number of considerations such as Security policy, System hardening, System security configuration management, Systems administration and management (access control), Monitoring and logging systems (audits, intrusion detection systems), Firewall deployment, Social engineering attack countermeasures (protocols and procedures), use of encryption mechanisms, multilevel security, use of biometrics, physical security, emission security, Military CND tools and techniques, operators and maintainers training, etc. (Zehetner, 2004). The design of C4ISR systems must therefore evolve, catering to the best practices of these security considerations coupled with the best practices of the Cyber security and while utilizing appropriate architecture framework. Additional references are listed at the end to provide further information to interested readers in these areas for improving security of C4ISR systems. Another important consideration and best practice for addressing cyber security in C4ISR systems is certification and testing of the systems prior deployment. IATAC is a centralized forum for USDoD for similar purpose. It provides information on Information Assurance emerging technologies in system vulnerabilities, research and development, models, and analysis to support the development and implementation of effective defense against Information Warfare attacks for the DoD (IATAC, 2010). IATAC provides three types of reports i.e. SOAR (State of the Art Reports), CR/TA(Critical Reviews and Technology Assessments) and Tool Reports. Tool Reports for Firewall, Intrusion Detection and Vulnerability Analysis are available for implementation and reference in this regard. A very relevant SOAR report is regarding Measuring Cyber Security and Information Assurance (CS/IA).

GENERAL SECURITY OF PROTOCOLS IN TCP/IP FAMILY

TCP/IP is used in the Internet like core network used for C4ISR systems and NCW. It is quite paradoxical that the TCP/IP protocols had no in-built security features despite the fact that they were developed under support and funding from the US-DoD, a highly security centric organization. Internet Protocol (IP) packets in the original specifications of TCP/IP traveled in plain-text and could be subject to undetected modification. This modification could even be in the packets header fields containing source and destination addresses. Hence a receiver could not even be sure of the source of the packet. Nevertheless, with its open for all approach for participation and eagerness to evolve, the Internet community under the Internet Engineering Task Force (IETF) has developed standard protocols which add security to all aspects of TCP/IP. Several approaches have been taken from the datalink layer to the application layer as shown in figure 9. The figure maps TCP/IP security protocols to the seven layer OSI Reference Model. Example communication and security protocols are mentioned at each level and the list should not be considered exhaustive. Security protocols, if implemented at lower levels tend to provide security transparently to all applications, e.g. TLS, IPSec and PPP-ECP. At higher levels the security protocols tend to be application specific like S/MIME, SSH, etc. Another aspect high-lighted in the figure is the link-level only versus end-to-end nature of the security protocol. In practice, multiple security protocols are concurrently being used. For example, secure end to end TLS sessions between client and server applications are many a times additionally secured by transporting them within encrypted IPSec VPN tunnels established across public networks by routers and gateways.

The approach taken by the Internet community is to leverage the development in the field of information security rather than re-inventing the wheel. Hence Internet security protocols have been defined in a generalized and modular way. They define the security mechanisms and message formating to be used and leave choice of actual algorithms used to the end users as per their security requirements. Hence the concept of the cipher suites in these security protocols. A cipher suite is a specification of the combination of al-

Figure 9. Security protocols added to TCP/IP protocol suite mapped to the OSI reference model

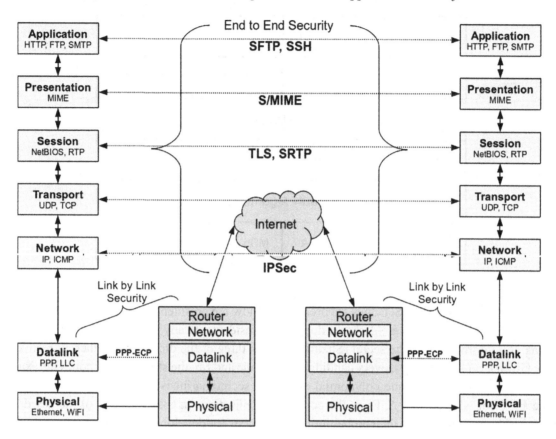

gorithms to be used for key agreement for the communication session, bulk encryption of data exchanged during the session, digital signature used for message integrity and non-repudiation and the hash function calculations within the digital signature. The well known, widely used and implemented security protocols/services, mechanisms and algorithms and their inter-relationship is shown in figure 10. Secret and Public Key types of cryptographic algorithms are used for encryption in TLS/SSL, IPSec and PPP-ECP protocols/services. Some commonly used secret key algorithms are the Advanced Encryption Standard (AES) and Triple Data Encryption Standard (3DES). MD-5 and SHA-1 are the security algorithms used for hashing. RSA and DSA are popularly used for digital signatures. DSA has analogs which are based on Elliptic Curves which are considered most secure and yet are computa-

tionally efficient public key encryption techniques. Finger prints and iris comparison are commonly used Biometric techniques. RSA or Diffie-Hellman protocols may be used for key exchange or agreement, respectively, during the beginning of a communications session. The development and use of large variety of mechanisms, algorithms and cryptographic primitives is justified as a single mechanism or primitive is not able to fulfill all information security requirements. The security features achievable through different cryptographic primitives are summarized in Table 1.

Another historical development in cryptographic technology were the Threshold Secret Sharing schemes which were driven by the need to secure access codes for strategic weapon systems. Secret sharing schemes can be very useful for general use also, as in banks for opening a

Figure 10. Security protocols, mechanisms and algorithms with concrete realizations

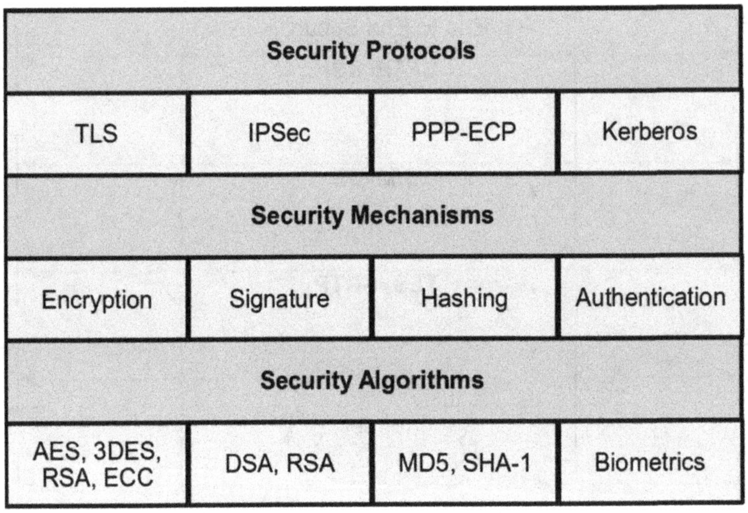

safe. Shamir's (k, n) Threshold Schemes Theorem states that any subset of up to $k - 1$ shares does not leak any information on the secret (Shamir, 1979). Given $k - 1$ shares (x_i, y_i), every candidate secret S corresponds to a unique polynomial of degree $k - 1$ for which $q(0) = S$. From the construction of the polynomials, all their probabilities are equal. Thus, $H(S) = \log |S|$ which is the maximum possible Shannon's entropy for S. Thus secret sharing is perfectly secure, and does not depend on the computational power of any party. As an example, the secret code for firing a nuclear weapon can be shared as follows for a $(3, n)$ threshold scheme. The president – 3 shares, the vice president – 2 shares and the directors – 1 share each. A $(3, n)$ threshold scheme will thus allow the president acting alone, or the two, vice president and any one of the three directors, and all three of the directors together, to recover the code and fire the strategic weapon. This example of secret sharing is meant to highlight the military applications in C4ISR as one of the key driving forces for developments in cryptography.

SECURITY FEATURES IN DIFFERENT PARTS/ COMPONENTS OF C4ISR SYSTEMS

C4ISR is composed of different types of hardware and software. The security features can be either implemented through appropriately designed

Table 1. Summary of security features of different cryptographic primitives

Cryptographic Primitive	Confidentiality	Authentication	Integrity	Key Management	Non-repudiation
Symmetric Encryption	Yes	No	No	Yes	No
Public Key Encryption	Yes	No	No	Yes	No
Digital Signature	No	Yes	Yes	No	Yes
Key Agreement	Yes	Optional	No	Yes	No
One Way Hash Function	No	No	Yes	No	No
Message Authentication Codes	No	Yes	Yes	No	No

hardware or software. The software components can be operating systems (OS), the embedded system software such as firmware or an embedded OS, the application software for displaying COP and operating through an operator, instant messenger, e-mail software, etc. The requirement and use of different types of hardware and software components with appropriate cyber security features are discussed in ensuing paragraphs.

The Operating Systems

The selection of an Operating System (OS) is an important factor while designing a C4ISR system. Initially being defense oriented projects, proprietary type of products were being used in C4I systems. However, considering the high cost of proprietary/military products, focus is now shifting to Commercial Off the Shelf (COTS) and open source solutions. The operating systems being designed now are security focused. Certain security requirements and features, as discussed earlier, are part of the newer operating systems. Even commercial operating systems such as Windows NT and its successor operating systems from Microsoft have security features such as access control, authentication, application and use of digital certificates, etc. After appropriate evaluation Microsoft Windows NT Server and Workstation 3.5 were granted the C2 security rating by the National Security Agency of the United States.

Among the commercial Unix type of operating systems, Trusted Solaris is a security hardened version of the Solaris Unix operating system. Its main security features includes auditing of all tasks, authentication on plugins, mandatory access control, fine-grained access control and authentication through additional physical devices. Trusted Solaris 8 received the EAL4 certification under the Common Criteria, an international security evaluation standard since 1999. The Trusted Solaris features have now been added to main stream Solaris 10 as Solaris Trusted Extensions.

In Linux, a leading open source Unix type of operating system, there have been different secure distributions. Some of them with their major features are discussed here briefly. Openwall Project has a non-executable userspace stack. It also has race condition protection and access control restrictions. It uses and supports Blowfish password encryption. Immunix distribution of Linux included cryptographic signing of executables, race condition patches and format string exploit guarding code. VPN-gateways, firewalls, intrusion detection systems and authentication are security features to be found in the small distribution Hardened Linux. It also includes GCC stack smashing, protection GRSecurity and PaX. LynxSecure® is a secure embedded hypervisor and separation kernel which provides high-assurance virtualization services and software security in embedded systems. As an embedded system OS, LynxSecure has the certification of DO-178B level A and EAL-7. It has a robust environment and without compromising on security, reliability and data integrity. Multiple OSes can run on top of it, including Linux (Wikipedia, 2010b).

High-performance UNIX workstations were being used by GCCS system to run its associated software. However, there is an exponential increase in power and processing capabilities of Intel Microprocessors and Personal Computer products based on them, hence GCCS is not hardware dependent. The operating systems associated with Intel PCs have also been matured such as Windows NT and Java/Web oriented multi-user OS. Hence migration from only UNIX, Wintel, Macintosh, etc. based machines to Windows NT and JAVA / Web environments in being carried out inclemently for GCCS/JC2 systems.

Recently, NATO has adopted Windows Vista for ensuring the security of the computers and IT systems. NATO worked directly with the Microsoft and suggested ways to improve security of the Microsoft desktop operating system considering the Enterprise requirements of NATO. Hence Windows Vista Security Guide (WVSG) was developed for deployment with NATO (Microsoft, 2008).

On the other hand, the French government is now inclined to the use of open source software. French military has chosen this option after a lengthy discussion which started in year 2003 and ended in year 2007. The purpose of adopting open source software was to get all possible independence in technological and commercial fields. Hence they are using Linux instead of Windows and OpenOffice instead of Microsoft Office.

E-mail Protection

Electronic Mail or e-mail is one of the most widely used and regarded network services. In its original incarnation the Internet mail transported through SMTP protocol is not secure. Email may be inspected either in transit or by suitably privileged users on destination system. Pretty Good Privacy (PGP) was a program invented by Philip Zimmermann in the early 1990s. It became a popular method to use to encrypt Internet email. It used MD5 (Message-Digest 5) hash function and RSA public key cryptosystem to generate digital signatures on messages. RSA public key cryptosystem was also used to encrypt message keys. The messages themselves were encrypted using the International Data Encryption Algorithm (IDEA), a symmetric bulk encryption algorithm of European origin. PGP implementations became readily available for UNIX, DOS, and Macintosh platforms. PGP also offers some variations of functionality, like compression, that other email security system may not. Multiple key pairs can be generated and placed on public and private key rings. Hence enhancement with respect to Confidentiality (protection from disclosure), authentication (of sender of message), message integrity (from modification protection) and non-repudiation (protection of origin from denial by sender) may all be achieved using PGP.

As opposed to the ad-hoc and de-facto nature of PGP, the IETF developed Secure Multipurpose

Internet Mail Extensions (S/MIME) as a standard protocol to secure TCP/IP based email on end to end basis supporting integration with X.509 based Digital Certificates and PKI. It uses SHA-1 and MD5 as hash functions, DSA and RSA for digital signatures, ElGamal and RSA for session key encryption and Triple-DES, RC2/4 for message encryption. It has a procedure to decide which algorithms to use. S/MIME features are available in various applications such as Outlook Express, Mozilla Thunderbird, etc.

Trustedbird is an email client based on Mozilla Thunderbird. Two branches are currently available, namely, Trustedbird 3.1 and Trustedbird 2. Trustedbird 3.1 is based on Mozilla Thunderbird 3.1.x and has Enhanced Security Services for S/MIME based on RFC 2634 i.e Signed Receipts, Security Labels. Trustedbird 2 is based on Mozilla Thunderbird 2.0.0.x and has Enhanced Security Services for S/MIME based on RFC 2634 i.e. Triple Wrapping (sign, encrypt, and sign again), Signed Receipts, Security Labels, DSN (Delivery Status Notification – the backend is now integrated in Mozilla Thunderbird 3), SMTP PRIORITY extension, Secure Headers / SASL EXTERNAL (for XIMFMAIL add-on). French Military has adopted Trustedbird and has also demonstrated it to NATO. Generally, it also qualifies the NATO's closed messaging services requirements. The French military now uses Mozilla's Thunderbird/Trustedbird mail software. It has also been extended to the ministries of Finance, Interior and Culture. It is in use on about 80,000 computers in the government sector (Michelson, 2009).

HAIPE (High Assurance Internet Protocol Encryptor)

HAIPE is acronym of High Assurance Internet Protocol Encryptor which is an encryption device. HAIPE is used in GIG network by DoD for Information Assurance. It is based mostly on IPSec and has additional restrictions and enhancements. It is compliant to National Security Agency specifications. It requires loading the same key on all HAIPE devices that will participate in the multicast session in advance of data transmission. Basically, HAIPE is a secure gateway that permits two separate enclaves to transmit and receive data through an untrusted link or a network having lower classification. HAIPE devices available include KG-245X/A, KG240A by L-3 Communications, KG250 by ViaSat, KG-175 by General Dynamics. HAIPE uses Internet Engineering Task Force (IETF) protocols to provide its traffic protection, networking, and management capabilities. The HAIPE IS specifies the use of the IETF Encapsulating Security Payload version 3 (ESPv3) to encapsulate plain-text IPv4 or IPv6 traffic. HAIPE uses the IETF's Simple Network Management Protocol version 3 (SNMPv3) to support over-the-network management and the IETF's Routing Information (CNSS, 2007).

Data Links

Data Links are needed for exchange of air/surface/subsurface tracks, Intelligence or EW data and C2 data. Various types of links are in use in the world, however, few are discussed below to provide an overview and better understanding of C4ISR systems.

Link 11/Link 11B is the technology of 1950s and 1960s. Its also known as TDL A/B (Tactical Data Link A/B). It is designed to work at High Frequency (HF) and low data rates. Link 11 is secure but is not an ECM resistant link. Link 16 is another Tactical Data Link which is used with Anti-Air Warfare (AAW). Aircraft control requirements are completely catered in Link 16. The US and NATO have applied it as the primary tactical data link in Theatre Missile Defence.

Link 22 is a tactical data link designed and used for maritime operations. It also caters to Link 16 operations. It has an open systems architecture. The interfaces between various components are well defined and it has a layered communications stack. Seven countries have been involved in the design and development of Link 22. These were Germany, France, Italy, Canada, Netherlands, UK and USA. It is also known as NILE (NATO Improved Link Eleven) System. The components of NILE are System Network Controller (SNC), Link-Level COMSEC (LLC), Signal Processing Controllers (SPCs), Radios, Operator Interface System-D Tactical Data System/Data Link Processor/(TDS/DLP). Link 22 employs an integral encryption/decryption device and hence is considered to a strong COMmunications SECurity (COMSEC) system. This encryption/decryption device is formally named as the Link Level COMSEC (LLC). Other security feature of Link 22 is transmission security which can be a configuration of frequency hopping in radios having the facility. The LLC device in Link 22 is KIV-21. Additionally, a Data Terminal Device (DTD) is required and used with LLCs for loading the keys. (Lockheed, 2010).

The Link Y Mk2 system (Thales, 2010) is another data link system being produced by Thales. It is one of the family of Link 11 and Link 16 and is being used by non-NATO countries. It gives better performance than Link 11. It is a reliable link for data transfer amongst naval forces through an encrypted radio network.

Public Key Infrastructure (PKI)/ Common Access Card (CAC)

PKI is an IT infrastructure that enables users of an unsecured public network (such as the Internet) to securely and privately exchange data by using trusted public keys distributed as part of Digital Certificates signed by trusted third parties called Certification Authorities (CA). Using public key cryptography for key exchange/agreement in conjunction with symmetric encryption for bulk data and digital signatures, it can provide confidentiality (assurance that the person receiving is the intended recipient), integrity (verification that no unauthorized modification of data has occurred), authentication (proof that the sender is whom he claims to be) and non-repudiation (assurance that the person sending cannot deny participation). In order make the digital certificates portable and enable two factor authentication Smartcards can be used as part of a PKI. The US-DoD smartcard initiative is the Common Access Card (CAC). The CAC is truly a multi-purpose card and not just an ID card. It contains a computer chip, barcodes, and a magnetic stripe which allow it to be used to: access buildings and controlled spaces, login to computer systems and networks, and digitally sign and encrypt E-mail messages. When a user receives a new CAC, new PKI certificates are placed on the CAC. These certificates can be used with standard software through use of middle-ware such as Windows CryptoAPI and PCSC or OpenSC libraries. Since PKI is a public key cryptography system two keys are generated for each individual. One of these keys is kept private and protected by a PIN, in case of a smartcard, and is hence termed the private key. The other key is widely published and is termed the public key (US-DoD, 2005). Three DoD PKI certificates, containing public and private keys, are loaded on a CAC. These certificates allow the user to provide digital identification, sign E-mail, and encrypt E-mail. DISA provides the engineering for the DoD PKI program. Similarly, NATO has its own PKI arrangements governed by the NATO PKI Certificate Authority located at NIATC NCSA (NATO, 2010). To implement a Key Escrow service recently the DoD PKI program completed an implementation of a new Key Recovery Authority (KRA) password scheme on the key escrow servers and Automated Key Recovery Agent (ARA) systems. The KRAs utilize 20 character passwords to recover keys on the key escrow servers. This feature allows recovering messages and data in situations where key owners may have lost their private keys or may have left the organization.

Identification, Friend or Foe (IFF)

IFF is widely used in C2 systems for identification of ships, vehicles and aircrafts. Basically, IFF is a type of cryptosystem (IFF, 2010). IFF systems are also known as secondary radar. They consist of two parts, the interrogator and the transponder. Interrogator transmits at a standardized frequency of 1030 MHz whereas the transponder transmits at 1090 MHz. It helps in identifying an aircraft, ship, vehicles, and even forces as friend or foe. The air traffic controllers in non-military environments also use it for the same purpose. Historically, the Germans invented and used IFF in 1940s. It was called Erstling or IFF FuG-25a. British had a good intelligence work and developed Perfectos to cater the use of IFF FuG-25 by Germans. RAF Mosquitos were installed with Perfectos and were triggered by interrogators of FuG-25 and hence helped British to misguide Germans. Ultimately the Germans switched off the FuG-25 IFF as a countermeasure of Perfectos. Soviet and other older IFF Systems used CBI (Cross-Band Inter-rogation) from 1946 to 1991. Nowadays a KIR and KIT cryptography computer is used with IFF transponders. Such crypto devices are not used with civilian aircrafts.

Different modes are used in IFF systems by different types of organizations. Modes A, C and S are used by Civilian aircrafts. Mode A is also known as mode 3/A as it is similar to military mode 3. Military uses Modes 1, 2, 3, 4 and 5. Modes 1, 2 and 3 are also known as Selective Identification Feature (SIF) modes. NATO forces use mode 4 and 5 in different combinations. Mode 4 is crypt-secure. Mode 5, Levels 1 and 2 utilizes crypto-secure with Enhanced encryption, Spread Spectrum Modulation, and Time of Day Authen-tication. Mode 5, Level 1 is similar to Mode 4 information but contains an Aircraft Unique PIN. Aircraft position and other attributes are included in Mode 5, Level 2 (Wikipedia, 2010a).

IFF systems are not failure-proof. There are several examples of friendly fire destroying friendly forces. The reported incidents of friendly fire in World War-II, in Afghanistan, in Iraq, etc. force us to think into the likely causes of failure of IFF systems despite technological advancement. Likely causes of negative identification can be wrong setting of encryption keys, physical damage to the system, poor RF propagation conditions etc.

RECENT DEVELOPMENTS AND INITIATIVES IN CYBER SECURITY OF C4ISR SYSTEMS

In this section we describe several recent developments and initiatives under progress for enhancing the cyber security of C4ISR systems. Many of the examples provided in this section have been possible through the CIWD which is an initiative of the US DoD. Coalition Warrior Interoperability Demonstration (CWID) is a forum initially started by US Army about 17 years ago. It has established series of Secure Tactical Data Network (STDN) and has demonstrated emerging command, control, communications and computer (C4) capabilities. The Joint Staff and DoD realized that they have to keep pace with the rapid advancements in communication and IT by Public sector. The aim was to enhance and bring improvement in coalition and joint command, control, communications, computers, intelligence, surveillance and reconnaissance (C4ISR) architecture. Few of the technology demonstrations are discussed in following sub sections.

Network Defense

As we have already established that C4ISR systems are distributed systems, a network of networks (Internet like core utilizing TCP/IP), system of systems hence it requires a strong network defense and its security. An operational view of network defense and security can be provided by main-taining a database of sensors data from intrusion detection sensors, vulnerability scanners, log files, mission data and asset information of a network. The correlation and fusion tools are required to acquire information from multiple database servers, perform analysis, and report results back as "cyber alerts". These are displayed as spreadsheets and graphically, in a Network Operations Center, and enhance the situational awareness of the operator. The NetD-COP (Network Defense Common Operation Picture) is such a system demonstrated at CWID forum. It used Secure Sockets Layer, interfaced with the Data Extraction Unit, to extract, integrate and normalize data from sensor systems including Snort, firewalls, and system logs. Snort® is an open source network intrusion prevention and detection system (IDS/IPS) developed by Sourcefire. Combining the benefits of signature, protocol and anomaly-based inspection, Snort is the most widely deployed IDS/IPS technology worldwide (Snort, 2010). The system utilizes three integrated visualization systems namely VisAlert, VIAssist, and Flexviewer. These help the cyber war fighters in event analysis, attack recognition and impact assessments when on a mission.

Secure, Trusted and Easy Collaboration Across Networks

An important aspect of C4ISR cyber security is requirement of operation collaboration between networks e.g. US top secret/secret networks, Allied & Coalition networks and the unclassified networks. The collaboration in coalition environment is a gigantic task. Various types of services such as text chat, whiteboarding, sharing of information/data and web are required for inter-network collaboration. Different solutions in this regard have been demonstrated at international forums.

During technology demonstration in 2009, the Cross Domain Collaborative Information Environment (CDCIE) solution (CWID, 2009a) helped the coalition forces to share the data and information using text chat, whiteboarding, and

SOAP (Simple Object Access Protocol) (W3C, 2007) based web services. This collaboration and sharing of information of different networks (having different classification levels) of DoD and non-DoD networks which included coalition partners, other government agencies, and non-governmental organizations. BAE DataSync Guard (DSG) was used for achieving cross-domain XML and fixed-format ASCII transfer. DataSync Guard 4.0 transfers critical information among individual endpoints in multiple domains. DataSync Guard's (DSG) inspection and filtering capabilities are defined by the user and enforce local security policies to ensure secure and speedy cross-domain data transfers (BAE, 2009). The Web Service Gateway (WSG) was used to achieve cross domain web services. The TransVerse chat client was used to carry out cross-domain text chat.

Collaborative Advanced Planning Environment (CAPE)(CWID, 2009b) is another tool-set and gateway for exchange of C4ISR situational awareness data. It provides a secure environment to enhance collaboration between various mission planners in a coalition environment. It helps in sharing of weather reports, notices to aviation/flight operations, secure chat and video, real-time PowerPoint briefings and a data "Mash-up" routine to facilitate collaboration between disparate CAPE-enabled workstations. CAPE demonstrated easy and secure transfer of critical data between different security enclaves.

Classification Stateless, Trusted Environment (CSTE)(CWID, 2009b) is yet another technology demonstration with assured electronic environment. It provides cyber structure to protect all data objects. The demonstration of CSTE showed rapid and secure sharing of unclassified/classified information amongst coalition networks. The CSTE data carries meta-data information such as the classification level of the data object, access privileges, and the history of the data object. The identification of users in CSTE is carried out through the user's location, the processing environment, and method of identification, authentication,

and authorization. CSTE tagged, encrypted and controlled access to data at rest and in transit based upon access privileges and sensitivity levels within existing networks, providing easy information sharing between authorized users.

Security of Military Wiki Systems

Wiki is described as the simplest on-line database that is updated and maintained by users (Wiki, n.da). A wiki is commonly understood to be a website that allows users to add and update content on the site using their own Web browser. This is made possible by Wiki software that runs on the Web server. Wikis end up being created mainly by a collaborative effort of the site visitors (Wiki, n.db). In multi-nation coalition environment of the military Wiki there can be various systems Wiki networks/systems depending on security classification of the data to be shared. As there can be secret Wiki Database (as in case of US-DoD it is operated on SIPRNET), other coalition nations may have their own Wiki database and a generic TS Wiki Database. There is a requirement of defining appropriate access control for accessing and editing the information.

Multi-Level Wiki (ML Wiki) is a military Wiki used by multi-nations in coalition and has multi-level security environment. It works best with the open source web browser Mozilla Firefox. Coalition partners can create, edit and share content among authorized users in a secure way. Once the information is published it is available to authorized users everywhere on the net. The Intelligence Community Standards for Information Security Markings (ICSISM) are assigned to each paragraph. Strong authentication mechanism, comprehensive auditing and granular access control are the key security features exercised to control access to sensitive information. ML Wiki is an easy and secure tool to create, edit, and share information containing various classification levels across multiple networks of different classification levels (CWID, 2009b).

Role Based Access Control with Thin Client

There is growing requirement in organizations to have thin clients with role based access control. A single workstation when connected with one wire should have the ability to securely access and transfer data from one domain to another. A thin client is also known as a lean or slim client. It is a computer or a computer program which depends heavily on some other computer (its server) to fulfill its traditional computational roles. This stands in contrast to the traditional fat client, a computer designed to take on these roles by itself (Wiki, n.dc).

Sun Secure Network Access Platform Solution (SNAP)(CWID, 2009b) is such a technology demonstration by Sun Microsystems Inc. SNAP runs on Sun Trusted Solaris OS. The said OS is a certified for Labeled Security Protection Profile, Role-based Protection Profile and Controlled Access Protection Profile. The SNAP solution is independent of platform and is certified by NSA (US) and CSE (Canada) for its ability to access and transfer data from one domain to another in secure way utilizing role-based solution on a single computer. Using SNAP the operators could work with MS Office tools (Word, Excel, PowerPoint) and Adobe Acrobat seamlessly. The users can also access multiple security enclaves as per defined and authorized security policies and profiles through a single computer.

Service Oriented Architecture: Standards Based Reusable Provisioning Systems

The service oriented architecture has three layers i.e. the application layer, service layer and the network layer. Service layer provides common services (based on common and inter-operable standards) to all applications connected to different networks through network layer. On these services the missions are dependent and are provided whenever the situation arises and the operator demands the particular service. It is done seamlessly without the knowledge to the operators. Cyber security features similar to as discussed in section are applicable to SOA solutions. Similar idea named as Service-Oriented Infrastructure Grid Appliance (SOIG-App)(CWID, 2009b) was demonstrated in CWID 2009. It demonstrated the provisioning of automatic services to the war fighters depending on the SOIG-App capability. Open source software TrustedOffice was used to demonstrate multi level security and access to the services, automatic provisioning of complex systems with secure exchange of documents with large file size.

SICCAM Network Enable Capable Information Centric (SICCAM-NECIC) (CWID, 2009b) is C2 system of the Italian Air Force utilizing SOA. The Web services are utilized by SICCAM-NECIC and the Italian Common ISR Capability Module. The SICCAM NECIC web portal demonstration provided an accurate and precise display and hence real-time situational awareness to the operator.

Network-centric Commanders Decision Services (netCDS) (CWID, 2009b) is an other SOA example which works on web-enabled, network-centric environment. netCDS has incorporated several Web applications which allow users to view, manipulate, distribute and receive data from multiple staff and command organizations for quick collaboration for arriving at mission-critical decisions.

Coalition Telecommunication Service (CTS) by DISA is another example of the service oriented architecture which is designed to provide net-centric services and transport to edge users through standards based applications for mobile applications. In this demonstration the handheld devices were connected to the larger network such as GIG through various wireless mediums e.g. Cellular, SATCOM, WiMAX, Tactical Radios etc. The services such as web browsing, Voice over IP, e-mail, streaming video and collaboration were demonstrated/provided to the users. Cell phones were used by warfighters to generate Keyhole Mark-up Language (KML) map mark-ups. These were sent to user workstations. CTS also used a biometric identification application through facial recognition and provided better and secure situational awareness.

Directorate Air Programmes, Canadian Department of National Defence demonstrated the Integrated Information Dashboard (IID)(CWID, 2009b). It is a decision support system utilizing SOA. IID is middle ware for information/data integration and demonstrated the capabilities of a military network centric operational framework (NCO). The software capability of the dashboard implementation included information sharing, information monitoring, application wrapping, assets visualization, data analysis and decision support.

Security Enabled Hand-Held/Mobile Devices

There is a need to have a unified end-to-end information security enabled hand-held device which can function as the end-user's interface to the C4ISR system. Such a device would allow standardizing and simplifying the user interface while allowing portability and personalization. Such a device will be a rugged one, made for the harsh military environment. Its software stack, consisting of the operating system and libraries, will be based on a secure and trusted operating system such as a security enhanced version of the Linux operating system. Use of Linux and open source will level the playing field for all vendors. Popularity of Linux for such portable platforms can be judged by the choice of Linux by Google for its Android smartphone toolkit. Openmoko was one of the novel projects which extended the open source idea even to the hardware design of PDAs. A demonstration of some these ideas was undertaken through the Integration Communications Encryption (ICE) project by Fujistu, New Zealand. ICE is a fully integrated, self-powered, secure, mobile platform that enables a user to deploy anywhere in the world and operate without infrastructure (CWID, 2009b). ICE was intended for rapid deployment and use in all environments, under all conditions and to operate in a first-responder type of environment. ICE. has the ability to negotiate and integrate with an AES256 encrypted tunnel into the New Zealand Defence Force corporate network. ICE has the ability to integrate power and generation capability into small deployable form-factor design.

Another recent initiative on similar lines is the PDA-184 project (CWID, 2009b). In demonstrations PDA-184 successfully passed weather data among field and station assets using PDA-184 chat and email functionality utilizing UHF SATCOM radios. It also delivered laser targeting data to remote locations. Finally, it also proved inter-operable with Virtual Intercom (VICOM), providing chat capabilities with multiple files.

Tactical Cellular (TACTICELL) is yet another concept of use of netbooks and smartphones and applications such as streaming media and instant messaging by Special Operations Forces (SOF). TACTICELL is an IP based Cellular system that provides users with 1.8/3.1 Mbps data rates for transmission/reception. TACTICELL demonstrated streaming video, voice over secure IP, chat, and email capabilities between network workstations and dismounted devices utilizing the communications suite (CWID, 2009b).

Responding to Network Events and Adapting to Cyber Threats

One of the desirable features is to enable the specialized military systems to integrate with TCP/IP communication networks. This TCP/IP enabling of the devices such as RADARs, SONARs, Weapon Control Systems and Command and Control Systems would provide the fullest real-time integration with other information systems at the disposal of commanders. There is a down-side to this extension of the Internet Protocol

(IP) to the tactical edge (airborne and enclave networks). It introduces new cyber-threat entry points into the Global Information Grid (GIG) and other information infrastructure. MARIAAN project which stands for Mission Aware Reporting of Information Assurance for Airborne Networks augments mission assurance by providing and fusing mission relevant information with detected cyber activities, and providing actionable alerts with courses of action enhancing the warfighter's situational awareness. In various trials it demonstrated the mitigation of enclave network risks and enhanced mission survivability by relating cyber events and effects to potential impacts on mission operations. Thus war fighters can receive a better understanding of the threats which may allow them to select appropriate courses of action. MARIAAN appliances are installed on board ships, AWACS, airplanes, UAVs, etc. These appliances provided network event information from multiple sensing/ detection sources in real-time and forward this information in an efficient, threat prioritized manner to a Network Operations Security Center for further analysis (CWID, 2009b).

Another such project is the REACT. REACT stands for Responding to Network Events and Adapting to Cyber Threats (REACT). It uses the PoliWall which is a bridging security appliance that automates responding to cyber threats. The PoliWall utilizes intuitive graphical tools to create country and user-defined group based Internet Protocol (IP) network access controls. A pre-compiled exception lists allows millions of IP addresses to be excluded from or added to country filtering policies while still maintaining bandwidth. In addition, the operator can also configure automated responses to policy violations, including alerts, blocking, and bandwidth restrictions. In trials and demonstrations this bridging security appliance allowed administrators to create and bind pre-defined automated responses to cyber threats and network events, thereby controlling quality of service and preserving bandwidth as IP is deployed to extend the GIG to the warfighter.

It also facilitated managed network policies and determined message precedence levels that dictated delivery to a Network Operations Security Center (CWID, 2009b).

C4ISR Systems in Disaster Management Applications

Natural disasters such as earthquakes and floods affect large geographical areas. Rescue and relief operations benefit greatly from the use of information and communication technology (ICT). Affected areas are mapped with satellite images and divided into zones. The severity of damage is assessed with the imagery data analysis by advanced software. Rescue teams can coordinate with each other using MANET (Mobile Ad Hoc Network) and the status of injured patients can be relayed to hospitals using cellular network. Since the C4ISR system provides accurate situational awareness, it can be adapted in disaster management to enhance the effectiveness of the relief operation.

An application of C4ISR systems for disaster management and relief operations is demonstrated by the InRelief Project. InRelief.org is a combined effort between the US Navy and San Diego State University Research Foundation to provide integrated communication tools, data repositories, coordination spaces and public information sites and helped responders coordinate efforts and hand off information in transition from Disaster Relief to Humanitarian Assistance. InRelief is based on Google cloud computing technologies and open source applications for increased cooperation and situational awareness between first responders and organizations for Humanitarian Assistance and Disaster Relief events. InRelief site provided information resources and data tracking/mapping capabilities. It demonstrated the usability of web-based Google suite of products to support natural disaster activities in unclassified non-DoD environments. It was perceived in trials by the US DoD that the InRelief project increased

DoD capabilities to interact with national and international humanitarian organizations during disaster relief events. InRelief utilized Satellite Personal Tracker (SPOT) to track individuals and Google Chat (GChat) for enabling communication between government and non-governmental agencies (CWID, 2009b).

USE OF OPEN SOURCE AND COTS IN C4ISR SYSTEMS

The use of open source software and COTS (commercial off-the shelf) hardware and software is on the rise. COTS systems allowed the US Navy to take advantage of investments made in computing technologies by the civilian marketplace, and the US Navy has embraced COTS technologies for C4I systems to the extent that the majority of the information technology on naval ships now uses commercial hardware, software, and networks (Rand, 2009). The latest technology demonstrations covered in the previous sections also show the rising trend of using open source modules and products. We know the famous phrase that there is no requirement of reinventing the wheel. Working on applications and modules (covering security aspects as well) already developed and integrating them suitably can generate better systems. The use of open source and COTS may bring the undesired consequences of increased risk of cyber attacks and malware. Therefore stringent measures are needed to make sure that all computing equipment carries only authorized software components and users are unable to add new programs and features without due security validation process.

Use of Open Source by Sentek (USA)

One of the examples of Open Source penetration in C4ISR market is that of (Sentek, 2010) which has decades of experience in developing world class C4ISR systems and a big team of experts.

Sentek has been leveraging open source software in its C4ISR solutions for providing significant cost savings to its customers in the government and the military. By replicating the capabilities of best of breed C4ISR systems using Open Source software and COTS hardware modules, Sentek Global is able to offer cost-effective, secure, C4ISR solutions that meet user needs and provide the latest and most effective capabilities for military and disaster assistance requirements. The systems thus developed by Sentinel include, but are not limited to, Sentinel C4ISR Suite, Sentinel Airport Security System (SASS), Sentinel Blue Force Tracking System (BFTS), Mobile Thin Client (MTC) Solution for U.S. Navy, Sentinel Radio Interoperability System (RIOS), etc.

Open Source C4ISR SDK by Safir-Saab Systems Sweden

Safir (Software Architecture for Information and Realtime systems) (Saab, 2010) is an advanced platform for command, control and communication systems which has been developed by Saab Systems of Sweden. Safir has a decade long history and the design objective was to create a powerful, reliable, secure and easy-to-use software architecture with significant re-usability features. The customers of Safir include the Swedish Defence Material Administration and the Swedish Armed Forces. Systems built on have been delivered to Saab customers. Safir SDK is the set of core libraries which forms the development environment for command and control systems. Safir SDK is already used by different C2 system developers. Recently, Saab Systems has released Safir SDK Core as open source under the GNU/GPL License agreement. Applications built on Safir SDK are claimed to scale from applets for handheld devices up to large distributed data centers without modification.

Open Standards Based Sentry: C2 (Air)

Sentry is a US airspace C2 system based on open architecture utilizing COTS hardware and reusable software components (Janes, 2010). The system provides multi-radar tracking and identification through use of multifunction workstations running standard operating systems like Windows and Linux. Sentry displays an integrated picture utilizing different types of data i.e. geographic, radars, manual injected tracks, automatically received from other agencies etc. For continuous operations, feature of redundant elements having capability to take over automatically is present. The system identifies tracks using various sources, such as beacon, furnished Identification Friend or Foe (IFF)/Selective Identification Feature (SIF) and associated flight plans, Airspace Control Means (ACMs), as well as operator input (Sentry, 2010). Although the entire Sentry platform is not itself open source, almost all of the building blocks and technologies used to create the various Sentry solutions are open standards based and could possibly be built using open source libraries and toolkits.

CONCLUSION

We have reviewed a broad spectrum of issues and technological trends in Cyber Security of C4ISR systems. Our review is no doubt brief and can only serve to scratch the mere surface of this vast area. As penetration of information technology and its various components into military systems continues at an unrelenting pace Cyber Security of these systems will continue to provide challenging research problems. Our review shall serve to provide the interested researcher some grasp of the possibilities in this area. The discussion in this chapter has also highlighted how today's global economy has prompted militaries and other resource managers to seek low-cost, open architecture, high-speed command and control (C2)

solutions that offer the full capability spectrum from high-level command visibility to tactical control. Complete vertical integration across strategic, operational, and tactical functionality is a key ingredient in this arena. Due to intrinsic cost-effectiveness and lack of a vendor-lock open source modules are increasingly used in the software layer of C4ISR systems. As open source software modules receive the broadest review possible, due to their community based development model, security weaknesses can be promptly identified and fixed during development cycle. The future shall see more integration of open source projects leading eventually to complete open source community based C4ISR systems.

REFERENCES

W3C. (2007). *SOAP version 1.2, part 1: Messaging framework* (2ⁿᵈ ed.). Retrieved from http://www.w3.org/ TR/ soap12-part1/#intro

ABC. (2010, July 26). WikiLeaks reveals grim Afghan war realities. *ABC News*.

AFP. (2010, September 27). *Stuxnet worm rampaging through Iran.*

Alghamdi, A. S. (2009). Evaluating defense architecture frameworks for C4I system using analytic hierarchy process. *Journal of Computer Science, 5*(12), 1078-1084ISSN 1549-3636

Anthony, H. D. (2002). *C4ISR architectures, social network analysis and the FINC methodology: An experiment in military organizational structure.* Information Technology Division, Electronics and Surveillance Research Laboratory-DSTO-GD-0313.

BAE. (2009). *DataSync Guard 4.0 data transfers across multiple domains with flexibility and uncompromised security systems.* BAE Systems.

Brehmer, B. (2010). Command and control as design. *Proceedings of the 15th International Command and Control Research and Technology Symposium*, Santa Monica, California.

CBS. (2010, July 26). Wikileaks publishes Afghan War secret article. *CBS News*.

CNSS. (2007). Committee on National Security Systems. *CNSS Policy, 19*.

CNSS. (2010, April 26). *National information assurance glossary*. Committee on National Security Systems. Instruction CNSSI-4009 dated 26 April 2010.

CWID. (2009a). *Assessment brief-Top performing technologies. Coalition Warrior Interoperability Demonstration (CWID)*. Hampton, VA: JMO.

CWID. (2009b). *Assessment brief – Interoperability trials. Coalition Warrior Interoperability Demonstration (CWID)*. Hampton, VA: JMO.

Ericsson. (2006). *C4ISR for network-oriented defense*. Ericsson White Paper. Retrieved from http://www.ericsson.com/technology/whitepapers

IATAC. (2010). *Mission of Information Assurance Technology Analysis Center* (IATAC). Retrieved from http://iac.dtic.mil/iatac/mission.html

IFF. (2010). *Identification of friend & foe, questions and answers*. Retrieved from http://www.dean-boys.com/extras/iff/iffqa.html.

ISO/IEC. (2007). *Systems and software engineering — Recommended practice for architectural description of software-intensive systems*. ISO/IEC 42010 (IEEE STD 1471-2000).

Janes. (2010). *Sentry (United States) command information systems – Air*. Retrieved from http://www.janes.com.

Langer. (2010). *Stuxnet logbook*. Langer Production & Development.

Lockheed. (2010). *Lockheed Martin UK-Integrated systems & solutions*. Retrieved from http://www.lm-isgs.co.uk

Merriam-Webster. (2010). *Cybersecurity*. Retrieved September 13, 2010, from http://www.merriam-webster.com/dictionary/cybersecurity

Michelson, M. (2009). *French military donated code to Mozilla Thunderbird*. PCMag.com. 12.10.2009.

Microsoft. (2008). *Microsoft case study: NATO accelerates Windows Vista deployment using the Windows Vista security guide*. Retrieved from http://www.microsoft.com/casestudies/Case_Study_Detail.aspx?CaseStudyID=4000002826

MoD. (2004, November). *Network enabled capability handbook*. Joint Services Publication 777, UK Ministry of Defence. Retrieved from http://www.mod.uk

MoD. (2005a). *Architectural framework overview*, version 1.0.

MoD. (2005b). *Architectural framework technical handbook*, version 1.0.

NAP. (1999). *Realizing the potential of C4I: Fundamental challenges. Computer Science and Telecommunications Board (CSTB), Commission on Physical Sciences, Mathematics, and Applications, National Research Council*. Washington, DC: National Academy Press.

NAP. (2006). *C4ISR for future naval strike groups*. Naval Studies Board (NSB) Division on Engineering and Physical Sciences, National Research Council of The National Academies. Washington, DC: The National Academies Press. Retrieved from www.nap.edu.

NATO. (2007). *NATO architectural framework*, ver. 3 (Annex 1 to AC/322-D (2007) 0048).

NATO. (2010). *NATO information assurance*. Retrieved from http://www.ia.nato.int

Navsea. (2007). *Naval sea systems command.* Retrieved from https://www.djc2.org

Nilsson, P. (2003). Opportunities and risks in a network-based defence. *Swedish Journal of Military Technology, 3.* Retrieved from http://www.militartekniska.se/mtt.

Rand. (2009). *Controlling the cost of C4I upgrades on naval ships. A study report for USN RAND Corporation.* National Defense and Research Institute USA (2009).

Reuters. (2010a). *Update 2-Cyber attack appears to target Iran-tech firms.*

Reuters. (2010b). *What is Stuxnet?* Robinson, C. (2002). *Military and cyber-defense: Reactions to the threat.* Washington, DC: Center for Defense Information.

Saab. (2010). *Safir software development kit for truly distributed C4I systems.* Retrieved from http://www.safirsdk.com

Saenz, A. (2010). Stuxnet worm attacks nuclear site in Iran – A sign of cyber warfare to come on singularity hub.

Sentek. (2010). *C4ISR solutions.* Sentek Global. Retrieved from http://www.sentekconsulting.com/index.php

Sentry. (2010). *C2 / C4I systems: A strategic tool for extended air defense by ThalesRaytheon Systems* (TRS). Retrieved from http://www.armedforces-int.com/article/c2-c4i-systems-a-strategic-tool-for-extended-air-defense.html

Shamir, A. (1979). How to share a secret. *Communications of the ACM, 22*(11), 612–613. doi:10.1145/359168.359176

Snort. (2010). *Open source intrusion detection system.* Retrieved from http://www.snort.org

Stallings, W. (2003). *Cryptography and network security principles and practices* (3rd ed.).

Stanton, N. A., Baber, C., & Harris, D. (2008). *Modelling command and control: Event analysis of systemic teamwork.* Aldershot, UK: Ashgate.

Stokes, M. (2010). *Revolutionizing Taiwan's security – Leveraging C4ISR for traditional and non-traditional challenges.* Retrieved from www.project2049.net

Thales. (2010). *Link-Y brochure and specification document.* Retrieved on October 15, 2010, from http://www.thalesgroup.com/LinkY/?pid=1568

Thales. (2010). *Thales defence & security C4I systems division (DSC) research and contribution to the cyber security.* Retrieved from http://www.nis-summer-school.eu/presentations/Daniel_Gidoin.pdf

US-CERT. (2009). Quarterly trends and analysis report. *US CERT, 4*(1). Retrieved from http://www.us-cert.gov/press_room/trendsanalysisQ109.pdf

US-DoD. (1995). *DoD integrated architecture panel.* IEEE STD 610.12.

US-DoD. (1997). *C4ISR architecture working group.* (US) Department of Defense. C4ISR Architecture Framework Version 2.0.

US-DoD. (2005). *Guide to using DoD PKI certificates in outlook security evaluation.* (Group Report Number: I33-002R-2005).

US-DoD. (2007). *Department of Defense architecture framework v1.5.* Retrieved from http://www.defenselink.mil/nii/doc/DoDAF_V2_Deskbook.pdf

US-DoD. (2009). *Department of Defense architecture framework v2.0.* Retrieved from http://www.defenselink.mil/nii/doc/DoDAF_V2_Deskbook.pdf

USCESRC. (2009). *China's cyber activities that target the United States, and the resulting impacts on U.S. national security.* US China Economic and Security Review Commission 2009 Annual Report to Congress. Retrieved from http://www.uscc.gov

USDoD. (2005). *The implementation of network-centric warfare.* Force Transformation, Office of the Secretary of Defense. Retrieved from http://www.oft.osd.mil/library/library_files/document_387_NCW_Book_LowRes.pdf.

Wiki. (n.da). *What is wiki?* Wikiorg, The Free Encyclopedia. Retrieved October 15, 2010, from http://wiki.org/wiki.cgi?WhatIsWiki

Wiki. (n.db). *Thin client.* Techterms, The Free Encyclopedia. Retrieved October 15, 2010, from http://en.wikipedia.org/wiki/Thin_client

Wiki. (n.dc). *Techterms.* Techterms, The Free Encyclopedia. Retrieved October 15, 2010, from http://www.techterms.com/definition/wiki

Wikipedia. (2010a). *Identification friend or foe.* Retrieved October 21, 2010, from http://en.wikipedia.org/wiki/Identification_friend_or_foe

Wikipedia. (2010b). *Security focused operating system.* Retrieved October 21, 2010, from http://en.wikipedia.org/wiki/Security_focused_operating_systems

Wortzel, L. M. (2009). *Preventing terrorist attacks, countering cyber intrusions, and protecting privacy in cyberspace. U.S. China Economic and Security Review Commission, Testimony before the Subcommittee on Terrorism and Homeland Security.* United States Senate.

Zehetner, A. R. (2004). *Information operations: The impacts on C4I systems.* Australia: Electronic Warfare Associates.

ADDITIONAL READING

Anderson, R., & Fuloria, S. (2009), "Security Economics and Critical National Infrastructure," in Workshop on the Economics of Information Security 2009.

DHS (2009), *A Roadmap for Cybersecurity Research*, Technical Report by the Department of Homeland Security, November 2009.

IATAC CRTA Report (2002). Network Centric Warfare, 14 May 2002.

IATAC CRTA Report (2003). Wireless Wide Area Network (WWAN) Security 14 May 2003.

IATAC SOAR Report (2001). Modeling And Simulation for Information Assurance, 14 May 2001.

IATAC SOAR Report (2005). A Comprehensive Review of Common Needs And Capability Gaps, 21 July 2005.

IATAC SOAR Report (2007). Software Security Assurance 31 July 2007.

IATAC SOAR Report. (2008, October). The Insider Threat. *Information Systems*, 10.

IATAC SOAR Report (2009). Measuring Cyber Security and Information Assurance, 8 May 2009.

USAF Instruction(2005a). Communications security: Protected Distribution Systems (PDS). *Air Force Instruction 33-201, Volume 8 dated 26 April 2005*

USAF Instruction(2005a). Emission Security. *Air Force Instruction 33-203, Volume 1 dated 31 October 2005*

USAF Instruction(2005a). Emission Security. *Air Force Instruction 33-203, Volume 3 dated 2 November 2005*

Jenkins, D. P. Contributing author (2008). Modeling Command and Control: Event Analysis of Systemic Teamwork. Ashgate: Aldershot.

Salmon, P. M., Stanton, N. A., Walker, G. H., Jenkins, D. P., Ladva, D., Rafferty, L., & Young, M. S. (2009). Measuring situation awareness in complex systems: Comparison of measures study. *International Journal of Industrial Ergonomics, 39*(3), 490–500. doi:10.1016/j.ergon.2008.10.010

Walker, G. H., Stanton, N. A., Jenkins, D. P., & Salmon, P. M. (2009). From telephones to iPhones: Applying systems thinking to networked, interoperable products. *Applied Ergonomics, 40*(2), 206–215. doi:10.1016/j.apergo.2008.04.003

Walker, G. H., Stanton, N. A., Salmon, P., Jenkins, D. P., Monnan, S., & Handy, S. (2009). An evolutionary approach to network enabled capability. *International Journal of Industrial Ergonomics, 39*(2), 303–312. doi:10.1016/j.ergon.2008.02.016

Walker, G. H., Stanton, N. A., Salmon, P. M., Jenkins, D., Revell, K., & Rafferty, L. (2009). Measuring Dimensions of Command and Control Using Social Network Analysis: Extending the NATO SAS-050 Model. *International Journal of Command and Control, 3*(2), 1–46.

Walker, G. H., Stanton, N. A., Salmon, P. M., Jenkins, D., Stewart, R., & Wells, L. (2009). Using an integrated methods approach to analyse the emergent properties of military command and control. *Applied Ergonomics, 40*(4), 636–647. doi:10.1016/j.apergo.2008.05.003

Walker, G. H., Stanton, N. A., Salmon, P. M., & Jenkins, D. P. (2008). A review of sociotechnical systems theory: A classic concept for new command and control paradigms. *Theoretical Issues in Ergonomics Science, 9*(6), 479–499. doi:10.1080/14639220701635470

Walker, G. H., Stanton, N. A., Salmon, P. M., & Jenkins, D. P. (2009). How can we support the commander's involvement in the planning process? An exploratory study into remote and co-located command planning. *International Journal of Industrial Ergonomics, 39*(2), 456–464. doi:10.1016/j.ergon.2008.12.003

KEY TERMS AND DEFINITIONS

Active Attack: An attack in which the adversary undertakes unauthorized modification of data or information system assets.

Community of Interest (CoI): COI is a collaborative grouping of users who share and exchange information in the pursuit of common goals or missions.

COMSEC: Communication Security measures include using encryption and ciphering techniques for protecting the contents of data from being deciphered, if intercepted by an intruder/ eavesdropper.

Cyber Security: Cyber security is coordinated actions in order to prevent, analyze and react in case of cyber attacks.

INFOSEC: Information Security are measures which ensure the integrity, availability and confidentiality of data and IT related services.

Passive Attack: An attack in which the adversary does not modify data or system is and only observes data or system information or activity.

TEMPEST: Transient Electromagnetic Pulse Emanation Standard are the measures undertaken to ensure that the electromagnetic transmissions from equipment can't be intercepted to derive information about the equipment's operation and the data it processes.

APPENDIX: ACRONYMS

- **ACDS/SSDS:** Advanced Combat Direction System/Ship Self-Defense System
- **ACTD:** Advanced Concept Technology Demonstration
- **AEHF:** Advanced Extremely High Frequency
- **AES:** Advanced Encryption Standard
- **AHP:** Analytic Hierarchy Process
- **AIP:** Anti-surface Warfare Improvement Program, MPA (Maritime Patrol Aircraft
- **ATWCS/ TTWCS:** Advanced Tomahawk Weapon Control System/Tactical Tomahawk Weapon Control System
- **BGPHES:** Battle Group Passive Horizon Extension System
- **BLOS:** Beyond Line of Sight
- **C2:** Command & Control
- **C4ISR:** Command, Control, Communications, Computers, Intelligence, Surveillance & Reconnaissance
- **CDCIE:** Cross Domain Collaborative Information Environment
- **CDF:** Combat Direction Finding
- **CEC DDS:** Cooperative Engagement Capability Data Distribution System
- **COMSEC:** Communications Security
- **COP:** Common Operational Picture
- **COTS:** Commercial Off the Shelf
- **CSTE:** Classification Stateless, Trusted Environment
- **CV/TSC:** Carrier/Tactical Support Center
- **CWID:** Warrior Interoperability Demonstration
- **DES:** Data Encryption Standard
- **DJC2:** Deployable Joint Command and Control
- **DODAF:** Department of Defense Architecture Framework
- **DoS:** Denial of Service
- **DSCS:** Defense Satellite Communications System
- **DTD:** Data Terminal Device
- **EHF:** Extremely High Frequency
- **EMF:** Management Framework
- **ESM:** The Enterprise System Management
- **FOS:** Family of Systems
- **GAL:** Global Address List
- **GBS:** Global Broadcasting System, Inmarsat- International Maritime Satellite
- **GCCS:** Global Command and Control System
- **GIG:** Global Information Grid
- **HAIPE:** High Assurance Internet Protocol Encryptor
- **HF:** High Frequency
- **ICT:** Information and Communication Technology
- **IMINT:** Image Intelligence
- **INFOSEC:** Information Security
- **INTELSAT:** Intelligence Satellite

- **IPC:** Internet Protocol Convergence
- **JMPS:** Joint Mission Planning System
- **JSIPS-N:** Joint Services Imagery Processing System-Navy
- **JTIDS:** Joint Tactical Information Distribution System
- **JTRS WNW:** Joint Tactical Radio System Wideband Network Waveform
- **KRA:** Key Recovery Authority
- **LAMPS:** Light Airborne Multipurpose System
- **LLC:** Link Level COMSEC
- **LOS:** Line-of-Sight
- **MANET:** Mobile Ad-Hoc Network
- **MASINT:** Measurement and Signatures Intelligence
- **MD5:** Message-Digest 5
- **MODAF:** Ministry of Defense Architecture Framework
- **MPAs:** Maritime Patrol Crafts
- **MUOS:** Mobile User Objective System
- **NAF:** NATO Architecture
- **NAVSSI:** Navigation Sensor System Interface
- **NBD:** Network Based Defense
- **NCO:** Network Centric Operations
- **NCW:** Network Centric Warfare
- **NEC:** Network Enabled Capability
- **NetD-COP:** Network Defense Common Operational Picture
- **NIST:** National Institute for Standards in Technology
- **OS:** Operating System
- **PC:** Personal Computer
- **PEM:** Privacy Enhanced Email
- **S/MIME:** Secure/Multipurpose Internet Mail Extensions
- **SIGINT:** Signal Intelligence
- **SMS/NAVMACS:** Stores Management System/Naval Modular Automated Communications System
- **SNC:** System Network Controller
- **SOA:** Service Oriented Architecture
- **SPCs:** Signal Processing Controllers
- **STDN:** Secure Tactical Data Network
- **TACTICELL:** Tactical Cellular
- **TADIL:** Tactical Digital Information Link
- **TAMD:** Theater Air and Missile Defense
- **TBMCS/JTT:** Theater Battle Management Core Systems/Joint Tactical Terminal
- **TDS/DLP:** Operator Interface System-D Tactical Data System/Data Link Processor
- **TEMPEST:** Transient Electromagnetic Pulse Emanation Standard
- **TLS:** Transport Layer Security
- **TPT:** Top Performing Technologies
- **TRMS:** Type Commanders Readiness Management System
- **TSAT:** Transformation Satellite

- **UAVs:** Unmanned Aerial Vehicles
- **UFO:** Ultra High Frequency Follow-On
- **UHF LOS:** Ultra High Frequency Line of Sight
- **USW:** Undersea Warfare
- **VHF:** Very High Frequency
- **VPN:** Virtual Private Network
- **WGS:** Wideband Gapfiller System

Chapter 13
Practical Web Application Security Audit Following Industry Standards and Compliance

Shakeel Ali
Cipher Storm Ltd., UK

ABSTRACT

A rapidly changing face of internet threat landscape has posed remarkable challenges for security professionals to thwart their IT infrastructure by applying advanced defensive techniques, policies, and procedures. Today, nearly 80% of total applications are web-based and externally accessible depending on the organization policies. In many cases, number of security issues discovered not only depends on the system configuration but also the application space. Rationalizing security functions into the application is a common practice but assessing their level of resiliency requires structured and systematic approach to test the application against all possible threats before and after deployment. The application security assessment process and tools presented here are mainly focused and mapped with industry standards and compliance including PCI-DSS, ISO27001, GLBA, FISMA, SOX, and HIPAA, in order to assist the regulatory requirements. Additionally, to retain a defensive architecture, web application firewalls have been discussed and a map between well-established application security standards (WASC, SANS, OWASP) is prepared to represent a broad view of threat classification.

DOI: 10.4018/978-1-60960-851-4.ch013

INTRODUCTION

For the past two decades web technology has dramatically changed the way user interact and transact the information over the internet. From a simple corporate web site to the complex applications with rich functionality have been making their way to the internet for wider communication. Each application has been developed differently to perform certain tasks with different stacks of technology (Andreu, 2006). This exposes the applications and their deployment architectures radically in different ways. In the business world, vulnerabilities to web applications originate from multiple sources, for instance, the pressure on developers to reach the applicable deadlines, limited knowledge of security, no detailed security specification, inherited vulnerabilities of insecure components, and the unsuitability with underlying operating system or network. This logical security convergence between application server technologies has laid the foundation of critical threats and vulnerabilities. Generally, web applications may contain several components such as, login, session tracking, user permissions enforcement, role distribution, data access, application logic and logout function (Cross et al., 2007). In turn it divides the web application architecture into three basic tiers, namely, web server, application layer and data storage. Each tier's input or output represents its analytical processing structure and the possible dimension to various attacks. These attacks include, but are not limited to, SQL injection, cross-site scripting, buffer overflow, session hijacking, insufficient access control, path traversal, misconfiguration, information leakage and denial of service. In order to prevent such attacks and weaknesses surrounding the application, a customized testing process has been proposed in this chapter to discover, assess and verify the known vulnerabilities using free and open source tools. The process is typically driven by mixed knowledge of two open methodologies, OSSTMM and ISSAF. Furthermore, the selected tools will also satisfy the specific level of industry standards and compliance. This will not only ensure to meet the necessary compliance mandates at each stage of testing but also provide a legal view to the technical objectives. The concept of web application firewall (WAF) technology using two well-know tools, Modsecurity and WebKnight, has also been addressed to provide an adequate protection for web application infrastructure in the enterprise environment. Moreover, to visualize the number of application threats cloak around web architecture, three core application security standards have been mapped together to depict a generic view for better understanding and evaluation.

BACKGROUND

Security assessment is a process that can be incorporated into regular development lifecycle as a part of industry best practices. However, at many occasions this task is being performed by third-party contractor or outsider without any prior knowledge of the system. This phenomenon divides the view of application security assessment into two broad categories, such as Black box and White box. Black box approach is the one in which the entity performing a test has no knowledge about the target. While with the White box approach, it is assumed that a tester should know the internal system processes and functions. There are several types of security audits, and there are many types of IT standards that an audit may apply to. A successful audit may reveal potential vulnerabilities while unsuccessful audits do not ensure the security of a system or application (Wright, 2008). According to Navarrete (2010), there is a significant difference between the automated and manual security testing tools. Most automated tools are design to detect infrastructure-based and application-based vulnerabilities but fail to cover manual and business logic assessment. The basic goal of security testing is to ensure that no vulnerabilities should exist in the system which could allow an attacker to get unauthorized access or even in worst case manipulate the data. It is where the manual and business logic testing becomes more vital. Thus, taking any approach (black box or white box) with minimally focus automated and manual testing procedures will not only address technical issues but also reveal the complex vulnerabilities of applications, which otherwise are not detectable. Due to rapid adoption of web 2.0 in number of enterprise applications, the site ownership is more decentralized thus it opens a wide range of risks for controlling and evaluating the malicious content or code (Moyse, 2010). Generally, the advance use of Asynchronous JavaScript XML (AJAX), Cascading Style Sheets (CSS), Flash and ActiveX components constitute a Web 2.0 platform. This behavioral shift on the web allows users to customize their own web contents rather than sticking with the static ones, however, it raises number of security concerns. These include all issues surrounding Web 1.0 and their inheritance to Web 2.0 frameworks. For instance, Cross-site scripting (XSS) is a prevailing attack in Web 1.0 applications but get more opportunities in Web 2.0 applications due to rich attack surface offered by AJAX (Cannings, Dwivedi, & Lackey, 2007). In near future, the next-generation Web 3.0 technology will bring more advancements and challenges. Kroeker (2010) states that Web 3.0 will help find the wisdom of the crowd and that of its technology platform will move beyond Web 2.0 model with semantic technologies to facilitate interlinked data and customization. This transition between Web 2.0 and Web 3.0 will bring forward more critical security issues and may introduce new or variants of the existing attacks. Hence, performing the security audit and measuring the accuracy and efficiency of the results captured during application security assessment with CIA (confidentiality, integrity, availability) triads will provide in-depth view of known and unknown vulnerabilities. It is also advisable that the tools involved in the security testing process should remain consistent with an output at any given time.

It is considerably important because testers can inline these specific tools with industry standards and compliance to bridge the gap between testing solutions and regulatory acceptance. Application security assessment is a crucial process that has to be dealt thoroughly and in a timely fashion. But in a large enterprise environment where thousands of applications are hosted, make it impossible to test each one of them individually from cost and quality perspectives. So, by installing an edge protection for these applications using WAF (web application firewall) technology will simplify the security process and enforces the adequate protection to Layer-7 against most modern threats. Finally, to conclude my discussion, the main theme behind this chapter is to present a structured and systematic approach towards testing the security of web applications and highlighting number of tools that can be incorporated into testing process while satisfying the necessary level of standards and compliance.

Security Assessment Methodologies

Assessing the security of an application is a time-critical and challenging task depending on its size and complexity. There are various methodologies proposed by the industry to cover a basic need of security assessment process. Some of them focus on the technical side of a test, while others target the management criteria and a very few stay in between both strategies. The basic idea conveyed by practicing these methodologies is to follow the steps which execute different set of tests and scenarios to judge the security of a system under question. Two of such well-known methodologies have been discussed below to give an extended view of security testing process with their relevant features and benefits. This will assist industry professionals to assess and qualify the best strategy that could fit into their testing prototype. In the next section, a customized security testing process has been demonstrated using mix knowledge of both methodologies to initiate

Figure 1. Time and cost factor affecting security analysis methods

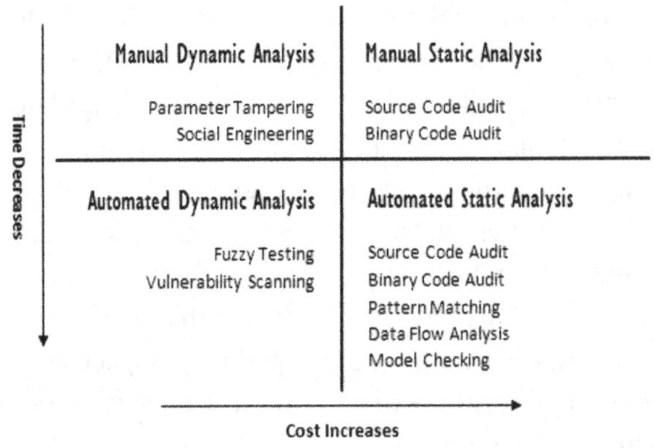

a practical roadmap for web application security testing. It is, however, important to notice that security is an on-going process and adapting to any one methodology does not necessarily reflect the completeness of application risk assessment process. There are wide range of solutions and methodologies, and many claim to be perfect in finding all security issues. But which solution finds what issues and which methodology suits your application criteria is what makes the selection perfect. Research by Bonvillain, Mehta, Miller, and Wheeler (2009) has acquainted the classification of security analysis methods on the basis of their usage, benefits, strengths and weaknesses. However, choosing the best one still requires proper knowledge of a system and judgment between the time and resource cost. A refined approach to these security assessment methods and their appropriate measurement by time and cost has been shown in Figure 1. Investing more capital and resources on security testing without taking an expert view of system requirements can put the business economy in danger.

Another interesting aspect is the use of Mortman-Hutton Model for simulating the vulnerabilities of a system or application on the principle of "exploit use" probability. This methodology illustrates a visionary approach towards black-hat motives and the classification of attacks at different levels (Mortman, Hutton, Dixon, & Crisp,

2009). Because the methodology is still in its infancy, it lacks the guidelines and procedures to follow to get a right direction for risk assessment process. Hence, different methodologies present different ways for assessing the security of a system or application. Choosing the right one depends on several factors including technical requirements, business objectives, regulatory concerns, technology availability, and expert knowledge. Furthermore, the two leading assessment methodologies, OSSTMM and ISSAF, are examined below with their core testing principles, features and benefits.

Open Source Security Testing Methodology Manual (OSSTMM)

The OSSTMM is a definitive process for security testing and analysis. It is also recognized as an international standard by most organizations. The methodology is mainly based on scientific method which helps measuring the operational security and its financial terms in relation with business objectives. Technically, it is divided into four main components, namely, Scope, Channel, Index and Vector. A scope defines the target operating environment including all of its assets. A channel provides the means of communication and interaction with these assets which further divides it into three broad categories, physical, spectrum,

Table 1. Classification of OSSTMM security test types

Test Types	Short Definitions	Exemplary Types
Blind	Requires no prior knowledge about the target, the target is notified in advance of the audit scope	Ethical Hacking, War Gaming
Double Blind	Requires no prior knowledge about the target, the target is not notified in advance of the audit scope	Black Box Audit, Penetration Test
Gray Box	Limited knowledge about the target, the target is notified in advance of the audit scope	Vulnerability Assessment
Double Gray Box	Limited knowledge about the target, the target is notified in advance of the audit scope and time frame of an audit, no channels or vectors are tested	White Box Audit
Tandem	Auditor and target both know in advance the audit scope, assess the protection level and controls of the target, test is conducted thoroughly	In-house Audit Crystal Box Audit
Reversal	Auditor holds full knowledge about the target, the target does not know how and when the auditor will be testing	Red-Teaming

and communication. Each of these channels represents unique set of security elements that has to be testified during the assessment. These involve human psychology, physical security, wireless communication medium, data networks and telecommunication. The index is a method for classifying the targets according to their unique identifications. Such as, IP address Mac address and Hostname. And finally, the use of vector determines the quantity of direction required to evaluate each functional asset. This overall combination of scope, channel, index and vector initiates a practical roadmap for an auditor known as "Audit Scope". Additionally, to complement different forms of security testing, the OSSTMM methodology has organized its terminology into six common functional security test types. The comparison between each one of them can be determined from Table 1.

The use of OSSTMM framework comes in handy to perform almost any type of security test in combination with test cases derived by five logical channels defined previously. These test cases collectively examine the target by testing its data controls, process security, access control security, perimeter protection, trust verification, physical location, security awareness level, fraud control level and many other mechanisms (ISECOM, 2008). The technical theme of OSSTMM focuses exactly on what needs to be tested, how

it should be tested, what measures should be in place before, during and after a test, and how to correlate the test results in a consistent and reliable manner. Security metrics are considered to be invaluable tools for characterizing and representing the current state of protection of a target. Hence, the OSSTMM methodology also encourages its practice via RAV (Risk Assessment Values). A RAV is usually developed from security analysis results, thus, computing the values of operational security, loss controls, and limitations will constitute the actual security value called "RAV Score". Using RAV score one can make security projections and define milestones that can be accomplished to achieve better protection. From a business standpoint, RAV can help restrict the amount of investment required on a particular solution thus leveraging the most return on investment.

Key Features

- It is an open source methodology maintained by Institute for Security and Open Methodologies (ISECOM).
- Its audit process provides an accurate measurement of operational security by substantially reducing false positives and false negatives.

- The OSSTMM is adaptable to many other audit types, such as, ethical hacking, penetration testing, vulnerability assessment, white-box audit, red-teaming and so forth.
- Ensures that the assessment was conducted thoroughly inclusive of all necessary channels, inline with the target's posture, and the results aggregated are quantifiable, consistent and repeatable.
- The methodology executes under four combined phases, namely, regulatory phase, definition phase, information phase and controls test phase. Each phase does acquire, assess and verify the specific information about a target.
- Security metrics are represented using RAV (Risk Assessment Values) method. The RAV evaluation is performed by calculating three set of values that are, operational security, loss controls and security limitations. And the RAV score is the final score based on the given values which represents the current state of security.
- The STAR (Security Test Audit Report) is a formal template presenting OSSTMM audit that can be added on the top of final report. The report summarizes different variables such as, testing criteria, risk assessment values and a comprehensive output from each test phase.

Benefits

- It is accepted as an international standard for security testing and provides industry-wide visibility and customer assurance.
- A certified OSSTMM audit aligned with all necessary requirements can be eligible for accreditation from ISECOM.
- The methodology can be coordinated with three types of compliance: government legislation, industry regulation, and business policy. These include, but are not limited to ISO 17799, CESG Check, ITIL,

PCI-DSS 1.0, NIST-800 series, Sarbanes-Oxley Act (SOX), Gramm-Leach-Bliley Act (GLBA), DoD FM 31-21 and many more.

- It is regularly updated with new tests for best practices, regulations, legislation, policies and ethical concerns.
- Training the qualified employees with OSSTMM standard and encouraging them to obtain professional certification from ISECOM not only improves the organization productivity but also cut-off the cost over hiring a third-party auditor.

Information Systems Security Assessment Framework (ISSAF)

ISSAF is another open source security assessment methodology. Its framework has been classified into various domains to reflect a complete process of information systems security assessment. Each of these domains support specific evaluation criteria and aim to provide field inputs for security assessment. The primary goal of this framework is to fulfill an organization's security testing requirements by defining a process that can be integrated into regular business lifecycle and give completeness, accuracy and efficiency to security engagements. The unifying idea behind the development of ISSAF was to integrate and address two broad areas of security testing, management and technical. The management side enforces the best practices and engagement management that should be covered during the assessment period. On the other hand, a technical spectrum provides necessary steps to follow to establish an effective security assessment process. It is important to notice that ISSAF defines the assessment as a process rather than audit. This is due to the fact that auditing may require more established body to promulgate the essential standards (OISSG, 2006). The framework is divided into five phase model which includes Planning, Assessment, Treatment, Accreditation and Maintenance. Each of these phases provide specific baseline or set of activities that are generic and flexible to any organization structure. The outputs of these phases constitute operational activities, management of security initiatives, and a full picture of vulnerabilities that may exist in a system. The assessment process uses the shortest path required to examine its target against severe vulnerabilities that can be exploited with minimal efforts. The overall methodical approach followed by ISSAF to assess the targets is bit similar to that of OSSTMM, but differs on the ground when dealing with technical issues.

ISSAF provides a wide and detailed security assessment framework to test range of processes and technologies. But, this incorporates another problem of maintenance, that it should be updated frequently to reflect new or updated technology assessment criteria. Hence, this activity requires more efforts to maintain such information. In comparison, OSSTMM is much less affected by desuetude issues because one can associate the same methodology over several security assessments using different tools and techniques. ISSAF as a broad framework pretends to provide up to date information regarding tools, techniques, best practices, and regulatory concerns to enhance your assessment engagement, while can be aligned with OSSTMM or any other assessment methodology. This overlap allows both assessment methodologies to complement each other. It is also important to notice that ISSAF is still immature and outdated in comparison with OSSTMM methodology.

Key Features

- It is a structured and open source framework maintained by Open Information Systems Security Groups (OISSG).
- It assesses the existing defenses in depth and breadth to detect vulnerabilities in order to strengthen organization's security process and technology, thus, returns a high value proposition for securing business.

- The framework stretches various domains of information security. These include engagement management, good practices, risk assessment, information security policy, business structure and management, and controls assessment.
- Technical controls implemented by ISSAF comprise of penetration testing methodology, physical security assessment, operations management, change management, security awareness, incident management, business continuity management, and legal and regulatory compliance.
- Penetration testing methodology is an absolute process to evaluate the network, system and application controls. ISSAF presented its methodology with more extensive focus on specific technology assessment. This includes the assessment of routers, switches, firewalls, intrusion detection systems, virtual private network, storage area network, AS 400 devices, Windows, Linux, Unix, web servers, databases, web applications and so on.

Benefits

- Organizations with ISSAF compliant assessment are eligible for the accreditation of ISSAF certification.
- Provides industry-wide visibility, satisfaction, customer trust, business reputation, better productivity and consistency with business objectives.
- Enable management to identify and understand the gaps in organization's security policies, controls and processes. Thus, reduces a potential risk by proactively addressing vulnerabilities before they are exploited.
- The framework bridges a gap between management and technical view of security assessment by implementing necessary controls that bring attention to both areas.

- Provides platform specific assessment guidelines, procedures and checklists to identify, assess, and verify critical vulnerabilities.

APPLICATION SECURITY TESTING PROCESS

Information security is a broad topic dealing with many factors in concern with various security threats. Securing the web applications is one of them. The most effective approach to secure applications would be marking security right from a design level to code level (Doraiswamy et al., 2009). However, on many occasions you may find applications developed irrespective of security integration. This leverages the practice of application security testing to assess number of threats that are specific to application infrastructure. The controls that can analyzed through security testing process may involve attacks and weaknesses like SQL injection, cross-site scripting (XSS), cross-site request forgery (CSRF), insecure indexing, insufficient access control, session prediction and fixation, buffer overflow, integer overflow, remote or local file inclusion, misconfiguration, path traversal, denial of service, information leakage and so forth. It is also wise to know that the increasing complexity in web technologies and attacks is seriously weaponizing the end users to commit cyber crimes without their knowledge or intention. These illegal activities include spamming, spreading malware, and stealing sensitive information. The attack space has dispersed from server-side to client-side by exploiting the vulnerabilities that exist in web browsers or any other third party application plug-ins (Smith, Ames, & Delchi, 2009). Thus, defending server-side applications is more crucial task and requires appropriate assurance mechanism to satisfy the maximum level of security. Understanding the application, extracting its threat profile, preparing the test plan, and executing test cases are some of the key areas that should be addressed properly.

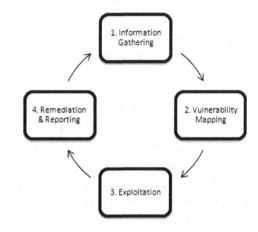

Figure 2. Application security testing process

This is where the importance of structured and systematic approach for testing web application security can be recognized. The approach presented in this section is a typical process that initiates the practical roadmap to application security assessment, as shown in Figure 2.

Each of these phases, from Figure 2, introduces number of free and open source tools that can be used to assess the application security and at the same time satisfy the best-known industry standards and compliance. The compliance mandates are measured according to the features and capabilities of the tools. This will provide handful information for those who are looking to test their applications but also want to be consistent with regulatory requirements.

Information Gathering

Information gathering (or reconnaissance) is the initial and most important phase of web application security testing. Such that, all the information accumulated is considered significant because it will help tester to understand its target in order to engage it properly. The technical areas covered under this phase provide information about target logistics, operating system, web server, application system, open ports, and other resource information. Logistics deal with information about the target network that can be obtained over the internet, such as IP addresses, organization emails, infrastructure information, administrative data, and DNS records. OS fingerprinting is an extremely valuable technique to discover the target operating system. Similarly, to discover web server technology a web-server fingerprinting technique can be employed. Moreover, the information about application system can be extracted by mapping open ports to identifiable services, analyzing error pages for information leakage, file types supported by the system, resource enumeration and source code mining. Additionally, to dig more about the target an information harvesting technique can be used to collect and organize unstructured information publicly accessible on the internet. The overall theme of this phase is to probe the target application system and its infrastructure. Tools that can automate this process faster and effectively have been discussed below.

Maltego

Maltego is a versatile information gathering and data mining tool. Its main purpose is to allow tester to enumerate the target network infrastructure and pull out personal information from internet resources. The information gathered then can be visually demonstrated to discover and understand the real world links between searched items and their relationships. Technically, it addresses two divisions of information gathering phase. The first is the infrastructure information which is comprised of enumerating Domain Names, Whois Data, DNS Names, Netblocks, and IP Addresses. The second is about extracting the personal information about a target which includes, email addresses, web site details, phone numbers, social networking groups, companies and organizations. It has also some specialized functions which allow auditor to perform email address verification, search blogs for tags and phrases, extract metadata from documents, and identify inbound or outbound links to website.

Compliance Mandates

Following regulatory requirements tie to Maltego usage: PCI-DSS 11.2, HIPAA 164.308(a)(8), GLBA 16CFR Part 314.4(c), FISMA RA-5, SOX A13.3

NMap

NMap is an extremely powerful and feature rich network mapping utility. It is used scan the IP address or hostname for open ports, operating system detection, service identification, and other network parameters. The real power of NMap comes into practice when different combination of scanning techniques and options are used. These techniques involve, SYN scan, TCP Connect scan, FIN scan, Xmas scan, Null scan, Ping scan, UDP scan, ACK scan, Window scan, RPC scan, List scan, Idle scan and FTP bounce scan. Other options like operating system fingerprinting, service detection (application name and version), host discovery, IP spoofing and structured output are also considered vital when taking security assignments in enterprise environment. It helps tester to assess the network with various characteristics that may draw a final outlook of network systems architecture.

Compliance Mandates

Following regulatory requirements tie to NMap usage: ISO 27001/27002 12.6, 15.2.2, PCI-DSS 11.3, 11.2, HIPAA 164.308(a)(8), GLBA 16 CFR Part 314.4 (c), FISMA RA-5, SI-2, SOX A13.3

SkipFish

SkipFish is a comprehensive tool used for enumerating web resources in an efficient and cognitive manner. By employing advanced techniques like recursive crawling and dictionary-based probing, it grabs all the possible web contents and generates interactive sitemap to provide a visual image of the web server resources. SkipFish also support the features like automatic dictionary construction from extracted contents, probabilistic scanning for time-bound assessments, heuristic scanning for ambiguous paths, and handle advanced procedures to capture path semantics based on application specific filtering rules. It is considerably useful for auditor to know the inner structure of a web server because it may turn to reveal some of the unknown facts about application deployment. These include deducing the supported file types, missing or broken links, sensitive data, default configuration, and possibly the source code.

Compliance Mandates

Following regulatory requirements tie to SkipFish usage: ISO 27001/27002 12.6, 15.2.2, PCI-DSS 6.3, HIPAA 164.308(a)(1)(i), GLBA 16 CFR 314.4(b) and (2), FISMA RA-5, SA-11, SI-2, SOX A12.4

DMitry

DMitry adds an excellent contribution towards information gathering phase. Its main functionality is to gather as much information as possible from multiple internet resources. Basic features included are whois lookup, email harvester, sub-domain locater, TCP port scanner, retrieve uptime information, operating system version and web server release. Additionally, its modular design extends the capabilities of a program by adding customized modules on the top of existing functional base. Thus, not only by using existing combination of options a tester can aggregate wide range of information about a target but is also allowed to integrate extra functionality to probe more useful data.

Compliance Mandates

Following regulatory requirements tie to DMitry usage: PCI-DSS 11.2, HIPAA 164.308(a)

(8), GLBA 16CFR Part 314.4(c), FISMA RA-5, SOX A13.3

Vulnerability Mapping

After taking enough intelligence on your target, it is now time to perform vulnerability identification and analysis. This phase utilizes a strategic plan to analyze a target for known and unknown vulnerabilities based on the input from information gathering phase. In order to address vulnerability mapping effectively, a finite set of criteria should be drawn that is specific to technology under assessment. This criterion employs unique techniques and set up solid directions to investigate potential flaws in the target application. It is highly recommended to refer OWASP (Open Web Application Security Project) and WASC (Web Application Security Consortium) guidelines which are explained in one of the next sections. These guidelines provide technical information regarding various attacks and weaknesses that can be demonstrated against the target application environment. During this whole process several automated tools can be referred to minimize the time and efforts required to achieve better application assessment. These tools can workout independently by pulling all the well-known vulnerabilities repository and test them against the target. However, there are situations where some tools should feed with data in order to verify the condition manually. In both cases, the output should be verified to minimize the false positives and false negatives. Thus, identifying and analyzing the critical vulnerabilities will provide stable ground to trek forward into exploitation phase.

Nessus

Nessus is a multi-purpose vulnerability scanner capable of auditing enterprise-class network, devices and applications. It comes with variety of test plug-ins that can be updated on regular basis. This range of plug-ins can be selected and enabled according to the testing criteria. Nessus also supports the modularity, such that, a tester with sound knowledge of Nessus Attack Scripting Language (NASL) can extend and customize its features. Some of the core security audits employed under Nessus are, network based vulnerability scanning, patch audits, configuration audits, web application security assessment, asset profiling, and other platform specific security tests. The attacks and weaknesses found by Nessus are then presented with their relevant remediation procedures and provide an option to generate a report. This robust and comprehensive functionality of Nessus make it a perfect tool for assessing web applications and the underlying server architecture.

Compliance Mandates

Following regulatory requirements tie to Nessus usage: ISO 27001-27002 12.6, 15.2.2, PCI-DSS 11.2, 6.6, HIPAA 164.308(a)(8), GLBA 16CFR Part 314.4(c), FISMA RA-5, SI-2, SOX A13.3

Burp Suite

Burp Suite is a combined set of tools with robust framework and integrated platform for testing web applications. These tools include proxy interceptor, scanner, repeater, spider, intruder, sequencer, comparer and decoder. This handful division of tools is designed to facilitate and speed up the process of security evaluation. Its extensible assessment process combines both manual and automated techniques to discover, analyze and attack the web application environment. Findings determined by one tool can be shared among others effectively that help us to reveal any security flaws that may exist in the application. The attack conditions that can be checked and verified against the target application involve client-side controls, authentication, session management, access control, injections, path traversal, cross-site scripting, application logic, and web server misconfiguration. In overall, Burp Suite provides

an auditor with true armory that can lead to successful determination of application security controls.

Compliance Mandates

Following regulatory requirements tie to Burp Suite usage: ISO 27001/27002 12.6, 15.2.2, PCI-DSS 6.3, HIPAA 164.308(a)(1)(i), GLBA 16 CFR 314.4(b) and (2), FISMA RA-5, SA-11, SI-2, SOX A12.4

Wapiti

Wapiti is another useful web vulnerability scanner which allows an auditor to test the web application using black-box approach. First it looks through all the web pages to find the interesting entry points for data and vulnerable scripts that may cause execution of malicious code. Once this list is extracted, it will be checked against number of security vulnerabilities and applied fuzzing techniques to identify vulnerable pages. Wapiti can measure the vulnerabilities like SQL injection, XPath injection, cross-site scripting, LDAP injection, command execution, session fixation, and other known set of application security problems. It helps auditor to think like an attacker and take this vision forward by hunting known and unknown application threats.

Compliance Mandates

Following regulatory requirements tie to Wapiti usage: ISO 27001/27002 12.6, 15.2.2, PCI-DSS 6.3, 11.3, 11.2, HIPAA 164.308(a)(1)(8)(i), GLBA 16 CFR 314.4 (b)(c)(2), FISMA RA-5, SA-11, SI-2, SOX A12.4, A13.3

SQLMap

SQLMap is a dedicated database security assessment tool. It assists in identifying and penetrating SQL injection vulnerabilities. Today, many web applications are developed using dynamic technology (ASP, PHP, JSP, etc) which may include a part of details that should be stored and retrieved from databases. This includes user authentication, customer profile, credit card data and other sensitive information. Due to the fact of technology integration between application tier and data tier, it opens a gate for an attacker to find the entry points from where the SQL queries can be injected in order to reveal all information from database. SQLMap automates this process by investigating every possible input inside the web application. It supports features like database fingerprinting, fetching data from a database, allow file system access and execute commands at operating system level.

Compliance Mandates

Following regulatory requirements tie to SQLMap usage: ISO 27001/27002 12.6, 15.2.2, PCI-DSS 11.3, 11.2, 6.6, HIPAA 164.308(a)(8), GLBA 16 CFR Part 314.4 (c), FISMA RA-5, SI-2, SOX A13.3

Exploitation

Starting this phase an auditor is fully armed with necessary information required to research a relevant exploit (program or script) which has been written to take advantage of discovered vulnerability. These exploits typically target some known software, like operating system, web server, or any other third-party application. It is also a known fact that these exploits are developed by some entities who publish their findings publicly over the internet or in a private group. Thus, it is ultimately an auditor's responsibility to research the vulnerability and find specific exploit that can finish the desired job. This section introduces an automated exploitation tool which can be used as a source to map the discovered vulnerability with any existing exploit or use it as an exploit development platform. It is extremely important to notice that the area of exploit development is

vast and requires enough knowledge and skills coupled with imagination and creativity. By assessing the target vulnerabilities, it will be assuring that whether or not it is susceptible to known and published exploits. This whole process emulates the attacker behavior and mindset, and put the auditor in a right path towards exploit research. Concerning various sources for the exploit data, finding and utilizing the published exploits repository, selecting and manipulating the exploit code based on vulnerability, are some of the key tasks to perform exploitation successfully. A responsible auditor is always be clear about the objectives for executing such exploits as they will present the basis for relevant follow-up business decisions.

Metasploit Framework

Metasploit is a powerful and automated exploitation framework. It comes with a comprehensive attack library including auxiliaries, exploits, payloads and encoders. Each of this subset represents different set of functionality that can assist in exploitation process. For instance, if an auditor has identified that the target is running a vulnerable web server and found the relevant exploit to take advantage of the same vulnerability from Metasploit database, then attaching the applicable payload will allow persistent or non-persistent access to target operating system depending on the exploit parameters and target architecture. The basic functionality of payload is to initiate a shellcode on target, which once executed, should return a call to attacker with attainable system privileges. Encoders assist in obfuscating such payload so that it would remain undetectable. On the other hand, auxiliaries are designed to test different network and application conditions that may influence the progress of penetration process. The overall framework takes streamlined approach to assess its target against known exploits. It is highly interactive, easy to use, dynamically extendable and robust.

Compliance Mandates

Following regulatory requirements tie to Metasploit Framework usage: ISO 27001/27002 12.6, 15.2.2, PCI-DSS 11.3, HIPAA 164.308(a)(8), GLBA 16 CFR Part 314.4 (c), FISMA RA-5, SI-2, SOX A13.3

Remediation and Reporting

Reporting plays an important role in any security assessment strategy from legal and ethical standpoints. Documenting the verified results, mitigation procedures and culminating of all your efforts provide a broad view of system weaknesses. The report constitutes a legal proof that the entity is in compliance with applicable standards or may require to resolve some issues in order to remain consistent with them. The lack of due diligence in this area can land the auditor into legal problems. By understanding the severity and importance of risks measured, a report should be constructed in clear terms to benefit both technical and management counterparts of the target organization. The report is usually made up of different sections like executive summary, risk matrix, affected resources, vulnerabilities discovered, attack data, recommendations, references, best practices, and the final summary. Apart from a report structure, the presentation of data must be tailored according to the intended recipients and their technical capabilities to interpret such information. It is also a common practice among many auditors to suggest alternate solutions to tackle critical security issues, however, fixes and remediation procedures should also be explained enough to provide better judgment from time and cost perspectives. Remediation procedures generally refer to the reactive and corrective steps that need to be taken under consideration in order to address security patches. Therefore, the final report must answer and relate each stage of testing by representing the factual data that could interest technical as well as management team at the target organization.

DEFENDING WEB APPLICATION INFRASTRUCTURE

Integrating the application security testing process into regular development lifecycle is the industry proven practice to cop known threats. But the increase in sophistication of attacks put all these major security solutions behind. As a general rule, security testing process must be revisited at every single change in application to check and verify any known and unknown vulnerability that may affect its confidentiality, integrity and availability. However, it is considerably expensive and time consuming task in the large enterprise environment where thousands of applications are developed and hosted. Remediation for one target application (e.g. Dot NET) works radically different from other application stack (e.g. J2EE). To overcome such limitations, a generic approach to edge-level (or network-level) protection has been introduced towards web application infrastructure. This next-generation defensive technology is called WAF (Web Application Firewall), which provides flexibility in protecting multiple web applications simultaneously. The solution can be deployed straightaway without touching application code or configuration of the production system. Web application firewall deeply inspects the web traffic and enforces reactive tactics so that the malicious traffic never reaches the application (Barnett, 2009). WAF is also known as "reverse proxy" server because there is no internet connection that can be directly established to the true web server host. It comes in the form of hardware appliance or software. WAFs offer deep application security by inspecting every single request and response flowing through them. It detects and blocks the malicious traffic by matching traffic pattern against known attack signatures or by tuning its anomaly model to detect abnormal traffic behavior that deviates from established security policy. Shah (2009) presented two approaches to secure web applications; one is by employing secure coding principles which takes longer time in fixing security issues and incur higher cost, while the other is application layer filtering solution "WAF" which can be tuned to work efficiently for longer period without any human intervention. Acting as a first line of defense, easy to manage, and implement new attack signatures are some of the key advantages of using web application firewall. Some of the inherent issues with signature-based systems (blacklisting) can be managed by utilizing anomaly-based (whitelisting) detection mechanism (Zanero & Criscione, 2009). Thus, by deploying both detection techniques one can completely eradicate a malicious traffic before it reaches the target application. As far as the edge of your enterprise network is protected, all the applications residing behind will be actively monitored to detect and prevent any critical threats.

Due to diverse functionality of various web technologies, there is a limited number of free and open source web application firewalls exist. Two of such prominent solutions have been discussed below highlighting their basic features, advantages and disadvantages. Each of these solutions does the most of what needs to be protected at the edge-level.

ModSecurity

ModSecurity provides a powerful protection against malicious web transactions by monitoring, logging and performing real-time analysis on HTTP traffic. Its software is highly scalable, flexible, tactical, and can operate as an Apache server module or as an independent entity. The protection mechanism is mainly based on the given ruleset whose function is to detect and prevent back-end web applications from known and unknown attacks. The attack prevention strategy works under three common approaches that are negative security model (blacklisting), positive security model (whitelisting) and the rules-set based on known weaknesses and vulnerabilities. Its robust architecture and deep inspection capability opens a wide range of options for achieving

better application security. ModSecurity workflow starts by capturing all the requests from external entity, performing canonicalization, testing against anti-evasion rules, execute input filtering data rules, execute output filtering rules, and log any data if required.

Advantages

1. Available as free and open-source.
2. Can be deployed as a reverse proxy, embedded-mode or network platform.
3. Advanced anti-evasion techniques.
4. Supports complex rule logic.
5. Encourages the use of regular expression (RegEx) in rule definitions.
6. Works on wide range of operating systems including flavors of Linux, Unix and Windows.

Disadvantages

1. In embedded mode, it can only protect the local application server and may consume good amount of resources like memory and processor.
2. In a reverse proxy mode, it sometimes fails to handle high amount of network traffic which may cause a single point of failure.
3. Performance degradation problems.
4. Signature-based (rule-set) security can be bypassed using zero-day attacks.

WebKnight

Webknight is another useful web application firewall (WAF). It uses ISAPI filter to detect and block malicious requests before they reach the desired application. By scanning all the incoming requests against filtering rules that have been set up by administrator, it assures and maintains the security of a web server. Once the attack signatures have been identified, an alert is triggered to inform the responsible entity and all the information is logged for future references. It supports rich set of application security filters, such as for SQL injection, cross-site scripting, character encoding, directory traversal, buffer overflow, and other attacks. Because it can easily be integrated with those web servers which support ISAPI filter, it works not just like a firewall or intrusion detection system but can be extended to protect encrypted traffic and more.

Advantages

1. Available as free and open-source.
2. Provide customization for preventing zero-day exploits.
3. Compatible with various web technologies, such as Cold Fusion, WebDAV, Sharepoint, Frontpage Extension etc.
4. Protect encrypted sessions over SSL.
5. Easy to deploy and configure.
6. Update configuration in run-time mode without restarting the web server.

Disadvantages

1. Only works for those web servers with ISAPI filter support.
2. Cannot handle heavy network traffic and may cause denial of service to back-end applications.
3. Performance issues arise in large enterprise environment.
4. Rule-based filtering can be bypassed using advanced attack techniques.

APPLICATION SECURITY STANDARDS MAPPING

A cross-domain map between three selected application security standards has been demonstrated below. These include Web Application Security Consortium (WASC) Threat Classification, Open Web Application Security Project (OWASP) Top Ten, and CWE-SANS Top 25 Most Dangerous

Programming Errors. This ideal presentation will let security auditors and developers to understand a true vision of application security by visualizing the classification of application threats. It can also be used as a reference while assessing the web application for various attacks and weaknesses. The map also provides flexibility to quickly audit your application according to the desired standard and achieve necessary certification. Additionally, it can be coordinated as a process into regular development lifecycle to accomplish greater productivity and security. It is worth noticing that these standards have been developed and maintained individually by their respective groups or organizations.

FUTURE RESEARCH DIRECTIONS

Securing web application is a challenging task and requires appropriate measures to be taken to protect its confidentiality, integrity and availability. Apart from practicing secure coding principles, security testing also plays an equal role in assuring better application security. Even though there are several automated security assessment tools exist that can evaluate the whole web infrastructure in shorter period. A manual approach is always encouraged for thorough and rigorous testing. Hence, by combining both strategies with industry proven assessment methodology may result in more accurate, efficient and reliable output. It is very important to note that the accuracy of these results may affect different factors surrounding the business environment. These could be a loss in reputation and intellectual property, compliance and regulation incompatibility, business investment risk, and more. Following a structured and systematic approach for testing web applications can help in validating all the technical and managerial controls as well as business logic. Thus, an auditor with true skills and knowledge can only devise proper assessment criteria. In today's typical network environment where thousands of

Table 2. Mapping between application security standards (WASC, SANS, OWASP)

WASC TC v2	CWE-SANS Top 25 2009	OWASP Top Ten 2010
01 - Insufficient Authentication	642 - External Control of Critical State Data	A3 - Broken Authentication and Session Management A4 - Insecure Direct Object References
02 - Insufficient Authorization	285 - Improper Access Control (Authorization)	A4 - Insecure Direct Object References A7 - Failure to Restrict URL Access
03 - Integer Overflows	682 - Incorrect Calculation	
04 - Insufficient Transport Layer Protection	319 - Cleartext Transmission of Sensitive Information	A10 - Insufficient Transport Layer Protection
05 - Remote File Inclusion	426 - Untrusted Search Path	
06 - Format String		
07 - Buffer Overflow	119 - Failure to Constrain Operations within the Bounds of a Memory Buffer	
08 - Cross-site Scripting	79 - Failure to Preserve Web Page Structure (Cross-site Scripting)	A2 - Cross-Site Scripting
09 - Cross-site Request Forgery	352 - Cross-Site Request Forgery (CSRF)	A5 - Cross-Site Request Forgery
10 - Denial of Service	404 - Improper Resource Shutdown or Release	A7 - Failure to Restrict URL Access
11 - Brute Force		A7 - Failure to Restrict URL Access
12 - Content Spoofing		
13 - Information Leakage	209 - Information Exposure Through an Error Message	
14 - Server Misconfiguration		A6 - Security Misconfiguration
15 - Application Misconfiguration		A6 - Security Misconfiguration
16 - Directory Indexing		
17 - Improper File system Permissions	732 - Incorrect Permission Assignment for Critical Resource 250 - Execution with Unnecessary Privileges	
18 - Credential/Session Prediction	330 - Use of Insufficiently Random Values	A3 - Broken Authentication and Session Management
19 - SQL Injection	89 - Improper Sanitization of Special Elements used in an SQL Command (SQL Injection)	A1 - Injection
20 - Improper Input Handling	20 - Improper Input Validation 73 - External Control of File Name or Path	
21 - Insufficient Anti-Automation		A7 - Failure to Restrict URL Access
22 - Improper Output Handling	116 - Improper Encoding or Escaping of Output	
23 - XML Injection		A1 - Injection
24 - HTTP Request Splitting		
25 - HTTP Response Splitting		
26 - HTTP Request Smuggling		
27 - HTTP Response Smuggling		
28 - Null Byte Injection		A1 - Injection
29 - LDAP Injection		A1 - Injection
30 - Mail Command Injection		A1 - Injection

continued on the following page

Table 2. Continued

WASC TC v2	CWE-SANS Top 25 2009	OWASP Top Ten 2010
31 - OS Commanding	78 - Improper Sanitization of Special Elements used in an OS Command (OS Command Injection)	A1 - Injection
32 - Routing Detour		
33 - Path Traversal	73 - External Control of File Name or Path 426 - Untrusted Search Path	A4 - Insecure Direct Object References
34 - Predictable Resource Location		A7 - Failure to Restrict URL Access
35 - SOAP Array Abuse		
36 - SSI Injection		A1 - Injection
37 - Session Fixation	732 - Incorrect Permission Assignment for Critical Resource	A3 - Broken Authentication and Session Management
38 - URI Redirector Abuse		A8 - Unvalidated Redirects and Forwards
39 - XPath Injection		A1 - Injection
40 - Insufficient Process Validation		
41 - XML Attribute Blowup		
42 - Abuse of Functionality		
43 - XML External Entities		
44 - XML Entity Expansion		
45 - Fingerprinting		
46 - XQuery Injection		A1 - Injection
47 - Insufficient Session Expiration	732 - Incorrect Permission Assignment for Critical Resource	A3 - Broken Authentication and Session Management
48 - Insecure Indexing		
49 - Insufficient Password Recovery		

enterprise applications are hosted, it is a common practice to deploy web application firewall (WAF) at the edge of network to detect and prevent any application-level threats. This will ensure the security of insecure applications without modifying a code or even test them individually. However, there are seamless challenges to this approach and new attacks are discovered on daily basis. The real objection to such technology may arise when transforming web applications from distributed network environment to cloud computing platform which may require researching and investigating new security technology or assessment strategy.

CONCLUSION

Addressing application security via defined assessment methodology or using a technology like web application firewall is the only way to ensure maximum level of security. Choosing the best assessment methodology in accordance with conformity of compliance and standards is a primary task that should be accomplished by auditor to cover both business and technical requirements. As you can see, today's auditor is solely responsible to conduct security testing not only from technical aspect but also from legal standpoint. The demand for maintaining existing system compliance, while auditing application security with selected tools and techniques that should not violate any business policy or regulatory framework, is a time critical and challenging issue. On the other hand, keeping up with web application firewall solution has obvious advantages over traditional assessment strategies. But it does not completely protect the application from zero-day attacks or weaknesses. Thus, combining the power of structured security testing process with firewall deployment at the edge of your network should resist any unnecessary attempts to break into the application.

REFERENCES

Andreu, A. (2006). *Professional pen testing for web applications*. Indianapolis, IN: Wiley Publishing.

Barnett, C. (2009). *WAF virtual patching challenge: Securing WebGoat with ModSecurity. Proceedings from Black Hat DC '09*. Crystal City, DC: Black Hat Briefings.

Bonvillain, D., Mehta, N., Miller, J., & Wheeler, A. (2009). *Cutting through the hype: An analysis of application testing methodologies, their effectiveness and the corporate illusion of security. Proceedings from Black Hat Europe '09. Moevenpick*. Amsterdam, The Netherlands: Black Hat Briefings.

Cannings, R., Dwivedi, H., & Lackey, Z. (2007). *Hacking exposed Web 2.0: Web 2.0 security secrets and solutions*. New York, NY: McGraw-Hill Osborne.

Cross, M., Palmer, S., Kapinos, S., Petkov, P. D., Meer, H., & Shields, R. ... Temmingh, R. (2007). *Web application vulnerabilities: Detect, exploit, prevent*. Burlington, MA: Syngress Publishing.

Doraiswamy, A., Pakala, S., Kapoor, N., Verma, P., Singh, P., Nair, R., & Gupta, S. (2009). *Security testing handbook for banking applications. Ely*. Cambridgeshire, UK: IT Governance Publishing.

ISECOM. (2008). *OSSTMM Lite: Introduction to the open source security testing methodology manual (3.0)*. New York, NY: Pete Herzog.

Kroeker, L. (2010). Engineering the web's third decade. *Communications of the ACM, 53*(3), 16–18. doi:10.1145/1666420.1666428

Mortman, D., Hutton, A., Dixon, J., & Crisp, D. (2009). *A Black Hat vulnerability risk assessment. Proceedings from Black Hat USA '09*. Las Vegas, NV: Black Hat Briefings.

Moyse, I. (2010, May 10). Securing Web 2.0. *Security Acts, 3*, 21–22.

Navarrete, C. (2010, February 15). Security testing: Automated or manual. *Security Acts, 2*, 20–21.

OISSG. (2006). *ISSAF: Information systems security assessment framework (draft 0.2.1A & 0.2.1B)*. Colorado Springs, CO: Rathore et al.

Shah, S. (2009). Application defense tactics and strategies: WAF at the gateway. *Proceedings from HITBSecConf '09*. Dubai, DB: HITB Security Conference Series.

Smith, V., Ames, C., & Delchi. (2009). Dissecting Web attacks. *Proceedings from Black Hat DC '09*. Crystal City, DC: Black Hat Briefings.

Wright, C. S. (2008). *The IT regulatory and standards compliance handbook: How to survive an information systems audit and assessments*. Burlington, MA: Syngress Publishing.

Zanero, S., & Criscione, C. (2009). *Masibty: An anomaly based intrusion prevention system for web applications. Proceedings from Black Hat Europe '09. Moevenpick*. Amsterdam, The Netherlands: Black Hat Briefings.

ADDITIONAL READING

Bagajewicz, J., & Thruaisingham. (2004). *Database and Applications Security: Integrating Information Security and Data Management.* Boca Raton, FL: CRC Press.

Barnett. (2009). *The Web Hacking Incident Database.* Retrieved May 5, 2010, from http://www.xiom.com/whid

Burns, G., Manzuik, G., & Killion, B. Biondi. (2007). *Security Power Tools.* Sebastopol, CA: O'Reilly Media.

Dowd, McDonald, & Schuh. (2006). *The Art of Software Security Assessment: Identifying and Preventing Software Vulnerabilities.* Boston, MA: Addison Wesley Professional.

Erlingsson, Livshits, & Xie. (2007). End-to-end web application security. *Proceedings of the 11th USENIX workshop on Hot topics in operating systems* (Article No: 18). Berkeley, CA: USENIX Association.

Ford, (Ed.). (2008). *Infosecurity 2008 Threat Analysis.* Burlington, MA: Syngress Publishing.

Foster, C. (2007). *Metasploit Toolkit for Penetration Testing, Exploit Development, and Vulnerability Research.* Burlington, MA: Syngress Publishing.

Grossman, H. Petkov, D., Rager, & Fogie. (2007). *XSS Attacks: Cross Site Scripting Exploits and Defense.* Burlington, MA: Syngress Publishing.

Hamiel, & Moyer. (2009). Proceedings from Black Hat USA '09: *Weaponizing the Web: More Attacks on User Generated Content.* Las Vegas, NV: Black Hat Briefings.

Harris, H. Eagle, & Ness. (2007). *Gray Hat Hacking: The Ethical Hacker's Handbook* (2nd ed.). New York, NY: McGraw-Hill Osborne.

Huang, Y., Tsai, Lin, Huang, S., Lee, & Kuo. (2005). A testing framework for Web application security assessment. *The International Journal of Computer and Telecommunications Networking,* *48*(5), 739–761.

Huang, Y., & Huang, S. Lin, & Tsai. (2003). Web application security assessment by fault injection and behavior monitoring. *Proceedings of the 12th international conference on World Wide Web. Session: Data integrity* (pp. 148-159). New York, NY: Association for Computing Machinery.

Liu, Holt, & Cheng. (2007). A Practical Vulnerability Assessment Program. *IT Professional,* *9*(6), 36–42. doi:10.1109/MITP.2007.105

Livshits, & Lam, S. (2005). Finding security vulnerabilities in java applications with static analysis. *Proceedings of the 14th conference on USENIX Security Symposium: Vol. 14.* (pp. 18-18). Baltimore, MD: USENIX Association.

McClure. Scambray, & Kurtz. (2009). *Hacking Exposed 6: Network Security Secrets and Solutions.* New York, NY: McGraw-Hill Osborne.

Nanda, Lam, & Chiueh. (2007). Dynamic multi-process information flow tracking for web application security. *Proceedings of the 2007 ACM/IFIP/USENIX international conference on Middleware companion. Session: Experience papers* (Article No: 19). New York, NY: Association for Computing Machinery.

Noureddine, A., & Damodaran. (2008). Security in web 2.0 application development. *Proceedings of the 10th International Conference on Information Integration and Web-based Applications and Services. Session: iiWAS 2008 and ERPAS 2008* (pp. 681-685). New York, NY: Association for Computing Machinery.

Peltier, R., & Peltier. (2002). *Managing a Network Vulnerability Assessment.* Boca Raton, FL: CRC Press.

Rasheed, & Chow, Y. C. (2009). Automated Risk Assessment for Sources and Targets of Vulnerability Exploitation. *Proceedings of the 2009 WRI World Congress on Computer Science and Information Engineering: Vol. 1.* (pp. 150-154). Washington, DC: IEEE Computer Society.

Rawat, & Saxena. (2009). Application security code analysis: a step towards software assurance. *International Journal of Information and Computer Security, 3*(1), 86-110.

Said, E., & Guimaraes, A. Maamar, & Jololian. (2009). Database and database application security. *Proceedings of the 14th annual ACM SIGCSE conference on Innovation and technology in computer science education. Session: Networking* (pp. 90-93). New York, NY: Association for Computing Machinery.

Shezaf. (2006). *Web Application Firewall Evaluation Criteria* (1.0) [PDF document]. Retrieved May 5, 2010, from http://projects.webappsec. org/f/wasc-wafec-v1.0.pdf

Stuttard, & Pinto. (2007). *The Web Application Hacker's Handbook: Discovering and Exploiting Security Flaws.* Indianapolis, IN: Wiley Publishing.

Sullivan. (2009). Proceedings from Black Hat USA '09: *Defensive URL Rewriting and Alternative Resource Locators.* Las Vegas, NV: Black Hat Briefings.

Thuraisingham. (2009). Data Mining for Malicious Code Detection and Security Applications. *Proceedings of the 2009 IEEE/WIC/ACM International Joint Conference on Web Intelligence and Intelligent Agent Technology: Vol. 2.* (pp. 6-7). Washington, DC: IEEE Computer Society.

Tryfonas, & Kearney. (2008). Standardising business application security assessments with pattern-driven audit automations. *Computer Standards & Interfaces, 30*(4), 262-270.

Ventuneac, Coffey, & Salomie. (2003). A policy-based security framework for Web-enabled applications. *Proceedings of the 1st international symposium on Information and communication technologies. Session: WWW applications* (pp. 487-492). Dublin, Ireland: Trinity College Dublin.

Walden, D. Welch, A., Whelan. (2009). Security of open source web applications. *Proceedings of the 2009 3rd International Symposium on Empirical Software Engineering and Measurement* (pp. 545-553). Washington, DC: IEEE Computer Society.

Walden. (2008). Integrating web application security into the IT curriculum. *Proceedings of the 9th ACM SIGITE conference on Information technology education. Session 2.5.1: integrating advanced topics II* (pp. 187-192). New York, NY: Association for Computing Machinery.

Wang, Y., Lively, M., & Simmons, B. (2009). Software security analysis and assessment model for the web-based applications. *Journal of Computational Methods in Sciences and Engineering, 9*(1), 179–189.

Whitaker, & Newman. (2005). *Penetration Testing and Cisco Network Defense.* Indianapolis, IN: Cisco Press.

KEY TERMS AND DEFINITIONS

Automated Exploitation: It is a process of exploiting the target vulnerabilities using the automated tools like Metasploit, Core impact and Canvas. It coordinates activities like penetrating the target, taking administrator privileges and maintaining the consistent access.

Edge Level Protection: The deployment strategy for network security system that filters all the external requests before allowing them to enter into a trusted zone. This could be an intrusion detection system, application firewall, or any other monitoring system. Usually these devices are employed at the edge of a network to filter internet traffic against malicious threats.

Enterprise Environment: The network infrastructure combining all the segments of IT systems and communication links. This includes components like application servers, firewalls, database management systems, routers, switches, backup storage, and other business platforms.

Layer-7: A part of OSI (Open System Interconnection) model which is divided into seven consecutive layers. Each layer represents different functionality and supports various methods and protocols that lay the foundation of network communication. Layer-7 or Application layer supports several protocols that help in process-to-process communication. These protocols include HTTP, DNS, FTP, SMTP and many more.

Malware: It is a kind of malicious software that is intended to harm, infiltrate or attack the computer systems. This term is collectively used for viruses, worms, trojans, bots and spywares.

Risk Assessment: The Risk assessment is a process to measure the effectiveness of organization security controls and provide quantitative or qualitative value of risk associated with each asset.

Spamming: Spam is a digital abuse of sending unsolicited bulk messages via email or newsgroups. This activity is accomplished by using automated application that is capable of sending thousands of messages to pre-defined recipients in a shorter period.

Threat Profile: A set of activities responsible for collecting information on target application environment. Such as application users, purpose of application, sensitive data involved, performing the desired actions and refinement of attack language that clearly states all the possible threats.

Vulnerability Assessment: A vulnerability assessment is a process to identify, quantify and prioritize the system vulnerabilities. The major steps include in this process are target scoping, enumeration, network assessment, compliance evaluation, and reporting.

Compilation of References

Abadi, M., & Needham, R. (1996). Prudent engineering practice for cryptographic protocols. *IEEE Transactions on Software Engineering, 22*, 122–136. doi:10.1109/32.481513

Abadi, M., & Rogaway, P. (2002). Reconciling two views of cryptography (The computational soundness of formal encryption). *Journal of Cryptology, 15*(2), 103–127.

Abadi, M., & Fournet, C. (2001). *Mobile values, new names, and secure communication*. In Symposium on Principles of Programming Languages (pp. 104-115).

Abadi, M., & Gordon, A. D. (1998). A calculus for cryptographic protocols: The Spi calculus. *Research Report 149*.

ABC. (2010, July 26). WikiLeaks reveals grim Afghan war realities. *ABC News*.

Adda, M., Valtchev, P., Missaoui, R., & Djeraba, C. (2007). Toward recommendation based on ontology-powered Web-usage mining. *IEEE Internet Computing, 11*(4), 45–52. doi:10.1109/MIC.2007.93

AFP. (2010, September 27). *Stuxnet worm rampaging through Iran*.

Agrawal, R., & Srikant, R. (1994). Fast algorithms for mining association rules in large databases. *Proceedings of 1994 Int. Conf. Very Large Data Bases (VLDB'94)*, (pp. 487-499), Santiago, Chile, Sept.

Agrawal, R., & Srikant, R. (1995). Mining sequential patterns. *Proc. 1995 Int. Conf. Data Engineering (ICDE'95)*, (pp. 3-14). Taipei, Taiwan.

Aguirre, S. J., & Hill, W. H. (1997). *Intrusion detection fly-off: Implications for the United States Navy*. (MITRE Technical Report MTR 97W096).

Aho, A. V., Lam, M. S., Sethi, R., & Ullman, J. D. (2006). *Compilers—Principles, techniques, and tools* (2nd ed.). Addison-Wesley.

Akyildiz, I., & Wang, X. (2009). *Wireless mesh networks*. West Sussex, UK: Wiley and Sons. doi:10.1002/9780470059616

Alba, M. (1988). *A system approach to smart sensors and smart actuator design*. (SAE paper 880554).

Albrecht, M. R., Watson, G. J., & Paterson, K. G. (2009). *Plaintext recovery attacks against SSH*. In IEEE Symposium on Security and Privacy (pp. 16-26).

Alghamdi, A. S. (2009). Evaluating defense architecture frameworks for C4I system using analytic hierarchy process. *Journal of Computer Science, 5*(12), 1078-1084ISSN 1549-3636

Alkabani, Y., & Koushanfar, F. (2008, July). Extended abstract: Designer's hardware trojan horse. In *Proceedings of IEEE International Workshop on Hardware-Oriented Security and Trust*, HOST 2008, (pp. 82-83). Washington, DC: IEEE Computer Society.

All Facebook. (2010). *Facebook application leaderboard*. Retrieved September 2010, from http://statistics.allfacebook.com/applications/leaderboard/

American Gas Association (AGA). (2006). *Cryptographic protection of SCADA communications part 1: Background, policies and test plan (AGA12, Part1)*. Retrieved from http://www.aga.org/NR/rdonlyres/B797B50B-616B-46A4-9E0F-5DC877563A0F/0/0603AGAREPORT12.PDF

American Petroleum Institute. (API). (2007). *Developing a pipeline supervisory control center*. (API Publication No. RP 1113). Washington, DC: American Petroleum Institute.

American Petroleum Institute. (API). (2009). *Pipeline SCADA security.* (API Publication No. API-1164). Washington, DC: American Petroleum Institute.

Amini, F., Mišic, V. B., & Mišic, J. (2007). Intrusion detection in wireless sensor networks. In Y. Xiao (Ed.), *Security in distributed, grid, and pervasive computing* (pp. 112-127). Boca Raton, FL: Auerbach Publications, CRC Press.

Anantvalee, T., & Wu, J. (2007). A survey on intrusion detection in mobile ad hoc networks. In Xiao, Y., Shen, X. S., & Du, D.-Z. (Eds.), *Wireless network security* (pp. 19–78). Springer, US. doi:10.1007/978-0-387-33112-6_7

Andreu, A. (2006). *Professional pen testing for web applications.* Indianapolis, IN: Wiley Publishing.

ANS/IEEE, C37.1. (1987). Definition, specification, and analysis of systems used for supervisory control and data acquisition, and automatic control.

Ante, S. (2010). *Dark side arises for phone apps.* Retrieved June 3, 2010, from http://online.wsj.com/article/SB10001424052748703340904575284532175834088.html

Anthony, H. D. (2002). *C4ISR architectures, social network analysis and the FINC methodology: An experiment in military organizational structure.* Information Technology Division, Electronics and Surveillance Research Laboratory-DSTO-GD-0313.

APEC. (2008). *Guide on policy and technical approaches against botnet.* Lima, Peru.

Arapinis, M., Delaune, S., & Kremer, S. (2008). From one session to many: Dynamic tags for security protocols. In *Logic for Programming* (pp. 128–142). Artificial Intelligence, and Reasoning.

Arbor Networks. (2010). *Peakflow SP & Peakflow-X.* Retrieved from http://www.arbornetworks.com/peakflowsp, http://www.arbornetworks.com/peakflowx

Argyroudis, P. G., Verma, R., Tewari, H., & D'Mahony, O. (2004). Performance analysis of cryptographic protocols on handheld devices. *Proc. 3rd IEEE Int. Symposium on Network Computing and Applications,* (pp. 169-174). Cambridge, Massachusetts.

AusCERT. (2002). Increased intruder attacks against servers to expand illegal file sharing networks. (Advisory AA-2002.03). Retrieved March 27, 2010, from http://www.auscert.org.au/render.html?it=2229&cid=1

Axelsson, S. (1999). *Research in intrusion-detection systems: A survey. Technical Report.* Goteborg, Sweden: Chalmers University of Technology.

Bace, R., & Mell, P. (2001). *Guide to intrusion detection and prevention systems (IDPS)* (pp. 1–127). National Institue of Standards Special Publication on Intrusion Detection Systems.

Bacioccola, A., Cicconetti, C., Eklund, C., Lenzini, L., Li, Z., & Mingozzi, E. (2010). IEEE 802.16: History, status and future trends. *Computer Communications, 33*(2), 113–123. doi:10.1016/j.comcom.2009.11.003

BAE. (2009). *DataSync Guard 4.0 data transfers across multiple domains with flexibility and uncompromised security systems.* BAE Systems.

Baeza-Yates, R. A., & Gonnet, G. H. (1992, October). A new approach to text search. *Communications of the ACM, 35*(10), 74–82. doi:10.1145/135239.135243

Bagajewicz, J., & Thruaisingham. (2004). *Database and Applications Security: Integrating Information Security and Data Management.* Boca Raton, FL: CRC Press.

Bailey, M., Cooke, E., Jahanian, F., Xu, Y., & Karir, M. (2009). A survey of botnet technology and defenses. Paper presented at the 2009 Cybersecurity Applications \& Technology Conference for Homeland Security.

Barnett, C. (2009). *WAF virtual patching challenge: Securing WebGoat with ModSecurity. Proceedings from Black Hat DC '09.* Crystal City, DC: Black Hat Briefings.

Barnett. (2009). *The Web Hacking Incident Database.* Retrieved May 5, 2010, from http://www.xiom.com/whid

Baronti, P., Pillai, P., Chook, V. W. C., Chessa, S., Gotta, A., & Hu, Y. F. (2007). Wireless sensor networks: A survey on the state of the art and the 802.15.4 and ZigBee standards. *Computer Communications, 30*(7), 1655–1695. doi:10.1016/j.comcom.2006.12.020

Barry, B. I. A., & Chan, H. A. (2010). Intrusion detection systems. In Stavroulakis, P., & Stamp, M. (Eds.), *Handbook of information and communication security* (pp. 193–205). Berlin, Germany: Springer-Verlag. doi:10.1007/978-3-642-04117-4_10

Barry, B. I. A. (2009). Intrusion detection with OMNeT++. In *Proceedings of the 2nd International Conference on Simulation Tools and Techniques*.

Basin, D. A., Mödersheim, S., & Viganò, L. (2005). OFMC: A symbolic model checker for security protocols. *International Journal of Information Security*, *4*(3), 181–208. doi:10.1007/s10207-004-0055-7

Bellovin, S. M., Benzel, T. V., Blakley, B., Denning, D. E., Diffie, W., Epstein, J., & Verissimo, P. (2008). Information assurance technology forecast 2008. *IEEE Security and Privacy*, *6*(1), 16–23. doi:10.1109/MSP.2008.13

Bengtson, J., Bhargavan, K., Fournet, C., Gordon, A. D., & Maffeis, S. (2008). *Refinement types for secure implementations*. In IEEE Computer Security Foundations Symposium (pp. 17-32).

Bennett, C. H. (1992). Quantum cryptography using any two nonorthogonal states. *Physical Review Letters*, *68*(21), 3121–3124. doi:10.1103/PhysRevLett.68.3121

Bennett, C. H., Bessette, F., Brassard, G., Salvail, L., & Smolin, J. (1992). Experimental quantum cryptography. *Journal of Cryptology*, *5*(1), 3–28. doi:10.1007/BF00191318

Bennett, C. H., & Brassard, G. (1989). The dawn of a new era for quantum cryptography: The experimental prototype is working. *SIGACT News*, *20*(4), 78. doi:10.1145/74074.74087

Bennett, C. H., Brassard, G., Breidbart, S., & Wiesner, S. (1982). *Quantum cryptography or unforgettable subway tokens. Advances in Cryptography: Proceeding of Crypto '82* (pp. 267–275). New York, NY: Plenum.

Bennett, C. H., Brassard, G., Crépeau, C., & Maurer, U. M. (1995). Generalized privacy amplification. *IEEE Transactions on Information Theory*, *41*(6), 1915. doi:10.1109/18.476316

Bennett, C. H., Brassard, G., & Robert, J.-M. (1988). Privacy amplification by public discussion. *Society for Industrial and Applied Mathematics Journal on Computing*, *17*(2), 210–229.

Bennett, C. H., Mor, T., & Smolin, J. A. (1996). The parity bit in quantum cryptography. *Physical Review A.*, *54*(4), 2675–2684. doi:10.1103/PhysRevA.54.2675

Bennett, C. H., & Brassard, G. (1984). Quantum cryptography: Public key distribution and coin tossing. *Proceedings of IEEE International Conference on Computers, Systems, and Signal Processing, Bangalore* (p. 175). New York, NY: IEEE.

Berg, M., & Stamp, J. (2005). *A reference model for control and automation systems in electric power*. Sandia National Laboratories. Retrieved from http://www.sandia. gov/scada/documents/sand_2005_1000C.pdf

Bergstrand, P., Borryd, K., Lindmark, S., & Slama, A. (2009). Botnets: Hijacked computers in Sweden (No. *PTS-ER, 2009*, 11.

Bhargavan, K., Fournet, C., & Gordon, A. D. (2006). *Verified reference implementations of WS-Security protocols*. In Web Services and Formal Methods (pp. 88-106).

Bhargavan, K., Fournet, C., & Gordon, A. D. (2010). *Modular verification of security protocol code by typing*. In Symposium on Principles of Programming Languages (pp. 445-456).

Bhargavan, K., Fournet, C., Gordon, A. D., & Tse, S. (2006). *Verified interoperable implementations of security protocols*. In Computer Security Foundations Workshop (pp. 139-152).

Bhuse, V., & Gupta, A. (2006). Anomaly intrusion detection in wireless sensor networks. *Journal of High Speed Networks*, *5*, 33–51.

Biham, E., & Shamir, A. (1997). Differential fault analysis of secret key cryptosystems. In *Proceedings of the 17th Annual International Cryptology Conference on Advances in Cryptology, 1294*, (pp. 513-525). London, UK: Springer-Verlag.

Blanchet, B. (2008). A computationally sound mechanized prover for security protocols. *IEEE Transactions on Dependable and Secure Computing*, *5*(4), 193–207. doi:10.1109/TDSC.2007.1005

Blanchet, B. (2009). Automatic verification of correspondences for security protocols. *Journal of Computer Security*, *17*(4), 363–434.

Blanchet, B. (2001). *An efficient cryptographic protocol verifier based on prolog rules*. In IEEE Computer Security Foundations Workshop (pp. 82-96).

Boneh, D., DeMillo, R. A., & Lipton, R. J. (1997). On the importance of checking cryptographic protocols for faults. In *Proceedings of the 16th Annual International Conference on Theory and Application of Cryptographic Techniques*, (pp. 37-51). Berlin, Germany: Springer-Verlag.

Bonvillain, D., Mehta, N., Miller, J., & Wheeler, A. (2009). *Cutting through the hype: An analysis of application testing methodologies, their effectiveness and the corporate illusion of security. Proceedings from Black Hat Europe '09. Moevenpick*. Amsterdam, The Netherlands: Black Hat Briefings.

BookRags. (2010). *Research*. Retrieved January 12, 2010, from http://www.bookrags.com/research/aqueduct-woi/

Bort, J. (2007). How big is the botnet problem? Network World. Retrieved March 27, 2010, from http://www.networkworld.com/research/2007/070607-botnets-side.html

Boyd, D. (2010). *Why privacy is not dead*. Retrieved September 2010, from http://www.technologyreview.com/web/26000/

Brackin, S. (1998). *Evaluating and improving protocol analysis by automatic proof*. In IEEE Computer Security Foundations Workshop (pp. 138-152).

Brehmer, B. (2010). Command and control as design. *Proceedings of the 15th International Command and Control Research and Technology Symposium*, Santa Monica, California.

Bresson, E., Chevassut, O., & Pointcheval, D. (2007). Provably secure authenticated group Diffie-Hellman key exchange. [TISSEC]. *ACM Transactions on Information and System Security*, *10*(3). doi:10.1145/1266977.1266979

Breuer, M. A. (1973, March). Testing for intermittent faults in digital circuits. *IEEE Transactions on Computers*, *22*(3), 241–246. doi:10.1109/T-C.1973.223701

Brier, E., Clavier, C., & Oliver, F. (2004). Correlation power analysis with a leakage model. In *Proceedings of Cryptographic Hardware and Embedded Systems–LNCS 3156*, (pp. 135-152). Springer-Verlag.

Brown, T. (2005, Jun./Jul.). Security in SCADA systems: How to handle the growing menace to process automation. *IEE Comp. and Control Eng.*, *16*(3), 42–47. doi:10.1049/cce:20050306

Burmester, M., & de Medeiros, B. (2009). On the security of route discovery in MANETs. *IEEE Transactions on Mobile Computing*, *8*(9), 1180–1188. doi:10.1109/TMC.2009.13

Burns, G., Manzuik, G., & Killion, B. Biondi. (2007). *Security Power Tools*. Sebastopol, CA: O'Reilly Media.

Burrows, M., Abadi, M., & Needham, R. (1990). A logic of authentication. *ACM Transactions on Computer Systems*, *8*(1), 18–36. doi:10.1145/77648.77649

Callegari, C., Giordano, S., & Pagano, M. (2009). New statistical approaches for anomaly detection. *Security and Communication Networks*, *2*(6), 611–634.

Canadian Standards Association (CSA). (2008). *Security management for petroleum and natural gas industry systems, Z246.1*. Retrieved from http://www.shopcsa.ca/onlinestore/GetCatalogDrillDown.asp?Parent=4937

Canavan, J. (2005). The evolution of malicious IRC bots.

Cannings, R., Dwivedi, H., & Lackey, Z. (2007). *Hacking exposed Web 2.0: Web 2.0 security secrets and solutions*. New York, NY: McGraw-Hill Osborne.

Cao, G., Zhang, W., & Zhu, S. (Eds.). (2009). Special issue on privacy and security in wireless sensor and ad hoc networks. *Ad Hoc Networks*, *7*(8), 1431–1576. doi:10.1016/j.adhoc.2009.05.001

Cardenas, A. A., Roosta, T., & Sastry, S. (2009). Rethinking security properties, threat models, and the design space in sensor networks: A case study in SCADA systems. *Ad Hoc Networks*, *7*(8), 1434–1447. doi:10.1016/j.adhoc.2009.04.012

Carlsen, U. (1994). *Cryptographic protocol flaws: Know your enemy*. In IEEE Computer Security Foundations Workshop (pp. 192-200).

Carvalho, M. (2008). Security in mobile ad hoc networks. *IEEE Privacy and Security, 6*(2), 72–75. doi:10.1109/MSP.2008.44

CBS. (2010, July 26). Wikileaks publishes Afghan War secret article. *CBS News.*

Center for Strategic and International Studies (CSIS). (2008). *Securing cyberspace for the 44th presidency: A report of the CSIS Commission on Cybersecurity for the 44th Presidency.* Washington, DC: Government Printing Office.

CERT Coordination Center. (2006). List of CSIRTs with national responsibility. Retrieved from http://www.cert.org/csirts/national/contact.html

Chen, L., & Leneutre, J. (2009). A game theoretical framework on intrusion detection in heterogeneous networks. *IEEE Transaction on Information Forensics and Security, 4*(2), 165–178. doi:10.1109/TIFS.2009.2019154

Chen, R.-C., Hsieh, C.-F., & Huang, Y.-F. (2010). An isolation intrusion detection system for hierarchical wireless sensor networks. *Journal of Networks, 5*(3), 335–342.

Chen, S., & Tang, Y. (2004). *Slowing down internet worms.* IEEE ICDCS.

Chen, L., Pearson, S., & Vamvakas, A. (2000). *On enhancing biometric authentication with data protection.* Fourth International Conference on Knowledge –Based Intelligent Engineering System and Allied Technologies, Brighton, UK.

Chen, Q., Su, K., Liu, C., & Xiao, Y. (2010). *Automatic verification of web service protocols for epistemic specifications under Dolev-Yao model.* In International Conference on Service Sciences (pp. 49-54).

Cisco. (2009). Cisco ASA botnet traffic filter. Retrieved March 27, 2010, from http://www.cisco.com/en/US/prod/vpndevc/ps6032/ps6094/ps6120/botnet_index.html

Cisco. (2009). Infiltrating a botnet. Retrieved March 27, 2010, from http://www.cisco.com/web/about/security/intelligence/bots.html

Cisco. (2010). *IOS flexible network flow.* Retrieved from http://www.cisco.com/go/netflow

Clark, A. (1990). *Do you really know who is using your system?* Technology of Software Protection Specialist Group.

Clark, J., Leblanc, S., & Knight, S. (in press). Compromise through USB-based hardware trojan horse device. *International Journal of Future Generation Computer Systems, 27*(5). Elsevier B.V.

Clark, J., & Jacob, J. (1997). *A survey of authentication protocol literature: Version 1.0* (Technical Report).

Cluley, G. (2010). *How to protect yourself from Facebook Places.* Retrieved September 17, 2010, from http://www.sophos.com/blogs/gc/g/2010/09/17/protect-facebook-places/

Cluley, G. (2010). *Twitter "onmouseover" security flaw widely exploited.* Retrieved September 21, 2010, from http://www.sophos.com/blogs/gc/g/2010/09/21/twitter-onmouseover-security-flaw-widely-exploited/

CNet News. (Jan 2010). InSecurity complex, Behind the China attacks on Google (FAQ). Retrieved from http://news.cnet.com/8301-27080_3-10434721-245.html?tag=mncol;txt

CNSS. (2007). Committee on National Security Systems. *CNSS Policy, 19.*

CNSS. (2010, April 26). *National information assurance glossary.* Committee on National Security Systems. Instruction CNSSI-4009 dated 26 April 2010.

Cole, A., Mellor, M., & Noyes, D. (2007). Botnets: The rise of the machines. Paper presented at the 6th Annual Security Research Associates Spring Growth Conference.

Common Criteria. (2009). *Information Technology security evaluation and the common methodology for Information Technology security evaluation.* Retrieved from http://ww.commoncriteriaportal.org/index.html

Common Malware Enumeration (CME). (2007). Data list. Retrieved from http://cme.mitre.org/data/list.html

Comon, H., & Shmatikov, V. (2002). Is it possible to decide whether a cryptographic protocol is secure or not? *Journal of Telecommunications and Information Technology, 4*, 5–15.

Comon-Lundh, H., & Cortier, V. (2008). *Computational soundness of observational equivalence.* In ACM Conference on Computer and Communications Security (pp. 109-118).

Cooke, E., Jahanian, F., & Mcpherson, D. (2005). The zombie roundup: Understanding, detecting, and disrupting botnets. In Workshop on Steps to Reducing Unwanted Traffic on the Internet (SRUTI), (pp. 39–44).

Corner, M. D., & Noble, B. D. (2002). Zero interaction authentication. In *Proceeding of the ACM International Conference on Mobile Computing and Communications* (MOBICOM'02), Atlanta, Georgia, USA.

Corner, M. D., & Noble, B. D. (2002). *Protecting applications with transient authentication.* MOBICOM'02, Atlanta, Georgia, USA.

Cortier, V., & Delaune, S. (2009). Safely composing security protocols. *Formal Methods in System Design, 34*(1), 1–36. doi:10.1007/s10703-008-0059-4

Cranton, T. (2010). Cracking down on botnets. Retrieved March 27, 2010, from http://microsoftontheissues.com/cs/blogs/mscorp/archive/2010/02/24/cracking-down-on-botnets.aspx

Cremers, C. J. F. (2006). *Feasibility of multi-protocol attacks* (pp. 287–294). In Availability, Reliability and Security.

Creti, M. T., Beaman, M., Bagchi, S., Li, Z., & Lu, Y.-H. (2009). Multigrade security monitoring for ad-hoc wireless networks. In *Proceedings of the 6th IEEE International Conference on Mobile Ad-hoc and Sensor Systems.*

Cross, M., Palmer, S., Kapinos, S., Petkov, P. D., Meer, H., & Shields, R. ... Temmingh, R. (2007). *Web application vulnerabilities: Detect, exploit, prevent.* Burlington, MA: Syngress Publishing.

Cui, W., Katz, R. H., & Tan, W.-T. (2005, April). *BINDER: An extrusion-based break-in detector for personal computers.* Usenix Security Symposium.

CWID. (2009a). *Assessment brief-Top performing technologies. Coalition Warrior Interoperability Demonstration (CWID).* Hampton, VA: JMO.

CWID. (2009b). *Assessment brief – Interoperability trials. Coalition Warrior Interoperability Demonstration (CWID).* Hampton, VA: JMO.

Dagon, D., Gu, G., Zou, C., Grizzard, J., Dwivedi, S., Lee, W., et al. (2005). A taxonomy of botnets. Paper presented at the CAIDA DNS-OARC Workshop.

De, P., Liu, Y., & Das, S. K. (2009). Deployment-aware modeling of node compromise spread in wireless sensor networks using epidemic theory. *ACM Transactions on Sensor Networks, 5*(3), 1–33. doi:10.1145/1525856.1525861

De Mulder, E., Buysschaert, P., Ors, S. B., Delmotte, P., Preneel, B., Vandenbosch, G., & Verbauwhede, I. (2005). Electromagnetic analysis attack on an FPGA implementation of an elliptic curve cryptosystem. In *Proceedings of the IEEE International Conference on Computer as a Tool.* EUROCON 2005, (pp. 1879-1882).

Debar, H., Dacier, M., Wespi, A., & Lampart, S. (1998). *A workbench for intrusion detection systems.* IBM Zurich Research Laboratory.

Denmac Systems, Inc. (1999). *Network based intrusion detection: A review of technologies.*

Denning, D. E. (1987). An intrusion detection model. *IEEE Transactions on Software Engineering, 13*(2), 222–232. doi:10.1109/TSE.1987.232894

Department of Homeland Security (DHS). (2009). *Strategy for securing control systems: Coordinating and guiding federal, state and private sector initiatives.* Retrieved from http://www.us-cert.gov/control_systems/pdf/Strategy%20for%20Securing%20Control%20Systems.pdf

Ding, X., Mazzocchi, D., & Tsudik, G. (2007). Equipping smart devices with public key signatures. *ACM Transactions on Internet Technology, 7*(1). doi:10.1145/1189740.1189743

DKIM. (2009). DomainKeys identified mail (DKIM). Retrieved March 27, 2010, from http://www.dkim.org/

Dolev, D., & Yao, A. C.-C. (1983). On the security of public key protocols. *IEEE Transactions on Information Theory, 29*(2), 198–207. doi:10.1109/TIT.1983.1056650

Doraiswamy, A., Pakala, S., Kapoor, N., Verma, P., Singh, P., Nair, R., & Gupta, S. (2009). *Security testing handbook for banking applications. Ely.* Cambridgeshire, UK: IT Governance Publishing.

Dowd, McDonald, & Schuh. (2006). *The Art of Software Security Assessment: Identifying and Preventing Software Vulnerabilities.* Boston, MA: Addison Wesley Professional.

Drapeau, M., & Wells, L. (2009). *Social software and security: An initial net assessment.* Washington, DC: Center for Technology and National Security Policy, National Defense University.

Du, J., & Peng, S. (2009). Choice of Secure routing protocol for applications in wireless sensor networks. In. *Proceedings of the International Conference on Multimedia Information Networking and Security, 2,* 470–473. doi:10.1109/MINES.2009.14

DuMouchel, W. (1999). *Computer intrusion detection based on Bayes factors for comparing command transition probabilities.* Tech. Rep. 91, National Institute of Statistical Sciences.

Durante, L., Sisto, R., & Valenzano, A. (2003). Automatic testing equivalence verification of Spi calculus specifications. *ACM Transactions on Software Engineering and Methodology, 12*(2), 222–284. doi:10.1145/941566.941570

Durgin, N. A., Lincoln, P., & Mitchell, J. C. (2004). Multiset rewriting and the complexity of bounded security protocols. *Journal of Computer Security, 12*(2), 247–311.

Durst, R., Champion, T., Witten, B., Miller, E., & Spagnuolo, L. (1999). Testing and evaluating computer intrusion detection systems. *Communications of the ACM, 42*(7), 53–61. doi:10.1145/306549.306571

Dwyer, C., Hiltz, S. R., Poole, M. S., Gussner, J., Hennig, F., & Osswald, S. … Warth, B. (2010). *Developing reliable measures of privacy management within social networking sites.* 43rd Hawaii International Conference on System Sciences, (pp. 1-10).

Eirinaki, M., & Vazirgiannis, M. (2003, February). Web mining for Web personalization. *ACM Transactions on Internet Technology, 3*(1), 1–27. doi:10.1145/643477.643478

Ericsson. (2006). *C4ISR for network-oriented defense.* Ericsson White Paper. Retrieved from http://www.ericsson.com/technology/whitepapers

Erlingsson, Livshits, & Xie. (2007). End-to-end web application security. *Proceedings of the 11th USENIX workshop on Hot topics in operating systems* (Article No: 18). Berkeley, CA: USENIX Association.

Escobar, S., Meadows, C., & Meseguer, J. (2009). *Maude-NPA: cryptographic protocol analysis modulo equational properties.* In Foundations of Security Analysis and Design (pp. 1-50).

ESISAC. (2010). *Electronic security guide.* Retrieved from http://www.esisac.com/publicdocs/Guides/SecGuide_ElectronicSec_BOTapprvd3may05.pdf

EU. (2008). About European Union. Retrieved March 27, 2010, from http://europa.eu/index_en.htm

Evans, A., & Kantrowitz, W. (1994). *A user authentication schema not requiring secrecy in the computer.* ACM Annual Conf. M.I.T. Lincoln Laboratory and Edwin Weiss Boston University.

Fábrega, F. J. T., Herzog, J. C., & Guttman, J. D. (1999). Strand spaces: Proving security protocols correct. *Journal of Computer Security, 7*(2/3), 191–230.

Facbook. (2010). *Privacy policy.* Retrieved September 2010, from http://www.facebook.com/privacy/explanation.php#!/policy.php

Facebook. (2010). *Developers.* Retrieved September 2010, from http://developers.facebook.com/

Falco, J., Stouffer, S., Wavering, A., & Proctor, F. (2002). *IT security for industrial control.* MD: Gaithersburg.

Farooqi, A. S., & Khan, F. A. (2009). Intrusion detection systems for wireless sensor networks: a survey. In Ślęzak, D. (Eds.), *Communication and networking* (pp. 234–241). Berlin, Germany: Springer-Verlag. doi:10.1007/978-3-642-10844-0_29

Farrell, N. (2007, November). Seagate hard drives turn into spy machines. *The Inquirer.*

Fawcett, T. (2005). *An introduction to ROC analysis.* Elsevier.

Fawcett, T. (2004). *ROC graphs: Notes and practical considerations for researchers.* HP Laboratories Technical Report, Palo Alto, USA.

Ford, (Ed.). (2008). *Infosecurity 2008 Threat Analysis.* Burlington, MA: Syngress Publishing.

Foster, C. (2007). *Metasploit Toolkit for Penetration Testing, Exploit Development, and Vulnerability Research.* Burlington, MA: Syngress Publishing.

freed0. (2007). ASN/GeoLoc reports and what to do about them. Retrieved March 27, 2010, from http://www.shadowserver.org/wiki/pmwiki.php/Calendar/20070111

F-Secure. (2009). Email-Worm: W32/Waledac.A. Retrieved March 27, 2010, from http://www.f-secure.com/v-descs/email-worm_w32_waledac_a.shtml

F-Secure. (2009). Mydoom.M. Retrieved April 07, 2010, from http://www.f-secure.com/v-descs/mydoom_m.shtml

Fung, C.-H., Tamaki, K., & Lo, H.-K. (2006). Performance of two quantum key distribution protocols. *Physical Review A., 73*(1), 012337. doi:10.1103/PhysRevA.73.012337

Gandhi, M., Jakobsson, M., & Ratkiewicz, J. (2006). Badvertisements: Stealthy click-fraud with unwitting accessories. *Journal of Digital Forensic Practice, 1*(2). doi:10.1080/15567280601015598

Ganger, G., Economou, G., & Bielski, S. (2002). Self-securing network interfaces: What, why, and how. (Carnegie Mellon University Technical Report, CMU-CS-02-144).

Garcia-Teodoro, P., Diaz-Verdejo, J., Macia-Fernandez, G., & Vazquez, E. (2009). Anomaly-based network intrusion detection: Techniques, systems and challenges. *Computers & Security, 28*(1-2), 18–28. doi:10.1016/j.cose.2008.08.003

Gast, M. S. (2005). *802.11 wireless networks: The definitive guide* (2nd ed.). Sebastopol, CA: O'Reilly Media.

Gates, G. (2010). *Facebook privacy: A bewildering tangle of options.* Retrieved May 12, 2010, from http://www.nytimes.com/interactive/2010/05/12/business/facebook-privacy.html

Ghosh, A. K., & Swaminatha, T. M. (2001). Software security and privacy risks in mobile e-commerce. *Communications of the ACM, 44*(2), 51–57. doi:10.1145/359205.359227

Giannetous, T., Kromtiris, I., & Dimitriou, T. (2009). Intrusion detection in wireless sensor networks. In Y. Zhang, & P. Kitsos (Ed.), *Security in RFID and sensor networks* (pp. 321-341). Boca Raton, FL: Auerbach Publications, CRC Press. Jackson, K. (1999). *Intrusion detection system product survey.* (Laboratory Research Report, LA-UR-99-3883). Los Alamos National Laboratory.

Giordano, S. (2002). Mobile ad hoc networks. In Stojmenovic, J. (Ed.), *Handbook of wireless networks and mobile computing* (pp. 325–346). New York, NY: John Wiley & Sons, Inc. doi:10.1002/0471224561.ch15

Gobby, C., Yuan, Z., & Shields, A. (2004). Quantum key distribution over 122 km of standard telecom fiber. *Physical Review Letters, 84*(19), 3762–3764.

Godwin, B., et al. (2008). *Social media and the federal government: Perceived and real barriers and potential solutions.* Retrieved December 23, 2008, from http://www.usa.gov/webcontent/documents/SocialMediaFed%20Govt_BarriersPotentialSolutions.pdf

Gottesman, D., Lo, H.-K., Lütkenhaus, N., & Preskill, J. (2004). Security of quantum key distribution with imperfect devices. *Quantum Information and Computation, 4*(5), 325–360.

Goubault-Larrecq, J., & Parrennes, F. (2005). *Cryptographic protocol analysis on Real C Code* (pp. 363–379). In Verification, Model Checking, and Abstract Interpretation.

Green, J., Marchette, D., Northcutt, S., & Ralph, B. (1999). Analysis techniques for detecting coordinated attacks and probes. Paper presented at the Intrusion Detection and Network Monitoring, Santa Clara, California, USA.

Gritzalis, S., Spinellis, D., & Sa, S. (1997). *Cryptographic protocols over open distributed systems: A taxonomy of flaws and related protocol analysis tools.* In International Conference on Computer Safety, Reliability and Security (pp. 123-137).

Grossman, H. Petkov, D., Rager, & Fogie. (2007). *XSS Attacks: Cross Site Scripting Exploits and Defense*. Burlington, MA: Syngress Publishing.

Gu, G. (2008). Correlation-based botnet detection in enterprise networks. Unpublished Dissertation, Georgia Institute of Technology, Georgia.

Gu, Y., McCullum, A., & Towsley, D. (2005). *Detecting anomalies in network traffic using maximum entropy estimation*. ACM/Usenix Internet Measurement Conference (IMC).

Gu, Y., Shen, Z., & Xue, D. (2009). *A game-theoretic model for analyzing fair exchange protocols*. In International Symposium on Electronic Commerce and Security (pp. 509-513).

Gupta, S. (1995). *CAN facilities in vehicle networking* (pp. 9-16). (SAE paper 900695).

Hamiel, & Moyer. (2009). Proceedings from Black Hat USA '09: *Weaponizing the Web: More Attacks on User Generated Content*. Las Vegas, NV: Black Hat Briefings.

Han, Y., Zou, X., Liu, Z., & Chen, Y. (2008). Efficient DPA attacks on AES hardware implementations. *International Journal of Communications. Network and System Sciences, 1*, 1–103.

Hardjono, T., & Seberry, J. (2002). *Information security issues in mobile computing*. Australia.

Hariri, S. (1991, May). A hierarchical modeling of availability in distributed systems. *Proceedings International Conference on Distributed Systems*, (pp. 190-197).

Harris, H. Eagle, & Ness. (2007). *Gray Hat Hacking: The Ethical Hacker's Handbook* (2nd ed.). New York, NY: McGraw-Hill Osborne.

Hazen, T. J., Weinstein, E., & Park, A. (2003). Towards robust person recognition on handheld devices using face and speaker identification technologies. *Proc. 5th Int. Conf. Multimodal Interfaces*, (pp. 289-292). Vancouver, British Columbia, Canada.

Hewlett-Packard Development Company. L.P. (2005). *Wireless security*. Retrieved January 12, 2010, from http://h20331.www2.hp.com/Hpsub/downloads/Wireless_Security_rev2.pdf

Hirschberg, D. S. (1977). Algorithms for the longest common subsequence problem. *Journal of the ACM, 24*(4), 664–675. doi:10.1145/322033.322044

Honeynet Project. (2005). Know your enemy: GenII honeynets. Retrieved from http://old.honeynet.org/papers/gen2/

Honeynet Project. (2006). Know your enemy: Honeynets. Retrieved March 27, 2010, from http://old.honeynet.org/papers/honeynet/

Hu, W.-C., Yeh, J.-h., Chu, H.-J., & Lee, C.-w. (2005). Internet-enabled mobile handheld devices for mobile commerce. *Contemporary Management Research, 1*(1), 13–34.

Hu, W.-C., Yang, H.-J., Lee, C.-w., & Yeh, J.-h. (2005). World Wide Web usage mining. In Wang, J. (Ed.), *Encyclopedia of data warehousing and mining* (pp. 1242–1248). Hershey, PA: Information Science Reference. doi:10.4018/978-1-59140-557-3.ch234

Hu, W.-C., Ritter, G., & Schmalz, M. (1998, April 1-3). Approximating the longest approximate common subsequence problem. *Proceedings of the 36th Annual Southeast Conference*, (pp. 166-172). Marietta, Georgia.

Huang, Y., Tsai, Lin, Huang, S., Lee, & Kuo. (2005). A testing framework for Web application security assessment. *The International Journal of Computer and Telecommunications Networking, 48*(5), 739–761.

Huang, Y., & Huang, S. Lin, & Tsai. (2003). Web application security assessment by fault injection and behavior monitoring. *Proceedings of the 12th international conference on World Wide Web. Session: Data integrity* (pp. 148-159). New York, NY: Association for Computing Machinery.

Hui, M. L., & Lowe, G. (2001). Fault-preserving simplifying transformations for security protocols. *Journal of Computer Security, 9*(1/2), 3–46.

Huima, A. (1999). *Efficient infinite-state analysis of security protocols*. In Workshop on Formal Methods and Security Protocols.

Hwang, W.-Y. (2003). Quantum key distribution with high loss: Toward global secure communication. *Physical Review Letters, 91*(5), 057901. doi:10.1103/PhysRevLett.91.057901

IAB. (2008). IAB documents and current activities. Retrieved March 27, 2010, from http://www.iab.org/documents/index.html

IATAC. (2010). *Mission of Information Assurance Technology Analysis Center* (IATAC). Retrieved from http://iac.dtic.mil/iatac/mission.html

Iclink. (2010). *Products*. Retrieved from http://www.iclinks.com/Products/Rtu/ICL4150.html

Idaho National Laboratory (INL). (2005), *A comparison of cross-sector cyber security standards*, Robert P. Evans. (Report No. INL/EXT-05-00656). Idaho Falls, ID.

IEEE. (1987). *Fundamentals of supervisory systems*. (IEEE Tutorial No. 91 EH-03376PWR).

IEEE. (2000). *IEEE recommended practice for data communications between remote terminal units and intelligent electronic devices in a substation*. (IEEE Std 1379-2000. Revision of IEEE Std 1379-1997).

IET. (2005). The celebrated maroochy water attack. *Computing & Control Engineering Journal*, *16*(6), 24–25.

IETF. (2010). Operational security capabilities for IP network infrastructure (OPSEC). Retrieved March 27, 2010, from http://datatracker.ietf.org/wg/opsec/charter/

IFF. (2010). *Identification of friend & foe, questions and answers*. Retrieved from http://www.dean-boys.com/extras/iff/iffqa.html.

Ilgun, K., Kemmerer, R. A., & Porras, P. A. (1995, March). State transition analysis: A rulebased intrusion detection approach. *IEEE Transactions on Software Engineering*, *21*(3), 181–199. doi:10.1109/32.372146

Inamori, H., Lutkenhaus, N., & Mayers, D. (2001). *Unconditional security of practical quantum key distribution*.

Ingham, K. L., & Inoue, H. (2007). *Comparing anomaly detection techniques for HTTP*. Symposium on Recent Advances in Intrusion Detection (RAID).

Institute of Electrical and Electronics Engineering (IEEE). (1994). *IEEE standard definition: Specification, and analysis of systems used for supervisory control, data acquisition, and automatic control – Description*. Washington, DC: IEEE Standards Association.

Intel. (2002). *Biometric user authentication fingerprint sensor product evaluation summary*. ISSP-22-0410. (2004). *Policy draft: Mobile computing*. Overseas Private Investment Corporation.

International Council of System Engineering (INCOSE). (2010). *International Council on Systems Engineering*. Retrieved from http://www.incose.org/

International Instrument Users' Associations – EWE (IIUA). (2010). *Process control domain-security requirements for vendors*, (Report M 2784-X-10). Kent, United Kingdom: International Instrument Users' Associations – EWE.

ISECOM. (2008). *OSSTMM Lite: Introduction to the open source security testing methodology manual (3.0)*. New York, NY: Pete Herzog.

ISO/IEC CD 29128. (2010). *Verification of cryptographic protocols*. Under development.

ISO/IEC. (2007). *Systems and software engineering — Recommended practice for architectural description of software-intensive systems*. ISO/IEC 42010 (IEEE STD 1471-2000).

ITU. (2008). ITU botnet mitigation toolkit: Background information.

ITU. (2010). About ITU. Retrieved March 27, 2010, from http://www.itu.int/net/about/#

Janes. (2010). *Sentry (United States) command information systems – Air*. Retrieved from http://www.janes.com.

Jeon, C.-W., Kim, I.-G., & Choi, J.-Y. (2005). *Automatic generation of the C# Code for security protocols verified with Casper/FDR*. In International Conference on Advanced Information Networking and Applications (pp. 507-510).

Jin, Y., & Makris, Y. (2008). Hardware trojan detection using path delay fingerprint. In *Proceedings of IEEE International Workshop on Hardware-Oriented Security and Trust*, HOST 2008, (pp. 51-57). Washington, DC: IEEE Computer Society.

Jung, J., Paxson, V., Berger, A. W., & Balakrishnan, H. (2004). *Fast portscan detection using sequential hypothesis testing*. IEEE Symp Sec and Priv.

Jürjens, J. (2005). *Verification of low-level crypto-protocol implementations using automated theorem proving*. In Formal Methods and Models for Co-Design (pp. 89-98).

Kabiri, P., & Ghorbani, A. A. (2005). Research on intrusion detection and response: A survey. *International Journal of Network Security*, *1*(2), 84–102.

Kahate, A. (2003). *Cryptography and network security* (1st ed.). Tata, India: McGraw-Hill Company.

Kaliski, B. (1993, December). A survey of encryption standards. *IEEE Micro*, *13*(6), 74–81. doi:10.1109/40.248057

Kamoun, N., Bossuet, L., & Ghazel, A. (2009). Experimental implementation of DPA attacks on AES design with Flash-based FPGA technology. In *Proceedings of 6th IEEE International Multi-Conference on Systems, Signals and Devices*, SSD'09, Djerba.

Karlof, C., & Wagner, D. (2003). Secure routing in wireless sensor networks: Attacks and countermeasures. *Ad Hoc Networks*, *1*(2-3), 293–315. doi:10.1016/S1570-8705(03)00008-8

Karrer, R. P., Pescapé, A., & Huehn, T. (2008). Challenges in second-generation wireless mesh networks. *EURASIP Journal on Wireless Communications and Networking*, *2008*, 1–10. doi:10.1155/2008/274790

Kejariwal, A., Gupta, S., Nicolau, A., Dutt, N. D., & Gupta, R. (2006). Energy efficient watermarking on mobile devices using proxy-based partitioning. *IEEE Transactions on Very Large Scale Integration (VLSI). Systems*, *14*(6), 625–636.

Keller, M., Held, K., Eyert, V., Vollhardt, D., & Anisimov, V. I. (2004). Continuous generation of single photons with controlled waveform in an ion-trap cavity system. *Nature*, *431*(7012), 1075–1078. doi:10.1038/nature02961

Kelsey, J., Schneier, B., & Wagner, D. (1997). *Protocol interactions and the chosen protocol attack*. In Security Protocols Workshop (pp. 91-104).

Khanum, S., Usman, M., Hussain, K., Zafar, R., & Sher, M. (2009). Energy-efficient intrusion detection system for wireless sensor network based on musk architecture. In Zhang, W., Chen, Z., Douglas, C. C., & Tong, W. (Eds.), *High performance computing and applications* (pp. 212–217). Berlin, Germany: Springer-Verlag.

Khayam, S. A. (2006). *Wireless channel modeling and malware detection using statistical and information-theoretic tools*. PhD thesis, Michigan State University (MSU), USA.

Koashi, M. (2004). Unconditional security of coherent-state quantum key distribution with a strong phase-reference pulse. *Physical Review Letters*, *93*(12), 120501. doi:10.1103/PhysRevLett.93.120501

Kocher, P. (1996). Timing attacks on implementations of Diffie-Hellman, RSA, DSS and other systems. In N. Koblitz (Ed.), *Proceedings of Annual International Conference on Advances in Cryptology, LNCS 1109*, (pp. 104–113). Springer-Verlag.

Kocher, P., Jaffe, J., & Jun, B. (1999). Differential power analysis. In *Proceedings of the 19th Annual International Cryptology Conference on Advances in Cryptology, LNCS 1666*, (pp. 388–397). Heidelberg, Germany: Springer-Verlag.

Komninos, N., & Douligeris, C. (2009). LIDF: Layered intrusion detection framework for ad-hoc networks. *Ad Hoc Networks*, *7*(1), 171–182. doi:10.1016/j.adhoc.2008.01.001

Koopman, P. (2004, July). Embedded system security. *IEEE Computer Magazine*, *37*(7).

Kroeker, L. (2010). Engineering the web's third decade. *Communications of the ACM*, *53*(3), 16–18. doi:10.1145/1666420.1666428

Krontiris, I., Benenson, Z., Giannetsos, T., Freiling, F. C., & Dimitriou, T. (2009). Cooperative intrusion detection in wireless sensor networks. In Roedig, U., & Sreenan, C. J. (Eds.), *Wireless sensor networks* (pp. 263–278). Berlin, Germany: Springer-Verlag. doi:10.1007/978-3-642-00224-3_17

Krontiris, I., Dimitriou, T., & Freiling, F. C. (2007). Towards intrusion detection in wireless sensor networks. In *Proceedings of the 13th European Wireless Conference* (pp. 1-10).

Krontiris, I., Dimitriou, T., & Giannetsos, T. (2008). LIDeA: A distributed lightweight intrusion detection architecture for sensor networks. In *Proceeding of the fourth International Conference on Security and Privacy for Communication*.

Kulik, J., Heinzelman, W., & Balakrishnan, H. (2002). Negotiation-based protocols for disseminating information in wireless sensor networks. *Wireless Networks, 8*(2-3), 169–185. doi:10.1023/A:1013715909417

Küsters, R. (2005). On the decidability of cryptographic protocols with open-ended data structures. *International Journal of Information Security, 4*(1-2), 49–70. doi:10.1007/s10207-004-0050-z

Kyasanur, P., & Vaidya, N. H. (2005). Selfish MAC layer misbehavior in wireless networks. *IEEE Transactions on Mobile Computing, 4*(5), 502–516. doi:10.1109/TMC.2005.71

Lakhina, A., Crovella, M., & Diot, C. (2004). *Diagnosing network-wide traffic anomalies.* ACM SIGCOMM.

Lakhina, A., Crovella, M., & Diot, C. (2005). *Mining anomalies using traffic feature distributions.* ACM SIGCOMM.

Lakhina, A., Crovella, M., & Diot, C. (2004). *Characterization of network-wide traffic anomalies in traffic flows.* ACM Internet Measurement Conference (IMC).

Langer. (2010). *Stuxnet logbook.* Langer Production & Development.

Lauf, A. P., Peters, R. A., & Robinson, W. H. (2010). A distributed intrusion detection system for resource-constrained devices in ad-hoc networks. *Ad Hoc Networks, 8*(3), 253–266. doi:10.1016/j.adhoc.2009.08.002

Law, Y. W., Palaniswami, M., Hoesel, L. V., Doumen, J., Hartel, P., & Havinga, P. (2009). Energy-efficient link-layer jamming attacks against wireless sensor network MAC protocols. *ACM Transactions on Sensor Networks, 5*(1), 1–38. doi:10.1145/1464420.1464426

Lazarevic, A., Kumar, V., & Srivastava, J. (2005). Intrusion detection: A survey. In Kumar, V., Lazarevic, A., & Srivastava, J. (Eds.), *Managing cyber threats* (pp. 19–78). New York, NY: Springer-Verlag. doi:10.1007/0-387-24230-9_2

Lazarevic, A., Ertoz, L., Kumar, V., Ozgur, A., & Srivastava, J. (2003). *A comparative study of anomaly detection schemes in network intrusion detection.* SIAM International Conference on Data Mining (SDM).

LBNL/ICSI. (2010). *Enterprise Tracing Project.* Retrieved from http://www.icir.org/enterprise-tracing/download.html

Lemos, R. (2007). Estonia gets respite from web attacks. Security Focus. Retrieved from http://www.securityfocus.com/brief/504

Li, W., Joshi, A., & Finin, T. (2010). (accepted for publication). Security through collaboration and trust in MANETs. *ACM/Springer. Mobile Networks and Applications.* doi:10.1007/s11036-010-0243-9

Li, C., Jiang, W., & Zou, X. (2009). Botnet: Survey and case study. Paper presented at the Fourth International Conference on Innovative Computing, Information and Control (ICICIC).

Li, W., Joshi, A., & Finin, T. (2010). Coping with node misbehaviors in ad hoc networks: A multi-dimensional trust management approach. In *Proceedings of the 11th IEEE International Conference on Mobile Data Management* (pp. 85-94).

Lima, M. N., dos Santos, L. A., & Pujolle, G. (2009). A survey of survivability in mobile ad hoc networks. *IEEE Communications Surveys and Tutorials, 11*(1), 1–28. doi:10.1109/SURV.2009.090106

Lincoln Lab, M. I. T. (1998-1999). *DARPA-sponsored IDS evaluation.* Retrieved from www.ll.mit.edu/IST/ideval/data/dataindex.html

Lippmann, R. P., Haines, J. W., Fried, D. J., Korba, J., & Das, K. (2000). The 1999 DARPA offline intrusion detection evaluation. *Computer Networks, 34*(2), 579–595. doi:10.1016/S1389-1286(00)00139-0

Lippmann, R. P., Fried, D. J., Graf, I., Haines, J. W., Kendall, K. R., & McClung, D. … Zissman, M. A. (2000). *Evaluating intrusion detection systems: The 1998 DARPA off-line intrusion detection evaluation.* DISCEX, 2, (pp. 12-26).

Liu, Holt, & Cheng. (2007). A Practical Vulnerability Assessment Program. *IT Professional, 9*(6), 36–42. doi:10.1109/MITP.2007.105

Livshits, & Lam, S. (2005). Finding security vulnerabilities in java applications with static analysis. *Proceedings of the 14th conference on USENIX Security Symposium: Vol. 14.* (pp. 18-18). Baltimore, MD: USENIX Association.

Lockheed. (2010). *Lockheed Martin UK-Integrated systems & solutions*. Retrieved from http://www.lm-isgs.co.uk

Lohr, S. (2010, February 28). *Redrawing the route to online privacy*. New York Times. Retrieved March 27, 2010, from http://www.nytimes.com/2010/02/28/technology/internet/28unbox.html

Lowe, G. (1996). Breaking and fixing the Needham-Schroeder public-key protocol using FDR. *Software - Concepts and Tools, 17*(3), 93-102.

Lowe, G. (1998). *Towards a completeness result for model checking of security protocols*. In IEEE Computer Security Foundations Workshop (pp. 96-105).

Lowrance, R., & Wagner, R. A. (1975). An extension of the string-to-string correction problem. *Journal of the ACM, 22*(2), 177–183. doi:10.1145/321879.321880

Ma, X., Fung, C.-H. F., Dupuis, F., Chen, K., Tamaki, K., & Lo, H.-K. (2006). Decoy-state quantum key distribution with two-way classical post-processing. *Physical Review A., 74*(3), 032330. doi:10.1103/PhysRevA.74.032330

Ma, X., Qi, B., Zhao, Y., & Lo, H.-K. (2005). Practical decoy state for quantum key distribution. *Physical Review A., 72*(1), 012326. doi:10.1103/PhysRevA.72.012326

MAAWG. (2010). MAAWG published documents. Retrieved March 27, 2010, from http://www.maawg.org/published-documents

Madhavi, S., & Kim, T., H. (2008). An intrusion detection system in mobile ad-hoc networks. *International Journal of Security and Its Applications, 2*(3), 1–17.

Maggi, P., & Sisto, R. (2002). *Using SPIN to verify security properties of cryptographic protocols*. In SPIN Workshop on Model Checking of Software (pp. 187-204).

Mahoney, M. V., & Chan, P. K. (2003). *Network traffic anomaly detection based on packet bytes*. ACM SAC.

Mahoney, M. V., & Chan, P. K. (2001). *PHAD: Packet Header anomaly detection for identifying hostile network traffic*. (Florida Tech technical report CS-2001-4).

Mahoney, M. V., & Chan, P. K. (2002). *Learning models of network traffic for detecting novel attacks*. (Florida Tech, technical report CS-2002-08).

Mahoney, M. V., & Chan, P. K. (2003). *An analysis of the 1999 DARPA/Lincoln Laboratory evaluation data for network anomaly detection*. Symposium on Recent Advances in Intrusion Detection (RAID).

Mandala, S., Ngadi, M. A., & Abdullah, A. H. (2008). A survey on MANET intrusion detection. *International Journal of Computer Science and Security, 2*(1), 1–11.

Marschke, G. (1988). *The directory authentication framework*. (. CCITT Recommendation, X, 509.

Masek, W. J., & Paterson, M. S. (1980). A faster algorithm for computing string edit distances. *Journal of Computer and System Sciences, 20*, 18–31. doi:10.1016/0022-0000(80)90002-1

Mayers, D. (2001). Unconditional security in quantum cryptography. *Journal of Association for Computing Machinery, 48*(3), 351–406.

McAfee Corporation. (2005). McAfee virtual criminology report: North American study into organized crime and the Internet.

McCarthy, C. (2010). *Facebook phishing scam snares company board member*. Retrieved May 10, 2010, from http://news.cnet.com/8301-13577_3-20004549-36.html?

McClure. Scambray, & Kurtz. (2009). *Hacking Exposed 6: Network Security Secrets and Solutions*. New York, NY: McGraw-Hill Osborne.

McCullagh, D., & Broache, A. (2006). *FBI taps cell phone mic as eavesdropping tool*. CNET News.

McHugh, J. (2000). *The 1998 Lincoln Laboratory IDS evaluation* (a critique). Symposium on Recent Advances in Intrusion Detection (RAID).

McIntyre, A., Stamp, J., Richardson, B., & Parks, R. (2008). *I3P Security Forum: Connecting the business and control system networks*. Albuquerque, NM: Sandia National Lab.

Meadows, C. A. (1996). The NRL protocol analyzer: An overview. *The Journal of Logic Programming, 26*(2), 113–131. doi:10.1016/0743-1066(95)00095-X

Meadows, C. A. (2001). A cost-based framework for analysis of denial of service in networks. *Journal of Computer Security, 9*(1), 143–164.

Merriam-Webster. (2010). *Cybersecurity*. Retrieved September 13, 2010, from http://www.merriam-webster.com/dictionary/cybersecurity

Messerges, T. S., Dabbish, E. A., & Sloan, R. H. (2002, May). Examining smart-card security under the threat of power analysis attacks. [IEEE Computer Society.]. *IEEE Transactions on Computers, 51*(5), 541–552. doi:10.1109/TC.2002.1004593

Messmer, E. (2009). America's 10 most wanted botnets. Retrieved March 27, 2010, from http://www.networkworld.com/news/2009/072209-botnets.html

Michelson, M. (2009). *French military donated code to Mozilla Thunderbird*. PCMag.com. 12.10.2009.

Micro, A. T. (2006). Taxonomy of botnet threats.

Microsoft. (2006). Sender ID. Retrieved March 27, 2010, from http://www.microsoft.com/mscorp/safety/technologies/senderid/default.mspx

Microsoft. (2008). *Microsoft case study: NATO accelerates Windows Vista deployment using the Windows Vista security guide*. Retrieved from http://www.microsoft.com/casestudies/Case_Study_Detail.aspx?CaseStudyID=4000002826

Microsoft. (n.d.). Windows products. Retrieved March 27, 2010, from http://www.microsoft.com/windows/products/

Milenković, A., Otto, C., & Jovanov, E. (2006). Wireless sensor networks for personal health monitoring: Issues and an implementation. *Computer Communications, 29*(13-14), 2521–2533. doi:10.1016/j.comcom.2006.02.011

Milner, R. (1999). *Communicating and mobile systems: The Pi-Calculus*. Cambridge University Press.

Misbahuddin, S. (2006). A performance model of highly available multicomputer systems. *International Journal of Simulation and Modeling, 26*(2), 112–120.

Mishra, A., Nadkarni, K., & Patcha, A. (2004). Intrusion detection in wireless ad hoc networks. *IEEE Wireless Communications, 11*, 48–60. doi:10.1109/MWC.2004.1269717

Mobasher, B., Cooley, R., & Srivastava, J. (2000). Automatic personalization based on Web usage mining. *Communications of the ACM, 43*(8), 142–151. doi:10.1145/345124.345169

MoD. (2004, November). *Network enabled capability handbook*. Joint Services Publication 777, UK Ministry of Defence. Retrieved from http://www.mod.uk

MoD. (2005a). *Architectural framework overview*, version 1.0.

MoD. (2005b). *Architectural framework technical handbook*, version 1.0.

Mödersheim, S., & Viganò, L. (2009). *The open-source fixed-point model checker for symbolic analysis of security protocols*. In Foundations of Security Analysis and Design (pp. 166-194).

Molva, R., & Michiardi, P. (2003). Security in ad hoc networks. In M. Conti et al. (Eds.), *Personal Wireless Communications, 2775*, 756-775. Berlin, Germany: Springer-Verlag.

Monniaux, D. (1999). *Decision procedures for the analysis of cryptographic protocols by logics of belief*. In IEEE Computer Security Foundations Workshop (pp. 44-54).

Mortman, D., Hutton, A., Dixon, J., & Crisp, D. (2009). *A Black Hat vulnerability risk assessment. Proceedings from Black Hat USA '09*. Las Vegas, NV: Black Hat Briefings.

Moyse, I. (2010, May 10). Securing Web 2.0. *Security Acts, 3*, 21–22.

Mueller, P., & Shipley, G. (2001, August). Dragon claws its way to the top. *Network Computing*. Retrieved from http://www.networkcomputing.com/1217/1217f2.html

Mulliner, C., & Miller, C. (2009, July). *Fuzzing the phone in your phone*. Las Vegas, NV: Black Hat.

Myers, L. (2006, October). Aim for bot coordination. Paper presented at 2006 Virus Bulletin Conference (VB2006).

Nanda, Lam, & Chiueh. (2007). Dynamic multi-process information flow tracking for web application security. *Proceedings of the 2007 ACM/IFIP/USENIX international conference on Middleware companion. Session: Experience papers* (Article No: 19). New York, NY: Association for Computing Machinery.

NAP. (1999). *Realizing the potential of C4I: Fundamental challenges. Computer Science and Telecommunications Board (CSTB), Commission on Physical Sciences, Mathematics, and Applications, National Research Council.* Washington, DC: National Academy Press.

NAP. (2006). *C4ISR for future naval strike groups.* Naval Studies Board (NSB) Division on Engineering and Physical Sciences, National Research Council of The National Academies. Washington, DC: The National Academies Press. Retrieved from www.nap.edu.

National Infrastructure Security Co-Ordination Centre. (2004). Border gateway protocol.

National Institute of Standards and Technology. (2009). *Special publications 800-114, 800-124.*

National Institute of Standards and Technology (NIST). (2009). *Special publication 800-53, revision 3: Recommended security controls for federal information systems and organizations.*

National Transportation Safety Board (NSTB). (2005). *Supervisory Control and Data Acquisition (SCADA) in liquid pipeline safety study.* (Report No. NTSB/SS-05/02, PB2005-917005). Retrieved from http://www.ntsb.gov/publictn/2005/ss0502.pdf

NATO. (2007). *NATO architectural framework,* ver. 3 (Annex 1 to AC/322-D (2007) 0048).

NATO. (2010). *NATO information assurance.* Retrieved from http://www.ia.nato.int

Navarrete, C. (2010, February 15). Security testing: Automated or manual. *Security Acts, 2,* 20–21.

Naveen, S., & David, W. (2004). Security considerations for IEEE 802.15.4 networks. In *Proceedings of the ACM Workshop on Wireless Security* (pp. 32-42). New York, NY: ACM Press.

Navsea. (2007). *Naval sea systems command.* Retrieved from https://www.djc2.org

Needham, R., & Schroeder, M. (1978). Using encryption for authentication in large networks of computers. *Communications of the ACM, 21*(12), 993–999. doi:10.1145/359657.359659

Negin, M., Chemielewski, T. A. Jr, Salgancoff, M., Camus, T., Chan, U. M., Venetaner, P. L., & Zhang, G. (2000, February). An iris biometric system for pubic and personal use. *IEEE Computer, 33*(2), 70–75.

NERC. (2006). *Cyber security standards.* Retrieved from http://www.nerc.com/~filez/standards/Cyber-Security-Permanent.html

Neves, P., Stachyra, M., & Rodrigues, J. (2008). Application of wireless sensor networks to healthcare promotion. *Journal of Communications Software and Systems, 4*(3), 181–190.

Next-Generation Intrusion Detection Expert System (NIDES). (2010). *NIDES Project.* Retrieved from http://www.csl.sri.com/projects/nides/

Ng, H. S., Sim, M. L., & Tan, C. M. (2006). Security issues of wireless sensor networks in healthcare applications. *BT Technology Journal, 24*(2), 138–144. doi:10.1007/s10550-006-0051-8

Nicholson, A. J., Corner, M. D., & Noble, B. D. (2006, November). Mobile device security using transient authentication. *IEEE Transactions on Mobile Computing, 5*(11), 1489–1502. doi:10.1109/TMC.2006.169

Nilsson, P. (2003). Opportunities and risks in a network-based defence. *Swedish Journal of Military Technology, 3.* Retrieved from http://www.militartekniska.se/mtt.

Noble, B. D., & Corner, M. D. (September 2002). The case for transient authentication. In *Proceeding of 10th ACM SIGOPS European Workshop,* Saint-Emillion, France.

Noureddine, A., & Damodaran. (2008). Security in web 2.0 application development. *Proceedings of the 10th International Conference on Information Integration and Web-based Applications and Services. Session: iiWAS 2008 and ERPAS 2008* (pp. 681-685). New York, NY: Association for Computing Machinery.

OECD Ministerial Background Report. (2008). DSTI/ICCP/REG(2007)5/FINAL, malicious software (malware): A security threat to the Internet economy.

OISSG. (2006). *ISSAF: Information systems security assessment framework (draft 0.2.1A & 0.2.1B).* Colorado Springs, CO: Rathore et al.

Omar, M., Challal, Y., & Bouabdallah, A. (2009). Reliable and fully distributed trust model for mobile ad hoc networks. *Computers & Security, 28*(3-4), 199–214. doi:10.1016/j.cose.2008.11.009

Ono, K., Kawaishi, I., & Kamon, T. (2007). Trend of botnet activities. Paper presented at 41st Annual IEEE International Carnahan Conference on Security Technology.

OpenSSL Team. (2009). *OpenSSL security advisor*. Retrieved from http://www.openssl.org/news/secadv_20090107.txt

Ors, S. B., Gurkaynak, F., Oswald, E., & Prencel, B. (2004). Power analysis attack on an ASIC AES implementation. In *Proceedings of the International Conference on Information Technology: Coding and Computing*, ITCC'04, Las Vegas, NV, Vol. 2 (p. 546). Washington, DC: IEEE Computer Society.

Otway, D., & Rees, O. (1987). Efficient and timely mutual authentication. *Operating Systems Review, 21*(1), 8–10. doi:10.1145/24592.24594

Pang, R., Allman, M., Bennett, M., Lee, J., Paxson, V., & Tierney, B. (2005). *A first look at modern enterprise traffic*. ACM/Usenix Internet Measurement Conference (IMC).

Pang, R., Allman, M., Paxson, V., & Lee, J. (2006). The devil and packet trace anonymization. *ACM CCR, 36*(1).

Parker, J., Pinkston, J., Undercoffer, J., & Joshi, A. (2004). On intrusion detection in mobile ad hoc networks. In *23rd IEEE International Performance Computing and Communications Conference - Workshop on Information Assurance*.

Paulson, L. (1998). The inductive approach to verifying cryptographic protocols. *Journal of Computer Security, 6*(1-2), 85–128.

Peltier, R., & Peltier. (2002). *Managing a Network Vulnerability Assessment*. Boca Raton, FL: CRC Press.

Permann, R. M., & Rohde, K. (2005). *Cyber assessment methods for SCADA security*. Retrieved from http://www.inl.gov/scada/publications/d/cyber_assessment_methods_for_scada_security.pdf

Perrig, A., Szewczyk, R., Tygar, J., Wen, V., & Culler, D. E. (2002). SPINS: Security protocols for sensor networks. *Wireless Networks, 8*, 521–534. doi:10.1023/A:1016598314198

Pipeline and Hazardous Material Safety Administration (PHMSA). (2010). *Pipeline basics*. Retrieved from http://primis.phmsa.dot.gov/comm/PipelineBasics.htm?nocache=5000

Pironti, A., & Sisto, R. (2010). Provably correct Java implementations of Spi calculus security protocols specifications. *Computers & Security, 29*(3), 302–314. doi:10.1016/j.cose.2009.08.001

Pironti, A., & Sisto, R. (2007). *An experiment in interoperable cryptographic protocol implementation using automatic code generation*. In IEEE Symposium on Computers and Communications (pp. 839-844).

Porras, P. (2009). Directions in network-based security monitoring. *IEEE Privacy and Security, 7*(1), 82–85. doi:10.1109/MSP.2009.5

Potkonjak, M., Nahapetian, A., Nelson, M., & Massey, T. (2009). Hardware trojan horse detection using gate-level characterization. In *Proceedings of the 46th Annual ACM IEEE Design Automation Conference*, CA, ACM.

Pozza, D., Sisto, R., & Durante, L. (2004). *Spi2Java: Automatic cryptographic protocol Java code generation from Spi calculus*. In Advanced Information Networking and Applications (pp. 400-405).

Prevelakis, V., & Spinellis, D. (2007, July). The Athens affair. *IEEE Spectrum, 44*(7), 26–33. doi:10.1109/MSPEC.2007.376605

Ptacek, T. H., & Newsham, T. N. (1998). *Insertion, evasion, and denial of service: Eluding network intrusion detection*. Secure Networks, Inc.

Pugliese, M., Giani, A., & Santucci, F. (2009). Weak process models for attack detection in a clustered sensor network using mobile agents. In Hailes, S., Sicari, S., & Roussos, G. (Eds.), *Sensor systems and software* (pp. 33–50). Berlin, Germany: Springer-Verlag.

Puketza, N., Chung, M., Olsson, R. A., & Mukherjee, B. (1997). A software platform for testing intrusion detection systems. *IEEE Software, 14*(5), 43–51. doi:10.1109/52.605930

Puketza, N. F., Zhang, K., Chung, M., Mukherjee, B., & Olsson, R. A. (1996). A methodology for testing intrusion detection systems. *IEEE Transactions on Software Engineering, 22*(10), 719–729. doi:10.1109/32.544350

Puri, R. (2003). Bots & botnet: An overview.

Puttaswamy, K. P. N., & Zhao, B. Y. (2010). *Preserving privacy in location-based mobile social applications.* Paper presented at HotMobile'10, Annapolis, Maryland.

Qingling, C., Yiju, Z., & Yonghua, W. (2008). A minimalist mutual authentication protocol for RFID system & BAN logic analysis. In *International Colloquium on Computing* (pp. 449–453). Communication, Control, and Management. doi:10.1109/CCCM.2008.305

Rafsanjani, M. K., Movaghar, A., & Koroupi, F. (2008). Investigating intrusion detection systems in MANET and comparing IDSs for detecting misbehaving nodes. *World Academy of Science. Engineering and Technology, 44*, 351–355.

Raghavendra, C. S., Sivalingam, K. M., & Znati, T. (Eds.). (2004). *Wireless sensor networks.* Berlin/Heidelberg, Germany: Spriger-Verlag. doi:10.1007/b117506

Rajab, M. A., Zarfoss, J., Monrose, F., & Terzis, A. (2006). A multifaceted approach to understanding the botnet phenomenon. Paper presented at 6th ACM SIGCOMM conference on Internet measurement.

Rand. (2009). *Controlling the cost of C4I upgrades on naval ships. A study report for USN RAND Corporation.* National Defense and Research Institute USA (2009).

Rao, L. (2010). *Twitter seeing 6 billion API calls per day, 70k per second.* TechCrunch. Retrieved from http://techcrunch.com/2010/09/17/twitter-seeing-6-billion-api-calls-per-day-70k-per-second/

Rasheed, & Chow, Y. C. (2009). Automated Risk Assessment for Sources and Targets of Vulnerability Exploitation. *Proceedings of the 2009 WRI World Congress on Computer Science and Information Engineering: Vol. 1.* (pp. 150-154). Washington, DC: IEEE Computer Society.

Rawat, & Saxena. (2009). Application security code analysis: a step towards software assurance. *International Journal of Information and Computer Security, 3*(1), 86-110.

Reuters. (2010a). *Update 2-Cyber attack appears to target Iran-tech firms.*

Reuters. (2010b). *What is Stuxnet?* Robinson, C. (2002). *Military and cyber-defense: Reactions to the threat.* Washington, DC: Center for Defense Information.

Ringberg, H., Rexford, J., Soule, A., & Diot, C. (2007). *Sensitivity of PCA for traffic anomaly detection.* ACM SIGMETRICS.

Robert Bosch. (1991). *CANS specification, ver. 2.0.* Stuttgart, Germany: Robert Bosch GmbH.

Roesch, M. (1999). *Snort – Lightweight intrusion detection for networks.* USENIX Large Installation System Administration Conference (LISA).

Rowan, D. (2010). *Six reasons why I'm not on Facebook.* Retrieved September 18, 2010, from http://www.wired.com/epicenter/2010/09/six-reasons-why-wired-uks-editor-isnt-on-facebook/

Ryan, P., & Schneider, S. (2000). *The modelling and analysis of security protocols: The CSP approach.* Addison-Wesley Professional.

Saab. (2010). *Safir software development kit for truly distributed C4I systems.* Retrieved from http://www.safirsdk.com

Sabahi, V., & Movaghar, A. (2008). *Intrusion detection: A survey.* In Third International Conference on Systems and Networks Communications (pp.23-26).

Saenz, A. (2010). Stuxnet worm attacks nuclear site in Iran – A sign of cyber warfare to come on singularity hub.

Saha, B., & Gairola, A. (2005). Botnet: An overview.

Said, E., & Guimaraes, A. Maamar, & Jololian. (2009). Database and database application security. *Proceedings of the 14th annual ACM SIGCSE conference on Innovation and technology in computer science education. Session: Networking* (pp. 90-93). New York, NY: Association for Computing Machinery.

Scadalink. (2010). *Support.* Retrieved from http://www.scadalink.com/support/scada.html

Schechter, S. E., Jung, J., & Berger, A. W. (2004). *Fast detection of scanning worm infections.* Symposium on Recent Advances in Intrusion Detection (RAID).

Schmeh, K. (2003). *Cryptography and public key infrastructure on the internet*. West Sussex, England: John Wiley & Sons.

Schneider, S. (1996). *Security properties and CSP*. In IEEE Symposium on Security and Privacy (pp. 174-187).

Sellke, S., Shroff, N. B., & Bagchi, S. (2005). *Modeling and automated containment of worms*. DSN.

Sentek. (2010). *C4ISR solutions*. Sentek Global. Retrieved from http://www.sentekconsulting.com/index.php

Sentry. (2010). *C2 / C4I systems: A strategic tool for extended air defense by ThalesRaytheon Systems* (TRS). Retrieved from http://www.armedforces-int.com/article/c2-c4i-systems-a-strategic-tool-for-extended-air-defense.html

Shabtai, A., Kanonov, U., & Elovici, Y. (2010, August). Intrusion detection for mobile devices using the knowledge-based, temporal abstraction method. *Journal of Systems and Software, 83*(8), 1524–1537. doi:10.1016/j.jss.2010.03.046

Shah, S. (2009). Application defense tactics and strategies: WAF at the gateway. *Proceedings from HITBSecConf '09*. Dubai, DB: HITB Security Conference Series.

Shamir, A., Rivest, R., & Adleman, L. (1978). *Mental poker (Technical Report)*. Massachusetts Institute of Technology.

Shamir, A. (1979). How to share a secret. *Communications of the ACM, 22*(11), 612–613. doi:10.1145/359168.359176

Shannon, C., & Moore, D. (2004). The spread of the Witty worm. *IEEE Security & Privacy, 2*(4), 46–50. doi:10.1109/MSP.2004.59

Sharp, R. I. (2004). *User authentication*. Technical University of Denmark.

Shezaf. (2006). *Web Application Firewall Evaluation Criteria* (1.0) [PDF document]. Retrieved May 5, 2010, from http://projects.webappsec.org/f/wasc-wafec-v1.0.pdf

Shipley, G. (1999). ISS RealSecure pushes past newer IDS players. *Network Computing*. Retrieved from http://www.networkcomputing.com/1010/1010r1.html

Shipley, G. (1999). Intrusion detection, take two. *Network Computing*. Retrieved from http://www.nwc.com/1023/1023f1.html

Shrestha, R., Sung, J.-Y., Lee, S.-D., Pyung, S.-Y., Choi, D.-Y., & Han, S.-J. (2009). A secure intrusion detection system with authentication in mobile ad hoc network. In *Proceedings of the Pacific-Asia Conference on Circuits, Communications and Systems* (pp.759-762).

Shyu, M.-L., Sarinnapakorn, K., Kuruppu-Appuhamilage, I., Chen, S.-C., Chang, L., & Goldring, T. (2005). Handling nominal features in anomaly intrusion detection problems. *Proc. 15th Int. Workshop on Research Issues in Data Engineering (RIDE 2005)*, (pp. 55-62). Tokyo, Japan.

Siciliano, R. (2010). *Social media security: Using Facebook to steal company data*. Retrieved May 11, 2010, from http://www.huffingtonpost.com/robert-siciliano/social-media-security-usi_b_570246.html

Sink, C. (July 2004). Agobot and the kit.

Smith, H. L., & Block, W. R. (1993, January). RTUs slave for supervisory systems. *Computer Applications in Power, 6*, 27–32. doi:10.1109/67.180433

Smith, V., Ames, C., & Delchi. (2009). Dissecting Web attacks. *Proceedings from Black Hat DC '09*. Crystal City, DC: Black Hat Briefings.

Snort. (2010). *Open source intrusion detection system*. Retrieved from http://www.snort.org

Song, D. X., Berezin, S., & Perrig, A. (2001). Athena: A novel approach to efficient automatic security protocol analysis. *Journal of Computer Security, 9*(1/2), 47–74.

Sophos. (2010). *Security threat report*. Retrieved January 2010, from http://www.sophos.com/sophos/docs/eng/papers/sophos-security-threat-report-jan-2010-wpna.pdf

Soule, A., Salamatian, K., & Taft, N. (2005). *Combining filtering and statistical methods for anomaly detection*. ACM/Usenix Internet Measurement Conference (IMC).

SPF. (2008). Sender policy framework.

Stallings, W. (2003). *Cryptography and network security principles and practices* (3rd ed.).

Standaert, F. X., Ors, S. B., Quisquater, J. J., & Prencel, B. (2004). Power analysis attacks against FPGA implementations of the DES. In *Proceedings of the International Conference on Field-Programmable Logic and its Applications (FPL), LNCS 3203*, (pp. 84-94). Heidelberg, Germany: Springer-Verlag.

Stanton, N. A., Baber, C., & Harris, D. (2008). *Modelling command and control: Event analysis of systemic teamwork*. Aldershot, UK: Ashgate.

Stojmenovic, I. (Ed.). (2002). *Handbook of wireless networks and mobile computing*. New York, NY: John Willy & Sons. doi:10.1002/0471224561

Stojmenovic, I. (Ed.). (2005). *Handbook of Sensor Networks*. England: John Willy & Sons. doi:10.1002/047174414X

Stokes, M. (2010). *Revolutionizing Taiwan's security – Leveraging C4ISR for traditional and non-traditional challenges*. Retrieved from www.project2049.net

Stolfo, S. J., Hershkop, S., Hu, C.-W., Li, W.-J., Nimeskern, O., & Wang, K. (2006). Behavior-based modeling and its application to email analysis. *ACM Transactions on Internet Technology*, 6(2), 187–221. doi:10.1145/1149121.1149125

Stouffer, K., Falco, J., & Scarfone, K. (2008). *Guide to Industrial Control Systems (ICS) security*. (Report No. NIST SP 800-82). Retrieved from http://www.nist.gov

Stuttard, & Pinto. (2007). *The Web Application Hacker's Handbook: Discovering and Exploiting Security Flaws*. Indianapolis, IN: Wiley Publishing.

Subhadrabandhu, D., Sarkar, S., & Anjum. F. (2006). *A statistical framework for intrusion detection in ad hoc networks*. IEEE INFOCOM.

Sullivan. (2009). Proceedings from Black Hat USA '09: *Defensive URL Rewriting and Alternative Resource Locators*. Las Vegas, NV: Black Hat Briefings.

Susilo, W. (2002). Securing handheld devices. *Proc. 10th IEEE Int. Conf. Networks*, (pp. 349-354).

Sybase Inc. (2006). *Afaria—The power to manage and secure data, devices and applications on the front lines of business*. Retrieved June 10, 2010, from http://www.sybase.com/files/Data_Sheets/Afaria_overview_datasheet.pdf

Symantec Internet Security Statistics. (2008). *Symantec Internet security threat reports I–XI*.

Symantec MessageLabs. (2009). MessageLabs intelligence: Q2/June 2009.

Symantec. (2007). W32.Randex.E. Retrieved March 27, 2010, from http://www.symantec.com/security_response/writeup.jsp?docid=2003-081213-3232-99

Symantec. (2010). *Security response*. Retrieved from http://securityresponse.symantec.com/avcenter

Symantec. (n.d.). Learn more about viruses and worms.

Szor, F. P. a. P. (2003). An analysis of the slapper worm exploit.

Takahashi, J., & Fukunaga, T. (2010, January). Differential fault analysis on AES with 192 and 256-bit keys. In *Proceedings of Symposium on Cryptography and Information Security*. SCIS, Japan, IACR e-print archive.

Ten, C., Govindarasu, M., & Liu, C. C. (2007, October). *Cyber security for electric power control and automation systems* (pp. 29-34).

Thales. (2010). *Link-Y brochure and specification document*. Retrieved on October 15, 2010, from http://www.thalesgroup.com/LinkY/?pid=1568

Thales. (2010). *Thales defence & security C4I systems division (DSC) research and contribution to the cyber security*. Retrieved from http://www.nis-summer-school.eu/presentations/Daniel_Gidoin.pdf

The Shadowserver Foundation. (2007). Botnets. Retrieved March 27, 2010, from http://www.shadowserver.org/wiki/pmwiki.php/Information/Botnets#toc

The Sydney Morning Herald. (2007). Cyber attacks force Estonian bank to close website. Retrieved from http://www.smh.com.au/news/breaking-news/cyber-attacks-force-estonian-bank-to-close-website/2007/05/16/1178995171916.html

The, N. S. S. Group. (2001). *Intrusion detection systems group test* (2nd ed.). Retrieved from http://nsslabs.com/group-tests/intrusion-detection-systems-ids-group-test-edition-2.html

Thuraisingham. (2009). Data Mining for Malicious Code Detection and Security Applications. *Proceedings of the 2009 IEEE/WIC/ACM International Joint Conference on Web Intelligence and Intelligent Agent Technology: Vol. 2.* (pp. 6-7). Washington, DC: IEEE Computer Society.

Tiri, K., & Verbauwhede, I. (2004). A logic level design methodology for a secure DPA resistant ASIC or FPGA implementation. In *Proceedings of the Conference on Design, Automation and Test.* IEEE Computer Society.

Tobler, B., & Hutchison, A. (2004). *Generating network security protocol implementations from formal specifications.* In Certification and Security in Inter-Organizational E-Services. Toulouse, France.

Transportation Security Administration (TSA). (2008). *Transportation Security Administration: Pipeline security guidelines, rev. 2a.* Washington, DC: TSA.

Trendmicro. (2003). POLYBOOT-B*. Retrieved from http://threatinfo.trendmicro.com/vinfo/virusencyclo/default5.asp?VName=POLYBOOT-B*

Trividi, K. (1990, July). Reliability evaluation of fault tolerant systems. *IEEE Transactions on Reliability, 44*(4), 52–61.

Tryfonas, & Kearney. (2008). Standardising business application security assessments with pattern-driven audit automations. *Computer Standards & Interfaces, 30*(4), 262-270.

Turneaure, F. E., & Russell, H. L. (1916). *Public water-supplies – Requirements, resources, and the construction of works.* New York, NY: John Wiley & Sons, Inc.

Turner, N. C. (1991, September). *Hardware and software techniques for pipeline integrity and leak detection monitoring.* Society of Petroleum Engineers, Inc. Paper presented at meeting of the Offshore Europe Conference, Aberdeen, Scotland.

Twitter Blog. (2010). *Links and Twitter: Length shouldn't matter.* Retrieved June 8, 2010, from http://blog.twitter.com/2010/06/links-and-twitter-length-shouldnt.html

Twitter Blog. (2010). *State of Twitter spam.* Retrieved March 23, 2010, from http://blog.twitter.com/2010/03/state-of-twitter-spam.html

Twitter Blog. (2010). *Trust and safety.* Retrieved March 9, 2010, from http://blog.twitter.com/2010/03/trust-and-safety.html

Twitter Help Resources. (2009). *About the Tweet with your location feature.* Retrieved November 12, 2009, from http://twitter.zendesk.com/forums/26810/entries/78525

Twycross, J., & Williamson, M. M. (2003). *Implementing and testing a virus throttle.* Usenix Security.

University of Central Florida. (2007). *Security of mobile computing, data storage, and communication devices.* University of Central Florida.

US-CERT. (2009). Quarterly trends and analysis report. *US CERT, 4*(1). Retrieved from http://www.us-cert.gov/press_room/trendsanalysisQ109.pdf

USCESRC. (2009). *China's cyber activities that target the United States, and the resulting impacts on U.S. national security.* US China Economic and Security Review Commission 2009 Annual Report to Congress. Retrieved from http://www.uscc.gov

US-DoD. (1995). *DoD integrated architecture panel.* IEEE STD 610.12.

US-DoD. (1997). *C4ISR architecture working group.* (US) Department of Defense. C4ISR Architecture Framework Version 2.0.

US-DoD. (2005). *Guide to using DoD PKI certificates in outlook security evaluation.* (Group Report Number: I33-002R-2005).

USDoD. (2005). *The implementation of network-centric warfare.* Force Transformation, Office of the Secretary of Defense. Retrieved from http://www.oft.osd.mil/library/library_files/document_387_NCW_Book_LowRes.pdf.

US-DoD. (2007). *Department of Defense architecture framework v1.5.* Retrieved from http://www.defenselink.mil/nii/doc/DoDAF_V2_Deskbook.pdf

US-DoD. (2009). *Department of Defense architecture framework v2.0.* Retrieved from http://www.defenselink.mil/nii/doc/DoDAF_V2_Deskbook.pdf

Vamosi, R. (2008). Koobface virus hits Facebook. *CNET.* Retrieved December 4, 2008, from http://news.cnet.com/koobface-virus-hits-facebook/

Van Eck, W. (1985). Electromagnetic radiation from video display units: An eavesdropping risk. [Oxford, UK: Elsevier Advanced Technology Publications.]. *Computers & Security, 4*(4), 269–286. doi:10.1016/0167-4048(85)90046-X

Vascellaro, J. (2010). *Facebook glitch exposed private chats*. Retrieved May 5, 2010, from http://online.wsj.com/article/SB10001424052748703961104575226314165586910.html

Ventuneac, Coffey, & Salomie. (2003). A policy-based security framework for Web-enabled applications. *Proceedings of the 1st international symposium on Information and communication technologies. Session: WWW applications* (pp. 487-492). Dublin, Ireland: Trinity College Dublin.

Viganò, L. (2006). Automated security protocol analysis with the AVISPA tool. *Electronic Notes in Theoretical Computer Science, 155*, 61–86. doi:10.1016/j.entcs.2005.11.052

Vishnubhtla, S. R., & Mahmud, S. M. (1988). *A centralized multiprocessor based control to optimize performance in vehicles*. IEEE Workshop on Automotive Applications of Electronics, Detroit, MI.

Voydock, V. L., & Kent, S. T. (1983). Security mechanisms in high-level network protocols. *ACM Computing Surveys, 15*(2), 135–171. doi:10.1145/356909.356913

Vu, T. M., Safavi-Naini, R., & Williamson, C. (2010). Securing wireless sensor networks against large-scale node capture attacks. In *Proceedings of the 5th ACM Symposium on Information, Computer and Communications Security* (pp. 112-123).

W3C. (2007). *SOAP version 1.2, part 1: Messaging framework* (2nd ed.). Retrieved from http://www.w3.org/TR/ soap12-part1/#intro

Wagner, R. A., & Fischer, M. J. (1974). The string-to-string correction problem. *Journal of the ACM, 21*(1), 168–173. doi:10.1145/321796.321811

Wagner, R. A. (1975). On the complexity of the extended string-to-string correction problem. *Proc. 7th Annual ACM Symp. on Theory of Computing,* (pp. 218-223).

Walden, D. Welch, A., Whelan. (2009). Security of open source web applications. *Proceedings of the 2009 3rd International Symposium on Empirical Software Engineering and Measurement* (pp. 545-553). Washington, DC: IEEE Computer Society.

Walden. (2008). Integrating web application security into the IT curriculum. *Proceedings of the 9th ACM SIGITE conference on Information technology education. Session 2.5.1: integrating advanced topics II* (pp. 187-192). New York, NY: Association for Computing Machinery.

Walters, J. P., Liang, Z., Shi, W., & Chaudhary, V. (2007). Wireless sensor network security: A survey. In Y. Xiao (Ed.), *Security in distributed, grid, and pervasive computing* (pp. 367-311). Boca Raton, FL: Auerbach Publications, CRC Press.

Wang, W., Man, H., & Liu, Y. (2009). A framework for intrusion detection systems by social network analysis methods in ad hoc networks. *Security and Communication Networks, 2*(6), 669–685.

Wang, Y., Lively, M., & Simmons, B. (2009). Software security analysis and assessment model for the web-based applications. *Journal of Computational Methods in Sciences and Engineering, 9*(1), 179–189.

Wang, F., Huang, C., Zhao, J., & Rong, C. (2008). ID-MTM: A novel intrusion detection mechanism based on trust model for ad hoc networks. In *Proceedings of the 22nd International Conference on Advanced Information Networking and Applications* (pp. 978-984).

Ward, R. (2008). *Laptop and mobile computing security policy*. Devon PCT NHS.

Weaver, N., Staniford, S., & Paxson, V. (2004). *Very fast containment of scanning worms*. Usenix Security.

Weinstein, E., Ho, P., Heisele, B., Poggio, T., Steele, K., & Agarwal, A. (2002). Handheld face identification technology in a pervasive computing environment. *Short Paper Proceedings, Pervasive 2002*, Zurich, Switzerland.

Whitaker, & Newman. (2005). *Penetration Testing and Cisco Network Defense*. Indianapolis, IN: Cisco Press.

Wiesner, S. (1983). Conjugate coding. *S/GACT News, 15*(1), 78-88.

Wiki. (n.da). *What is wiki?* Wikiorg, The Free Encyclopedia. Retrieved October 15, 2010, from http://wiki.org/wiki.cgi?WhatIsWiki

Wiki. (n.db). *Thin client.* Techterms, The Free Encyclopedia. Retrieved October 15, 2010, from http://en.wikipedia.org/wiki/Thin_client

Wiki. (n.dc). *Techterms.* Techterms, The Free Encyclopedia. Retrieved October 15, 2010, from http://www.techterms.com/definition/wiki

Wikipedia. (2010). *Wikipedia main page.* Retrieved from http://en.wikipedia.org/

Wikipedia. (2010a). *Identification friend or foe.* Retrieved October 21, 2010, from http://en.wikipedia.org/wiki/Identification_friend_or_foe

Wikipedia. (2010b). *Security focused operating system.* Retrieved October 21, 2010, from http://en.wikipedia.org/wiki/Security_focused_operating_systems

Williamson, M. M. (2002). *Throttling viruses: Restricting propagation to defeat malicious mobile code.* ACSAC.

Winpcap. (2010). *Winpcap homepage.* Retrieved from http://www.winpcap.org/

WiSNet. (2008). *Bibliography of network-based anomaly detection systems.* Retrieved from http://www.wisnet.seecs.nust.edu.pk/downloads.php

WiSNet. (2010). *WiSNet ADS comparison homepage, November 2010.* Retrieved from http://www.wisnet.seecs.nust.edu.pk/projects/adeval/

Wong, C., Bielski, S., Studer, A., & Wang, C. (2005). *Empirical analysis of rate limiting mechanisms.* Symposium on Recent Advances in Intrusion Detection (RAID).

Woodcock, J., Larsen, P. G., Bicarregui, J., & Fitzgerald, J. (2009). Formal methods: Practice and experience. *ACM Computing Surveys, 41*(4), 1–36. doi:10.1145/1592434.1592436

Woodward. (2010). *Document.* Retrieved from http://www.woodward.com/pdf/ic/85578.pdf

Wortzel, L. M. (2009). *Preventing terrorist attacks, countering cyber intrusions, and protecting privacy in cyberspace. U.S. China Economic and Security Review Commission, Testimony before the Subcommittee on Terrorism and Homeland Security.* United States Senate.

Wright, P. (1987). *Spycatcher – The candid autobiography of a senior intelligence officer.* Australia: William Heinemann.

Wright, C. S. (2008). *The IT regulatory and standards compliance handbook: How to survive an information systems audit and assessments.* Burlington, MA: Syngress Publishing.

Wu, S. X., & Banzhaf, W. (2010). The use of computational intelligence in intrusion detection systems: A review. *Applied Soft Computing, 10*(1), 1–35. doi:10.1016/j.asoc.2009.06.019

Wu, S., & Manber, U. (1992). Text searching allowing errors. *Communications of the ACM, 35*(10), 83–91. doi:10.1145/135239.135244

Wu, B., Chen, J., Wu, J., & Cardei, M. (2006). A survey on attacks and countermeasures in mobile ad hoc networks. In Xiao, Y., Shen, X., & Du, D.-Z. (Eds.), *Wireless/mobile network security* (pp. 170–176). Berlin/Heidelberg, Germany: Spriger-Verlag.

Xiao, Y., Chen, H., & Li, F. H. (Eds.). (2010). *Handbook on sensor networks.* Hackensack, NJ: World Scientific Publishing Co.doi:10.1142/9789812837318

Yafen, L., Wuu, Y., & Ching-Wei, H. (2004). *Preventing type flaw attacks on security protocols with a simplified tagging scheme.* In Symposium on Information and Communication Technologies (pp. 244-249).

Yang, H., Ricciato, F., Lu, S., & Zhang, L. (2006). Securing a wireless world. *Proceedings of the IEEE, 94*(2), 442–454. doi:10.1109/JPROC.2005.862321

Ylonen, T. (1996). *SSH - Secure login connections over the internet.* In USENIX Security Symposium (pp. 37-42).

Yocom, B., & Brown, K. (2001). Intrusion battleground evolves. *Network World Fusion.* Retrieved from http://www.nwfusion.com/reviews/2001/1008bg.html

Zanero, S., & Criscione, C. (2009). *Masibty: An anomaly based intrusion prevention system for web applications. Proceedings from Black Hat Europe '09. Moevenpick.* Amsterdam, The Netherlands: Black Hat Briefings. ADDITIONAL READING SECTION.

Zehetner, A. R. (2004). *Information operations: The impacts on C4I systems.* Australia: Electronic Warfare Associates.

Zhang, Z., Ho, P.-H., & Naït-Abdesselam, F. (2010). (in press). RADAR: A reputation-driven anomaly detection system for wireless mesh networks. *Wireless Networks.* doi:10.1007/s11276-010-0255-1

Zhang, Y., & Lee, W. (2000). Intrusion detection in wireless ad-hoc networks. In *Proceedings of the 6th Annual International Conference on Mobile Computing and Networking* (pp. 275-283).

Zheng, D., Liu, Y., Zhao, J., & Saddik, A. E. (2007, June). A survey of RST invariant image watermarking algorithms. *ACM Computing Surveys, 39*(2), article 5.

Zhou, L., & Haas, Z. (1999). *Securing ad hoc networks. (Technical Report, TR99-1772).* Ithaca, NY: Cornell University.

Zou, C. C., Gao, L., Gong, W., & Towsley, D. (2003). *Monitoring and early warning of Internet worms.* ACM Conference on Computer and Communications Security (CCS).

About the Contributors

Junaid Ahmed Zubairi is currently a Professor at the Department of Computer and Information Sciences in the State University of New York at Fredonia, USA. Dr. Zubairi received his BE (Electrical Engineering) from NED University of Engineering, Pakistan and MS and Ph.D. (Computer Engineering) from Syracuse University, USA. He worked in Sir Syed University Pakistan and Intl' Islamic University Malaysia before joining State University of New York at Fredonia. Dr. Zubairi is a recipient of many awards including Malaysian Government IRPA award, National Science Foundation MACS grant, SUNY Scholarly Incentive award, and SUNY individual development award. He has authored several chapters and scholarly articles in books, international journals, and conference proceedings. His research interests include information security, network traffic engineering, performance evaluation of networks, and network applications in medicine.

Athar Mahboob is an Associate Professor at the National University of Sciences & Technology, Pakistan. Dr. Athar Mahboob obtained a Ph.D. in Electrical Engineering from National University of Sciences & Technology, Pakistan in 2005. Earlier, he had obtained BS and MS degrees in Electrical Engineering both from Florida State University, USA (1988-1996). Dr. Athar Mahboob is a specialist in implementing enterprise information services using Linux, information security and cryptology, computer networks, and internetworking using TCP/IP protocols, digital systems design and computer architectures. Dr. Athar Mahboob's Ph.D. research was focused on "Efficient Hardware and Software Implementations of Elliptic Curve Cryptography," an area in which he has obtained several international publications.

* * *

Rania Abdelhameed received the B.Sc. degree (First Class (HONORS)) in Electronics Engineering (Computer Engineering) from the Sudan University of Science and Technology (SUST), Khartoum, Sudan, in 2001, and the Postgraduate Diploma in Information Technology (IT) (Advanced Networking and Telecommunications) from the International Institute of Information Technology (I2IT), Pune, India, in 2003, and the M.Sc. and PhD degree in Computer Systems Engineering from the University Putra Malaysia (UPM), Kuala Lumpur, Malaysia, in 2005 and 2011, respectively. In May 2009, she earned the IEEE Wireless Communication Professional (IEEE WCP) certificate of the Wireless Communication Engineering Technology (WCET) Exam.

Nizar Al-Holou is a Professor and a Chair of Electrical and Computer Engineering Department at the University of Detroit Mercy, Detroit, Michigan. His research interest is in the areas In-vehicle and Intra-vehicle networking; Intelligent Transportation Systems (ITS); Distributed and parallel processing systems with an emphasis on automotive applications; Digital and Embedded systems. He is a member of IEEE Computer Society and Education society and the American Society for Engineering Education (ASEE). Dr. Al-Holou is a Senior Member of IEEE since 1996. He has served as Chairman and Vice Chair of the Computer Chapter for IEEE/SEM for over ten years. He received numerous awards for his professional services such as IEEE/SEM Outstanding Chapter Involvement Award for 1998, The Most Active Chapter award for 1994-95, IEEE-Computer Chapter Outstanding Chapter award for 1995-96 for being the most active chapter worldwide, IEEE Outstanding Involvement Award 1998, IEEE-EIT 2000 Award, and FIE 98 Best Paper Award. Moreover, he was nominated for IEEE/SEM Millennium Medal Awards, 1998, and the University of Detroit Mercy Distinguished Faculty Award, 2005. Also, he was selected and published at Who's Who In Midwest, 1994, Who's Who among American Teachers, 1998 and Madison Who's Who, 2010. He was the chair of ASEE/NCS conference. Dr. Al-Holou has received over $1,000,000 of funding in the last five years and has published over one hundred refereed papers. Dr. Al-Holou is an ABET program evaluator (PEV). He holds the Bachelor of Engineering Degree from Damascus University, the Master of Science from Ohio State University, Columbus, OH, and a Ph.D. Degree from the University of Dayton, all in Electrical Engineering.

Sellami Ali earned his B.Sc. from University of Mohamed Khider, Biskra, Algeria, in 1998. Next, he earned his M.Sc. from International Islamic University Malaysia, 2006. Finally, he earned his PhD from International Islamic University Malaysia, 2010. He has held some academic posts at Biskra's University (Algeria) and International Islamic University Malaysia.

Shakeel Ali is a CTO and co-founder of Cipher Storm Ltd, UK. His expertise in security industry has put up marvelous benefits to various businesses and government institutions. He is also an active and independent researcher who has been evangelizing security practices via articles, journals, and blogs at Ethical-Hacker.net. Shakeel has assessed and measured the security of several business applications and network infrastructures for global organizations. He also presented his security vision in a collective interview conducted by President of OdinJobs (Careers section) which gave clear highlights on skills, knowledge, and experience required to deal with today's technical and managerial goals. Shakeel has also coordinated in BugCon Conferences to present the best of breed cyber security threats and solutions, and industry verticals. This joint venture has attracted many audiences from different sectors including government, education, media, commercial, banking, and other respective institutions.

Ayesha Binte Ashfaq has an MS degree in Information Technology from the School of Electrical Engineering and Computer Science (SEECS), National University of Sciences and Technology (NUST). She is currently pursuing her PhD from SEECS, NUST, specializing in network security. Her research interests include malware analysis, network security, network traffic monitoring and network performance measurement, and modeling. In her research career, she has been able to publish in some of the leading conferences and symposiums in security. She also worked as a consultant for the Silicon Valley Company, WiChorus. Ayesha has won quite a few national awards including the NCR National IT Excellence Award and the National Youth Award to mention a few.

Muhammad Naeem Ayyaz received his Bachelor's degree in electrical engineering from the prestigious University of Engineering and Technology, Lahore Pakistan, and M.Sc. and Ph.D. in electrical engineering with emphasis on computer engineering from Syracuse University, New York, USA. His research interests span diverse areas including embedded systems, bioinformatics, and computer networks. His research has been published in various reputed journals. He has been part of faculty of electrical engineering at the University of Engineering and Technology, Lahore for more than previous twenty years where he holds the title of Professor and is also Chairman Department of Electrical Engineering. Apart from this, he holds a consultant position at the Al-Khawarizmi Institute of Computer Science.

Babar Bhatti is the CEO and Co-founder of MutualMind, a platform for social media intelligence and management. Babar has over 12 years of experience in managing and delivering enterprise and Web applications. Babar holds dual Master's from MIT in Technology and Policy and Civil and Environmental Engineering. Babar is a Certified Information Systems Security Professional (CISSP). He is based in Dallas, Texas.

Muhammad Farooq-i-Azam received his B.Sc. in electrical engineering from the prestigious University of Engineering and Technology Lahore (Taxila Campus), Pakistan and M.Sc. in computer science from the University of the Punjab, Lahore, Pakistan. By serving at various engineering positions in reputed organizations, he has accumulated hands-on experience in the development of digital systems. He has also extensive work experience with computer networks and UNIX based systems, Solaris, VAX/VMS machines and various distributions of Linux. He is part of a team of developers as project administrator of an open source project, IPGRAB, at sourceforge.net, which is a light-weight packet sniffer, distributed with Debian Linux originally authored by Mike Borella. He is founder of an information and computer security company ESecurity and has also been organizing an annual information security event, CHASE, in Pakistan since 2006. Currently he is part of faculty at the Department of Electrical Engineering, COMSATS Institute of Information Technology, Lahore, Pakistan.

Arif Ghafoor holds B.Sc, EE from UET, Pakistan and M.S., M.Phil, and PhD degrees, all in Electrical Engineering from Columbia University, USA. He served in the Dept. of Electrical and Computer Engineering, Syracuse University, New York prior to joining the School of Electrical and Computer Engineering at Purdue University in 1991 where currently he is a Professor, and Director of Distributed Multimedia Systems Laboratory. Dr. Ghafoor has been actively engaged in research areas related to parallel and distributed computing, information security, and multimedia Information Systems. He has published over 170 technical papers in leading journals and conferences. He has been consultant to GE, the DoD, and the UNDP. He has served on the editorial boards and a guest editor of numerous journals including ACM/Springer Multimedia Systems Journal, IEEE Transactions on Knowledge and Data Engineering, IEEE Journal on Selected Areas in Communication, and Journal of Parallel and Distributed Databases. He has co-edited a book entitled "Multimedia Document Systems in Perspectives" (Kluwer Publisher), and has co-authored a book entitled "Semantic Models for Multimedia Database Searching and Browsing" (Kluwer Publisher). Dr. Ghafoor is an IEEE Fellow and has received the IEEE Computer Society Technical Achievement Award (2000) in recognition to his contributions in the field of multimedia systems.

Morgan Henrie, PhD, PMP, is President of MH Consulting, Inc., a national and international Project and Program Management consulting and training company. Dr. Henrie has advanced educational degrees in system science and project management (Master of Science from The George Washington University and a Doctorate in systems science and engineering management from Old Dominion University). Dr. Henrie's SCADA activities including leading American Petroleum Institute 2009 *Pipeline SCADA Security* standard revision, consulting with crude oil transportation pipeline companies SCADA cyber security programs consulting, resilient system research and publishing several articles. He is a member of the Department of Energy Sector Control Systems Working Group where he assists in identifying areas of critical energy sector infrastructure cyber security research, research peer reviews and a contributing author. He was also a member of the Infrastructure for Information Infrastructure Protection (I3P) advisory board representing the oil and gas sector.

Wen-Chen Hu received a BE, an ME, an MS, and a PhD, all in Computer Science, from Tamkang University, Taiwan, the National Central University, Taiwan, the University of Iowa, and the University of Florida, in 1984, 1986, 1993, and 1998, respectively. He is currently an Associate Professor in the Department of Computer Science of the University of North Dakota. He is the Editor-in-Chief of the International Journal of Handheld Computing Research (IJHCR), and has served as editor and editorial advisory/review board members for over 20 international journals/books and chaired more than 10 tracks/sessions and program committees for international conferences. Dr. Hu has been teaching more than 10 years at the US universities and advising more than 50 graduate students. He has published over 90 articles in refereed journals, conference proceedings, books, and encyclopedias, edited five books and proceedings, and solely authored a book. His current research interests include handheld computing, electronic and mobile commerce systems, Web technologies, and databases.

Naima Kaabouch received a B.S. and an M.S. from the University of Paris 11 and a PhD from the University of Paris 6, France. She is currently an Assistant Professor and the Graduate Director in the Department of Electrical Engineering at the University of North Dakota. Her research interests include signal/image processing, bioinformatics, robotics, embedded systems, and digital communications.

Adil Khan specializes in the field of image processing, pattern recognition, and digital signal processing in which he has obtained several publications. He obtained his BS in Avionics and MS in Computer Engineering from College of Aeronautical Engineering, NUST and Center for Advanced Studies in Engineering (CASE), Pakistan respectively. Adil Khan is currently a PhD student at National University of Sciences and Technology, Pakistan in the field of Information Security and Cryptology.

Syed Ali Khayam has a PhD degree in Electrical Engineering from Michigan State University. Since February 2007, he has been serving as an Assistant Professor at the School of Electrical Engineering & Computer Science (SEECS), National University of Science and Technology (NUST), Pakistan. His research interests include analysis and modeling of statistical phenomena in computer networks, network security, cross-layer design for wireless networks, and real-time multimedia communications. Dr. Khayam has over 50 publications in some of the most prestigious conferences and journals in his areas of interest. He has received research awards from Nokia Research, Korean Research Foundation, and Pakistan National ICT R&D Fund. He currently has 4 patents pending at USPTO, some of which were indigenously drafted and filed by him. He serves on the Technical Program Committees (TPCs) of many conferences (including RAID, IEEE ICC, and IEEE Globecom) in his areas of expertise. He also works as a consultant for technology companies in the Silicon Valley. Dr. Khayam has won many national and international awards. Among these awards, he is most proud of the nation-wide award for the "Best University Teacher of the Year 2009" given to him by the Higher Education Commission (HEC) of Pakistan.

Ashfaq Ahmad Malik is a PhD scholar at PN Engg College, National University of Sciences and Technology, Karachi, Pakistan. His area of research is "Design of C4I systems using COTS and Open Source Software". He got commission in Pakistan Navy in July 1992. He graduated as BE(Electrical) from PN Engg College/NEDUET, Karachi in 1994. He qualified Weapon Engg Application Course (WEAC) from PN Engg College, Karachi in 1997. He did ME (Computer Systems) from NED University of Engg and Technology, Karachi, Pakistan in 2003. Ashfaq Ahmad Malik has almost 18-20 years of experience of working with respect to maintenance and operation of different weapons, sensors, communication systems, fire control systems, command & control systems, et cetera onboard different PN ships of US/UK/French/Chinese origin.

Syed Misbahuddin received BE in Electronics from Dawood College of Engineering & Technology, Karachi Pakistan in 1983, MS in Electrical and Computer Engineering from King Fahd University of Petroleum and Minerals, Dhahran, Saudi Arabia in 1988 and Doctor of Engineering in Electrical and Computer Engineering from the University of Detroit Mercy, Detroit, MI, USA in 1998. He started his career as an Assistant Professor in Computer Systems department, NED University of Engineering and Technology, Karachi, Pakistan in 1988. He remained at NED University until 1992. From 2000 to 2010, Syed Misbahuddin was serving as faculty member in King Fahd University of Petroleum and Minerals and University of Hail, Saudi Arabia. He also has served North American Auto and Financial industry as IT consultant. Misbahuddin has contributed more than twenty research publications in international journals and conference proceedings. He has co-authored three chapter books and one Internet draft. His research interests are in embedded systems, parallel and distributed computing, and data reduction algorithms. Presently, Syed Misbahuddin is a Professor in Computer Engineering department, Sir Syed University of Engineering and Technology, Karachi, Pakistan.

S. Hossein Mousavinezhad received his Ph.D. in Electrical Engineering from Michigan State University, East Lansing, Michigan. He is currently a Professor and the Chair of the Department of Electrical Engineering Computer Science (EECS), Idaho State University, Pocatello, Idaho. His research interests include digital signal processing, bioelectromagnetics, and communication systems. Dr. Mousavinezhad is a recipient of the Institute of Electrical and Electronics Engineers (IEEE) Third Millennium Medal. He received American Society for Engineering Education (ASEE) Electrical and Computer Engineering Division's Meritorious Service Award in June 2007. Professor Mousavinezhad is a program evaluator for the Accreditation Board for Engineering and Technology (ABET).

Alfredo Pironti is a post-doctoral researcher in formal methods for security protocols and security-aware applications at Politecnico di Torino. His main research interests are on formal methods applied to security protocols and security-aware applications. In particular, he focused on sound automatic implementation generation of security protocols from formally verified specification, and on black-box monitoring of legacy security protocols implementations. He is a member of the research group led by Prof. Riccardo Sisto. Moreover, he is participating in the CryptoForma initiative, aimed at bridging the gap between formal and computational models of cryprography. Alfredo Pironti received his PhD in 2010, and his M.S. in computer engineering in 2006, both at Politecnico di Torino.

Victor Pomponiu is a Ph.D. student and member of the Security and Network group at the Computer Science Department, Università degli Studi di Torino, Italy, since January 2009. He received his B.Sc. and M.Sc. in Computer Science from the Polytechnic University of Bucharest in 2006 and 2008, specializing in communication systems. His areas of research include multimedia security (image/video/audio encryption, watermarking, digital fingerprinting, authentication, forensics, digital rights management), communication and network security (intrusion detection, malware, and bots detection), and ad-hoc networks.

Davide Pozza graduated in Computer Engineering in 2002, and received a PhD degree in Computer Engineering in 2006, both from Politecnico di Torino, Torino, Italy. He is currently a post doctoral researcher at the Department of Computer Engineering at that institution. His current research interests include: processes, methodologies, and techniques that address software security, reliability, and safety, static analysis techniques to detect software vulnerabilities, formal methods for modelling and analyzing network vulnerability and cryptographic protocols, and automatic code generation of cryptographic protocols by starting from their formal specifications. He teaches courses on network and distributed programming, and on secure software engineering. He also provides consultancies in the area of reliable and secure software.

Rashid A. Saeed received his BSc in Electronics Engineering from Sudan University of Science and Technology (SUST), and PhD in Communication Engineering, UPM. He served as senior researcher in MIMOS Berhad and then in Telekom Malaysia R&D where he awarded the "platinum badge" for outstanding research achievement Award. Since 2010 he is Assistant Professor in electrical engineering, UIA Malaysia. He published over 70 research papers/tutorials/talks/book chapters on UWB, cognitive radio, and radio resources management. He is also successfully awarded 2 U.S patents and other 8 filed. Rashid is a certified WiMAX engineer (RF and core network). He is also Six Sigma™, certified Black Belt based on DMAIC++ from Motorola University. He is a senior member of IEEE, IEM Malaysia, and Sigma Xi. He is one of the contributors of IEEE-WCET wireless certification in its earlier stages.

Riccardo Sisto received the M.Sc. degree in electronic engineering in 1987, and the Ph.D degree in computer engineering in 1992, both from Politecnico di Torino, Torino, Italy. Since 1991 he has been working at Politecnico di Torino, in the Computer Engineering Department, first as a researcher, then as an Associate Professor and, since 2004, as a Full Professor of computer engineering. Since the beginning of his scientific activity, his main research interests have been in the area of formal methods applied to software engineering, communication protocol engineering, distributed systems, and computer security. On this and related topics he has authored or co-authored more than 70 scientific papers. Dr. Sisto has been a member of the Association for Computing Machinery (ACM) since 1999.

Hung-Jen Yang received a BS in Industrial Education from the National Kaohsiung Normal University, an MS in Industrial Technology from the University of North Dakota, and a PhD in Industrial Education and Technology from the Iowa State University in 1984, 1989, and 1991, respectively. He is currently a Professor in the Department of Industrial Technology Education and the director of the Center for Instructional and Learning Technology at the National Kaohsiung Normal University, Taiwan. His research interests include computer networks, automation, and technology education.

Index